Secrets of Statistics

Eighth Edition

Nicholas Noviello

University of California Irvine

WILEY

CUSTOM SERVICES

Cover images from top to bottom:
  Swans: © Corbis Digital Stock
  Field of Sunflowers in Bavaria, Germany: © PhotoDisc, Inc.
  Hotels and Bars in Germany: © PhotoDisc, Inc.
  Many Satelite dishes with a blue sky: © Digital Vision
  Aerial view of parking lot: © Digital Vision

This custom textbook includes materials submitted by the author for publication by John Wiley & Sons, Inc. The material has not been edited by Wiley and the author is solely responsible for its content.

Printed in the United States of America.

ISBN-13 978-0-471-77726-7
ISBN-10 0-471-77726-9
10 9 8 7 6 5 4 3 2 1

CONTENTS

CHAPTER 8 PROBABILITY

CHAPTER 9 BINOMIAL SAMPLING DISTRIBUTIONS

CHAPTER 10 DESCRIBING PROBABILITY DISTRIBUTIONS

CHAPTER 14   DIFFERENCES BETWEEN TWO POPULATIONS

CHAPTER 15   INFERENCE ABOUT NOMINAL VARIABLES: χ^2

CHAPTER 16   ONE WAY ANALYSIS OF VARIANCE

CHAPTER 17   TWO WAY FACTORIAL ANALYSIS OF VARIANCE

CHAPTER 21   USING CORRELATION AND REGRESSION WISELY

Preface

I've taught over eight thousand students elementary statistics. Over the years I've tried to listen carefully to many students as they described the problems and misunderstandings associated with learning this subject. The large classes I've dealt with have been invaluable, because they have guaranteed me the opportunity to meet numerous bright, lucid, motivated students who have been more than willing to let me know what was working well for them, what was not working well, and often, what would work much better.

Each chapter briefly introduces a technique, describes what it can be used for, why people came up with it, and shows how to do any necessary computations. The emphasis is on *concepts* like error, relationships between variables, significance, strength, etc. The computations covered are almost all presented in forms that contribute to understanding the concepts. It's been my experience that students benefit from learning how to compute deviations from the mean, sums of squares, etc, *if* every computation reviews the definition of the term for them, and *if* every computation is clearly related to a goal they understand. I've never met anyone who really understands the concepts of statistics who hasn't carried out these basic computations at least once.

Many short practice problems involving very small sets of data are provided, with answers. I've tried to provide several different examples of every conceivable question that could be asked about a given statistical technique or concept. This allows apprehensive students to see clearly how much they are expected to know, and to practice with feedback as much as they need to.

Extensive real world examples are not included in the text. I always supplement the text with lectures and handouts about current journal articles and statistics in newspapers and magazines.

A software package, Secrets Software, which supplements this text, is available at no charge. This software allows computation of all the statistics covered in the text. Unlike commercial software packages, the *computations* may be displayed, so students may use the software to quickly check their work. Demonstrations illustrating regression line fit and sampling distributions are also included.

Acknowledgements

Bob Newcomb inspired me and encouraged rigor. Bernie Grofman helped me enjoy various statistical applications. Russ Dalton, Christine Lofgren, Mary-Louise Kean, Mike Braunstein, Mike Burton, Ted Wright and Joan Murray have made helpful suggestions about content and examples. Amjad Toukan and other teaching assistants have shared their ideas. Mike Migalski, Jerry Keys, Gerald Langiewicz and Tamar Peddie aided in the process of developing, debugging and installing the software. Caesar Sereseres, Vicki Ronaldson and Rene Martin helped me to survive dealing with large classes. Jennifer Loh has made many helpful suggestions, and many other former students have made my work easier by letting me know just what was needed.

CHAPTER 1

INTRODUCTION

1.1 SOME GOALS

ASSESSING TRUTH

The people who devised the techniques you'll be learning about in this class were motivated by a desire to *objectively* assess the *truth* of interesting statements. They make the assumption that many interesting statements are best viewed as neither definitely true nor definitely false. Why?

> A) Today, in the late twentieth century, scientists (including social scientists) are much more sophisticated about the notion of "truth" than they were in earlier centuries, or even earlier in this century. People realize that the interesting statements in sciences are typically *generalizations*, and generalizations often turn out to be incorrect.

> B) No one doing new research is very interested in the areas within a field that everyone agrees on! The *interesting* questions are those which so far remain *unanswered*. Those unanswered questions which spark people's curiosity often lead to differences of opinion. Later in this course you'll see how probability and statistics provide relatively objective methods to settle such differences of opinion.

SUMMARIZING DATA

Another goal of statistics is to *summarize* large batches of numbers in a neat, meaningful way. You may be surprised to find out that statistics helps *minimize* the use of numbers! One statistic, or one graph can clearly summarize thousands of separate numbers.

1.2 PROBABILITY

Numbers between 0 and 1 are used to indicate the "degree of truth" that statements have, and to indicate the likelihood that events occur. We'll call these numbers "probability estimates", or simply "probabilities".

If a statement is definitely *false* it has a probability value of 0.
If a statement is definitely *true* it has a probability of 1.
If a statement is *equally likely* to be true or false its probability is .5.

So you can think of the probability of a *statement* as a rating of "how likely the statement is to be true,", on a scale ranging from 0 to 1. Similarly, the probability of an *event* rates "how likely the event is to occur," on a scale ranging from 0 to 1.

1.3 WHAT IS A STATISTIC?

The term 'statistic' is used in two common ways in statistics classes:

1) A statistic is a *rule* for computing one number used to describe a bunch of scores. For example, 'the mean' is a statistic, and when you define the mean as 'the number you get when you add up the scores and divide by the number of scores' you are stating a *rule*.

2) The term 'statistic' is also applied to the actual value (often a number) you get when you use a rule like the one above. For example, in the statement "The mean of the scores was 7.6", the number 7.6 is a statistic.

Fortunately it will always be clear from the context which of the two versions of the term is intended.

Techniques for *displaying* data clearly in pictorial form are also commonly considered part of the field of statistics.

1.4 EXAMPLE 1:   THE ESAT TEST

Consider the following example, "Dr. Jones ESAT experiment":

Dr. Jones, a hypothetical, possibly mad, scientific type, has concocted a drug he refers to as "Substance X", which he believes can cause people to have ESP abilities. He thinks that these abilities will allow the people who take Substance X to sense things using previously undiscovered sensory channels.

Although Dr. Jones has confidence in the ESP-enhancing power of Substance X, he understands that the world will be *skeptical* about his claims. He is motivated by a strong desire to *prove* to others that Substance X actually can cause ESP ability in average people.

He does not want to waste his time conducting an experiment which might produce ambiguous or questionable results; his goal is to conduct an experiment such that if Substance X does work,

1) the results of the experiment will clearly and obviously indicate that Substance X has produced ESP, and

2) no one will be able to claim that there was some *other* effect involved, something other than Substance X, that caused the apparent ESP.

Dr. Jones has Dr. Plon, his favorite pharmacist, prepare two bottles of identical looking pills, arbitrarily labelled A and B. One bottle contains pills with Substance X, the other bottle contains *placebos*, pills with no active ingredients. Dr. Plon does not indicate to Dr. Jones which bottle actually contains Substance X until *after* the experiment is concluded.

Dr. Jones uses a table of random numbers to pick seats in a classroom at random and uses 20 students picked in this way as participants in his experiment. He gives the first 10 participants picked pills from bottle A, and the next 10 participants pills from bottle B.

Then Dr. Jones gives the ESAT, a 10 question True-False test to all 20 participants. He "beams" 10 questions to all participants, using only ESP, and the participants attempt to answer the questions. Scores on the ESAT range from 0 to 10 depending on the number of questions answered correctly.

Finally, after the tests are collected and scored, Dr. Jones calls Dr. Plon and they "Break the code", i.e., Dr. Plon tells Dr. Jones which bottle contained Substance X.

The ESAT test is an example of a ***double-blind**, **controlled**, **randomized** experiment*. Many examples we discuss will not be so "scientific", but it's good to start with an example like this to illustrate the terminology of experiments and the kind of reasoning process involved in doing experiments, the "*logic*" behind the experimental design.

1.5 CRUCIAL TERMINOLOGY

To be able to follow the discussion in all chapters below it is essential that you *memorize* the definitions of these terms!

In many cases, a familiar word such as 'relationship' has a specific meaning in statistics, unrelated to the more common meaning which is familiar to you.

POPULATION (PRECISE DEFINITION)

" THE POPULATION YOU CAN GENERALIZE TO "

Studies which use statistics always refer to a collection of measurements, usually the result of measuring a bunch of things, called *cases* or *elements*.

The *population* (precise definition) for a particular study is the set of all things that the study is *really* about, or the set of all things that might have been *measured* by the person conducting a study, *as the study was actually carried out*. Note that if all cases in the sample are *treated* in some way (e.g., given a medication) then the population 'you can generalize to' is restricted to cases that are *treated* that way.

POPULATION (INFORMAL DEFINITION)

" THE KIND OF CASES YOU WISH TO STUDY "

A more informal definition of population is also commonly used: The set of all cases that are similar to the ones actually studied, even if they could not actually have been included in your sample. The cases involved may actually be objects, animals, plants, people, events, etc.

EXAMPLES:

A psychiatrist may study a population of 'all patients at Charter Oak Hospital in 1991 who have obsessive-compulsive disorder and who are treated with Prozac'.

A city planner may consider the population of "all left turns within the city of Irvine on May 21, 1992."

A biologist might study a population of all fish in a certain pond.

Physicists sometimes study populations such as all atoms in a certain film of metal, or all collisions between two specific types of particles.

Political scientists deal with populations such as "all voters in California' or 'all countries with a particular form of government."

CASE (OR ELEMENT)

One of the people, things or events in the population being studied.

ALTERNATE TERMS:

In experimental studies in which the cases are humans, the cases are referred to as *participants*. In other social sciences, e.g. sociology and anthropology, cases are often called *respondents*.

SAMPLE

The subset of the population that is picked by the researcher and *actually measured* by the researcher.

SAMPLE SIZE

The number of cases chosen from the population to be in the sample. This is typically designated 'n'.

SIMPLE RANDOM SAMPLE

DEFINITION

A sample that is chosen in such a way that *each possible sample* from the population has an equal chance to be the sample that is chosen.

This also guarantees that each case in the population has an equal chance to be included in the sample chosen.

CHOOSING RANDOM SAMPLES

We can guarantee that we'll obtain a simple random sample if we choose the sample in one of these ways:

1) Using a container of **tokens**, where there is one token for every case (or element) in the population. You mix up the tokens and choose 'n' of them, where 'n' is the size of the sample you are picking. The tokens must, of course, be designed so that the person picking them can't tell which token corresponds to which case.

2) Using a **random number table**, where a random number that occurs in the table forces you to pick one specific case from the population. You assign each case in the population a number. Then you use a random number table to pick the first 'n' numbers that come up in the random number table.

3) Using a **computer program** which generates random numbers.

VARIABLE

Something that the different cases can differ *with respect to*.
Some quality (or 'aspect') that is *not the same* for all of the cases.
A *way* in which the different cases differ from each other.

ALTERNATE TERMS:

In mathematical descriptions of statistics a variable may be defined as a *vector* or an *ordered list of scores*.

NOMINAL SCALE VARIABLE

A variable that merely divides the cases into *categories*.

If two cases get different scores on a nominal scale variable, we can only conclude that they are in different categories. We can't conclude anything meaningful about which case is "higher" or "lower" than the other, because the categories do not imply any order.

Cases' *scores* on nominal scale variables are usually indicated by *words*, not numbers. The scores name one category (of several possible categories) E.g., 'Honda', 'Female', 'Schizophrenic' are scores on nominal scale variables.

EXAMPLES OF NOMINAL SCALE VARIABLES:

A person's gender, blood type, eye color, marital status, ethnicity, "whether the person has had mumps", "whether the person has ever...(fill in any event that can happen to a person.)."

An automobile's brand, model, body type, country of manufacture

A country's type of government, climate, main industry

ORDINAL SCALE VARIABLE

A variable that "ranks" the cases, i.e. it puts the cases in an *order* from lowest to highest (or vice versa).

If two cases get different scores on an ordinal scale variable, we can conclude that one of them is "higher" than the other or "greater" than the other on some dimension measured by the variable.

Scores on ordinal scale variables are often the *ordinal* numbers: 1st, 2nd, 3rd, etc.. However sets of words such as "low", "medium" or "high" also may be used as scores on ordinal scale variables.

EXAMPLES OF ORDINAL SCALE VARIABLES:

A song or album's *rank* in the Billboard top 100.

An athlete's *order* of finish in a race.

A job applicant's *order* of preference according to some hiring committee.

> For example the statement "Lopez is our *second* choice, Smith is our *first* choice." Implies that Smith's score on the ordinal variable "order of preference" is 1, Lopez' score is 2, and the preference for Smith is greater than for Lopez. (We can't conclude, of course, that the preference for Smith is "twice as great.")

A city's *rank* in crime rate, e.g., "Detroit ranks third in homicide rate".

INTERVAL SCALE VARIABLE

We'll use this working definition: In research in the social sciences, variables are generally assumed to be interval scale variables if they are numerical, represent quantities, and are *not obviously ordinal* scale variables.

EXAMPLES OF INTERVAL SCALE VARIABLES:

A person's height, weight, pulse rate, IQ, score on the statistics test, income

A car's weight, horsepower, price, top speed, air drag coefficient, EPA mileage, G-force (when turning!)

A city's area, population, mean income, illness rate (for any specific illness), actual crime rate (E.g. "New York's homicide rate is 3/10,000")

SCORE

The result of measuring one case (or element) on one variable. The 'measurement' of the case (or element) on the variable may be done by mere observation (E.g., when an interviewer notes 'Female' or 'Male' on a form) or by physical measurement of a case (As height, weight, blood pressure are typically measured) or by psychological tests (I.Q. scores, scores on personality scales), or by obtaining a respondent's answers to some survey questions.

ALTERNATE TERMS:

Often the word *attribute* is used to describe a score on a variable, particularly when nominal scale variable is being referred to.

MEASUREMENT

We'll refer to *any* process that assigns one score (or attribute) to each case as **measurement**. This very general definition is helpful in the long run.

Some authors don't like using 'measurement' to describe the process of assigning scores on nominal scale variables, but there is no single alternative term that is generally accepted.

If you liked algebra courses you may prefer to think of measurement using this mathematical definition: A measurement process defines a *function* from the set of cases into the set of scores.

1.6 RELATIONSHIPS BETWEEN VARIABLES

(1.6.1) A *relationship* exists between two *variables*...

- **if *information* about one variable
        (the independent variable)
    enables you to better *predict* the other variable
        (the dependent variable)**

- **if knowing a case's score on one variable
        (the independent variable)
    usually helps you make a *better estimate* of the
    case's score on the other variable
        (the dependent variable).**

TIP: Statistical relationships are *not* relationships between *cases*, they are relationships between *variables!*

EXAMPLE:
Dr. Jones' hunch is that "There is a relationship between the *variable* drug level, or treatment, and the *variable* ESAT score."

EXAMPLE:
Let's say that drivers of *red* cars swerve more on the freeway. Then, we can state that there is a relationship between the *variable* "car color", and the *variable* "amount of swerving."

RELATIONSHIPS MAY, OR MAY NOT, BE CAUSAL

When information about one variable allows you to make a better prediction of some other variable, then there *is* a relationship between the variables, *but* it doesn't have to be "*causal*"!

A relationship between two variables does not imply that either *causes* the other! The *independent* variable is the one you have information about, the *dependent* variable is the one you try to predict based on that information.

EXAMPLE:
A study of presweetened cereal consumption and amount of Saturday morning television viewing might show that high quantities of sweetened cereal consumption was related to more hours of televised cartoon viewing on Saturday mornings, but we would *not* conclude that the relationship was *causal.* That is, we would *not* conclude that eating a lot of presweetened cereal *caused* people to turn to their televisions on Saturday mornings! (We might note that children eat more presweetened cereals and they would be expected to watch more cartoons on Saturday mornings.)

INDEPENDENT VARIABLE (OR PREDICTOR)

The variable that 'does the causing or effecting' (*If* the relationship is a causal one)

The variable that you 'have information about'

The 'treatment' variable (Which usually indicates whether the participant received the treatment or a placebo)

DEPENDENT VARIABLE (OR CRITERION)

The variable that 'gets affected' by some treatment

The variable that you are trying to *predict*

The variable that measures the possible *effect* of some treatment

HOW TO CHECK FOR A RELATIONSHIP BETWEEN VARIABLES

In the first examples of relationships we'll cover, the independent variable will always be *nominal* scale, and the dependent variable will be *interval* scale. In these examples, you can quickly and easily check to see if there's a relationship between the variables as follows:

1) Separate all the cases into groups according to their scores on the independent variable.

2) Compute the mean (average) of each group on the dependent variable.

3) If the means of the different groups are *not* equal, then there *is* a relationship between the independent variable and the dependent variable. If the means of the groups *are* equal, then there is *no* relationship between the variables.

EXAMPLE:
Suppose in the ESAT example above, the group that got Substance X (the Treatment Group) got an average ESAT score of 7.6, and the group that got the Placebo (the Control Group) averaged 4.9 on the ESAT.

We'd say there *is* a relationship between the treatment and ESAT score in the data obtained from this sample.

Later we'll cover techniques for measuring how *strong* a relationship is, how *significant* it is, etc.

PARAMETERS vs. STATISTICS

Few terms are *misused* as often as the term *parameter*. ("Paradigm" is a close competitor in this regard!) Luckily, there is *one* and only one common statistical definition for a parameter, and it's easy to remember. A parameter is the value of a statistic, *when the statistic is computed for an entire population.* Parameters are often contrasted with statistics computed from *samples* from a population. E.g.
> "Using the *sample* mean (a statistic) which was 102.3, we estimated the *population* mean (a parameter)."

Parameters are often designated with Greek letters corresponding the first letter of the statistic. E.g., 'μ' (*mu*, the Greek letter 'm') designates the parameter 'the *population* mean'.

1.7 EXPERIMENTS

DEFINITION:

An *experiment* is a study in which the *researcher* performs some action that causes the cases to have certain scores on the independent variable. The most obvious example is one like the ESAT demo, where Dr. Jones gives the participants either the drug or a placebo, and whether they get the drug or placebo determines their score on the independent variable. In cases like this the independent variable is often called "Treatment", "Drug Level", or "Experimental Group", to indicate that it is categorizing the cases according to which *treatment* they got.

SINGLE-BLIND EXPERIMENT

An experiment in which the *participants* don't know which treatment (e.g. 'drug' vs. 'placebo') they got, though the researcher may know.

DOUBLE-BLIND EXPERIMENT

An experiment in which neither the *participants* nor the *experimenter* know which treatment the participants got, until *after* completion of the experiment.

EXPERIMENTAL GROUP (OR "TREATMENT GROUP")

The group of participants in the *sample* that get the '*treatment*' or 'active ingredient'. They get the level of the independent variable that the experimenter thinks should produce some effect.

CONTROL GROUP

The group of participants in the sample that get a ***placebo***, or *no treatment* . They are not expected to show any actual reaction to the independent variable (only a possible 'placebo effect'). This group is included only for comparison to the experimental group.

1.8 OBSERVATIONAL STUDIES

Recall that in an *experimental* study the *researcher* controls the value of the variable of interest. For example, in the ideal version of the ESAT experiment, the researcher decides, for each participant, whether that participant receives the drug or placebo. Other ways of saying this are: "The experimenter determines which cases are in the treatment group and the control group." or "The independent variable is under the *control* of the experimenter."

Some variables, such as gender and age, *cannot* be changed by the experimenter. The differences between two people with regard to gender or age have already been determined *by nature*. Hence, if a researcher wants two groups of people, male and female, for a study, she is definitely not going to be able to *randomly assign* participants to the male group or the female group!

DEFINITION:

Studies in which *nature*, not the experimenter, determines which group a participant is in are called ***observational studies (or passive-observational studies)***. That is, if the researcher *does not* take some action that determines each case's score on the independent variable the study is *observational*.

This general, inclusive definition of 'observational' includes a variety of *specific* kinds of studies to be discussed later, including:

- quasi-experimental studies
- naturalistic observation
- surveys
- unobtrusive measures

EXAMPLE:

If you wanted to study whether caffeine in coffee makes people more alert, an *observational* study would find out who in the population has *already chosen* to drink coffee, and who hasn't, and would compare both groups.

An *experimental* study, on the other hand, would require that you *randomly select* people and give half coffee with caffeine, and the other half "placebo" coffee without caffeine, and would then compare.

In observational studies, *confounding* is very likely, conclusions about causality are suspect.

CONFOUNDING OF VARIABLES

Confounding occurs when you are trying to study the effect of some independent variable on some dependent variable, and *other* variables are systematically affecting the dependent variable. Confounding can occur in either observational or experimental studies, but it is *more* likely to occur in *observational* studies.

1.9 SUMMARY of ALTERNATE TERMINOLOGY

We mentioned above that there are a variety of ways to refer to some of the basic concepts in statistics. You don't need to memorize this table (except for the top row!) to get by in this class, but a familiarity with these common alternate terms will help you use your knowledge later. The top row shows the most common ones in general use (which we'll use); the other rows show alternate terms common in several specific fields.

SECRETS	Case (or element)	Variable	Score, or Value
Experimental Psychology	Participant (human) Subject	Variable	Level
Anthropology	Respondent		Attribute
Survey Research	Respondent, Case	Item	Response
Mathematics	Element, Point	Vector	Scalar
Computer Software	Case	Variable	Value

1.10* RESEARCH DESIGNS

SAMPLING IN GROUP DESIGNS

In a *group* research design, two or more groups of cases are compared, and the differences between groups are interpreted. Typically one group receives some kind of treatment and is referred to as the **treatment group**. The other group, which doesn't receive the treatment, is referred to as the **control group** (or **comparison group**). If the treatment group does better than the control group, the evidence seems to imply that the treatment works.

PARTICIPANT ASSIGNMENT AND GROUP FORMATION

RANDOM SELECTION

Random selection of *large* samples generally results in samples that are *like* the entire population on most variables. The goal is to allow us to generalize to the entire population that the sample came from. If our treatment works well in the sample, we can say "The treatment worked in the sample, and the sample was *representative of* the population."

RANDOM ASSIGNMENT

In random assignment, each *participant* in the sample has the same chance to be assigned to each *group*. The *goal* of the random assignment is *control*. We try to assure that the treatment group and the control group are *not* very different on any extraneous (or confounding) variables. This is the same as saying that we have *controlled for* all relevant extraneous variables, so we can conclude that differences are *caused* by the treatment.

GROUP EQUIVALENCE

If random assignment succeeds *perfectly*, then the groups will be *equivalent* on all extraneous, or nuisance variables. Random assignment is much more likely to succeed in producing equivalent groups when the size of groups is *large*.

DEFINITIONS RELEVANT TO RESEARCH DESIGNS

Between-groups (or Between participants) designs manipulate the independent variable by administering *different levels* of the independent variable to *different participants*.

Within-subjects designs administer *different levels* of the independent variable at *different times* to a *single group* of participants.

Single-subject designs manipulate the independent variable as the within-subjects designs do, but focus on the performance of a *single participant* rather than the average of a group of participants.

Mixed (or '**split-plot**') designs *combine* aspects of the within-subjects and between-subjects designs.

* Starred sections are optional

SELECTED GROUP DESIGNS

The notation used below has become the standard for describing research designs.

NOTATION:

R   Random assignment of participants to groups was used.

nonR   The participants were *not* randomly assigned to groups.

O   Observation of the participants on the dependent variable.

X   The participants receive a treatment on the independent variable.

X_A This usually designates that participants receive the *active* or *new* treatment on the independent variable.

X_B This usually designates that participants receive the *control or comparison* treatment on the independent variable.

(blank)   The participants receive the *control* or *comparison* treatment on the independent variable.

TRUE EXPERIMENTAL DESIGNS

These are the designs that can provide evidence of *causality*, *if* they are conducted correctly. These designs can provide the most convincing evidence that the *treatment* is responsible for the differences between the two groups.

Posttest-Only Control Group Design

$$\text{Group 1} \rightarrow \quad R \quad X_A \quad O_1$$
$$\text{Group 2} \rightarrow \quad R \quad X_B \quad O_2$$

We randomly assign participants to two groups, give one group the treatment, and then measure the groups on the dependent variable. (The ESAT example was like this)

In this design we *don't* measure participants prior to the treatment, so we can't be *sure* that the two groups were equivalent prior to the treatment. However, random assignment of the participants to groups does tend to make the groups equivalent prior to treatment, especially if the size of the groups is large.

Pretest-Posttest Control Group Design

$$\text{Group 1} \rightarrow \quad R \quad O_1 \quad X_A \quad O_2$$
$$\text{Group 2} \rightarrow \quad R \quad O_2 \quad X_B \quad O_4$$

We randomly assign participants to two groups, measure each group on the dependent variable (pretest), then give one group the treatment, and finally measure the groups again (posttest) on the dependent variable.

In this design we *do* measure participants prior to the treatment, so we can check that the two groups are equivalent prior to the treatment. We can be more confident that differences between the groups after the treatment were *due to* the treatment.

QUASI-EXPERIMENTAL DESIGNS

These designs lack one component that true experimental designs possess, usually random assignment of participants to groups. They are not as convincing as true experiments.

Pretest-Posttest Nonequivalent Control Group Design

$$\text{Group 1} \rightarrow \quad nonR \quad O_1 \quad X_A \quad O_2$$
$$\text{Group 2} \rightarrow \quad nonR \quad O_2 \quad X_B \quad O_4$$

Individuals in two groups are compared. We measure each group on the dependent variable (pretest), then we give one group the treatment, and finally we measure the groups again (posttest) on the dependent variable. However the participants are *not* randomly assigned to groups.

In this design we *do* measure participants prior to the treatment, so we can check that the two groups were equivalent on the dependent variable prior to the treatment. However, the two groups may be different on many confounding variables that make it difficult to conclude that the treatment was what caused group differences.

Another possible drawback is associated with all pretests: There may be a *sensitization* effect due to the pretest. That is, the treatment may *not* work as well *without* the pretest!

PRE-EXPERIMENTAL DESIGNS

These designs are seldom seen in modern times in publications claiming to provide convincing evidence. They provide no evidence that the treatment had any effect.

One-Group Posttest Only Design ('One-Shot Case Study')

Group 1 $\rightarrow$ X O_1

Participants in one group receive the treatment, and then are each measured on the dependent variable. There is *no* control group, so there is no way to tell if the scores on the dependent variable were affected by the treatment.

One-Group Pretest-Posttest Design

Group 1 $\rightarrow$ O_1 X O_2

Participants in one group are measured on the dependent variable, then all receive the treatment, and then are each measured again on the dependent variable. There is *no* control group, so there is no way to tell if the scores on the dependent variable were affected by the treatment. If the pretest and posttest scores are different, we can't be sure that the change was due to the independent variable.

Posttest-Only Nonequivalent Control Group Design

Group 1 $\rightarrow$ nonR X_A O_1
Group 2 $\rightarrow$ nonR X_B O_2

Individuals in two groups are compared. We give one group the treatment, and then we measure the groups on the dependent variable. However the participants are *not* randomly assigned to groups.

In this design we *do not* measure participants prior to the treatment, so we cannot check that the two groups were equivalent on the dependent variable prior to the treatment. There is no way to know if any differences between the groups after treatment were due to the treatment or to preexisting differences between the groups.

CORRELATIONAL or 'Ex Post Facto' DESIGNS

These involve measuring participants on two variables, usually numerical, neither of which has been manipulated by the experimenter.

Typically a *correlation coefficient* is then computed, which measures how strong a relationship there is between the independent variable and the dependent variable.

1.11 REVIEW: RELATIONSHIPS BETWEEN VARIABLES

Hopefully, you'll never forget this *crucial* definition!

There's a *relationship* between an *independent* variable and a *dependent* variable if, *knowing* the scores on the independent variable helps you to *better predict* scores on the dependent variable.

Here are some rules of thumb for quickly spotting the independent and dependent variables in word problems.

TIPS: IDENTIFYING INDEPENDENT AND DEPENDENT VARIABLES

SPOTTING THE INDEPENDENT VARIABLE

- It's the one you *get information about*

- It's the one you'll *use in making predictions*

- In an *experimental* study, it's the one the experimenter *manipulates*.
    (E.g. a treatment variable)

- In *observational studies* about nominal participant variables such as Gender, Ethnicity, Sexual Orientation, Immigrant Status, etc. these variables are most often the independent variables. (E.g. if a study is called "The *effect* of Gender and Ethnicity on…" or "The *relationship between* Gender, Ethnicity and…" you can be sure Gender and Ethnicity are the *independent* variables.

- *If* a study describes a *causal* relationship, then the *independent* variable is the cause. E.g. "The effect of early abuse on later hostility…" implies the 'level of early abuse' is the independent variable since it's obviously supposed to be causing some variation in hostility.

- If some *condition* or *event* is supposed to predispose people to have certain illnesses, diagnoses, personality traits, etc., then information about whether the participant experienced the *condition* or *event* is the *independent* variable.

SPOTTING THE DEPENDENT VARIABLE

- It's the one you try to *predict* or *estimate.*

- In an *experimental* study, it's the one *not manipulated* by the experimenter, but merely observed.

- *If* a study describes a *causal* relationship, then the *dependent* variable is the *one being caused.*

- If some *condition* or *event* is supposed to predispose people to have certain illnesses, diagnoses, personality traits, etc., then information about whether the participant *has* the illness, diagnosis or personality trait, etc. is the dependent variable.

EXERCISES FOR CHAPTER 1

----

1. 200 patients in a psychiatric hospital are studied to see if "Handedness" (Whether the patient is "Left Handed" or "Right Handed") is related to the patient's diagnostic category. What does "Left Handed" represent in this example?

2. What does "Handedness" represent?

----

3. Suppose that a *relationship* exists between the variables X and Y, and that Sue and Joe have both been measured on each of the variables X and Y. You can conclude that...
   (READ ALL ANSWERS)
       A) knowing Sue's score on X would help you predict her score on Y.
       B) knowing Sue's score on X would help you to predict Joe's score on Y.
       C) Sue's score on X causes (at least in part) her score on Y.
       D) there must be some relationship between Sue and Joe, though it may
           not be causal, and it might only be platonic.
       E) more than one of the above must be true.

Suppose we obtain and record from a group of 8 people, the person's gender (male or female), and their marital status (single, married, divorced)

4. Are the data obtained in this study nominal, ordinal, or interval scale data? Explain.

5. How many variables are involved?

6. What is the total number of scores appearing in the raw data?

Fast Eddie, a horseplayer, states "My horse, 'Halcion' placed (finished second) and paid $7.60."

7. If the horse Eddie bet on is the *case (or element)*, what two *variables* are involved here?

8. What are the two *scores*?

9. What is each variable's level of measurement, or 'type of scale'? (nominal, ordinal, or interval)

----

10. What is true *only* of observational studies but never true of experimental studies?

Dr. C. conducts an experiment to support the statement: "Vitamin B supplements will cause an *increase* in the math scores of 3rd grade students in the Amityville N.Y. school district." The school district has two different elementary schools with 3rd grade students available for the study: School A, an "old" school constructed in 1963, and School B, a "new" school built in 1990.

During fall 1990, Dr. C. personally picks 18 of the 3rd grade students from Ms. Johnson's 3rd grade class in School B. She contacts the parents of these students and 12 of the children's parents agree to have their children participate in the study. Dr. C. arranges to have these 12 children given a B-vitamin supplement daily throughout the school term.

During fall 1991, Dr. C. personally picks 12 children from Mr. Simpson's 3rd grade class in School A and gives them each a placebo tablet at the start of the day. No parental permission is obtained for this group.

Each group of 12 students is assessed by Dr. C. at the end of their school year, using a standardized math test.

11. Does the selection of the 24 students studied using the above procedure (based only on information supplied above) constitute *simple random sampling*? Explain.

12. This study is:
    A) observational, not controlled
    B) experimental, not controlled
    C) observational, controlled
    D) experimental, controlled

13. All participants in the *treatment* group were 3rd grade students from _____ class who _____ picked by Dr. C.
    A) Ms Johnson's, were not
    B) Mr. Simpson's, were not
    C) Ms Johnson's, were
    D) Mr. Simpson's, were
    E) either, were

14. All participants in the *control* group were 3rd grade students from _____ class who _____ picked by Dr. C.
    A) Ms Johnson's, were
    B) Mr. Simpson's, were
    C) Ms Johnson's, were not
    D) Mr. Simpson's, were not
    E) either, were not

15. Assume that neither group of students in the study knew whether they were receiving the supplement or the placebo. Based on this information, was this study *single*, or *double blind*? Explain.

16. What was the effect of the supplement confounded with:
    A) the effect of "teacher" (Johnson vs Simpson)   B) the effect of "year" (1990 vs 1991)
    C) the effect of "school" (School A vs School B)   D) all of the above
    E) none of the above

17. (HARD!) What was the *population actually studied* by Dr. C.? I.e., *exactly* what group of people could Dr. C. correctly generalize to, based on this study?

18. What was the *independent* variable?

19. What was the *dependent* variable?

20. What was the *sample*?

21. How many scores on the *independent* variable appear in the entire set of raw data for Dr. C's study?

ANSWERS TO EXERCISES

1 - 2. "Left Handed" is a *score* on the *variable* "Handedness".

3. A

    Relationships exist between variables *not* between cases; therefore, knowing *one* case's score on X can only help you predict *that case's* score on Y, it cannot help you predict scores for other cases!

4. The data are *nominal* scale data because both variables divide the cases into categories (i.e., they are qualitative not quantitative.)

5. There are two variables: gender and marital status.

6. Each case gets one score on each variable; therefore, since there are 8 cases and 2 variables, the total number of scores in the raw data is 16. (Measuring 8 cases on 2 variables produces 16 scores)

    ----
7. "Order of finish in the race" and "Amount the horse paid"

8. 2nd, $7.60

9. Ordinal, Interval

    ----
10. With observational studies, *nature* (ie., factors outside of the control of the experimenter) assigns the participants to different groups or categories.

----

11. No. No technique involving *human judgement* is simple random sampling. Since Dr. C. personally picked the students who would participate, the selection does not constitute simple random sampling. Simple random sampling is a process which *guarantees* that *each case* in the population has an *equal chance* of being in the sample.

12. D

The *researcher*, not nature, determined which category each student was in (ie. received supplement or placebo). This is a *controlled* study since there is a treatment and control group against which to measure the results.

13. C

The treatment group are those students who received the Vitamin B supplement and were personally picked by Dr. C.

14. B

The control group are those students who received the placebo and were picked by Dr. C.

15. This was a single blind study because the students did not know which group they were in at the time the study was conducted. (If *neither* the researcher nor the students knew which group the participants were in, then this would have been *double* blind).

16. D

The effect of the vitamins was confounded by all of these effects because the cases differed on all of these variables, not just the variable of interest (ie. vitamin). Because of this, there may be confusion about which variable is causing the effect.

17. The population was the set of all cases that might have been picked to be in the sample. In this case, this set is quite difficult to explain precisely. It consists of all students:
   1) whom Dr. C. would choose, *and*
   2) who are *either*
      a) in Ms. Johnson's class and able to get permission, *or*
      b) in Mr. Simpson's class.

18. The *independent variable* was the variable which specified whether a student received the Vitamin B or the placebo.

19. The *dependent variable* was the student's performance on the standardized math test.

20. The *sample* consisted of all 24 students who were measured, i.e., all students who received the Vitamin B or the placebo.

21. 24

Measuring 24 cases on one independent variable produces 24 scores on that variable.

CHAPTER 2
DISPLAYING DATA

2.1 RAW DATA AND FREQUENCY DISTRIBUTIONS

RAW DATA (DATA MATRICES)

In any study involving statistics there must be a set of *raw data*, i.e., a list of all the scores the different cases got on the variables when they were measured. Sets of raw data are also referred to as **data matrices**. Computer programs sometimes refer to them as **rectangular data sets**.

No matter how advanced the statistics you are using may be, you should *always* keep the raw data in mind. If you are reading about a study, it's helpful to stop and picture the cases being measured on each variable, and to picture the set of raw data that must have been recorded. The format for presenting raw data is standard:

1) *Variable names* are *column* headings, which appear on one top line from left to right.

2) The *scores* on each variable appear in the rows of a column under the variable name.

A list of the cases' names, or a set of id. numbers for referring to individual cases are *optional*. The cases' *names* or *id's* are not usually considered a necessary part of the data.

EXAMPLE: TABLE 2.1.1

Case	Name	Treatment	ESAT Score
1.	Al	A	6
2.	Bijan	A	7
3.	Cal	A	8
4.	Den	A	8
5.	Ed	A	9
6.	Fab	B	9
7.	Glee	B	10
8.	Hal	B	10
9.	Ivy	B	10
10.	Jay	B	10

The *raw data* in Table 2.1.1 above consist of the columns labeled "TREATMENT" and "ESAT". The sequence numbers and names are optional.

There is one (horizontal) row in the raw data for each case (or case), and one (vertical) column for each variable.

Ten cases were measured, so there are 10 scores on each variable, and 20 scores appear altogether in the raw data.

> **(2.1.1)   The number of *scores* appearing in a set of raw data is always:**
>
> **(the number of cases measured)(the number of variables)**
> **or**
> **(n)(the number of variables)**

The number of cases in a set of data is always designated by "N" or "n".

The upper case "N" is used when it is known that the data represent a *whole population*, not just a sample from a population.

The lower case "n" is used when it is known that the data represent a sample from some population.

FREQUENCY DISTRIBUTIONS

These contain all of the information in the raw data for *one* variable, but in a more compact form. You can always create a frequency distribution from a set of raw data, and you can always go back and recreate the raw data from the data in the frequency distribution.

DEFINITION:

A frequency distribution for a variable lists all possible scores on the variable, and for each score, a frequency that indicates how many cases got that score.

EXAMPLE:

Here's the frequency distribution for the variable ESAT based on the raw data in Table 2.1.1 above.

TABLE 2.1.2

ESAT	f
6	1
7	1
8	2
9	2
10	4

n = 10

The frequency distribution consists of the two columns above and their headings.

It's always a good idea to total the "f" or frequency column, and check that this total matches n, the number of cases measured.

DISTRIBUTIONS 'BY PERCENT'

We can convert any frequency to a percent as follows:

Percent = (100%)(f / n)

A distribution which is like a frequency distribution, but lists percents instead of frequencies is called a percentage distribution or "distribution of scores by percent".

Table 2.1.3 below shows the distribution of ESAT scores by percent. The second column has been converted from frequency to percent For example, 4 of the 10 cases got scores of 10 on the ESAT, and (100%)(4/10) = 40%, which appears to the right of the score 10 in the column labeled "%".

TABLE 2.1.3

ESAT	%
6	10%
7	10%
8	20%
9	20%
10	40%
	100%

RELATIVE FREQUENCY DISTRIBUTIONS AND PROBABILITY DISTRIBUTIONS

Similarly we could convert frequencies to *relative frequencies* or *proportions* as follows:

Proportion = f / n

Proportions for the ESAT data appear in the right column in TABLE 2.1.4 below.

TABLE 2.1.4

ESAT	Relative frequency or Proportion
6	.1
7	.1
8	.2
9	.2
10	.4
	1.0

TIP:

>Students who have been away from math for a while sometimes forget that *proportions* and *percents* measure exactly the same thing, on different scales. You can always convert from a proportion to a percent or vice versa:

$$percent = (100\%)(proportion)$$

$$proportion = percent/(100\%)$$

PROPORTIONS AND PROBABILITIES

Very often, *proportions* are interpreted as *probabilities* (and vice versa). For example, we could say accurately, "If one case is picked at random from the sample described in TABLE 2.1.4, the *probability* of picking a case with a score of 9 is .2".

Probabilities *look* just like proportions, and it will create no problems if we assume that whenever the right column in a distribution has values between 0 and 1.0 which add up to 1.0, the numbers can represent *either* proportions *or* probabilities. The distribution in question can be interpreted as a "distribution of scores by proportion," or, as a "probability distribution".

2.2 BAR GRAPHS

Histograms and bar graphs can represent *many* cases' scores on *one* single variable. With these displays you can quickly and easily visualize patterns in data that would be difficult to describe with numbers alone.

The *horizontal* axis on a histogram or bar graph always represents a set of possible scores on one variable.

The *vertical* axis or the "height" of a bar graph or histogram always tells you *how many* cases got a particular score.

DRAWING BAR GRAPHS

To display *nominal* scale (or 'qualitative') data the appropriate display is a *bar graph*, in which separate vertical bars are used to indicate how many cases are in each category.

The height of the bars may be based on *frequency*, or *percent*, or *proportion*.

TABLE 2.2.1

COLOR	f
Blue	3
Green	2
Orange	1
Red	2

n = 8

EXAMPLE: FIGURE 2.2.1

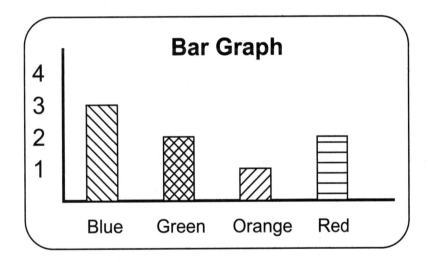

Note that the information in the bar graph above is equivalent to the data in the frequency distribution. From either, we could conclude that '8 cases were measured on a nominal scale variable, and 3 cases scored Blue, etc.'

ALTERNATIVES TO BAR GRAPHS

TABLE 2.2.2 below shows the color data with columns added indicating the relative frequency (or proportion) and percent for each color. Figures 2.2.3 and 2.2.4 show a '3D BAR CHART' and a 'pie chart' for the color data. These formats, seen often in popular publications such as USA Today, are easily produced using word processing program and spreadsheet programs such as Microsoft Word and Microsoft Excel.

TABLE 2.2.2

COLOR	Frequency f	Relative frequency or Proportion	Percent %
Blue	3	3/8 = .375	37.5%
Green	2	2/8 = .250	25%
Orange	1	1/8 = .125	12.5%
Red	2	2/8 = .250	25%
	n = 8	total = 1.000 √	total = 100% √

FIGURE 2.2.3   RELATIVE FREQUENCY DISTRIBUTION

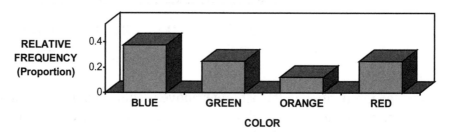

FIGURE 2.2.4   PIE CHART

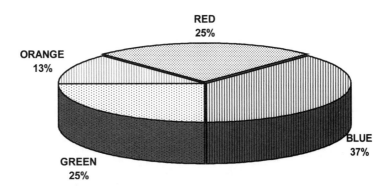

2.3 HISTOGRAMS and FREQUENCY POLYGONS

CONTINUOUS DATA

Continuous (numerical) data are numerical data in which, at least in theory, every pair of possible scores has another possible score between them. Examples of variables usually measured on continuous scales are height, weight, temperature, speed, length, and blood pressure.
Often in the social sciences, data which are not truly continuous are treated *as if* they were continuous. Income, debt, IQ scores and personality test scores are common examples.

DISPLAYING CONTINUOUS DATA

To display *continuous* numerical data (typically interval scale data) either *histograms* , *frequency polygons*, or *density histogram*s may be used. Density histograms are described below in Section 2.4.

DISCRETE NUMERICAL DATA

Discrete numerical data are numerical data which are *not* continuous.

In discrete data there are "gaps" in the scale.

Typically discrete data represent *counts* ("How many children do you have") or *ranks* ("How many runners beat you in the marathon")

DISPLAYING DISCRETE DATA

To display *discrete* numerical data (typically ordinal scale data) *histograms* are typically used. Histograms are drawn like bar graphs, but the vertical bars are connected, i.e., they are drawn right next to each other.

DRAWING HISTOGRAMS:

EXAMPLE

Suppose the data below in Table 2.3.1 have been collected from a small sample of 8 families, where 'X' represents the number of children:

TABLE 2.3.1

X	f
0	1
1	2
2	3
3	2

FIGURE 2.3.1   **HISTOGRAM FOR TABLE 2.3.1**

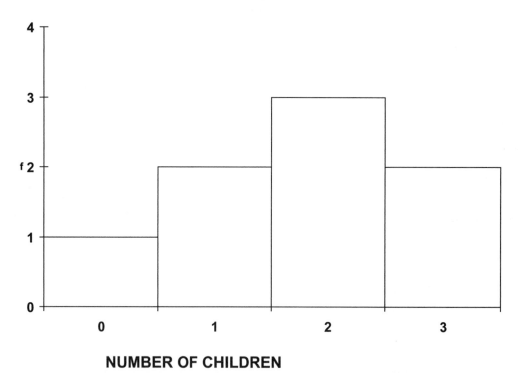

NUMBER OF CHILDREN

In the histogram the *vertical* axis represents the frequency of each score, and the *horizontal* axis represents the scores themselves. Boxes are drawn above each score, centered around the score itself. The *height* of the box indicates the *frequency* of the score.

DRAWING FREQUENCY POLYGONS:

EXAMPLE
Suppose the data below in Table 2.3.2 have been collected from a small sample of 8 families, where 'X' represents the monthly income in thousands of dollars.

TABLE 2.3.2

Income	f
0	1
1	2
2	3
3	2

FIGURE 2.3.2   FREQUENCY POLYGON FOR TABLE 2.3.2

MONTHLY INCOME

Frequency polygons are more often used when the data are *continuous*. Frequency polygons and histograms contain exactly the same kinds of information. As in a histogram, the *vertical* axis represents the frequency of each score, and the *horizontal* axis represents the scores themselves.

However, in a frequency polygon, a point is placed above each score. The *height* of the point indicates the *frequency* of the score. The points are then connected.

2.4* DENSITY HISTOGRAMS

DENSITY SCALES

When a percentage (or proportion) histogram is created for **continuous** numerical data, the vertical scale is referred to as a *density* scale (Often as a '*probability density*').

The tricky thing about histograms that use *density* scales is that the vertical axis indicates *proportion per unit.* (or equivalently, 'percent per unit').

Here's an example of what '*proportion per unit*' means:

Suppose all we know about some data is that '.4 of all cases scored between 5 and 9'. I.e., the *proportion* of all cases that scored between 5 and 9 is .4.

It would be misleading to conclude that ".4 scored between 5 and 6" or that ".4 scored between 8 and 9". We *don't know* exactly what proportion of the cases scored between 5 and 6, but the most *reasonable guess* would be *.1*.

Why? There are 4 'units' *between* 5 and 9. (This is just another way of saying that 9 - 5 is equal to 4, or that the distance from 5 to 9 is 4.) And .4 of the cases scored in that range, which is 4 units wide.

We figure that, on the average, the *density* of cases in the range 5 to 9 is ' .1 per unit ', because .4/4 = .1. We'd make the *height* of a density histogram .1 in the range 5-9 to indicate this.

In general:

(2.4.1)

The "proportion per unit", or the *density*, is the *height* of a density histogram.

It is computed by *dividing* the *proportion* of cases scoring in a certain interval by the *width* of that interval.

$$\text{density} = \frac{\text{proportion of elements}}{\text{width of interval}}$$

---

* asterisks denote optional sections.

GROUPED FREQUENCY DISTRIBUTIONS

Sometimes we may know how many cases scored within certain *intervals*, (also called *class intervals* or *ranges*), of scores, but we may not know each individual case 's score precisely. In such cases we summarize the data in a *grouped* frequency distribution. A grouped frequency distribution specifies a set of intervals, and a frequency for each interval. Here's a simple grouped frequency distribution:

TABLE 2.4.1A

X	f
0 - 20	120
20 - 60	80

n = 200

This table tells us that 200 cases were measured on the variable X, with 120 cases scoring between 0 and 20 on X, and 80 cases scoring between 20 and 60. The score 0 is referred to as the **lower limit** of the first interval; 20 is its **upper limit**.

THE ENDPOINT CONVENTION FOR GROUPED DATA

If Joe scored 20 on X, is Joe one of the 120 people included in the first interval, or one of the 80 in the second interval? The answer is that Joe scored 'between 20 and 60', and is included in the second interval. Intervals, by longstanding convention, include their *lower* limits, but not their *upper* limits.

DRAWING DENSITY HISTOGRAMS:

EXAMPLE

To graph a density histogram for grouped data, we must first compute the densities for each interval.

Suppose the variable X in Table 2.4.1 represents incomes of 200 families:

.6 of the families had incomes between 0 and 20. Since there are 20 units between 0 and 20, we estimate that the *density* in that interval is .6/20 or .03.
The interval's *width* is always the upper limit minus the lower limit.

Similarly for the 20 - 60 interval the density is .4/40, or .01. See TABLE 2.4.1B for a summary of the computations. The check mark (√) under the proportion column indicates that you can always *check* your computations by making sure that this column total is close to 1.0

TABLE 2.4.1B

X	f	proportion	width	density
0 - 20	120	.6	20	.03
20 - 60	80	.4	40	.01

n = 200   1.0 √

FIGURE 2.4.2   DENSITY HISTOGRAM FOR TABLE 2.4.1

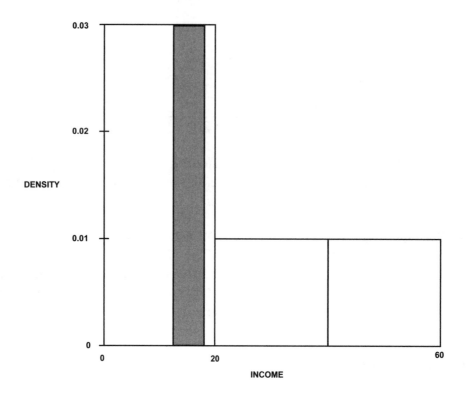

Note that the *height* of a density histogram over each interval is the *density* (in proportion *per unit*) for that interval. This density histogram shows a height of '.03 per unit' above the incomes between 0 and 20 and a height of '.01 per unit' above the incomes 20 to 60.

AREA REPRESENTS PROPORTION (OR PROBABILITY) IN DENSITY HISTOGRAMS

Density histograms are used to answer questions like "What proportion of the cases scored between 15 and 18?". Later we'll use density histograms to answer questions like "What is the probability that a case picked at random scored between 15 and 18?".

Both questions above can be answered by computing the *area* between the scores 15 and 18 in the graph. (shaded in Figure 2.4.2 above). The shaded area between scores 15 and 18 is *3 units wide* (there's one unit between 15 and 16, one between 16 and 17, and one between 17 and 18), and it's *.03 'proportion per unit'* high. To obtain the area we multiply the width by the height. Multiplying *3* times *.03* we get *.09*, and so we can estimate that .09 of all cases obtained scores between 15 and 18.

EXERCISES, CHAPTER 2

Here is a hypothetical weekly box office summary for some year in the near future:

Film	Rank	Gross	Theatres	Weeks	Company
I Know What You Did!	1st	27.2	2,334	13	Disney
Scream 17	2nd	16.3	1,984	27	Warner
Being Somebody Else	3rd	12.2	958	2	Miramax
What Is It About Mary?	4th	8.9	17	1	Disney

1. The table above describes 4 different films measured on _____ *variables*.
      A) 20   B) 4   C) 5   D) 6   E) 16

2. In the table above, "Disney" represents a(n)
      A) nominal scale variable   B) case   C) statistic   D) score or value

3. "Scream 17" is a(n)
      A) nominal scale variable   B) case   C) statistic   D) score or value

4. "Rank" is a(n)
      A) nominal scale variable   B) score on a nominal scale variable
      C) ordinal scale variable   D) score on an ordinal scale variable
      E) none of the above

5. "1st" is a(n)
      A) nominal scale variable   B) score on a nominal scale variable
      C) ordinal scale variable   D) score on an ordinal scale variable
      E) none of the above

---

6. Is the score 2.5 included in the class interval 1.5 to 2.5?

Suppose that 60% of all the cases in a study scored between 40 and 70.

*7. What is the width of this interval?
      A) .5   B) 1.5   C) 30   D) 20   E) none of the above.

*8. If a density histogram is drawn, what would be the height (density) for the above interval?
      A) .005   B) .02   C) .2   D) .6   E) none of the above is correct

*9. Which type of data are most appropriate for density histograms?
      A) Qualitative   B) Discrete   C) Continuous
      D) All of the above are equally appropriate   E) Any numeric data are equally appropriate

---

The next three questions refer to these data:

INCOME	f
0-50	30
50-60	20

*10. The data above are presented in a frequency distribution in which the values of the variable are represented by *ranges*, or *intervals* of scores.
     The type of data which are most often presented in this form is
           A) continuous quantitative (interval scale)
           B) discrete quantitative (usually ordinal scale)
           C) continuous qualitative
           D) discrete qualitative (nominal scale)

*11. In the type of histogram most appropriate for data such as this, the *height* of the histogram represents
           A) the score a case received
           B) the frequency of a particular score
           C) proportion per unit, or density
           D) proportion

*12. In the density histogram representing the distribution of income, the height of the graph above the interval 0 - 50 would be
           A) .06 B) .04 C) 40 D) .012 E) .6

REVIEW EXERCISES   CHAPTERS 1 - 2

DATA: 10, 7, 10, 10, 8, 6, 10, 9, 9, 10

13. Create the appropriate frequency distribution. Assume the scores were measured on the variable X.

     OPTIONAL PREVIEW QUESTIONS:
*14. The *mean* is the *average* of all the scores, the sum divided by the number of scores.
     What is the mean of the above 10 scores?

*15. The *mode* is the most frequent score. What is the mode?

*16. The *median* is the *middle* case 's score. What is the median?

We'll define this type of distribution, in which the mean is less than the median, as *negatively skewed.*

There are 316 left handed male asthma patients at University Hospital in Philadelphia. From these, 16 are chosen randomly to participate in a study. Each individual is asked whether he smokes or not, and each is given a test to rate the severity of his symptoms. 9 of the 16 men report that they don't smoke.

17. What kind of study is this?

18. What is the population?

19. What is the sample?

20. What is the control group?

21. What's the independent variable?

22. What's the dependent variable?

23. What are some variables the independent variable might be *confounded* with?

TABLE 1

X	f
0 - 8	80
8 - 12	80
12 - 22	40

*24. What is the height of the density histogram for TABLE 1 above the range 0 - 8 ?

*25. What is the height of the density histogram for TABLE 1 above the range 8 -12 ?

*26. What's the density for the range 12 - 14 ?

*27. What does the vertical axis represent in a histogram for data like this ?

*28. Estimate the percent of cases that scored between 6 and 10.

*29. Estimate the percent of cases that scored between 11 and 16.

---

* optional (or preview) questions

ANSWERS TO EXERCISES   CHAPTER 1-2

---

1. C) 5   Rank, Gross, Theatres, Weeks, Company. "Film" is just the ID of the case, and is not usually considered one of the variables.

2. D) score or value

3. B) case

4. C) ordinal scale variable

5. D) score on an ordinal scale variable

---

6. No, but the score 1.5 is included. Class intervals include the left, or lower endpoint, not the right, or higher endpoint.

---

*7. C

The range of scores in the interval is 40 - 70, to determine the interval width, subtract the lowest score in the range from the highest score. (i.e. 70 - 40 = 30)

*8. B

Density is calculated by dividing proportion by the interval width:

Range of Scores	Width	Proportion	Density
40-70	30	.60	.60/30 = .02

*9. C

*10. A Since the data are presented in a grouped frequency distribution, using ranges of scores.

     Data presented in this form are always interval scale data.

*11. C This represents the best estimate of the proportion of cases that got a certain score.

*12. D The height of the graph above the interval 0 - 50 would be the *density* or *proportion per unit*. To calculate:

Income	f	Width	Proportion	Proportion/Unit
0-50	30	50	.6	.60/50 = .012

    (We calculate proportion by dividing f, in this case 30, by n, in this case 50, 30/50 = .6)

ANSWERS TO REVIEW EXERCISES

13.

X	f
6	1
7	1
8	1
9	2
10	5

*14. 8.9 = 89/10

*15. 10 5 cases scored 10. No other score occurred as frequently in these data.

*16. 9.5 When there are an even number of scores, the convention is to *average* the two middle scores, which in this case are 9 and 10

17. A controlled observational study

18. All left handed male asthma patients at University Hospital

19. The set of 16 men actually measured

20. The men who reported not being smokers

21. "Smoking", or whether the men smoke or not

22. Severity of asthma symptoms

23. Age, other illnesses, lifestyle variables such a drinking and/or drug use, medication, whether the patient was raised by smokers, etc. (*Not* gender or handedness in this sample, because gender and handedness were constant in this sample)

TABLE 1

X	f	%	WIDTH	% PER UNIT
0 - 8	80	40%	8	5
8 - 12	80	40%	4	10
12 - 22	40	20%	10	2

*24. 5 percent per unit

*25. 10 percent per unit

*26. 2 percent per unit

*27. Density in percent per unit

*28. 30%
> Each unit between 0 and 8 is estimated to contain 5%. There are 2 of these units included in the interval 6 to 10, (6-7 and 7-8)
> Each unit between 8 and 12 contains 10%. There are two of these units in the interval 6-10. (8 to 9, and 9 to 10).
> So in the interval 6-10 we have 2 units at 5% plus 2 units at 10% = 30%.

*29. 18%
> 1(10%) + 4(2%) as in #5

----

* optional (or preview) questions

CHAPTER 3
MEASURES OF LOCATION

3.1 MEASURES OF LOCATION, OR CENTRAL TENDENCY

The mean, mode, and median are three different statistics, each designed to summarize a bunch of scores by indicating 'how high' or 'how low' the scores are *generally* or *typically*.

If we picture a bunch of scores displayed in a histogram, with lower scores on the left and higher scores on the right, it's easy to see why these statistics are called "measures of location." They each give us one number that summarizes where the scores tend to be *located*, from left to right.

Here are brief definitions to begin with:

THE MEAN
is the number obtained when you add up a set of scores on an *interval scale* variable and then divide by the number of cases that were measured.

THE MODE
is the score that occurs most often in a given set of scores. In a frequency distribution, it's the *score* with the highest frequency.

THE MEDIAN
is found by *ordering,* or *ranking,* a set of ordinal or interval scale scores from low to high (or from high to low)
If an *odd* number of cases were measured, then the *middle* score is the median.
If an *even* number of cases were measured, then the *mean* of the *two middle scores* is the median.

3.2 HOW TO COMPUTE THE MEAN

COMPUTING THE MEAN FROM RAW DATA

NOTATION:
$\overline{X}$ represents the mean of the variable X, for a *sample*
n   represents the number of cases in a *sample*

μ_X (pronounced "mu sub X") represents the *mean* of the variable X, for an *entire population*. When some statistic is computed for an entire population it is called a *population parameter*, and is usually designated with a Greek letter.
N   represents the number of cases in a *population*.

(3.2.1) FORMULAS FOR COMPUTING THE MEAN (FROM RAW DATA ONLY)

$\overline{X}$ = the total of all scores / the number of scores

or

$$\overline{X} = \frac{\Sigma X}{n}$$

EXAMPLE 1: COMPUTING THE MEAN FROM RAW DATA

Here's a set of 10 scores that we'll compute the mean of three times in this chapter. Note that 10 cases were measured on one variable, so there are 10 scores.

```
                        X
                        1
                        2
                        2
                        3
                        3
                        3
                        3
                        4
                        4        mean, or X
                        5         /
            total  30/10 = 3
                     /    \
        total of all scores   number of scores
```

SUMMATION NOTATION

The symbol Σ may be read as "The sum of all ...".

Sums denoted by Σ are taken *after* multiplying, but *before* adding, unless parentheses indicate that addition or subtraction should be done first.

E.g. "$\Sigma 3X+4$" says "*first* multiply each score by 3, then add the results, then add 4 to the sum.", but "$\Sigma(3X+4)$" says "*first* multiply each score by 3, then add 4 to each result, *then* add the results." We do the computations inside the parentheses *before* adding.

A series of different cases' scores on a variable will be denoted by a *column* headed by the variable name. When a whole set of scores is changed by adding, or multiplying, etc., *new columns* will be created to illustrate the result.

EXAMPLE: COMPUTING SUMS USING "Σ" NOTATION

$\underline{X}$	$\underline{3X}$	$\underline{3X+4}$
4	12	16
2	6	10
$\underline{6}$	$\underline{18}$	$\underline{22}$
$\Sigma X = 12$	$\Sigma 3X = 36$	$\Sigma(3X+4) = 48$ but, $\Sigma 3X+4 = 36+4 = 40$!

COMPUTING THE MEAN FROM A FREQUENCY DISTRIBUTION

(3.2.2) FORMULA FOR THE MEAN (OF A FREQUENCY DISTRIBUTION)

$$\overline{X} = \frac{\sum fX}{\sum f} = \frac{\sum fX}{n}$$

EXAMPLE 2: THE MEAN OF THE FREQUENCY DISTRIBUTION BASED ON EXAMPLE 1

Here are the *same* 10 scores used in Example 1 above, shown in frequency distribution form. Note that it takes only *five* rows in this table to describe *all 10* scores, because several rows represent *more than one case* . For example, the third row represents the four cases that scored 3 on X-- note the 'f' value of 4.

possible scores \\ $\underline{X}$	how many cases got each score \\ $\underline{f}$	(frequency)(score) / $\underline{fX}$
1	1	1 (1x1)
2	2	4 (2x2)
3	4	12 (4x3)
4	2	8 (2x4)
5	$\underline{1}$	$\underline{5}$ (1x5)
	$n = \Sigma f = 10$	$\Sigma fX = 30$

number of cases that got measured   sum or total of all scores

$$\overline{X} = \Sigma fX/n = 30/10 = 3$$

```
┌─────────────────────────────────────────────────────────┐
│  TIP  3.2                                                 │
│      Be careful!                                          │
│      Be sure to divide by n, the                          │
│                                                           │
│                  number of  cases                         │
│                                                           │
│      when computing the mean of a frequency              │
│      distribution !                                       │
│              not the number of rows !                    │
│              not the number of different scores !        │
└─────────────────────────────────────────────────────────┘
```

TIP 3.2 warns you away from this kind of *frequent* error: Erroneously computing a mean of *6* for the data above in EXAMPLE 2, by dividing 30 by 5! They say "there were 5 scores, 1 to 5, and they added up to 30, so I divided 30 by 5." Hopefully you see that there were *10* scores. obtained by the *10* cases that must have been measured. The number 5 *is* the number of *different values* obtained on the variable X by these cases, but that number *does not* figure into any of our statistical computations! It's *n*, the number of cases that were measured that matters. (Recall that the frequency distribution above is interpreted: "1 *case* scored 1, 2 cases scored 2, 4 cases scored 3...etc.")

COMPUTING THE MEAN FROM A PROBABILITY (OR 'RELATIVE FREQUENCY') DISTRIBUTION

```
┌─────────────────────────────────────────────────────────┐
│                                                           │
│      (3.2.4)  FORMULA FOR THE MEAN OF A PROBABILITY        │
│                 DISTRIBUTION                               │
│                                                           │
│                      X  = ΣpX                             │
│                                                           │
│      (Where p designates probability of the score X,      │
│      or the proportion of cases that scored X)            │
│                                                           │
└─────────────────────────────────────────────────────────┘
```

$$\overline{X} = \Sigma pX$$

This formula states: "To compute the mean, first multiply each possible score by the *proportion* of cases that got that score. Then add."

EXAMPLE 3: THE MEAN OF THE PROBABILITY DISTRIBUTION BASED ON EXAMPLE 1

possible scores \\	proportion of cases that got each score \\	(proportion)(score) /
X	p	pX
1	.1	.1 (.1x1)
2	.2	.4 (.2x2)
3	.4	1.2 (.4x3)
4	.2	.8 (.2x4)
5	.1	.5 (.1x5)
	Σp = 1.0	$\overline{X}$ = ΣpX = 3.0

check: sum of proportions is always 1.0   mean

3.3 SHAPES OF HISTOGRAMS AND MEASURES OF LOCATION

Sketching distributions can help you to quickly develop the right intuitions about all of the commonly used statistics. It's very helpful at first to write out frequency distributions, draw sketches, try to estimate the mean, mode, median (and after the next chapter, the range and standard deviation as well), and *then* do the computations and check your estimates.

Actually, when real cases do get measured, the resulting distributions don't often end up looking very complicated.

The following definitions and rules will help you to
     1) categorize distributions using the correct vocabulary, and
     2) estimate some statistics just by inspection of a histogram.

SYMMETRICAL DISTRIBUTIONS

Distributions in which the left half is a "mirror image" of the right half are called "*symmetrical*", which corresponds to our usual use of that term. Some people describe them this way: "If you draw a vertical line through the center of a symmetrical distribution and fold on that line, the two sides will match up."

In symmetrical distributions, the mean and the median are the same. If a symmetrical distribution is unimodal, i.e., if it has only one mode, the mode will be the same as the mean and the median. Note that symmetry is defined in terms of *shape*, not in terms of statistics. Not *all* distributions in which the mean equals the median are symmetrical in shape.

OUTLIERS

Sometimes most of the scores in a distribution are close to the middle, while a few scores are very far from the center (The "center" is usually indicated by the median in such cases). The scores far from the middle are called *outliers*.

NEGATIVELY SKEWED DISTRIBUTIONS

We'll define distributions in which the mean is *less than* the median as *negatively skewed*. Such distributions often, but not always, have a shape indicating "low outliers" or a tail that is "longer and shallower on the left."

A nice intuition regarding negatively skewed distributions: The "low outliers" affect the mean, pulling it *down*. The median, being unaffected by outliers, remains "in the middle."

POSITIVELY SKEWED DISTRIBUTIONS

Distributions in which the mean is *greater than* the median are defined as *positively skewed*. Such distributions often, but not always, have a shape indicating "high outliers" or a tail that is "longer and shallower on the right."

Typically in **positively** skewed distributions, the "high outliers" affect the mean, pulling it *up*. The median, being unaffected by outliers, remains "in the middle."

EXAMPLES

(A) DATA: 1, 7   OR   X
                              1
                              7

(A) A SYMMETRICAL DISTRIBUTION

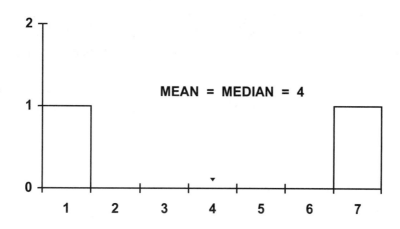

MEAN = MEDIAN = 4

(B) DATA: 1, 1, 7   OR   X   OR   X   f
                               1   *1*   2
                               1   7   1
                               7

(B) A SKEWED DISTRIBUTION

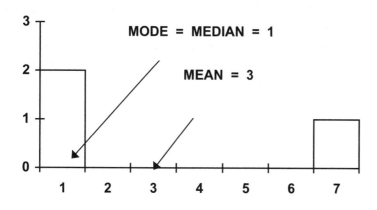

MODE = MEDIAN = 1

MEAN = 3

3.4 COMPARING THE MEAN, MEDIAN AND MODE

THE MEAN

PRO:

1) It is "closest" to the scores in this sense: If *total distance* is measured in the usual way (which involves *squaring* the distances from the mean to each score) the total distance from the *mean* to all the scores is less than it would be for any other number. In the next chapter, this important property will be restated as "the mean *minimizes* the sum of squared deviations."

2) It is "in the middle" of all the scores in this sense: The scores that are *higher* than the mean exactly *balance* the scores that are *lower* than the mean. In terminology explained in the next chapter, the "*positive* deviations from the mean exactly equal the *negative* deviations."

3) Most of the mathematics of prediction, estimation and inference has been developed using the mean.

4) If a number of samples are repeatedly drawn from the same population, the means of the samples will *vary less* than other statistics. This property is referred to as "low sampling error", or "high sampling stability".

CON:

1) The mean is strongly affected by *outliers*

2) In skewed or bimodal distributions the mean may not lie close to *any* of the cases' actual scores.

3) The mean cannot be used with nominal or ordinal scale data!

THE MEDIAN

PRO:

1) It is in the "middle" of the scores in the *ordinal* sense: The number of cases that are *higher* than the median is equal to the number of cases that scored *lower* than the median.

2) It is not affected by *outliers*.

3) It is generally preferred, even with interval level data, when the data are *skewed*.

4) It *can* be used with interval or ordinal scale data.

CON:

1) It is not necessarily *close* to the scores in terms of the numerical distance from the scores, as the mean is.

2) Since it doesn't have the ideal mathematical qualities of the mean, techniques for prediction and estimation using the median are not well developed.

3) It doesn't have the sampling stability of the mean; i.e., the medians of several samples from the same population are likely to vary a lot. As a result some samples may be *misleading*, in the sense that the sample median may be quite far from the population median.

THE MODE

PRO:

1) It can be computed for any type of data: nominal, ordinal or interval.
2) It's easiest to compute.
3) It represents the "most typical" score in this sense: If you pick a case at random, and you guess that case 's score to be the mode, you maximize your probability of being correct.
4) It is *never* affected by outliers.

CON:

1) The mode may *not even exist* for some sets of data. Some data are ***bimodal***, i.e., there are two different scores that both have the same frequency, which is higher than any other. "Flat" distributions, in which all scores have the same frequency are examples of distributions with *no* modes.
2) The mode has poor sampling stability, and is not easily dealt with mathematically.

EXERCISES, CHAPTER 3

----

1. What is the mean of the following list of scores?

$$1, 1, 1, 1, 1, 1, 8$$

2. What is the mode?

3. What is the median?

----

(4) - (10). Compute the mean, median and mode for each of the distributions (4) - (10) in the table below, and describe its skewness and/or symmetry. DRAW SKETCHES!

(4)		(5)		(6)		(7)		(8)		(9)		(10)	
X	f	X	f	X	f	X	f	X	f	X	f	X	f
0	1	0	3	19	1	0	1	19	1	0	4	0	9
1	1	1	1	20	2	19	1	20	2	2	2	3	1
2	1	2	1	21	1	20	2	21	1	4	2	6	9
3	3	3	1			21	1	40	1	6	1		

	X
TABLE 2	
Dave	0
Ely	0
Mark	0
Janet	4
Brandy	4
Shante	16

11. The *mean* of the set of scores on the variable X described by TABLE 2 above is
    A) 0   B) 2   C) 4   D) 5   E) 6

12. The *median* of X is
    A) 0   B) 2   C) 4   D) 5   E) 6

13. The *mode* of X is
    A) 0   B) 2   C) 4   D) 5   E) 6

14. When scores are presented as in TABLE 2 the format is called a
    A) set of raw data   B) frequency distribution   C) histogram   D) datagram

15. The distribution of scores on the variable X described in TABLE 2 is
    A) positively skewed   B) negatively skewed   C) symmetrical
    D) not skewed   F) skewy

16. The participant designated Shante in this distribution would be designated…
    A) modal   B) a wanderer C) devious   D) an outlier   E) a deviation

---

FIGURES:

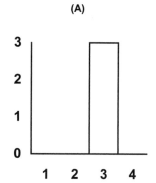
(A)

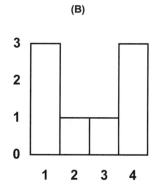
(B)

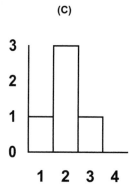
(C)

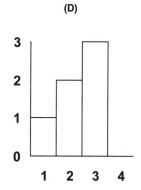
(D)

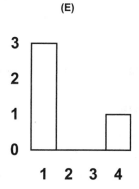
(E)

17. Which of the figures above obviously describes a variable with a mean of 2.5?
    A) A   B) B   C) C   D) D   E) E

18. Which of the figures above obviously describes a variable which is positively skewed?
    A) A   B) B   C) C   D) D   E) E

TABLE 4	X	p
	2	.5
	4	.4
	6	.1

TABLE 4 above is a probability distribution describing the variable X.

19. What is the mean of the variable X described in TABLE 4?
    A) 2.0   B) 3.2   C) 2.4   D) 4   E) none of the above

TABLE 5   X   f
                 2   5
                 4   4
                 6   1

20. When scores are presented as in TABLE 5 the format is called a
   A) set of raw data   B) frequency distribution   C) histogram   D) telegram

21. How many *scores* appear in the set of raw data described by TABLE 5?
   A) 2   B) 3   C) 6   D) 10   E) 16

22. The numeral '5' in TABLE 5 represents
   A) an interval scale variable   B) a score on an interval scale variable
   C) a frequency or 'count'   D) none of the above
   E) more than one of the above is correct

23. The *mean* of the variable X described in TABLE 5 is
   A) 2.0   B) 3.2   C) 2.4   D) 4   E) none of the above

ANSWERS TO EXERCISES, CHAPTER 3

----

1. 2   14/7

2. 1

3. 1

----

	(4)	(5)	(6)	(7)	(8)	(9)	(10)
Mean	2	1	20	16	24	2	3
Median	2.5	.5	20	20	20	2	3
Mode	3	0	20	20	20	0	none
Skewed?	neg.	pos.	no	neg.	pos.	no	no
Symmetrical?	no	no	yes	no	no	no	yes

11. C) 4

12. B) 2

13. A) 0

14. A) set of raw data

15. A) positively skewed

16. D) an outlier

----

17. B) B

18. E) E

----

19. B) 3.2

----

20. B) frequency distribution

21. D) 10

22. C) a frequency or 'count'

23. B) 3.2

CHAPTER 4

MEASURING ERROR AND DISPERSION

4.1 MEASURING THE ERROR OF ESTIMATES OR PREDICTIONS

ERROR: HOW MUCH THE ESTIMATE "MISSED BY"

Suppose a forecaster, A, predicts a high temperature today of 90 degrees, and the high actually turns out to be 95 degrees. We'd say the forecaster "was off by 5 degrees" or "underestimated by 5 degrees", because the *difference* between the estimate (90) and the true temperature (95) was 5 degrees.

Suppose another forecaster, B, predicted a high of 100 degrees today. Forecaster A and B are each off by 5 degrees, but in opposite directions.
We'd say that the errors they made were equal in *magnitude* but opposite in *sign*.

Which forecaster's error should be labeled "-5" and which should be labeled "+5"? The average person's intuition says that...

> forecaster A *under*estimated the actual temperature, so his error should be labeled "-5 degrees". That is, his estimate was "5 degrees too *low*".

> forecaster B *over*estimated the temperature; her estimate was 5 degrees too high. Label her error "+5 degrees".

This intuitive version of error can be computed this way:

(4.1.1)   ERROR OF AN ESTIMATE = THE ESTIMATE - THE TRUE VALUE

This intuitive notion of error will be referred to simply as "*error*", and if it occurs by *chance* (e.g., as a result of random sampling) it will be called "*chance error*". It tells you how much you have overestimated or underestimated by. If you *over*estimated, the sign of the error is *positive*; if you *under*estimated, the sign is *negative*.

RESIDUALS: ERRORS WITH THE *SIGN REVERSED*

In statistics, estimates and predictions are frequently made, and the accuracy of estimates is a very important topic.

An error in estimation in statistics is often referred to in a less intuitive way, as "*residual error*" or more simply a *residual*. Compared to the intuitive error estimates described above, the sign of a residual is *reversed*, and its interpretation is different.

(4.1.2) RESIDUAL ERROR =

THE TRUE VALUE - THE ESTIMATE

RESIDUAL ERROR = - ERROR

The residual tells you how much you'd have to add to the estimate to "fix it and make it correct."

In the example above, if the estimate is 90 and the true value is 95 the residual is +5. The interpretation of this is "to get from the estimate to the true value, you'd have to go *up* by an additional 5 degrees."

If the estimate is 100, but the true value is 95, the residual is -5. This indicates, correctly, that you'd have to *decrease* the estimate by 5 to 'make it correct'.

The residual error is always "what you'd need to *add* to the estimate to make it equal to the true value". This is expressed in an equation:

THE ESTIMATE + THE RESIDUAL ERROR   =   THE TRUE VALUE

4.2 COMBINING SEVERAL ERRORS

SQUARED ERROR AND R.M.S. ERROR (ROOT-MEAN-SQUARED ERROR)

If you *square* the error of an estimate, the sign of the error doesn't matter, so it doesn't matter whether the error was computed as a residual or as a simple error.

$$\text{SQUARED ERROR} = (\text{ERROR})^2 = (\text{RESIDUAL})^2$$

When we need to *combine* a bunch of errors together to come up with a measure of the overall error, we'll always *square* the errors first before *adding*, so the term *squared error* will be used frequently.

EXAMPLE 4.2

CASE	ESTIMATE	TRUE VALUE	ERROR	SQUARED ERROR
Al	8	5	+3	9
Bo	2	5	-3	9
Cal	6	5	+1	1
Deb	4	5	-1	1

20
/
SUM OF SQUARED ERRORS

Suppose Al, Bo, Cal and Deb each estimate the weight of a jar of jelly beans, and their estimates are 8, 2, 6 and 4. The jar actually weighs 5 pounds. Al's error is +3, because he *over*estimated by 3; Bo's error is -3, because he *under*estimated by 3, etc.

The *sum of squared errors* is one number that summarizes all the errors. The more the people's estimates were off by, the bigger the sum of squared errors will be. But this sum, which is 20 in this example, *doesn't* give us any indication of how far off a *typical* person's guess was. Nobody's guess was off by more than 3, and nobody's guess was off by less than 1.

You'd probably expect the number that would represent size of a *typical* error to be between 1 and 3. Most people would say, "Two of the estimators (Al and Bo) were off by 3, and two were off by 1, so the typical size of an error is 2, the mean of the amounts of error." Unfortunately, this kind of 'mean' or 'average error is *not* generally used to describe the size of a typical error in statistics!

Another, less obvious way of measuring typical error is required. It's called '*r.m.s. error*', which stands for '*root-mean-square error*', literally 'the square **root** of the *mean* of all the *squared* errors'.

Why is it necessary to introduce this new concept, which at first is so unintuitive? Because the use of *r.m.s.* error will later make the mathematics of estimation and prediction work out neatly, and more intuitively. Also, you'll need to *understand* a very common statistic called "the standard deviation", and the standard deviation *is* just a special case of an *r.m.s.* error.

Here's the formula for computing any *r.m.s.* error:

$$\text{(4.2.1)} \quad \text{R.M.S. ERROR} = \sqrt{\frac{\text{Sum of Squared Errors}}{n}}$$

In the example above, the sum of squared errors was 20 and there were 4 case s, so

$$\text{r.m.s. error} = \sqrt{20/4} = \sqrt{5} = 2.236$$

4.3 DEVIATIONS FROM THE MEAN

DEVIATIONS

We often need to refer to the numerical difference between a certain known *score* and one fixed value, usually the value of a certain *statistic.* There's a standard terminology and notation for this:

(4.3.1) DEFINITION:

The *deviation* of a score from the mean is the difference between the score and the mean.

DEVIATION　=　(THE SCORE) - (THE MEAN)

It's also the size of the *error* you'd make if you used
- the score to estimate the *mean,* or
- the *mean* to estimate the *score.*

EXAMPLE 4.3.1

Suppose the score is 9 and the mean is known to be 5.
What is the deviation from the mean in this case?

ANSWER:　　The deviation　=　(the score) - (the mean)
　　　　　　　　　　　　　=　9 - 5
　　　　　　　　　　　　　=　+4

We also say that if we had used the score (9) to *estimate* the mean (5), the *error* of that estimate would be +4.

PREVIEW

There will be some situations later in which the *mean* will be *known,* and the task will be to use the mean as an estimate of some unknown score. In that case, the deviation may be interpreted as *the residual,* that is, "how far you'd have to go from the mean to get to the score".

There will be other situations like the one in the example above, in which a *score* will be *known,* and the task will be to use the score as an estimate of the unknown mean. In that case, the deviation of the score from the mean is the *error.* I.e., the deviation is the 'amount you'd overestimate or underestimate the mean by, if you used the *score* as an estimate.'

4.4 THE STANDARD DEVIATION and VARIANCE

Each individual score has its own deviation (from the mean of all the scores). We need *one* number that will characterize the *typical* size of a deviation, for the whole set of scores. This number will tell you how far a *typical* score is from the mean. This number is called the *standard deviation* of the scores.

COMPUTATION OF THE *STANDARD DEVIATION* OF A SET OF RAW DATA:

$$(4.4.1) \quad \text{Standard Deviation} = SD \text{ or } s =$$

$$\sqrt{\frac{\Sigma(X-\overline{X})^2}{n}} = \sqrt{\frac{SS_X}{n}}$$

The square of the standard deviation also comes up frequently in statistics. It is called the *variance*.

COMPUTATION OF THE *VARIANCE* OF A SET OF RAW DATA:

$$(4.4.2) \quad \text{Variance} = SD^2 \text{ or } s^2 =$$

$$\frac{\Sigma(X-\overline{X})^2}{n} = \frac{SS_X}{n}$$

EXAMPLE 4.4.1

CASE	SCORE X	MEAN $\overline{X}$	DEVIATION X-$\overline{X}$	(DEVIATION)^2 (X-$\overline{X}$)^2
Al	8	5	+3	9
Bo	2	5	-3	9
Cal	6	5	+1	1
Deb	4	5	-1	1
			$\sqrt{}$ 0	20

SS = SUM OF SQUARED DEVIATIONS, or $\Sigma(X-\overline{X})^2$

SD = standard deviation = $\sqrt{SS/n} = \sqrt{20/4} = \sqrt{5} = 2.236$

SD^2 = variance = SS/n = 5

Note that computations are identical to those in example 4.2 above. However, the interpretation of the numbers is more specific here:

Suppose we used Al's score to estimate the mean of all four scores. The *error* of this estimate is +3, since the score, 8, is 3 more than 5, the true value of the mean. This error is referred to as 'Al's *deviation* from the mean of X' , or simply, 'Al's deviation'. Similarly, Bo's deviation is -3. The *typical* size of a deviation, called the *standard deviation* is 2.236.

The check mark (√) at the bottom of the deviations column is a reminder to add this column when you are doing computations like this, and check that the sum is zero. The sum of all cases' deviations should always be zero if computations have been done correctly.

COMPUTATION OF THE STANDARD DEVIATION OF A FREQUENCY DISTRIBUTION:

The computation of the standard deviation of a *frequency distribution* is different from the raw score computation in these ways:

You must *multiply* the squared deviations by the *frequencies* before adding to get the SS.

If you want to check that the sum of deviations equals 0, you must multiply the deviations by the frequencies first. This step, shaded below, is optional, but recommended.

COMPUTATION OF THE *STANDARD DEVIATION* OF A FREQUENCY DISTRIBUTION:

$$\textbf{(4.4.1)} \quad \textbf{Standard Deviation = SD } or \textbf{ s =}$$

$$\sqrt{\frac{\Sigma f(X - \overline{X})^2}{\Sigma f}} \quad = \quad \sqrt{\frac{SS_X}{n}}$$

EXAMPLE 4.4.2

SCORE X	f	MEAN $\overline{X}$	DEVIATION $X-\overline{X}$	f(DEVIATION) $f(X-\overline{X})$	(DEVIATION)² $(X-\overline{X})^2$	f(DEVIATION)² $f(X-\overline{X})^2$
10	1	6	+4	+4	16	16
8	2	6	+2	+4	4	8
6	3	6	0	0	0	0
4	4	6	-2	-8	4	16
n = Σf =	10			√ 0		40

SS = SUM OF SQUARED DEVIATIONS, or $\Sigma f(X-\overline{X})^2$

SD or s = STANDARD DEVIATION = $\sqrt{SS/n} = \sqrt{40/10} = \sqrt{4} = 2$

NOTATION

The sum of squared deviations is often abbreviated 'SS' or 'SS_X' and is referred to as 'the sum of squares'. It is the total squared error you'd make if you used the *mean* as an estimate of the *scores* (or vice versa).

The notation for the standard deviation of a set of scores is not entirely consistent in the literature of applied statistics! Texts, journal articles, computer programs and calculators all refer to this popular statistic. The most common designations are "s" or "SD". When it is necessary to specify which variable you are referring to, the variable name is added as a subscript: s_X or SD_X

PROPERTIES OF THE STANDARD DEVIATION

The standard deviation of a set of scores is...

1) the *r.m.s. error* of the mean when the *mean* is used as an 'estimate' of the *scores*. That is, if you used the mean to estimate each score (or to 'represent' all the scores), the standard deviation is the *typical* amount of error you'd make.

2) the *r.m.s. error* of the *scores* as estimates of the *mean*. For example, if we picked a score at random from a population, and used that *one score* as an estimate of the population mean, the *typical* amount we'd be "off by" is the standard deviation.

3) the most common measure of *dispersion*, or *spread* of a distribution. If the distribution for one variable, X, is obviously more 'spread out' and 'wider' than the distribution for another variable Y, the standard deviation of X will be greater than the standard deviation of Y.

4.5 THE RANGE

There's another common measure of dispersion, the *range*, which is easily and quickly computed, but usually less useful than the standard deviation.

COMPUTATION

> **(4.5.1) THE RANGE =**
>
> **(THE HIGHEST SCORE) - (THE LOWEST SCORE)**

EXAMPLE 4.5.1 COMPARING THE RANGE AND THE STANDARD DEVIATION

A) HIGH DISPERSION

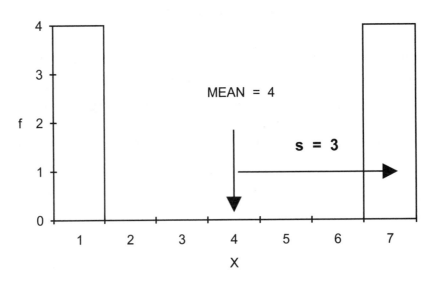

A) Here each case is either 3 below the mean or 3 above the mean, i.e., all the deviations are either -3 or +3. The standard deviation, s, is 3. This is just what we'd expect the *typical* deviation to be! The *range* is 7 - 1 = 6.

B) LOW DISPERSION

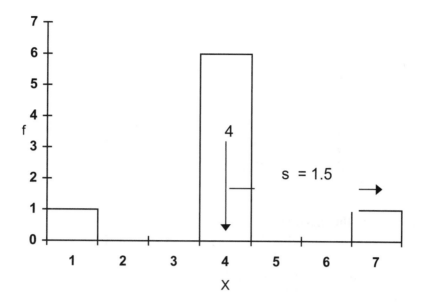

B) These scores are generally *less* dispersed than in A). Six scores have deviations of zero, and the other two are 3 units from the mean. The standard deviation, s, is much *less* than in A), only 1.5. (You might want to check this computation for practice.) The range is again 6. The range does *not* capture the tendency of the scores within the distribution to 'group' or 'clump' around the mean.

4.6 WHY THE MEAN IS THE BEST ESTIMATE

TWO IMPORTANT PROPERTIES OF THE MEAN

Recall that the mean has two properties which help explain why the mean is the statistic most frequently used in estimation. These properties can be better stated now that we can use the new definitions above:

A) THE SUM OF THE DEVIATIONS FROM THE MEAN IS *ZERO*

$$\Sigma(X - \overline{X}) = 0$$

This implies that the mean is an *unbiased* estimate of the scores (or vice versa); it neither overestimates nor underestimates the scores.

B) THE SUM OF SQUARED DEVIATIONS FROM THE MEAN IS *MINIMAL*

This implies also that the *r.m.s.* error of the *mean* is *less than* the *r.m.s.* error of *any other number*. In a sense, the mean is *closer* than any other number is, to the batch of scores it is the mean *of.*

EXERCISES FOR CHAPTER 4

TABLE 1

	X
Amy	0
Bob	2
Cab	4
Deb	6
Elmore	8
Fay	10
Gary	12

1. Bob's deviation from the mean is
   A) 4   B) -4   C) 0   D) 2   E) -2

2. The sum of all deviations from the mean for all 7 scores is
   A) 0   B) 24   C) -24   D) 112   E) 56

3. The sum of squared deviations from the mean, SS, is
   A) 0   B) 56   C) -24   D) 112   E) 24

4. The standard deviation, s (or SD), is
   A) 10.58   B) 2.85   C) 4   D) 2   E) 1

5. If you pick one case from among the seven above, and estimate that case 's score using the mean, how big will the typical error be? I.e., how much will you typically be 'off by'?
   A) 2   B) 2.85   C) 4   D) 6   E) 1

6. If you used Amy's score as an estimate of the mean, what would the *error* be?
   A) -6   B) 6   C) 0

ANSWERS TO EXERCISES FOR CHAPTER 4

1. B

2. A   The sum of deviations from the mean is *always* 0.

3. D

4. C

5. C   This is *just what* the standard deviation tells you!

6. A

CHAPTER 5
RESCALING AND STANDARDIZING

5.1 STANDARD DISTRIBUTIONS

A *standard* distribution is one with a mean of 0 and a standard deviation of 1. Standard distributions can have any shape! Figure 5.1 shows what some typical standard distributions look like when sketched.

FIGURE 5.1

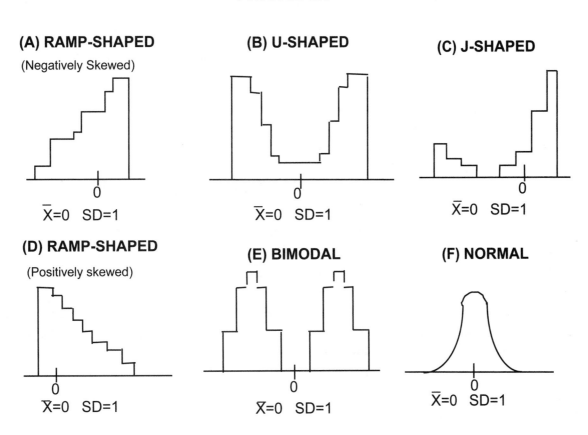

(A) RAMP-SHAPED
(Negatively Skewed)
$\bar{X}=0$ SD=1

(B) U-SHAPED
$\bar{X}=0$ SD=1

(C) J-SHAPED
$\bar{X}=0$ SD=1

(D) RAMP-SHAPED
(Positively skewed)
$\bar{X}=0$ SD=1

(E) BIMODAL
$\bar{X}=0$ SD=1

(F) NORMAL
$\bar{X}=0$ SD=1

These sketches should make it clear that standard distributions may have a variety of shapes; hence you cannot conclude anything about a distribution's shape based on the information that it is standard. Conversely, you cannot make any conclusions about whether a distribution is standard, based on information about its shape. In statistics, the term "standard" refers only to location (a mean of 0) and dispersion (a standard deviation of 1).

5.2 LINEAR TRANSFORMATIONS

DEFINITION AND NOTATION

Suppose you replace each score, X, on some interval scale variable by another, rescaled version of the score, obtained using this formula:

$$\text{rescaled } X = a + bX \qquad \text{where: } \begin{array}{l} a \text{ is any number} \\ b \text{ is any number other than } 0 \end{array}$$

We'd say that the scores on X have been *linearly transformed* or *linearly rescaled*.

If *b* is greater than zero, the rescaled variable is called a *positive linear transformation* of X.

Sometimes it's desirable to compare scores on two variables which have been measured on different scales. The best way to do this is to use the appropriate linear transformation to rescale one variable so that its mean and its SD match the other variable's.

Here's an example of linear rescaling:

TABLE 5.2.1   RESCALING THE VARIABLE X

	X	Y = 5 + 3X
Al	2	11
Bo	4	17
Cecil	5	20
Dino	6	23
Ellie	8	29

There are two scores for each case listed in TABLE 5.2.1: one score on the variable X, and one score on Y, which represents a linear rescaling of X. Each case's score on Y can be obtained from his/her score on X by multiplying by 3 and adding 5.

EFFECTS OF RESCALING

It might seem that some valuable information about the cases would be *lost* when their scores are rescaled. However, as long as the fact that the scores were rescaled is kept in mind, there is just as much information about the cases in the new rescaled scores as there was in the original data. If necessary, you could always go back and undo the rescaling process and recover the original data.

Suppose the variable X is linearly rescaled by replacing each score on X by Y, where

$$Y = a + bX$$

Here is a brief summary of the effects of this rescaling:

1) The mean of Y will equal $a + b$(mean of X)

2) The SD of Y will equal $|b|$(SD of X)

    $|b|$ represents "the *absolute value, or magnitude* of b".

3) The SS of Y will equal b^2(SS of X)

4) If b is positive, the order of all cases will be the same on Y as on X. That is, if Al beat Ben on X, Al will also beat Ben on Y. (If b is negative, the order of scores will be reversed.)

5) If b is positive, the shape of Y will be the same as the shape of X
(If b is negative, Y will have a shape that is a "mirror image" of X)

EXAMPLE

In TABLE 5.2.1, $\bar{X}$ is 5 and the SD of X is 2. We rescaled using $a = 5$ and $b = 3$.

Does the mean of Y $= a + b(5)$? That is, does $\bar{Y} = 5 + 3(5)$?

Does the SD of Y $= |b|(2)$? That is, does $s_y = 3(2)$?

Does Y have the same shape as X ?

Dino beat three other people on X (I.e., his score was higher than Al's, Bo's and Cecil's.) Did he beat the *same* three people on Y?

It's good practice to verify that the answer to all these questions is 'yes'.

5.3 STANDARDIZING DISTRIBUTIONS

HOW TO STANDARDIZE

Standardizing a distribution linearly rescales the distribution so that its mean becomes 0 and its SD becomes 1.   That is, standardizing a distribution 'makes it standard'

> **(5.3.1) To *standardize* a given set of scores on the variable X,**
> **rescale X by replacing each score on X by:**
>
> $$\text{STD X} = \frac{X - \bar{X}}{SD} \quad \text{or} \quad \frac{X - \mu}{\sigma}$$

Of course the first formula is used for a sample with mean $\bar{X}$ and standard deviation, s.
the second formula is used for an entire population with mean, μ, and standard deviation, σ.

Another way to describe standardization is "replace each score on X by its *deviation* divided by the *standard deviation*."

> **TERMINOLOGY**
>
> There is no universal standard designation for the 'standardized version of the score X'. We'll use '*STD X*'. The designation for the new scores, after standardization, is "*standard scores*".
>
> Some authors call standard scores "*z-scores*", a label we'll reserve for scores from the *standard normal* distribution (in Chapter 7).

Here's an example of standardization, using the variable X from TABLE 5.1 above:

TABLE 5.2   STANDARDIZING THE VARIABLE X

CASE	X	STD X
Al	2	-1.5
Bo	4	-.5
Cecil	5	0
Dino	6	+.5
Ellie	8	+1.5

Since $\bar{X}$ is 5 and the SD of X is 2, we compute STD X by replacing each score on X by

$$\text{STD X} = (X - \bar{X})/SD$$

In this case, the formula tells us to replace each score by

$$\text{STD X} = (X - 5)/2$$

PRACTICE: Check the computation in TABLE 5.2, and check that the mean of the variable STD X is 0 and the SD of the variable STD X is 1.

EFFECTS OF STANDARDIZING A DISTRIBUTION

Here's a brief summary of some of the effects of standardizing the variable X to create STD X:

1) The mean of STD X will be 0.

2) The SD of STD X will always be 1.

3) The shape of STD X will always be exactly the same as the shape of X! Specifically, STD X will not have a "more normal" shape than X!

4) Any case's percentile rank on STD X will be the same as its percentile rank on X.

5) STD X is another interval scale variable that contains just as much information about the cases as X does.

6) STD X tells you how far above or below the mean the score X is, in standard deviation units. That is, STD X tells you how many *'standard deviations'* above or below the mean X is.

WHY STANDARDIZE?

Standardizing two distributions that were originally measured on different scales allows you to compare scores from one distribution with scores from the other, directly.

Standard scores represent *interval* scale data, which provides more meaningful information about the cases than ordinal scale data. (Percentile ranks, which will be described in the next chapter only represent *ordinal* level data.)

In Chapter 7, we'll discuss the most common reason for standardizing a distribution: so the scores can be easily related to scores on the *standard normal* distribution. This procedure will allow us to *estimate* statistics such as percents, proportions, percentile ranks and percentiles. Later when we move on to inferential statistics, the same computations will allow us to *estimate* probabilities quickly and accurately.

'UN-STANDARDIZING': RECOVERING SCORES FROM STANDARD SCORES

Later we'll need to be able to *compute a score* on the variable X, given this information:
> the mean of X
> the SD of X
> an case's *standard score*, STD X

This procedure goes "backward" from the standard score back to the original score. A little thought and experimentation, or algebra, will show that this formula produces the correct result:

The case's original score, $X = \bar{X} + (STD\ X)(SD_x)$

That is, an case's original score on the variable X is *exactly* equal to the mean of X, plus the product of the case's standard score and the SD of the variable X.

EXAMPLE

Suppose we didn't know Al's *score* on X, but we did know that

$$\overline{X} = 70$$
$$SD = 20$$
$$\text{Al's standard score, STD X} = -1.5$$

We can conclude that Al's score on X must have been 40, because...

$$X = \overline{X} + (STD\ X)(SD_x)$$
$$= 70 + (-1.5)(20)$$
$$= 40$$

INTERPRETATION OF STANDARD SCORES

A case's **standard score** tells you...

- what the case's score would have been, *if* the variable had a mean of 0 and a SD of 1.

- how many 'standard deviations' above or below the mean the case scored.

In the preceding example, Al's standard score of -1.5 could also be expressed, "Al scored 1 ½ standard deviations *below* the mean". Since *one* SD is 20, '1 ½ standard deviations' is 1.5 times 20, or 30. This checks out, since Al's score of 40 is *30 below* the mean of X.

EXERCISES, CHAPTER 5

----

1. If you standardize any distribution by converting every score in that distribution to a standard score, the resulting distribution always...
     A) will be approximately normal   B) will have a mean of 1 and a SD of 0
     C) will have a SD of 1 and a mean of 0   D) will be bell shaped
     E) more than one of the above is correct

The mean of the scores on a test is 186 and the SD is 24. Len scored 150. Len's score on the test beat 32 other students' scores.

2. What is Len's standard score?

3. How many of the students did Len's *standard score* beat in the distribution of *standard scores*?
     A) 32   B) cannot be determined without additional information

----

4. Suppose a distribution of scores has a mean of 5, an SD of 3, and is positively skewed. If you *standardize* this whole distribution by standardizing every score, what will the resulting *standardized* distribution look like?

----

5. Justin's *standard score* was -1.2. The test his standard score was based on had a mean of 132 and an SD of 40. What was his score on the test?

    A) 84   B) 92   C) 180   D) 172   E) Cannot be determined

----

TABLE 1

X	f
0	1
4	3
6	2

6. How many scores are represented in TABLE 1 above?
7. Compute the mean of the variable X.
8. Compute the SD of X.

9. Standardize the distribution of scores in TABLE 1.

10. Abe got a 0 on X. How many cases beat Abe on X?

11. What was Abe's deviation from the mean? (On the original variable X)

12. What was Abe's standard score ?

TABLE 2

	X
Amy	0
Bob	2
Cab	4
Deb	6
Elmore	8
Fay	10
Gary	12

13. Bob's *deviation* from the mean is

    A) 4   B) -4   C) 0   D) 2   E) -2

14. The sum of all *deviations* from the mean for all 7 scores is

    A) 0   B) 24   C) -24   D) 112   E) 56

15. The sum of *squared* deviations from the mean is

    A) 0   B) 56   C) -24   D) 112   E) 24

16. The *standard* deviation is

    A) 10.58   B) 2.85   C) 4   D) 2   E) 1

17. If you pick one case from among the seven above, and *estimate* that case's score using the mean, how big will the typical error be? I.e. how much will you typically be off by ?

    A) 2   B) 2.85   C) 4   D) 6   E) 1

ANSWERS TO EXERCISES, CHAPTER 5

---

1. C   When a distribution is standardized, its mean becomes 0 and its SD becomes 1. Remember, standardizing *does not* change the *shape* of the distribution!

---

2. Standard Score $= \dfrac{X - \overline{X}}{SD} = \dfrac{150 - 186}{24} = \dfrac{-36}{24} = -1.5$

3. A

---

4. A positively skewed distribution with a mean of 0 and a SD of 1.

   Standardizing the scores rescales the distribution so that the mean is 0 and the SD is 1, but *the shape remains the same.*

---

5. A   To compute the *score* if you are given the standard score, the mean and the SD, use this formula:

$$X = \underline{X} + (\text{standard score})(SD)$$

   In this case:

$$X = 132 + (-1.2)(40)$$
$$X = 132 - 48$$
$$X = 84$$

---

6. 6

7. 4

8. 2

9. Standardized version of TABLE 1:   Each score has been replaced by $(X-\underline{X})/SD$

STD. X	f
-2	1
0	3
1	2

Extra Practice: Check that this distribution actually does have a mean of 0 and a SD of 1

10. 5   Three cases scored 4, two scored 6

11. -4

12. -2

----

13. B $\qquad$ $X - \bar{X} = 2 - 6 = -4$

14. A $\qquad$ The sum of deviations from the mean, for all cases, is *always* 0!

15. D

16. C

17. C $\qquad$ This is just one interpretation of the SD

CHAPTER 6

PERCENTILE RANKS and PERCENTILES

6.1 PERCENTILE RANKS

COMPUTING PERCENTILE RANKS FROM RAW DATA

> **(6.1.1)** The *percentile rank* of a *score* on the variable X
> is the percentage of all cases with scores
> *less than or equal to* that score

Of course, the scores referred to must be the results of measuring some case s on some variable. It's assumed that there is *one* variable we're referring to, and that variable must be measured on a scale that is at least *ordinal* level. Percentile rank is also referred to as *cumulative percent*.

The percentile rank of a *case* is the percentile rank of the case's *score*, i.e., it is the percent of all cases with scores less than or equal to that case's score. This is often stated, "An case's percentile rank is the percent of cases *beaten* or *tied* by that case." (This version of the definition assumes that you count the case as tying itself.)

TABLE 6.1: RAW DATA FOR A VARIABLE X

	X
Amy	10
Bob	10
Cale	13
Dee	13
Ely	90

The percentile rank of the score 10 is 40%, because 2 of the 5 cases got scores of 10 or less.

Dee's percentile rank is 80 percent because Di's score was 13, and 4 of the 5 cases scored 13 or less.

COMPUTING PERCENTILE RANKS FROM A FREQUENCY DISTRIBUTION

TABLE 6.2: FREQUENCY DISTRIBUTION FOR THE VARIABLE X

X	f	Cumulative frequency	Cumulative proportion	Cumulative % (Percentile Rank)
10	2	2	.4	40%
13	2	4	.8	80%
90	1	5	1.0	100%
n=	5			

TABLE 6.2 shows the frequency distribution for the raw data in TABLE 6.1. Three columns representing computations have been added: cumulative frequency, cumulative proportion and cumulative %., or *percentile rank*.

A score's *cumulative frequency* is the sum of the score's frequency and the frequencies of all lower scores. That is, the cumulative frequency states how many cases scored less than or equal to a particular score. Four cases got scores less than or equal to 13, so the cumulative frequency for the score 13 is 4.

The *cumulative proportion* for some score is the *proportion* of all cases who got that score or less. You compute this by dividing cumulative frequency by n, the number of cases.

Cumulative % is a synonym for percentile rank. To compute the cumulative %, you convert the cumulative frequency to a percent, i.e., you divide cumulative frequency by n, then multiply the result by 100%. Of course, you can also just multiply the cumulative proportion by 100%.

The computations described above produce *exact* percentile ranks, not estimates. The computations are based directly on definitions; there are no short cuts. E.g., to compute the percentile rank of 13 you *must* do some computation that's equivalent to counting up the number of cases with scores less than or equal to 13, and then you must convert that to a percent. Note that you must *know* the frequencies for all the scores at or below 13 to count them! E.g., if you didn't know how many cases got 10, you couldn't compute the percentile rank of 13, because you wouldn't be able to count the number of cases that scored less than 13.

Later, in Chapter 7, we'll describe a widely used *approximation* technique for estimating percentile ranks when you *don't* know the frequencies for all the scores.

STANDARDIZING DOES NOT AFFECT PERCENTILE RANKS

As mentioned in the previous chapter, positive linear transformations do not change the *order* of a set of scores. Standardizing is one kind of positive linear transformation. If Amy beat Zoe on X, Amy will also beat Zoe on 'STD X', the standardized version of X. Since cases' percentile ranks are determined completely by their *order*, standardizing will not affect any case's percentile rank.

6.2 PERCENTILES

> **(6.2.1)** For any percent i, the *i*th *percentile* is
> the *lowest* score with a percentile rank of
> *at least* i%.
>
> **(or, the *lowest* score with a percentile rank of *i% or more*)**

The term *percentile* is unambiguous, but some authors use **percentile point** or **percentile score** instead.

EXAMPLES

The 40th percentile of the variable X in TABLE 6.2 above is 10, because 10 is the lowest score with a percentile rank of 40% or more.

The 80th percentile is 13, because 13 is the lowest score with a percentile rank of 80% or more.

The 3rd percentile is 10, because 10 is the lowest score with a percentile rank of 3% or more.

The 81st percentile is 90, because 90 is the lowest score with a percentile rank of 81% or more.

Note that percentiles are *scores*; but percentile ranks are *percents*.

6.3 WHY CONVERT SCORES TO PERCENTILE RANKS?

PERCENTILE RANKS ARE EASY TO INTERPRET

Numerical variables are measured on many different scales. A group of students' weights may range from 90 to 240 lbs.; a group of temperatures for the same students may range from 97.6 to 100.2, and their scores on an exam may range from 0 to 16. The actual numerical scale used for a particular variable is arbitrary, and is just set by tradition. The numbers on the Centigrade and Fahrenheit temperature scales look different, but someone who is familiar with either one of the scales knows which numbers on their scale correspond to hot days, cool days, freezing water, etc.

Percentile ranks allow you to express a case's score on a variable in a way that is independent of the original numerical scale the case was measured on. You don't need to know anything about the original measurement scale to interpret a percentile rank based on that scale. For example, if I told you that Al got 90 on a test you'd really need to know something about the distribution of test scores to be able to say anything meaningful about Al's performance. You wouldn't know if 90 was good or bad; it would depend on the test. The score alone is meaningless without knowledge of the scale it was measured on.

However, if I told you "Al's percentile rank was 50%," instead of telling you Al's actual score, you'd know that Al was in the middle of the group that took the test, because you'd know that the percent of cases with scores less than or equal to Al's was 50%. Similarly, if Ben's percentile rank was 1%, he did poorly, and if Amy's was 100%, we can conclude that she got the top grade among the students she was compared to.

PERCENTILE RANKS ALLOW COMPARISONS BETWEEN VARIABLES

Percentile ranks also let you compare scores on variables that have been measured on different scales.

EXAMPLE

The most commonly administered personality test, the MMPI, measures a person on 13 different variables, each corresponding to a different personality trait. Each of the variables is measured on a different scale, with a different distribution. If someone scored 20 on scale Pa (originally designed to assess paranoia) and 20 on the Scale Sc (originally designed to assess schizophrenia), the two scores of 20 tell you nothing about the person directly, unless you are familiar with norms for the scales. However if you know that the percentile rank of 20 on the Sc scale is about 40%, and the percentile rank of 20 on the scale Pa is about 99%, then you know that the person who took the MMPI may be a very unusual individual who experiences considerable paranoia while maintaining relatively good contact with reality in most areas of his/her life. The percentile ranks in this case can *tell you more*, quickly, than the raw scores can.

6.4 CAUTION: PERCENTILE RANKS ARE ORDINAL NUMBERS

TABLE 6.4

6.4 (A) Three cases' weights

WEIGHT (As measured on a scale)	
Arnie	100 lbs.
Bennie	110 lbs.
Carrie	120 lbs.

6.4 (B) The cases' percentile ranks

PERCENTILE RANK on the variable 'weight'	
Arnie	10%
Bennie	20%
Carrie	30%

Some information is *lost* when you convert from an interval scale score to a percentile rank, because percentile ranks provide only *ordinal* data. Percentile ranks *can* tell you if Case A beat Case B, but *not* "by how much".

If the weights in TABLE 6.4(A) were measured on the usual *interval* scale, we can conclude that 'the difference in weight between Arnie and Bernie (10 lbs.) is *equal to* the difference in weight between Bennie and Carrie.' The difference in scores is 10 in each case, and these differences are meaningful for interval scales. You can picture Arnie holding a 10 lb. weight at one end of a seesaw balancing Bennie at the other; or Bennie holding the same 10 lb. weight balancing Carrie.

Suppose TABLE 6.4(B) shows the cases' *percentile ranks* on the variable weight, among a large group of people, *without* the original scores in lbs. (or kilograms). If we *only* had this information instead of the actual weights, we could *only* make these kinds of conclusions:

10% of the people weigh the same as Arnie, or less.

Bennie's weight equals or exceeds 20% of the people's weights.

Carrie's weight is greater than Bennie's, which is greater than Arnie's

If we *only* knew the percentile ranks in Table 6.4(B) we *could not* conclude that the difference between Bennie's weight and Arnie's is the same as the difference between Carrie's and Bennie's. Percentile ranks are *ordinal* numbers, and *differences* between percentile ranks do not tell you as much as differences between scores on interval scale variables.

6.5* *USING INTERPOLATION WITH CONTINUOUS DATA*

ESTIMATING PERCENTILE RANKS FROM CONTINUOUS, GROUPED DATA

Density histograms were presented in Chapter 2 as a meaningful way to describe continuous data which have been *grouped*. In the density histograms covered in Chapter 2, density was expressed in 'proportion per unit'. Since *proportion* and *percent* both measure the same thing, we can also express density as '*percent* per unit'. Table 6.5.1 shows the computations of density in percent per unit for the same data used in Chapter 2.4.

TABLE 6.5.1

X	f	percent	width	density (% per unit)
0 - 20	120	60%	20	3%
20 - 60	80	40%	40	1%
	n = 200	100% √		

There are only two *upper real limits* in this table: 20 is the upper real limit of the interval 0 - 20, and 60 is the upper real limit of the interval 20 - 60.

The percentile rank of the score 20 is easily seen to be 60%, since 60% of the cases scored below 20. The percentile rank of the score 60 is 100%.

* Optional section

But what is the percentile rank of the score 22? We can't tell! These data clearly don't contain sufficient information to let us compute exactly 'the percentage of cases with scores less than or equal to 22'. We can only *estimate* the percentile rank of the score 22 using a procedure called 'prorating' or **interpolation**.

60 percent of the cases scored below 20. We want to estimate the percent that scored below 22. We'll estimate the percent of the cases scoring between 20 and 22 and add that to 60% to get our estimate of the percentile rank of 22. There are 2 'units' inside the interval from 20 to 22, and the density in this interval is '1% per unit', so we estimate that 2 percent of the cases scored between 20 and 22. We add this 2% to the 60% below 20 and estimate that the percentile rank of the score 22 is 62%.

FIGURE 6.5.1   DENSITY HISTOGRAM FOR TABLE 6.5.1

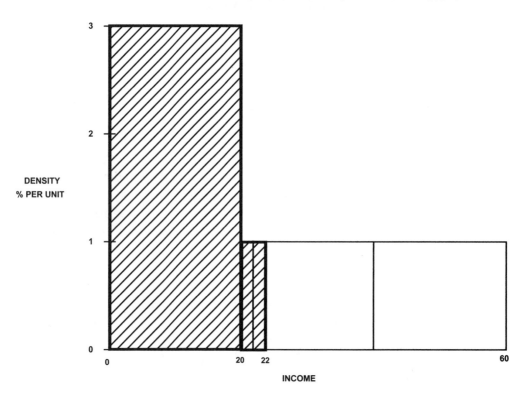

> **(6.5.1)   The *percent* of cases scoring within a certain range of scores is represented by *area* in a density histogram.**
>
> **To estimate the percentage of all cases scoring within a specific interval, multiply the *width* of the interval by the *density* for that interval:**
>
> **PERCENT = (WIDTH IN UNITS)(DENSITY IN PERCENT UNIT)**

ESTIMATING PERCENTILES FROM GROUPED DATA

We can reverse the interpolation process to estimate *percentiles*. The exact 75th percentile for the distribution can't be determined because the data have been grouped. We can say it lies somewhere between 20 and 60, since 20 is the 60th percentile and 60 is the 100th percentile.

Here's how to estimate which score is the 75th percentile, i.e. the lowest score with a percentile rank of 75% in figure 6.5.1:

We know the score 20 beats 60% of the cases. We need to figure out how many units *beyond* 20 we'll have to go to beat 15% more. (because 60% + 15% = 75%)

We estimate this by dividing the percent needed by the density...

$$\text{number of units} = \frac{\text{percent}}{\text{density}} = \frac{15\%}{1\% \text{ per unit}} = 15 \text{ units}$$

So we estimate we'll need to go to a score '15 units past 20' to beat 75% of the cases, i.e., we must go to the score 20 + 15 = 35.

ESTIMATING THE MEDIAN FOR A SET OF GROUPED DATA

If we use the percentile estimation process to estimate the *50th* percentile we will have an interpolated *estimate* of the *median*. The intuitive idea of the median is that it is the score that the *middle case* would receive, if all cases were rank ordered according to their scores.

The interpolation technique only produces an estimate, or approximation, of the middle case's score.

EXAMPLE
Estimate the median of the grouped frequency distribution in TABLE 6.5.1.

We want to estimate the 50th percentile, so we need to estimate the lowest score that will beat 50% of the cases. The score 20 beats 60% of the cases, but we can estimate a *lower* score that beats 50% of the cases. The density between 0 and 20 is 3 % per unit, so we can estimate the lowest score that beats 50% of the cases by dividing 50% by the density:

$$\text{UNITS} = \frac{\text{PERCENT}}{\text{DENSITY}} = \frac{50\%}{3\% \text{ per unit}} = 16.67$$

So we *estimate* that the median is 16.67, i.e., we estimate the middle case's score to be 16.67.

6.6 DISPLAYING CUMULATIVE DISTRIBUTIONS

FIGURE 6.6.1

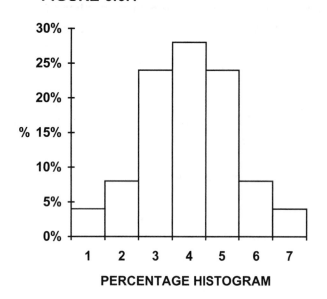

PERCENTAGE HISTOGRAM

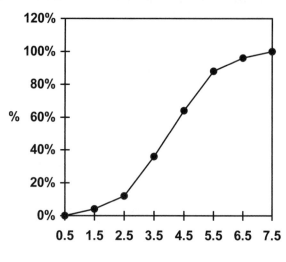

CUMULATIVE PERCENTAGE HISTOGRAM

TABLE 6.6.1

DISTRIBUTION

X	f	%
1	1	4%
2	2	8%
3	6	24%
4	7	28%
5	6	24%
6	2	8%
7	1	4%

CUMULATIVE DISTRIBUTION

U.R.L.	cum. f	cum %
1.5	1	4%
2.5	3	12%
3.5	9	36%
4.5	16	64%
5.5	22	88%
6.5	24	96%
7.5	25	100%

Table 6.6.1 shows a frequency distribution for scores on the variable X for 25 cases, along with the corresponding percentages for each score. Here, as usual, the *horizontal scale* shows all the possible scores and the *vertical* scale indicates how likely each score is.

To the right is the corresponding *cumulative* distribution showing cumulative frequency, along with the cumulative percent (or percentile rank). We'll assume that the variable is continuous and interval scale. In that case the usual is to use *upper real limits* (U.R.L.) for each score in the cumulative distribution-- we assume that each score, say '4' represents an interval from 3.5 to 4.5, so that the upper real limit is 4.5. This is realistic if the data have been 'rounded' to the nearest whole number.

The figures above show the histograms for each type of distribution. Note that the *cumulative* percentage histogram also uses *upper real limits*. The *vertical* scale in the cumulative percent histogram indicates what *percent* of the cases scored *below* each score.

EXERCISES FOR CHAPTER 6

(USE THE DEFINITIONS IN SECTIONS 6.1 and 6.2)

---   Data

Set 1

X	f
70	1
80	6
90	1

1. Suppose that Data Set 1 above represents a set of scores that a group of batteries got when they were tested to see how many hours they worked. What percent of the batteries actually worked for 70 hours or less? That is, what is the actual (not estimated) percentile rank of 70?

2. What is the percentile rank of the score 80?

3. In the list of raw data for this study, how many *scores* appear?

Data Set 2:

2, 2, 4, 4, 6, 8, 8, 8

4. The median of this set of scores is
   A) 8   B) 4   C) 6   D) 5   E) 5.2

5. The 62nd percentile is, by definition, the...
   A) percentage of cases with scores at or below 62
   B) highest score that beat 62% or less of the cases
   C) score achieved by 62% or more of the cases
   D) lowest score with a percentile rank of 62% or more
   E) lowest score with a percentile rank greater than 62%

6. For this set of data, the 62nd percentile is
   A) 4   B) 5   C) 6   D) 8   E) 62%

7. The first percentile, or "1%-ile", is
                    A) 2   B) 4   C) 6   D) 8

8. The 100th percentile is
                    A) 2   B) 4   C) 6   D) 8

9. The 50th percentile is
                    A) 2   B) 4   C) 6   D) 8

10. According to the definition provided in class and in handouts, this set of scores is...
                    A) negatively skewed
                    B) positively skewed
                    C) neither negatively skewed nor positively skewed

----

DATA SET 3

(A) ORIGINAL SCORES		(B) STANDARDIZED SCORES	
X	f	STD. X	f
0	1	___	1
3	4	___	4
6	6	___	6
9	4	___	4
12	1	___	1

11. DATA SET 3(A) above represents a set of scores. Tables which represent scores in this format are referred to as
                    A) crosstabulations
                    B) frequency distributions
                    C) raw data
                    D) percentiles
                    E) percentile ranks

12. Table 1(A) describes ___ scores altogether on _____.
                    A) 32... two variables
                    B) 32... one variable
                    C) 16... two variables
                    D) 16... one variable
                    E) none of the above is correct

13.* The set of scores described in Table 1(A) is...
(READ ALL ANSWERS)
A) approximately normal   B) skewed
C) standard   D) standard and approximately normal
E) more than one of the above is correct

14. The mean of the variable X is
A) 3   B) 6   C) 9   D) 0   E) none of the above

15. The standard deviation (SD, or s) of the variable X is
A) 3   B) 1   C) 2   D) 0   E) none of the above

16. If Jack got 3 on X, Jack's deviation from the mean is
A) 3   B) -3   C) -6   D) 6   E) -1

17. What is Jack's *exact* (not estimated) percentile rank on the variable X?
A) 31.25%   B) 62%   C) 68.75   D) 6.25%   E) none of the above

18. What is the 6th percentile for the variable X in Table 1(A)?
A) 5%   B) 95%   C) .5   D) .05   E) 0

19. What is the 45th percentile for the variable X in Table 1(A)?
A) 45%   B) 65%   C) 0   D) 3   E) 6

20. If you picked one score at random from the scores described in Table 1(A), and used that one score to estimate the mean of all scores, how far off would you typically be? I.e., how big would the error typically be?   A) 3   B) 6   C) 0   D) 1   E) 2

THE FOLLOWING QUESTIONS REFER TO THE *STANDARDIZED* VERSION OF THE VARIABLE X, WHICH IS LABELLED TABLE 1(B) ABOVE.

21. If Jack got a 3 on the variable X in Table 1(A), what will Jack's standard score be?
I.e., what will Jack's score be on the standardized variable in Table 1(B).
A) -1   B) -2   C) 0   D) +1   E) +2

22. The mean of all standard scores represented in Table 1(B) is
A) 1   B) 12   C) 6   D) 0   E) none of the above

23. The SD of all standard scores represented in Table 1(B) is
A) 1   B) 2   C) 0   D) 3   E) none of the above

----

24. Suppose Bill's percentile rank in a distribution is 42%. If you standardize the distribution, the percentile rank of Bill's *standard score* in the new standard distribution will be...
A) (42-50)/SD   B) 42%
C) more than 42%   D) less than 42%
E) cannot be determined from the information given

ANSWERS TO EXERCISES FOR CHAPTER 6

1.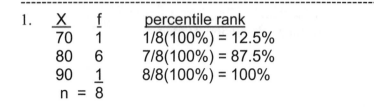

    So, the actual percentile rank for 70 is 12.5%.

2. 87.5%

3. $n = 8$, which means you have 8 cases , each measured on one variable, so there are 8 scores.

----

4. D   The median is the score between 4 and 6 and is therefore 5.

5. D

6. C   6 is the lowest score with a percentile rank of 62% or more

X	percentile rank
2	2/8(100%) = 25%
4	4/8(100%) = 50%
6	5/8(100%) = 62.5%
8	8/8(100%) = 100%

7. A

8. D

9. B

10. B   The mean is greater than the median

----

11. B

12. D

13.* A

14. B

15. A

16. B

17. A   Jack beat or tied 5 cases out of 16

      (100%) (5)/(16) = (100%)(.3125) = 31.25%

18. E   The percentile rank of the score 0 is 6.25%
        So, 0 is the lowest score with a percentile rank of 6% or more.
        By definition this makes 0 the sixth percentile..

19. E

20. A

The mean of X is 6 and the SD is 3, so the standardized version of X, STD X, is computed as shown:

(A) ORIGINAL SCORES				(B) STANDARDIZED SCORES	
X	f			STD. X	f
0	1	(0 - 6)/3 =		-2	1
3	4	(3 - 6)/3 =		-1	4
6	6	(6 - 6)/3 =		0	6
9	4	(9 - 6)/3 =		1	4
12	1	(12 - 6)3 =		2	1

21. A

22. D   It's always 0 for a *standardized* variable

23. A   It's always 1 for a *standardized* variable

----

24. B   Standardizing *doesn't affect* percentile ranks or percentiles

----

CHAPTER 7
NORMAL DISTRIBUTIONS AND ESTIMATION

7.1 THE NORMAL SHAPE

AN IDEALIZATION

Table A1 in the Appendix contains partial information about the *standard normal distribution*, which is usually designated the *z distribution*. The scores which are summarized in this distribution are called *z-scores*.

Our z Table contains some z-scores (from -3.49 to 3.49) and the *cumulative proportions* corresponding to those z-scores (from .0002 to .9998). Of course, the cumulative proportions can be converted into percentile ranks, or cumulative percents, by multiplying by 100%. The percentile ranks range from .02% to 99.98%.

It's possible to produce much more extensive versions of this table, which was generated using a computer program. For any number you can think of, no matter how small (say, minus 200 trillion!) the percentile rank of that number in any normal distribution is *not* 0%; so creating a *complete* table of percentile ranks is impossible.

The z, or standard normal distribution is an *idealization*, a *mathematical model* designed to describe an ideal version of a shape which many real distributions come close to. The mathematical versions of circles, spheres, cylinders, squares, cubes, etc., are perfectly analogous: There are no *perfect* circles or spheres in our world, but there are of course numerous things that come *close*. So a knowledge of the mathematics of circles and spheres enables engineers to design stadiums, piston rings, space shuttle O-rings, etc., and perhaps to understand bubbles, cells and basketballs better.

Just as there are no perfect circles in nature, *no* set of real cases ever obtained a complete set of z-scores, and no *actual* frequency distribution produced the percentile ranks in a z-table. Yet every elementary statistics text has a version of Table A1, and more attention is paid to the distribution it describes, the standard normal distribution, than to any distribution of *real* data.

Why? The particular 'bell shape' in Figure 7.1 is *not* familiar to every child, as 'circle', 'square', and even 'cylinder' (or 'soup can' shape) are. Why has *that particular* bell shape been chosen as the archetype that other distributions will routinely be compared to? The shape exists everywhere, but it's not visible until you draw a distribution.

FIGURE 7.1   THE STANDARD NORMAL DISTRIBUTION, z

This distribution is STANDARD because its mean is 0 and its SD is 1

This distribution is NORMAL because of its unique ideal shape

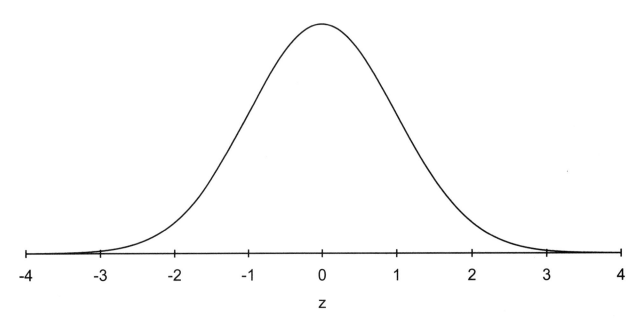

THE NORMAL SHAPE IS EVERYWHERE

When people describe things in the world around them using numbers, and create distributions of those numbers, they see one shape recurring in those distributions far more than any other. We'd say the real data they record have distributions that are 'approximately normal'. Some scientists have patiently recorded many thousands of observations by hand, and the distributions of scores they have collected look almost exactly like the smooth 'perfectly normal' shape in Figure 7.1. Robots have been programmed to carry out experiments millions of times and measure the results on numerical scales. The robot measurements have approximately normal distributions also; the 'approximately normal' shape is not introduced by a specifically human pattern of error.

People who are interested in the reasons for these phenomena now have a good idea why this one special shape shows up. Any time each case's score is affected by *many different factors* in combination, it can be proved that the distribution of scores will approximate a normal shape. It seems that, in our complex world, *most* things we might think of measuring are like that; they are affected by many separate factors whose effects get combined.

The mathematical description of the *perfect* normal shape is a mathematical model of a set of scores for cases that are being affected by an *infinite* number of independent random factors, each adding its own subtle effect to the combined effect of all the other factors.

Some people, *strict reductionists*, think that when all the factors are understood, along with their rules of combination, we'll be able, in theory, to predict complicated phenomena such as human behavior *exactly*. Other people think that no matter how many variables you might measure, there will always be some 'random' or 'unpredictable' part. Modern physics is more consistent with the latter, *probabilistic,* or nondeterministic view. This bothered Albert Einstein so much that he once stated "I shall never believe that God plays Dice with the universe", and tried to design experiments to prove quantum physics was wrong in that regard. (No, this will *not* be on the exam!)

There may be as many *nearly* normal distributions in our world as there are *nearly* perfect circles. Children don't learn the 'normal' shape at an early age only because *distributions* of scores must be *created*, they are not directly sensed or perceived. (Though it *can* be argued that some *decisions* and judgments made by children and even animals seem to be made *as if* they realized that certain variables have normal distributions!)

SPECIFYING A NORMAL DISTRIBUTION

You can't look at a sketch and tell if it's intended to represent part of a perfectly normal distribution. Only one very specific bell shape is the true normal shape. So representations of distributions with normal shapes will always be labeled as such.

There is *exactly one* normal shaped distribution for every possible mean and (nonzero) standard deviation.

So there's one normal distribution with a mean of 3 and a standard deviation of 3 million, one with a mean of 17,000,003 and a standard deviation of .01, etc. The one, single, normal shaped distribution with a mean of 0 and a standard deviation of 1 is the *standard normal*, because it's both *normal* (in shape) and *standard* (in location and dispersion).

Since we have already covered linear transformations, we can describe a nice way to picture the infinite family of all possible normal distributions:

The set of *all* normal distributions consists of:

A) The *standard* normal distribution, which has a mean of 0 and a SD of 1.
   This theoretical, ideal distribution is defined by a mathematical formula, not real data.
   Its scores are continuous and range from minus infinity to plus infinity.
   Percentile ranks for some scores from this distribution are listed in Table A1 (the z Table).
                    and...
B) *All other* normal distributions, which consist of all possible positive linear transformations of the z, or standard normal distribution.
   If you create a new distribution, z' by rescaling the z-scores this way...
$$z' = a + bz$$
   then the new rescaled normal distribution will have the *same normal shape*, but its mean will be *a* and its SD will be *b*.

7.2 USING THE STANDARD NORMAL TABLE

STANDARD NORMAL PERCENTILE RANKS

The percentile rank of a z-score is the percent of cases in the standard normal distribution with scores less than or equal to that z-score. We find percentile ranks of z-scores by looking the scores up in the z Table, finding the cumulative proportion, and multiplying by 100%. These percentile ranks are not approximations, they are the actual percentile ranks, accurate to 4 decimal places.

EXAMPLES   The percentile rank of the z-score 0 is 50%.

The percentile rank of the score -2.0 in the standard normal distribution is 2.28%

The percentile rank of -4.3 in the z distribution is *less than* 0.02%.   (Our table only goes down to $z = -3.49$, which has a Percentile Rank of 0.02%)

The percentile rank of 5 in the z Table is *greater than* 99.98%.   (Our table only goes up to $z = 3.49$, which has a Percentile Rank of 99.98%)

STANDARD NORMAL PERCENTILES

Percentiles of the standard normal distribution may be found by reversing the procedure for finding percentile ranks.

To find the ith percentile in the standard normal distribution:

1) Convert i% to a proportion by dividing i% by 100%.

2) Find the cumulative proportions in the body (not the margins) of the z Table that are closest to the cumulative proportion computed in Step 1.

3) The ith percentile is the *lowest* z score with a cumulative proportion as big as the cumulative proportion computed in Step 1.

EXAMPLE   Find the 70th percentile in the standard normal distribution.

1) 70% corresponds to the proportion 70%/100% = .70

2) z-scores with cumulative proportions close to .70 in the z table are:

z	Cum. pr.	P.R.
.53	.7019	70.19%
.52	.6985	69.85%

3) z = .53 is the *lowest* standard normal score with a cumulative proportion at or above .70, so .53 is the 70th percentile.

7.3 ESTIMATING PERCENTILE RANKS

APPROXIMATELY NORMAL DISTRIBUTIONS OF ACTUAL DATA

Distributions which are roughly symmetrical, and either bell-shaped or at least "concentrated" or "clumped together" near the center are generally termed *approximately normal*. We are concerned about this set of distributions because *only* approximately normal distributions can be approximated by the standard normal distribution.

As mentioned earlier, it is impossible to obtain a distribution from real data that is *perfectly* normal in shape, but you are likely to see data that produce an *approximately* normal shape. Here are a few examples of possible distributions that are or are not approximately normal in shape:

FIGURE 7.3.1

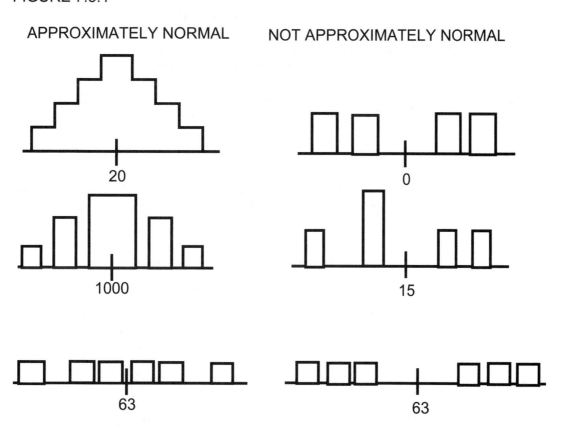

PROCEDURE FOR ESTIMATING PERCENTILE RANKS

You can use the set of percentile ranks for the standard normal distribution to *estimate* the percentile rank of a given score X from some *real* distribution, if and only if the following are all known:

A) The *mean* of all cases' scores, $\bar{X}$

B) The *standard deviation* of the scores, SD

C) *One* particular score, X (The one you want to estimate the percentile rank of)

D) The distribution of all scores is known to be *approximately normal.*

Here is the procedure to follow:

1) Standardize the score X, using the formula $STD\ X = (X - \bar{X})/SD$

2) Look up the STD X score in the z distribution *as if* it were a score in the standard normal distribution, and then look up the percentile rank for that score.

3) Use that percentile rank as an *estimate* of the score's percentile rank in the actual distribution of the variable X.

EXAMPLE

Bill scored 1088 on an aptitude test that had a mean of 1000 and a SD of 200. The distribution of aptitude test scores was approximately normal in shape. Estimate Bill's percentile rank on the aptitude test.

1) Bill's *standard score* is exactly $(1088 - 1000)/200 = 88/200 = .44$
      (This is *not* an estimate.)

2) We look up .44, Bill's standard score, in the z distribution, as if it were a z score. The cumulative proportion of .44 in the z distribution is .6700, so the percentile rank of .44 in the standard normal distribution is 67% (exactly).

3) We *estimate* Bill's percentile rank on the aptitude test to be 67%.

Don't forget that the 67% is only an *estimate*, not Bill's actual percentile rank! To obtain his *actual* percentile rank, we'd have to carry out the computation in the definition of percentile rank.

COMPARING <u>TRUE</u> PERCENTILE RANKS WITH <u>ESTIMATED</u> PERCENTILE RANKS

TABLE 1 shows the *true* percentile ranks (column A) for each of the scores 1 through 5, in an approximately normal distribution. Also, in column B, are the *estimated* percentile ranks that *would have been obtained* if each score were standardized and looked up in the z Table.

Of course we wouldn't need to estimate the percentile ranks if we had a complete set of data like this. But it is very helpful to do this comparison and ask "How *accurate* are the estimates?"

Note that this distribution is approximately normal, but is also quite coarse. It has only 5 possible scores. When we use a continuous distribution like the normal distribution to approximate a coarse distribution, errors can be quite large.

For example, look at the score 3 in the table below. Seven of the 10 cases got scores of 3 or less, so the true percentile rank of the score 3 is clearly 70%. But 3 is also the mean of this symmetrical distribution. When you standardize the score 3, the standard score will be zero. If you look up the standard score of zero in the standard normal distribution you find (of course!) that its percentile rank is 50%. In this case using the estimated percentile rank, 50%, will result in *underestimating* the true percentile rank by 20%! This should serve as a warning: Don't have too much confidence in normal estimates when they're applied to *coarse* real world distributions.

TABLE 1   COMPARING
A) True percentile ranks
B) Estimates based on *scores* and
C) Continuity Corrected Estimates based on *upper limits*

ORIGINAL DATA				B. Estimated P.R.		UPPER LIMIT	C. Corrected Estimated P.R.
Score X	f	A. True P.R.					
1	1	10%		3.4%		1.5	8.5%
2	2	30%		18.1%		2.5	32.3%
3	4	70%		50.0%		3.5	67.4%
4	2	90%		81.9%		4.5	91.3%
5	1	100%		96.6%		5.5	98.9%

THE CONTINUITY CORRECTION: IMPROVING ESTIMATES*

There's a way to improve normal estimates that works very well when distributions are coarse. It's called the **correction for continuity**. Instead of standardizing the score you're interested in, you instead standardize the *upper real limit* of the interval for that score.

Figure 7.3.2 Histogram for a coarse, approximately normal distribution

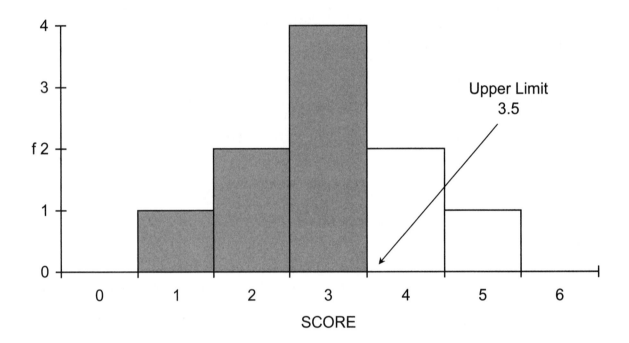

Notice on the histogram that the part of the histogram "above" the score 3 really includes a bar that goes from 2.5 to 3.5. Even if the data are *discrete*, when we use a normal approximation, we are acting *as if* the data were interval scale and *continuous*-- and it is appropriate to think of percentages as represented by *area*.

When we ask 'what percent of the cases got scores less than or equal to 3, we should really use *3.5* instead of 3, as the number to standardize. The total *shaded* area below 3.5 on the histogram is what corresponds to 'the percent of cases that scored less than or equal to 3'. 3.5 is called the *upper real limit* that corresponds to the score 3. Standardizing 3.5 produces an estimated percentile rank of *67.4%*, much closer to the true percentile rank of *70%*!

Figure 7.3.3 Percentile Ranks and Estimated Percentile Ranks

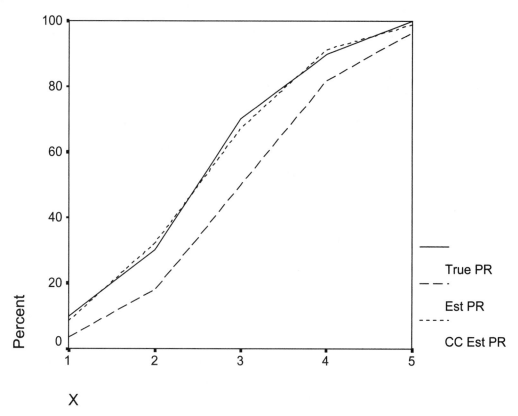

Figure 7.3.3 above shows graphically how much closer the continuity corrected estimates (CC Est PR) are to the true percentile ranks.

The reasoning behind this may not seem intuitive at first-- it's a little early in the course to introduce it. You won't be *required* to use continuity corrections on quizzes or exams, but it's good to be aware that continuity corrections can improve the accuracy of estimates.

7.4 ESTIMATING PERCENTILES

We can *reverse* the procedure used above and estimate percentiles for real world distributions, given appropriate information.

PROCEDURE FOR ESTIMATING PERCENTILES

You can use the z Table to *estimate* the ith percentile for some *real* distribution, if and only if the following are all known:

A) The *mean* of all cases' scores, $\overline{X}$

B) The *standard deviation* of the scores, SD

C) $i\%$ (One specific *percentile* you want to estimate)

D) The distribution of all scores is known to be *approximately normal.*

Here is the procedure to follow:

1) Find the ith percentile in the *z distribution*. That is, find the lowest z score with a percentile rank of at least $i\%$. Use that z score as an estimate of 'STD X', the standardized version of the score we are trying to find.

2) *Un*standardize the estimated 'STD X', using the formula   'X' = $\overline{X}$ + ('STD X')(SD)

3) Use the result, 'X', as an *estimate* of the ith percentile on X, i.e., the lowest score on X with a percentile rank of $i\%$ or more.

EXAMPLE

An aptitude test had a mean of 1000 and a SD of 200. The distribution of aptitude test scores was approximately normal in shape. Estimate the 67th percentile on the aptitude test.

1) We find the 67th percentile in the *z distribution*. That is, we find the lowest z score with a percentile rank of at least 67%. It is .44. We use that z score as an estimate of 'STD X', the standardized version of the score we are trying to find.

2) We *un*standardize the .44 (Our 'STD X'), using the formula

$$\text{'X'} = \overline{X} + (\text{'STD X'})(\text{SD})$$
$$= 1000 + (.44)(200)$$
$$= 1088$$

3) We use the 1088 as an *estimate* of the 67th percentile on X, i.e., the lowest score *on X* with a percentile rank of 67% or more.

EXERCISES, CHAPTER 7

----

1. The standard normal distribution...
   - A) is an ideal, theoretical distribution
   - B) ranges from "minus infinity" to "plus infinity"
   - C) has a mean of 0 and a SD of 1.
   - D) all of the above are correct.
   - E) only A) and C) are correct.

----

2. Ken and Deb each score 60, and Kay and Bob each score 100 on a new IQ test.
   This distribution of IQ scores is:
      A) symmetrical B) positively skewed C) negatively skewed

3. The distribution _____ approximately normal because it _____ .
   - A) is...is symmetrical.
   - B) is...is bell shaped.
   - C) is not...is not symmetrical
   - D) is not...is not bell shaped.
   - E) is not...is not standard.

4. What is Ken's deviation from the mean?

5. What is Ken and Deb's standard score?

6. Compute the 51st percentile of this distribution.

----

7. How many different *normal* distributions are there with a mean of 32.8?
      A) 0   B) 1   C) 2   D) infinitely many

----

8. What is the 20th percentile in the standard normal distribution?
      A) .84   B) .85   C) .2005   D) -.84   E) -.85

----

9. Sue beat or tied 20% of the students on a test which had a mean of 200 and a SD of 40.
   Assuming the distribution of scores was approximately normal, estimate Sue's score, i.e., estimate
   the 20th percentile.

Al's percentile rank is 33% on a variable which has an approximately normal distribution.

10. Estimate Al's standard score, if possible.

11. Assume further that the distribution above has a mean of 190 and a SD of 20.
    Estimate Al's score, if possible.

Refer to the graphs below to answer the next three questions:

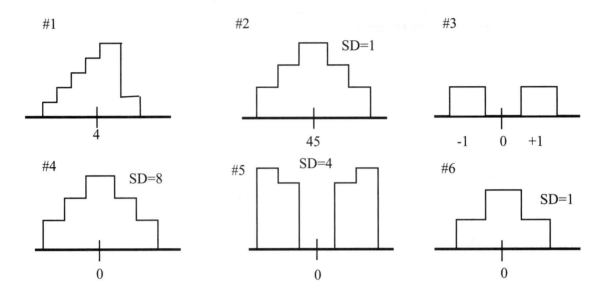

12. Using the criteria defined in this class, which of the distributions sketched above are
    approximately normal?
                    A) #6 only   B) #6 and #4 only
                    C) #6 and #4 and #2   D) #6 and #1 and #2
                    E) None of the above is correct

13. Which distribution(s) appear(s) to be standard?
                    A) #3 and #6 only   B) #6 only
                    C) #1 and #2 and #6 only   D) #1 and #2 and #4 and #6
                    E) None of the above is correct

14. Suppose you went through the complete standardization procedure, standardizing every score,
    for each of the distributions. For which of the distributions would the resulting distribution be
    "approximately standard normal"?
                    A) #4 only   B) #2 and #4 and #6 only
                    C) #4 and #6 only   D) #1 and #2 and #4 and #6
                    E) All of the distributions, because the process of standardizing a distribution
                       guarantees that the resulting distribution will be standard and approximately
                       normal.

----

15. In the standard normal distribution, the percentile rank of the score -1.22 is
                    A) 11.51% B) 11.12% C) 1.22% D) 88.49% E) 88.88%

---

16. Suppose Bill's percentile rank in a distribution is 42%. If you standardize the distribution, the percentile rank of Bill's standard score in the new standard distribution will be...

       A) (42-50)/SD   B) 42%

       C) more than 42%   D) less than 42%

       E) cannot be determined from the information given

---

17. In the standard normal distribution the 40th percentile is

       A) 40% B) -.26 C) -.25 D) -2.0 E) .25

---

18. Dr. Jones collects some data, and reports that the distribution of scores on the variable "Memory Impairment" was "approximately normal". Based on her statement, you can draw conclusions about...   (READ ALL ANSWERS)

       A) the mean of the scores on the variable

       B) the shape of the distribution of scores

       C) the SD of the distribution of scores

       D) the cause of Alzheimer's disease

       E) more than one of the above is correct

Satyan knows that his chemistry instructor, grades on a strict "curve", and always fails the lowest 20% of the students. He wants to figure out how many points he'll need to *beat or tie 21%* of the students, so he'll be sure to pass the class.

Satyan finds out that the total points for the course have averaged 1000 in the past, with a SD of 400. The shape of the distribution of total points has been approximately normal.

19. What is the 21st percentile in the standard normal distribution?

       A) 21% B) .21 C) .81 D) -.80 E) -.81

20. If scores this year follow the same pattern as in the past, how many points would you estimate that Satyan will need in order to pass? (Read all answers)

       A) exactly 680

       B) approximately 680 (estimated)

       C) approximately 1320 (estimated)

       D) approximately 600 (estimated)

       E) cannot be determined

Kim scores 480 on a test which had a mean of 500 and a SD of 100.

21. What was Kim's standard score?

22. Assume the test scores were approximately normal. Estimate Kim's percentile rank.

ANSWERS TO EXERCISES FOR CHAPTER 7

----

1. D

----

2. A

3. D

4. $X - \overline{X} = 60 - 80 = -20$

5.   Standard Score $= \dfrac{X - \overline{X}}{SD} = \dfrac{60 - 80}{20} = -1.00$

6.   100   The 51st percentile is the lowest score with a percentile rank of 51% or more.

X	percentile rank
60	2/4(100%) = 50%
100	4/4(100%) = 100%

----

7. D

There are infinitely many different *normal* distributions with a certain mean. It is only when the mean is fixed with a specific SD that it becomes one unique distribution.

----

8. D

The 20th Percentile in the standard normal distributions is the lowest z score with a percentile rank of 20% *or more*. A Percentile rank of 20% corresponds to a proportion of .20. A z score of -.84 has a cumulative proportion of .2005, so its percentile rank is 20.05%.

----

9. The 20th percentile in the z distribution is z = -.84 (lowest z score with a percentile rank of 20% or more). We need to estimate what score Sue would need to get to get a standard score of -.84.

$$X = \overline{X} + \text{(standard score)(SD)}$$
$$= 200 + (-.84)(40)$$
$$= 200 - 33.6$$
$$= 166.4$$

----

10. The 33rd percentile in the z distribution is z = -.44, because -.44 is the lowest z score with a percentile rank of 33% or more (33% corresponds to a proportion of .33). We *estimate* Al's standard score to be -.44.

11. estimated score, X
  $= \overline{X} + $ (estimated standard score)(SD)
  $= 190 + (-.44)(20)$
  $= 190 + -8.8$
  $= 181.2$

----

12. C These 3 distributions are roughly symmetrical and bell shaped.

13. A A standard distribution can have any shape but will always have a mean of 0 and a SD of 1.

14. B These are the only distributions that are approximately normal in shape.
  Any distribution which is approximately normal will be approximately *standard* normal after it is *standardized*.

----

15. B The cumulative proportion from the table is .1112. Multiplying by 100% we get 11.12%.

----

16. B Standardizing doesn't affect percentile ranks.

----

17. C -.25 is the lowest z score with a percentile rank of 40% or more.

----

18. B 'normal' is an adjective describing *shape* only! It says *nothing* about the mean, SD, etc! Of course the same goes for 'approximately normal'.

----

19. D -.80 is the lowest z score with a percentile rank of 21% or more.

20. B This is asking for an estimate of the 21st percentile.
  In a *normal* distribution, the standard score of -.80 is the 21st percentile.

  We're dealing with a real distribution, so we can *estimate* that the score which standardizes to -.80 is the 21st percentile. We find this score this way:

  $$\text{est X} = \overline{X} + (\text{est STD X})(\text{SD}) = 1000 + (-.80)(400) = 680$$

----

21. -.2
  $$\text{STD X} = \frac{X - \overline{X}}{\text{SD}} = \frac{480 - 500}{100} = -.2$$

22. 42.07%

CHAPTER 8
PROBABILITY

8.1 THREE APPROACHES

PROBABILITY

The ***probability*** of an *event* is a number between 0 and 1 which indicates how likely the event is to occur.

The ***probability*** of a *statement* is a number between 0 and 1 which indicates how likely the statement is to be true.

NOTATION: Events will be denoted by upper-case letters: A, B, C, etc.
The *probability* of some event A is denoted: P(A)

There are three distinct ways in which probabilities are obtained, and probability values are designated *subjective*, *empirical* or *rational*, depending on the method used to obtain them.

A) SUBJECTIVE PROBABILITY ESTIMATES

The term ***subjective probability*** (or *personal probability*) refers to an estimate of the probability of some event made by an individual. Such estimates typically differ from person to person. They can apply to events which may happen only one time.

EXAMPLE
Tamar thinks the probability that the Raiders will win the Super Bowl next year is .8, but Barb thinks it is only .4. In the preceding statement '.8' and '.4' are *subjective* probability estimates.

Note that the subjective estimates *disagree*, which is typical. The game referred to can happen only once. If the Raiders win, we still can't say which probability estimate was correct, because the event 'The Raiders win' is *possible* according to both estimates.

Personal probability estimates have been studied by psychologists who investigate people's decision making under risk, optimism, pessimism, and other traits. For example, people who are depressed and pessimistic tend to assign much higher probabilities to unpleasant events.

B) EMPIRICAL PROBABILITY ESTIMATES

The *empirical* approach to probability *always* involves *actually performing* some "experiment" a number of times. Each repetition of the experiment is called a *trial*. The proportion of trials in which some event occurs is computed and used as an estimate of the probability of the event.

**(8.1.1) The *empirical* probability estimate of the event A after
N trials is the proportion of trials in which A occurred,**

$$P(A) = \frac{\text{the number of trials in which A occurred}}{N, \text{ the number of trials conducted so far}}$$

**The empirical probability of the event A is the limit
that this proportion approaches, as the number
of trials becomes infinitely large.**

The empirical approach can only be used in cases where an event has many chances to occur in similar or identical circumstances.

EXAMPLE
Al suspects that a die is unfair. He rolls the die one hundred times and it comes up '6' forty times. Al estimates the probability of a '6' on the die to be 40/100, or .4. This is an empirical estimate because it is a proportion based on experimentation with the die.

C) RATIONAL PROBABILITIES

The *rational* (also called '*classical*', or '*logical*') *approach* to probability always involves considering a bunch of *outcomes* or possibilities which are always *assumed to be equally likely.* If there are N of these equally likely outcomes, each has probability equal to $1/N$. Note that no experiments are actually performed when this approach is used.

**(8.1.2) Assume that there are N possible outcomes
to some experiment.
Assume that each outcome is equally likely.
The *rational* (or, *classical*) probability of the
event A after N trials is the *proportion* of the
outcomes in which A occurs,**

$$P(A) = \frac{\text{the number of outcomes in which A occurs}}{N, \text{ the total number of outcomes}}$$

EXAMPLE

When a die is rolled, each of the six possible sides may end up facing up, so there are six possible outcomes. If the sides are labeled '1' through '6' as usual, what is the probability of the event 'an odd number comes up' when a fair die is rolled?

ANSWER:

If the die is fair, then each side has an equal chance to come up. Three of the six sides have odd numbers on them ('1', '3' and '5'), so the rational probability of an odd number coming up is 3/6, or .5. This is a *rational* probability because the die is not actually rolled, and each outcome has been assumed to have an equal probability.

EXAMPLE

A box contains three balloons, two red and 1 blue, two 'happy' and one 'sad', illustrated, sort of, in figure 8.1. A balloon will be picked at random from the box.
What is the probability of picking a red balloon?

FIGURE 8.1

A box of three balloons, each with a color and a mood

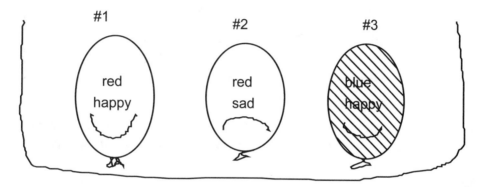

ANSWER: .667. We assume each of the three outcomes is equally likely. The number of outcomes in which the event occurs is 2, and N, the total number of outcomes is 3, so the rational probability is 2/3 = .667.

OUTCOMES versus EVENTS

Note that it is the *outcomes* that are assumed to be equally likely in the rational approach, not the *events*! The outcomes correspond to the different things that could physically happen when the experiment is conducted, without regard to scores on variables. In this example the outcomes are the different balloons that might be picked (#1, #2 or #3). If the sampling is done at random, we assume that each of these is equally likely.

After a balloon is picked, we can measure it on the variable 'color' and establish that its score is 'red', so that the event 'red balloon picked' would be said to have occurred. But we don't ever assume that because there are two events 'red' and 'blue', that these *events* are equally likely. Some textbooks call outcomes 'elementary events', or 'simple events' (E.g, Kirk, 1989).

SAMPLE SPACE

The set of all possible outcomes is referred to as the *sample space*, often designated *S*.

8.2 INDEPENDENT and DEPENDENT EVENTS

JOINT PROBABILITY

For any two events A and B, the *joint probability* of A and B, denoted P(A & B) or P(A and B), is the probability that the events A and B *both* occur.

CONDITIONAL PROBABILITY

> **(8.2.1) DEFINITION**
>
> **For any two events A and B, P(A|B), the conditional probability of A given B, is defined to be the probability that A occurs, *given* that we know that B occurs.**
>
> **COMPUTATION: P(A|B) = $\dfrac{\text{P(A \& B)}}{\text{P(B)}}$**

NOTATION

It's a good practice to quickly get used to reading "P(A|B)" as "The probability of A *given* B" or "The probability of A *given* that we know B occurred". (*Not* "A slash B"!)

EXAMPLE

If the probability that the boss arrives by train is .4, and the probability that she arrives by train *and* is late is .2, what's the conditional probability that she arrives late *given that* she arrives by train?

ANSWER .5

Let A be 'the boss arrives late' and B be 'the boss arrives by train'. From the information given, we know P(B) = .4 and P(A & B) = .2, so

$$P(A|B) = P(A \ \& \ B)/P(B) = .2 / .4 = .5$$

INDEPENDENCE

This important statistical concept is trickier than it seems to be at first. The statistical definition of independence is very specific. When you're dealing with two events, say "Event A" and "Event B", you'd say:

"Event A is *independent of* Event B if the probability of Event A remains *exactly the same* if we find out that Event B has occurred."

> **(8.2.2) Two events A and B are *independent* if**
>
> **P(A) = P(A|B) , or if P(B) = P(B|A)**

If either of the two equalities above is true, the other will be also. That is, if A is independent of B, then B will also be independent of A.

EXAMPLE

Consider the number that comes up in one roll of a die.

Let A be the event 'the number is evenly divisible by 3' and let B be the event 'the number is less than 4'.

Are A and B independent?

FIGURE 8.2 A SAMPLE SPACE FOR ONE ROLL OF A DIE

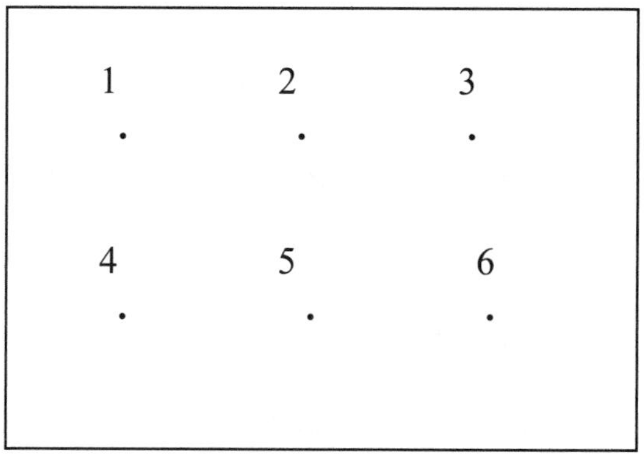

ANSWER: Yes, A and B *are* independent, because P(A) = 1/3 and P(A|B) = 1/3.

The sketch of the six outcomes in the sample space (Figure 8.2) shows that 2 of the 6 outcomes are 'evenly divisible by 3', so the probability of event A is 2/6, or 1/3. To find P(A|B), we restrict our attention to only those outcomes in which event B, 'less than 4' happens. These are the 3 outcomes in the top row. Among those 3 outcomes, only *one* is also in event A, so P(A|B) = 1/3.

(8.2.3)   Two events A and B are *not independent* if

P(A) $\neq$ P(A|B) , or if P(B) $\neq$ P(B|A)

Events which are not independent are called *dependent*, or *contingent*

NOTATION

The symbol " $\neq$ " just stands for "not equal". E.g., if P(A) = .2 and P(B) = .4 then we'd denote their *in*equality: "P(A) $\neq$ P(B)."

EXAMPLE

Consider the number that comes up in one roll of a die.

Let A be the event 'the number is odd', and let B be the event 'the number is less than 4'.

Are A and B independent?

ANSWER:

No, A and B are dependent (or contingent).

P(A) = 3/6 = 1/2, but P(A|B) is the proportion of outcomes which are *less than 4* which are *also* odd. This proportion is 2/3.

Another way to state this: Finding out that the number on the die is less than 4 would cause the probability of it being odd to *change* from 1/2 to 2/3, so the two events 'less than 4' and 'odd' are *not* independent.

EXAMPLE

Suppose the probability that a person watches Sesame Street is .02.

Also assume the probability that a person who is *under 10* watches the show is .15.

Is Event A, "person watches Sesame Street," *independent of* Event B, "the person is under 10"?

ANSWER:

P(A), the probability that a person watches Sesame Street, is .02.

P(A|B), the probability that a person watches Sesame Street, *given that* the person is under 10, is .15. (Note that we can conclude this from the second statement in the information above.)

Since P(A) is *not* equal to P(A|B) the events A and B are *not* independent.

Another way to state this: The probability of Event A *changes* (from .02 to .15) when we find out that Event B occurs. That is, P(A) = .02, but P(A|B) = .15. So A and B are not independent.

8.3 THE MULTIPLICATION RULE

The multiplication rule (or product rule) is used to figure out the joint probability that two events will *both* occur, given certain other probabilities. The need to use this rule is often indicated by the use of the words "*and*" or "*both*" in a word problem, e.g. "What is the probability that the Lakers *and* the Clippers will both win Saturday?"

(8.3.1) MULTIPLICATION RULE

For *any* two events A and B,

P(A & B) = P(A) P(B|A)   or   P(B) P(A|B)

EXAMPLE

Suppose the probability of picking a female is .6 and the probability that someone smokes *given that* they're female is .3. What is the probability of picking at random someone who is *both* female and a smoker, i.e., a female smoker?

ANSWER .18
Let A be 'female picked' and B be 'smoker picked'.
P(A) = .6 and P(B|A) = .3, so P(A & B) = P(A)P(B|A) = (.6)(.3) = .18

(8.3.2) MULTIPLICATION RULE FOR *INDEPENDENT* EVENTS:

For any two *independent* events A and B,

P(A & B) = P(A) P(B)

EXAMPLE

Suppose that you know that flips of a coin are independent of each other, and you accept that the probability of a Head on any coin flip is .5. What's the probability of getting two Heads *in a row*?

ANSWER .25

Let A be 'a Head on the first flip' and B be 'a Head on the second flip'

P(A) = .5 and P(B) = .5 and A and B are independent, so

P(A & B) = P(A)P(B) = (.5)(.5) = .25

EXAMPLE

Suppose the probability that a student studies *very* hard is .2 and the probability that a student gets an A+ is .05. Can you conclude that the probability that a student studies very hard *and* gets an A+ is (.2)(.05) = .01?

ANSWER
No, you can't tell, because you don't know whether the two events are *independent*. *Only* if the two events were *independent* would the joint probability be .01.

EXERCISES FOR CHAPTER 8, SECTIONS 8.1 - 8.3

---

1. Sabria is optimistic, and though she has never interviewed for a job, she feels that the probability she will get hired is .9. Sam interviews for three jobs, doesn't get hired, and concludes that the probability that he will ever get hired after an interview is 0. Ed reads in the LA times that there are 20,000 applicants and 4,000 jobs available, and he figures hiring is a random process wholly dependent on luck, so he computes the probability he will get hired to be 4,000/20,000 = .20. Which approach to probability is each using?

---

2. Izzy doesn't have a clue about question 1, which is a TRUE-FALSE question. He guesses at random. What is the probability he guesses right?

3. Izzy also has no idea about question 2, a five-choice multiple choice question. He guesses at random. What's the probability that he guesses question 2 right?

4. What's the probability that he guesses *both* questions right?

5. Assume that the class has *some* students who know *all* the answers, and some who don't. Kurt is a student picked at random from the class. Suppose 1/2 of the students get question 1 right, and only 1/5 get question 2 right. What's the probability that Kurt gets both questions right?

---

6. If Johnny plays Russian Roulette twice, by spinning a revolver containing one bullet in six chambers, what is the probability he *doesn't* shoot himself either time?

Suppose we added 1 balloon to the three described in Figure 8.1, and that the balloon added was BLUE and SAD. The four balloons would then be:

#1	#2	#3	#4
RED	RED	BLUE	BLUE
HAPPY	SAD	HAPPY	SAD

We will abbreviate each event by its first letter, i.e.: R: RED, B: BLUE, H: HAPPY, S: SAD

7. $P(S|R) = $ _____

8. $P(S \& R) = $ _____

*9. $P(S \text{ or } R) = $ _____

10. Are the events SAD and RED independent?

11. Are the events SAD and HAPPY independent?

Three individuals are to be picked at random from a pool of 5 candidates. Among the 5 candidates, 2 are female and 3 are male. Note that once a candidate is picked, that candidate is *not* returned to the pool, and cannot be picked again. That is, the sampling is being done *without replacement.*

We'll abbreviate the events as follows:

                 A: a male is picked on the first draw
                 B: a male is picked on the second draw

12. What is P(A)?

                 A) .2 B) .5 C) .6 D) .4 E) 1.0

13. What is P(B)?

HINT:
     Assuming you know nothing about the outcome of the *first* draw, the probability that something will happen on the *second* draw will remain *the same* as it was on the first draw.

                 A) .2 B) .5 C) .6 D) .4 E) 1.0

14. What is P(B|A)?

                 A) .2 B) .5 C) .6 D) .33 E) 1.0

15. To check whether A and B are independent events, we'd check to see if

                 A) P(A) = P(B|A)
                 B) P(B) = P(A and B)
                 C) A and B cannot both occur
                 D) P(B) = P(B|A)
                 E) P(B) = P(A|B)

16. Are A and B independent events in this case?

                 A) Yes B) No C) Cannot be determined

17. Suppose that two men in a row end up getting picked. What is the probability that that would happen,
     just by chance? (See description of A and B above)
                 A) .05 B) .10 C) .2 D) .3 E) .125

ANSWERS TO EXERCISES FOR CHAPTER 8.1 - 8.3

----

1. Sabria: subjective; Sam: empirical; Ed: rational

2. $1/2 = .5$

3. $1/5 = .2$

4. $.1 = (.5)(.2)$
    We assume the two events are *independent*, because he's just guessing at random in each case. (So he's equally likely to guess each choice, and each choice is equally likely to be the correct answer)

5. You can't tell!
    P(A), the probability that Kurt gets question 1 right is .5, and P(B), the probability that Kurt gets question 2 right is .2. But we can't multiply these probabilities to get P(A & B), unless the events are independent. (The events are probably not independent-- typically, a student who gets question 1 right will be more likely to get question 2 right than a student picked at random)

6. The probability that he shoots himself on each trial is 1/6, and the probability that he doesn't shoot himself is 5/6. Assuming that spinning the barrel is random sampling, and that the trials are independent, the probability that he *doesn't* shoot himself, *both* times, is $(5/6)(5/6) = .694$

7. $1/2 = .5$

8. $1/4 = .25$

9. $3/4 = .75$

10. Yes, because P(S) = 2/4 = .5; and P(S|R) = .5 That is, P(S) = P(S|R)

11. No, because P(S) = 2/4 = .5; but P(S|H) = 0

12. C   3 of 5, or .6 are male

13. C   Same as 12!

14. B   If one male is picked and removed, that leaves 2 males, 2 females

15. D   We know P(B) and P(B|A) from 13 and 14.

16. B   P(B) = .6; P(B|A) = .5 This is typical when sampling without replacement.

17. D   This is P(A & B), which equals P(A)P(B|A) = (.6)(.5) = .3

8.4 *INCOMPATIBLE EVENTS*

> **8.4.1 Two events A and B are *incompatible*
> (or *mutually exclusive*) if**
>
> **P(A & B) = 0**

When two events are incompatible, if you know that one happened, you know the other didn't. Common examples of pairs of events that our intuitions tell us are incompatible: heads and tails; alive and dead; right and wrong; even and odd; sane and insane, etc.

Any event with *zero* probability is obviously incompatible with every other event.

8.5 *THE ADDITION RULE*

The *addition rule* is used to figure out the probability that at least one of two events will occur. The need to use this rule is often indicated by the use of the word "or", or the phrase "at least one of", in a word problem, e.g. "What is the probability that Jones or Smith will be nominated?"

"P(A or B)" designates the probability that A occurs, or B occurs, or both A and B occur.

> **(8.5.1)   ADDITION RULE: For *any* two events, A and B,**
>
> **P(A or B) = P(A) + P(B) - P(A & B)**

EXAMPLE
   On a given work day, the probability that Al is late is .2.
   The probability that Al takes the Red Line is .1
   The probability that Al takes the Red Line and arrives late is .05
   What is the probability that Al is late *or* takes the Red Line?
           ANSWER .25
               P(A or B) = P(A) + P(B) - P(A&B) = .2 + .1 - .05 = .25

> **(8.5.2) ADDITION RULE FOR *INCOMPATIBLE* EVENTS:**
>
> **For any two events, A and B, which are
> *incompatible* (or mutually exclusive),**
>
> **P(A or B) = P(A) + P(B)**

EXAMPLE

Suppose that an agent knows that the probability that a customer has an income over $100,000 is .60, and the probability that customer is over 55 is .53. She has an appointment with a new customer at 1pm. What is the probability that the customer is over 55, *or* makes over $100,000 (or both) ?

ANSWER   You can't tell!

Designate the two events as follows

A: 'the customer has an income over $100,000'

B: 'the customer is over 55'

The task is to find P(A or B). If you knew P(A & B), you could use the addition rule (8.4.1) You don't know the events " being over 55" and "making over $100,000" are *incompatible*, so you can't use the addition rule for *incompatible* events (8.5.2). (Note that in this example, the probability of 'A or B' could be as low as .60 or as high as 1.00, but it couldn't possibly be equal to P(A) + P(B), which would be .60 + .53, or 1.13. *No* probability can be above 1.0!)

EXAMPLE

The probability that Al arrives late is .2.

The probability that Al stays home (hence never arrives) is .1.

What is the probability that Al does not arrive at work at the time he is expected?

ANSWER   .3

Al will *not* arrive on time if he is late *or* stays home.

P(Al is late *or* stays home) = P(Al is late) + P(Al stays home),

because these two events are incompatible (mutually exclusive)

EXERCISES FOR CHAPTER 8.4 - 8.5

Suppose that the probability that (A) Edie has a cold, in any given week, is .02, and the probability that (B) she sees a physician is .01.

1. Can you compute the probability that *both* of these events occur? If not, what more would you need to know?

2. Can you compute the probability that Edie either has a cold, *or* sees a physician, or both? What more would you need to know?

3. Would you estimate that these events are independent? (According to your personal estimate) Which personal probabilities would you have to check?

4. Would you estimate that the two events are mutually exclusive (incompatible)? What probability would you have to check?

In a group of adolescents in a treatment program, 20 used coke only, 70 used both coke and crystal, and 10 used crystal only. There were a total of 150 patients.

5. If you picked a patient at random, what is the probability that the patient used crystal *or* coke?

6. Are coke and crystal use *independent* events within this group?

7. Are coke and crystal use *mutually exclusive* (incompatible)?

ANSWERS TO EXERCISES FOR CHAPTER 8.4 - 8.5

---

1. No, you'd need to know either P(A|B), or P(B|A), or that the events are independent. (See the multiplication rules! *Only* the multiplication rules can be used to compute P(A&B) from other probabilities)

2. No, you'd need to know P(A&B), or that the events are mutually exclusive.

3. Most people would probably figure Edie would be *more* likely to see a physician given that she had a cold, so the events would not be independent. P(B|A) would be greater than P(B).

4. No, P(A&B) would not be expected to be 0; of course she *could* have a cold *and* see a physician.

---

5. .67   100 of the 150 patients used coke or crystal or both.

6. No. E.g. P(Coke) = .6, because 90 of 150 patients used coke. But P(Coke|Crystal) = .875, because of the 80 crystal users, 70 of them also use coke, so P(Coke|Crystal) = 70/80 = .875.

7. No, there were 70 patients who used *both* coke and crystal.

8.6 TREE DIAGRAMS

Tree diagrams do not allow you to compute any probabilities that could not be computed without them, but they do make it much easier to organize and keep track of *sequences* of events, or events that may happen in more than one *way*.

For example in Figure 8.6.1 below the event A2 can occur in two ways, by taking the *top* path or the *third* path, and its probability is P(A1 & A2) + P(B1 and A2)

FIGURE 8.6.1 FORMAT OF A TREE DIAGRAM

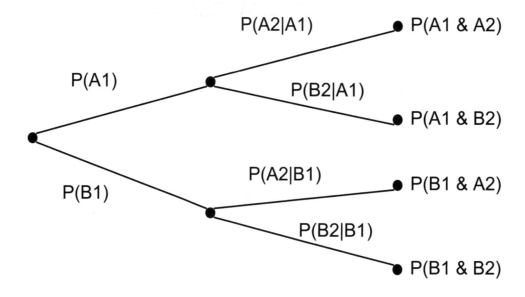

8.7 REVIEW OF IMPORTANT CONCEPTS

RATIONAL VS. EMPIRICAL APPROACHES

If you are answering a probability question that requires that you assume that each outcome has an equal chance of occurring, you are using the *rational* approach. Typically this will involve either looking at some physical object, like a coin or a die, <u>or</u> sampling at random from a population, where you know the scores of *all* the cases in the population.

EXAMPLE 1

"An experiment was run, and we know 5 of the 20 subjects improved. What's the probability that a subject picked at random from this group of 20 will be one that improved."

> ANS: .25

>> This is the *rational* approach. We are sampling from a group of 20 that we already know about, assuming each outcome is equally likely.

EXAMPLE 2

"An experiment was run, in which 20 subjects were picked at random from a large population. 5 of the 20 subjects improved. Estimate the probability that a subject from the population improves."

> ANS: .25

>> This is the *empirical* approach. We *don't* know the scores of everyone in the population. We're *estimating* a probability for a large population, knowing only about a small portion of its cases.

EXAMPLE 3

"Dr. Jones improved her treatment recently. She *estimates* the improvements will cause the probability of a patient's improving to increase to .25". Which approach to probability is involved?

> ANS: This is a *subjective estimate* or *personal probability*, based on one person's opinion.

INDEPENDENCE VS. INCOMPATIBILITY

Incompatible, or mutually exclusive events cannot *both* happen. If one of two mutually exclusive events happens, we can conclude that the other will not happen. Mutually exclusive events are never independent, (unless one of their probabilities is 0) because knowing that one happened tells us something about the probability that the other will happen.

E.g. "heads" and "tails" on one flip of a coin are mutually exclusive (because they can't *both* occur) but not independent. (Because, e.g., if you know the coin came up "heads", you know a lot about the probability that it came up "tails".)

Independent events are often said to "have nothing to do with each other". Consider these three events:

<blockquote>
A: Joe is ill
B: Joe's temperature is 99.9
C: Joe's sign is Scorpio
</blockquote>

Estimate $P(A)$, assuming Joe is a male Californian picked at random. Your estimate of $P(A|B)$ will surely be higher if you have the usual knowledge of fevers, temperature scales and illnesses. Based on most people's subjective estimates, $P(A) < P(A|B)$ and also $P(B) < P(B|A)$. Finding out about illness or high temperature makes the other event more likely, and we say the events are *dependent* (or 'associated' or 'related').

On the other hand, for most people's personal estimates, $P(A) = P(A|C)$. That is, knowing someone is a Scorpio does not make that person more or less likely to be ill. These events are generally viewed as *independent,* unrelated, or not connected to each other.

In these cases, your intuition can tell you which events are independent. In cases in which you must examine data and come to a conclusion based only on the data, there are no shortcuts. You must compute and then compare: $P(A)$ versus $P(A|B)$ or $P(B)$ versus $P(B|A)$.

JOINT PROBABILITY VS CONDITIONAL PROBABILITY

The *joint* probability that a coin comes up heads 6 times in a row is

$$(1/2)(1/2)(1/2)(1/2)(1/2)(1/2) = 1/64.$$

We can multiply probabilities here because we assume separate flips of a coin are *independent*.

The *conditional* probability that a coin will come up heads, *given that* it came up heads 5 times in a row already, is 1/2 ! This difference bothers people sometimes. It helps to picture a tree in which the joint probability requires that you start at the beginning of the tree and have 6 successes *in a row*, but the conditional probability just involves *one* success on the sixth flip.

EXERCISES FOR CHAPTER 8

POWERFUL ORANGE JUICE?
Suppose that on a ward, in any given week, a patient is equally likely to be judged "Improved" or "Not improved" by the staff who come in contact with the patients. Dr. Mennuti picks four patients at random and has his new medication slipped in their orange juice. All four patients are rated "Improved." Dr. Mennuti claims that his new medication must work. (Assume that the patients are *independent*, i.e. that one patient's improving doesn't affect the other patients' chances of improving.)

Dr. Jones is skeptical. He says "Those four patients might have gotten better just by chance, i.e. just by luck. Picking four patients who each get better is not that unusual or unlikely. I'm not impressed!"

1. How likely is it that all four patients picked would improve "just by chance"?
    Compute this probability as if the sampling were done with replacement.
    (There were no controls in this experiment. Do you think that's OK in this case?)

2.* What's the probability that exactly *three* of the four patients would "Improve," by chance?

3.* What's the probability that three or more of the four patients would be rated as "Improved", if
    the improvement were only due to chance?

4. What's the probability that the fourth patient improved?

Consider a case that is similar to the above, except that instead of being rated "Improved" or "Not Improved", the patients are rated on a five point scale, from "A: Much improved" to "E: Much worse".
Suppose that it is well known that patients in general are equally likely to get any of the five possible ratings. Suppose that *all four* patients in Dr. Mennuti's group get the rating "A".

5. How likely would this be, just by chance?

6.* What is the probability that *exactly three* of four patients would get the rating "A" by chance?

7. What's the probability that *three or more* of the four patients picked will get an "A" rating?

LUCKING OUT ON THE QUIZ?

We encourage the use of tree diagrams to "count the ways". This technique is appropriate for repeated experiments, or experiments with 2 or more "trials", as in the following exercise:

> Suppose you take a test with 2 questions.
> Question 1 is a true-false question, answered T or F.
> Question 2 is a 5-choice multiple choice question, answered A,B,C,D, or E.

8. How many *different ways* are there to answer the two questions on the test? (Please draw a *tree!*)

Suppose that T is the correct answer for question 1 and either B or E are acceptable answers for question 2.

9. If you guessed at random, what would be your chances of getting a *perfect* score? (*Both* right)

10. What's the probability of getting *at least 1* right? Note that this is the same as asking for the probability that you get the first question *or* the second right.

   What's the probability of getting ...

11. ... *neither* right? (*Both* wrong)

12. ... the *second* right, *given* that you got the first right? (Hint: Same as getting the *second right!*)

13. ... *both* right, *if* (or, *given that*) you got the first right? (Hint: Same as getting the *second right!*)

14. ... *both* right, *if* you got the second right? (Hint: Same as getting the *first right!*)

REVIEW MULTIPLE CHOICE QUESTIONS

TABLE 1:

Tx	Status	
A	I	EVENT A: Got Treatment A
A	I	EVENT B: Got treatment B
A	N	
A	W	EVENT I: Improved
B	I	EVENT W: Got worse
B	I	EVENT N: No change
B	N	
B	N	

TABLE 2:

#1:A I	#2:A I	#3:A N	#4:A W
#5:B I	#6:B I	#7:B N	#8:B N

Eight patients on a ward each has a score of A or B on the Tx variable, indicating which treatment the patient got.

Each patient also has a score on the variable status, indicating whether the patient 'Improved', got 'Worse' or showed 'No change'.

TABLE 1 describes the patients' scores in the usual raw data format. TABLE 2 lists the eight patients by number, along with their scores.

One patient will be picked at random. Abbreviations for the events being considered are described above.

15. P(I) =   A) .4   B) .5   C) .2   D) .1   E) .8

16. P(I|A) =   A) .4   B) 1.0   C) .2   D) .5   E) 0

17. P(A|N) = A) .4   B) .5   C) .33   D) .67   E) 1.0

18. P(A or I) = A) 1.0   B) .67   C) .33   D) 0   E) .75

19. Are the events A and I independent?
            A) Yes   B) No   C) Cannot be determined

20. Are the events A and N independent?
            A) Yes   B) No   C) Cannot be determined

21. Are the events A and B independent?
            A) Yes   B) No   C) Cannot be determined

22. How many different outcomes are there in this example?
            A) 5   B) 2   C) 16   D) 8   E) 4

---

23. The probability that a bettor wins the first race is .2.
    The probability that a bettor wins the last race is .4.
    The probability that a bettor wins *both* races is
            A) .6   B) .08   C) .2   D) .8   E) Cannot be determined

---

24. The probability that a package arrives damaged is .2.
        The probability that a package arrives by air is .5.
        10% of all the packages that arrive by air arrive damaged.
        What's the probability that a package picked at random arrived by air *and* arrived damaged?
        (HINT: Ignore the one *irrelevant* number)
            A) .05   B) .02   C) .1   D) .2   E) cannot be determined

---

----

25. Al, a bettor, only wins *one* race on July 20.

      The probability that Al wins the first race is .2.

      The probability that Al wins the last race is .4.

      The probability that Al wins the first race *or* the last race (or both) is

        A) .6 B) .08   C) .2   D) .06   E) Cannot be determined

----

26. The probability that a package arrives damaged is .2.

      The probability that a package arrives by air is .5.

      The probability that a package arrives by air and is also damaged is .1

      What's the probability that a package picked at random arrived by air *or* arrived damaged? (or both)

        A) .6   B) .01   C) .1   D) .7   E) cannot be determined

----

TABLE 3:

#	Tx	EXAM	
	Tx	EXAM	EVENT A: Got Treatment A
#1	A	L	EVENT B: Got treatment B
#2	A	M	
#3	A	H	EVENT L: Low
#4	B	L	EVENT M: Medium
#5	B	L	EVENT H: High
#6	B	L	
#7	B	M	
#8	B	H	
#9	B	H	

TABLE 4:

#1:AL	#2:AM	#3:AH
#4:BL	#5:BL	#6:BL
#7:BM	#8:BH	#9:BH

In a group of nine students (numbered #1 through #9 above), each has a score of A or B on the Tx variable, indicating which teacher the student had for a class.

Each student also has a score on the variable EXAM, indicating whether the student scored Low, Medium or High on an exam.

TABLE 3 describes the students' scores in the usual raw data format. TABLE 4 lists the nine students by number, along with their scores. For example "#1:AL" indicates "Student #1 was in group A and scored Low on the exam".

One student will be picked at random.

27. P(H) =   A) .444 B) .333 C) .667 D) .556 E) .222

28. P(H|A) =   A) .111 B) .222 C) .333 D) .444 E) .556

29. P(H or A) =   A) .111 B) .222 C) .333 D) .444 E) .556

30. P(H & A) =   A) .111 B) .222 C) .333 D) .444 E) .556

31. The events A and H are
    A) independent and mutually exclusive
    B) independent but not mutually exclusive
    C) mutually exclusive, but not independent
    D) neither mutually exclusive nor independent

32. The events A and L are
    A) independent and mutually exclusive
    B) independent but not mutually exclusive
    C) mutually exclusive, but not independent
    D) neither mutually exclusive nor independent

Two people will be picked at random from a group of five people.
The group of five people is composed of 3 women and 2 men.

Let M1 designate the event "A man is picked on the first pick"

Let M2 designate the event "A man is picked on the second pick"

33. If the sampling is done *with* replacement, what is P(M1 & M2)?
        A) .25 B) 0 C) .04 D) .16 E) .10

34. If the sampling is done *without* replacement, what is P(M1 & M2)
        A) .25 B) 0 C) .04 D) .16 E) .10

35. If the sampling is done *with* replacement, are M1 and M2 independent?
        A) Yes B) No

ANSWERS TO EXERCISES FOR CHAPTER 8

----

1. $(.5)(.5)(.5)(.5) = .0625$

       Fairly impressive, but not sufficient to convince most researchers today.

2.*   .25

3.*   .3125 (Or .25 + .0625)

4.   .5

----

5. $(.2)(.2)(.2)(.2) = .0016$

       Very impressive. Most researchers today would accept this as *impressive* evidence that Dr.
       Mennuti's medication was actually causing improvement, because these results are so *unlikely*
       to be due just to *luck*, or chance. Why do you think most people would allow the use of the
       word "cause" here?

6.*   .0256

       4 times $(.2)(.2)(.2)(.8)$, because there are four "ways" to get three patients with A's and one
       without an A, and each of these has probability $(.2)(.2)(.2)(.2)$. This can be computed more
       intuitively using a tree, or using the Binomial Formula.

7.   .0256 + .0016 = .0272

       So, if three of four patients in the medicated group got "A" ratings, that would still be fairly
       impressive evidence that the medication was working. Why? Because "The amount of
       improvement exhibited in the data is greater than we would expect by chance. It's pretty
       unlikely that it was just due to luck."

---

8. 10   TA, TB, TC, TD, TE, FA, FB, FC, FD, FE

9. .2

    You could get this by counting the ways, i.e., TB and TE are the correct ways, out of 10 possible ways, so the answer is 2/10 = .2
    You could also multiply (assuming independence) the probability of success on the first question, .5, by the probability of success on the second question, .4, to get .2

10. .7

    (You need to "count the ways" here-- you can't *add* .5, the probability of success on question 1, to .4, the probability of success on question 2, because success on the first is not *incompatible* with success on the second)

11. .3

12. .4

13. .4 (This is the same question as 12)

14. .5

REVIEW MULTIPLE CHOICE QUESTIONS

---

15. B $4/8 = .5$

16. D $2/4 = .5$

17. C $1/3 = .33$

18. E $6/8 = .75$

19. A   Because $P(I) = P(I|A) = .5$

20. B   No, because $P(A) = .5$, $P(A|N) = .33)$

21. B   No! $P(A) = .5$, $P(A|B) = 0$

22. D   Any one of 8 cases might be picked

---

23. E $P(A \& B) = P(A)P(B|A)$ or $P(B)P(A|B)$
             We don't know either of the conditional probabilities, $P(B|A)$ or $P(A|B)$

---

24. A $P(D|A) = .1$, $P(A) = .5$, $(.5)(.1) = .05$

---

25. A   He can't win *both* races, so the events are incompatible.

---

26. A   .2 + .5 - .1

---

27. B   3/9

28. C   1/3

29. E   5/9

30. A   1/9

31. B   P(H) = 1/3 and P(H|A) = 1/3, so H and A are independent.

                P(H & A) = 1/9 which is not 0, so H and A are not mutually exclusive.

32. D   P(A) = 1/3 and P(A|L) = 1/4, so A and L are not independent.

                P(A and L) = 1/9 which is not 0, so A and L are not mutually exclusive.

---

33. D   (2/5)(2/5) = (.4)(.4) = .16

34. E   (2/5)(1/4) = (.4)(.25) = .1

35. A

CHAPTER 9
BINOMIAL SAMPLING DISTRIBUTIONS

9.1 RANDOM VARIABLES AND PROBABILITY DISTRIBUTIONS

In the previous chapter we referred to a simple experiment in which balloons would be drawn at random from a box. The balloons differed on the variables COLOR and MOOD. Suppose we know that there are three red balloons, one green balloon and one blue balloon in the box. Before any balloons are drawn, we already know that the possible scores on the variable COLOR are red, green and blue, but we don't know which score will actually occur when a balloon is picked at random. Assuming that the rational approach is appropriate, we can compute the probability that each of the colors occurs. The variable COLOR in a case such as this is called a *random variable*. The set of all possible colors, along with a probability for each color, is called the *probability distribution* for the random variable COLOR.

(9.1.1)

A *random variable* is a variable in which a case's score is determined by some chance process. The chance process is often referred to as an experiment.

(9.1.2)

The *probability distribution* for the random variable X describes
  a) all possible values of X
  b) the probability that each value occurs

EXAMPLE

Table 9.1.1

COLOR	Probability
Red	.6
Blue	.2
Green	.2

Table 9.1.1 is the probability distribution for the variable COLOR as described above.

9.2 *SAMPLING DISTRIBUTIONS*

Previously we have computed statistics, such as the mean, SD, proportions, percents, etc., for sets of cases. Those sets of cases have been *either* samples *or* populations. The branch of statistics we have been using is called *descriptive statistics*, because we have been using statistics to *describe* the entire set of cases in a given sample or population.

We haven't yet dealt with these types of questions:

"If the *sample* correlation coefficient is -.3, can we conclude that there's a negative relationship in the whole *population*?"

"If 55% of the *population* actually support Jones, what are the chances that we pick a *sample* in which less than 50% support Jones."

"If the proportion of patients in the *population* that would improve if they were given Treatment X is .30, what is the probability that all 4 patients in a random *sample* will improve if they are given Treatment X?"

These questions mention both populations and samples, so they are in the domain of *inferential* statistics. Typically in inferential statistics we *infer* something about a population, but we only have scores from a sample.

(9.2.1)

Inferential statistics is the branch of statistics that deals with making inferences about entire populations, based upon samples from those populations.

Sampling distributions are the most important distributions used in *inferential* statistics. Sampling distributions are primarily about the set of all possible *samples*; *not* the set of scores in the population; *not* the set of scores in the sample!

(9.2.2) Given some specific population, statistic, and sample size, n,
The *sampling distribution* of the statistic is the probability distribution for values of the statistic.

The *sampling distribution* of the statistic specifies
a) each possible value of the statistic and
b) the probability of that value, assuming that samples of size n are being drawn at random.

9.3 PREVIEW OF HYPOTHESIS TESTS

"DR. ALTERNATE'S NEW TREATMENT"

To provide one clear example of the distributions and techniques used in inferential statistics, the following example will be used throughout the remainder of this chapter. It is also presented in class.

EXAMPLE ("DR. ALTERNATE'S NEW TREATMENT")

Dr. Alternate knows that the generally accepted cure rate for patients with a certain illness, given the standard treatment, is .3. That is, it is believed that in the population of all patients with the illness, the proportion of patients that will be cured is .3. Dr. Alternate has a new treatment which she feels will cause a cure rate much greater than .3. Dr. Null, a skeptical colleague, believes that Dr. Alternate's treatment produces no improvement in the cure rate.

Dr. Alternate proposes picking four patients at random and giving them her treatment.

TERMINOLOGY:
Nominal scale variables such as 'whether a patient got cured or not', which have two possible scores on a nominal scale, are called *dichotomous* variables. Such variables divide the population into two categories. The two categories are traditionally called '*success*' and '*failure*', even in cases in which these designations are arbitrary. In keeping track of scores on these variables, success is coded numerically as a '1', and failure is coded as a '0', so that the sum of scores for a sample is the same as the number of successes. This number is called the '*count*' and is usually designated '**k**'. In the example above, k may have any value from 0 to 4.

Many different procedures are essentially the same as 'picking one case and determining whether it represents success or failure'. They are all designated *Bernoulli Trials*.

**(9.3.1)   A *Bernoulli Trial* (or Bernoulli Experiment)
        is any procedure which
            a) always results in one of two events
                (labeled 'success' and 'failure'), and
            b) the probability of a success
                (designated p) is the same for all
                trials, and
            c) the trials are independent**

So **the *count*, *k*,** can also be described as the random variable which represents the number of successes which occur in n Bernoulli trials, where the probability of success on each trial is p.

Suppose that a sample of four patients is drawn, and that after these patients are given Dr. Alternate's treatment, *all four* of the patients are cured. We would like to confidently draw an inference about the population based on these results. Stated in the usual terminology, "k, the number of successes, is *4* in a sample of size *4*".

However, we must keep in mind that the experimental results are *consistent* with either Dr. Alternate's position or Dr. Null's position. That is, the results, which *do* seem to support Dr. Alternate's position, could be viewed in two different ways:

Dr. Null's position:
> "Even if the patients are all given your new treatment, the proportion of successes in the treated population will still be *equal to* .3, the same as it's always been. If you got a lot of successes in your sample, it just happened *by chance* or luck." [This "skeptical" position, which always specifies that *no* change, or *no* difference, or *no* improvement exists, is traditionally termed the **null hypothesis**.]

Dr. Alternate's position:
> "No, my new treatment has *raised* the success rate *above* .3. If I got a lot of successes in my sample it's *not* just due to chance, it's because the proportion of successes, with my treatment, is *greater than* .3!" [This position, which holds that there *has* been a *change*, a *difference*, or an *improvement*, is traditionally called the **alternate hypothesis**.]

9.4 IS THE EVIDENCE CONVINCING ?

The example is about the population of all patients with the illness, *if* they were given Dr. Alternate's treatment. What would *you* conclude about this population based on the data described above? That is, suppose you had been given only this information:

- Dr. Alternate believes the proportion of successes (cures) in the *population* is greater than .3

- Dr. Null believes that the proportion of successes in the *population* is equal to .3

- In a random sample of size 4 from the population there were 4 successes, that is, the *sample* proportion was 1.0

If you are like a typical student, your reasoning might be something like this:

"Either of the doctors *could* be right; we only know about four patients sampled from thousands."

"However, the data support Dr. Alternate's position, because the sample proportion is 1.0, showing a high success rate in the sample, which is what you'd expect if her treatment *was* working well."

"But, as Dr. Null claims, you *could* get 4 successes in a row just by luck. It's certainly possible that the population proportion is just .30, and the sample happened to favor Dr. Alternate's position only by chance."

"The evidence isn't convincing enough to convince *me*, but if *more* patients had been picked and they all improved then I would be convinced. *Ten* successes in a row would be *convincing*; 100 in a row would be almost *definite proof*".

Almost everyone sees that ten successes in a row would be more convincing than four in a row, but we seldom need to state the fundamental principle behind this reasoning:

> **(9.4.1)** **Suppose that the results of an experiment might be either**
> **a) due to some *effect*, or**
> **b) due to *luck*.**
> **The *less likely* the results of the experiment are to occur just by luck, the *more convincing* evidence they can provide for the existence of the effect.**

Most people have this intuition, that the occurrence of *rare*, or unlikely, or low probability events can provide strong evidence. Here's a more general, informal version of this important principle:

> **(9.4.2)** **Suppose an event occurs, and the occurrence of the event could either be**
> **a) due to some specific *cause*, or**
> **b) due to luck**
> **The *less* likely the event is to occur by luck, the *more* we are convinced it was due to the specific *cause*.**

In our example, four successes in a sample size of four is *not* impressive or convincing enough to most people because they don't see it as *rare*, or *unlikely* enough. It's too easy to imagine getting four successes in a row by chance. Exactly how *rare* is that event? We'll assess the probability of getting four successes in a row *three* different ways:

- We'll describe a classroom demonstration, using random numbers, to simulate the experiment, and *estimate* the probability.
  (Described in Section 9.5)

- We'll show how to compute the probability *exactly* using a tree diagram.
  (Described in Section 9.6)

- We'll show how to compute the probability *exactly* using the binomial formula.
  (Described in Section 9.7)

The probability that the results of an experiment happened just by chance, or just by luck is called "p" in statistics. It's referred to as the "obtained significance level." You should memorize this!

Italic "p" will never be used for anything other than this.

9.5 BINOMIAL PROBABILITIES: EMPIRICAL ESTIMATES

THE SAMPLING DISTRIBUTION OF k : A BINOMIAL DISTRIBUTION

Recall that the sampling distribution of a statistic lists each possible value of the statistic, along with the probability that you'll pick a random sample with that value.

The sampling distribution of the statistic k lists all possible values of k, along with their probabilities. Recall that k always represents the number of successes in a set of independent trials, where the probability of a success on each trial is the same. Probability distributions for variables like k are called *binomial distributions*.

**(9.5.1)   Given: p, the probability of success, and
            n, the number of trials.**

**The *Binomial Distribution*, designated B(n,p) is
the sampling distribution of the statistic k,
the *number of successes* in n Bernoulli trials.**

So there is *one* binomial distribution for each possible value of n, (the number of 'trials'), and p, (the probability of success on a given trial).

CLASSROOM DEMONSTRATION: ESTIMATING BINOMIAL PROBABILITIES

A *MONTE CARLO* SiMULATION

Each student represents a researcher conducting an experiment on a random sample of four patients. We assume that each patient had a .3 chance of improving (Which we labeled "success").

We use random numbers chosen at random from a table to represent randomly selected patients. If a random number was *00 through 29* or greater, that number is circled, to indicate it represents a patient who improved. Since .3 of all random numbers between 00 and 99 are between 00 and 29, this procedure is a good way to represent patients who have a .3 chance of improving.

In class we ask how many students had samples with 0 successes, 1 success, etc. We then compute the proportion of samples in our class with 0 successes, 1 success, etc. We are empirically *estimating the probability* that each value of k would occur. For example, if 14 of 156 students had samples in which 3 of the 4 patients "improved, we'd estimate the probability that k = 3 to be 14/156 = .09.

This kind of procedure, called ***Monte Carlo simulation***, can be used to estimate probabilities in many different situations.

9.6 *COMPUTING BINOMIAL PROBABILITIES USING TREES*

The probability referred to above, that k = 3 when p = .3 and n = 4, can be computed *exactly* using a tree diagram. You must count all the paths through the tree that have 3 successes and 1 failure, then add the probabilities for those paths.

The appropriate tree is shown on the following page in FIGURE 9.6.1. There are *four* paths through the tree with exactly 3 successes in 4 trials. Each has the same probability, .0189.

So the probability of obtaining 3 successes in four trials is the sum of the probabilities of taking these paths, or 4 times .0189, which is .0756.

FIGURE 9.6.1:   TREE REPRESENTING   P(S) = .3   P(F) = .7   4 TRIALS

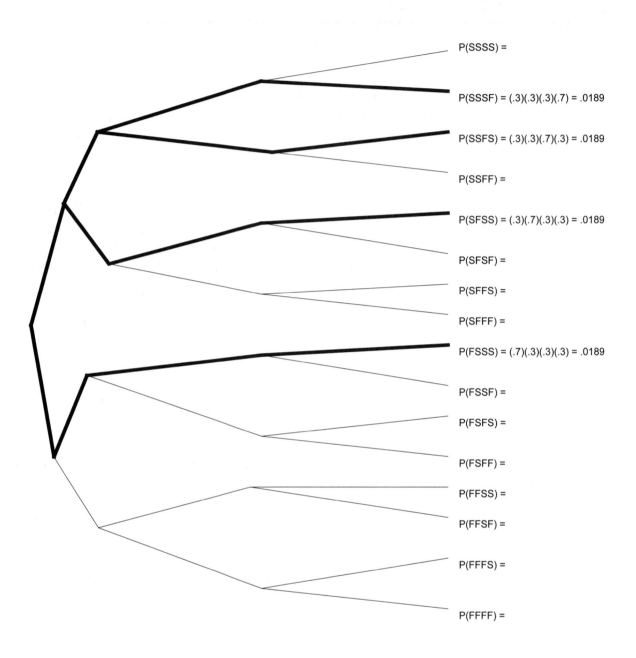

9.7 THE BINOMIAL FORMULA

Luckily, there's a *faster* way to compute binomial probabilities: a table of binomial coefficients can tell you how many paths there are through the tree with k successes. Each *path* represents *one* sequence of k successes and n-k failures. The probability for *each* of those paths will always be:

$$p^k(1-p)^{n-k}$$

This is the probability of getting k successes in n trials *in a specific order*.

In our example, k is 3 and n-k is 1. Each path with 3 successes and 1 failure has probability

$$p^k(1-p)^{n-k} = (.3)^3(.7)^1 = .0189$$

In our example, there were *four* such paths in the tree, so the probability of getting exactly 3 successes in *any* order is

$$P(k = 3) = \text{(The number of paths with 3 successes)} p^k(1-p)^{n-k}$$

$$= (4)(.3)^3(.7)^1 = (4)(.0189) = .0756$$

The probability of getting k successes can be computed this way in general using this well known formula:

(9.7.2) BINOMIAL FORMULA

The probability of obtaining exactly k successes in n Bernoulli trials is

(The *number of ways* of getting k successes in n trials)$p^k(1-p)^{n-k}$

USING THE TABLE OF BINOMIAL COEFFICIENTS

The *number of ways* of getting k successes in n trials is called the binomial coefficient for n and k. You can use the BINOMIAL TABLE (Table A2 in the Appendix) to quickly find the number of 'ways', so that the binomial formula can be used.

There are 20 rows in the binomial table, one for each possible value of n, the sample size (or "number of trials"). Since our sample size was 4, we'll look at the fourth row down in the table. The entries in that row read '1 4 6 4 1'.

The *columns* in the table correspond to the possible values of k, the number of "successes" in n trials. In our case, with 4 trials, the number of successes can range from 0 to 4.

How many ways are there to get exactly 3 successes in 4 trials? To find this number, you look up the entry in the *row* labeled 4 and the *column* labeled 3-- the entry is '4'. Note that if you patiently go through a tree, you come to the *same* conclusion: there are 4 paths through the tree with exactly 3 successes and one failure.

The probability of each one of these paths is the same: $(.3)(.3)(.3)(.7)$ or $(.3)^3(.7)^1$, which is .0189, because the probability of success is always .3 and the probability of failure must be 1 - .3, or .7. When you multiply the probabilities on a path that has three successes and one failure, you'll always multiply .3 three times and .7 one time.

Since there were 4 'ways' to get exactly three successes, and the probability of each 'way' is .0189, the probability of getting exactly three successes is $(4)(.0189) = .0756$, or about .08.

The probability of getting *four* consecutive successes in a row is $(.3)^4 = .0081$. This probability is so *low* that the typical statistician would say "If k = 4, that would constitute *convincing* evidence that p is greater than .3 in the population. k = 4 is very *unlikely* to happen just by luck."

COMPUTING BINOMIAL COEFFICIENTS (OPTIONAL)

The *number of ways* of getting k successes in n trials may also be *computed* using this formula:

$$\binom{n}{k} = \frac{n!}{k!(n-k)!} \quad \text{where } n! = (n)(n-1)(n-2)...(1)$$

That is, n!, called 'n factorial' is computed by multiplying n and all positive integers less than n together.

EXAMPLE

In our 'Dr. Alternate' example above, we were interested in the probability of getting 3 successes in 4 tries. That is, k = 3 and n = 4, so the number of 'ways' is

$$\binom{4}{3} = \frac{4!}{3!(4-3)!} = \frac{(4)(3)(2)(1)}{(3)(2)(1)(1)} = 4$$

9.8 THE BINOMIAL DISTRIBUTION, B(n,p)

COMPUTING ALL POSSIBLE BINOMIAL PROBABILITIES

Assume that we conduct n Bernoulli trials, each with probability of success equal to p.

We've shown how to compute the probability of obtaining exactly k successes in n trials.

Of course, k *could* be any number from 0 to n.

If we consider every possible value of k, and compute a probability for each, we have computed B(n,p), the binomial distribution with parameters n and p. For every positive integer n, and probability p, there is just one *binomial distribution* whose probabilities indicate how likely you are to obtain k successes in n trials.

(9.8.1) B(n,p), the *binomial distribution* with parameters
n and p, is the probability distribution with scores
0,1,.,k,.., n in which the probability of each score is

$$P(k) = \binom{n}{k} p^k (1-p)^{(n-k)}$$

EXAMPLE

Computing the probability of k successes, for all possible values of k in the 'Dr. Alternate' example above yields this binomial distribution:

TABLE 9.8.1   B(4, .3)

k	p(k)
0	.2401
1	.4116
2	.2646
3	.0756
4	.0081

√ 1.0000

TABLE 9.8.1 shows that we are *most* likely to see 1 success in 4 tries, if the probability of success is .3 on each try. 4 successes in a row is the *least* likely result, with probability .0081. The distribution is positively skewed. (We'll see later that the scores are 'clumped' close to the mean, which is (4)(.3) = 1.2. A k value of 1 represents the score that is closest to the distribution's mean of 1.2).

DISPLAYING A BINOMIAL SAMPLING DISTRIBUTION

The following probability histogram shows the binomial distribution B(4, .3) portrayed in the most common format. Across the horizontal axis are the possible values of the statistic, k. the vertical axis represents probability. The height above each possible value of k is the probability of obtaining that number of successes in 4 tries, when the probability of success on each trial is .3. This distribution is also called the *sampling distribution* for the statistic k.

FIGURE 9.8.1

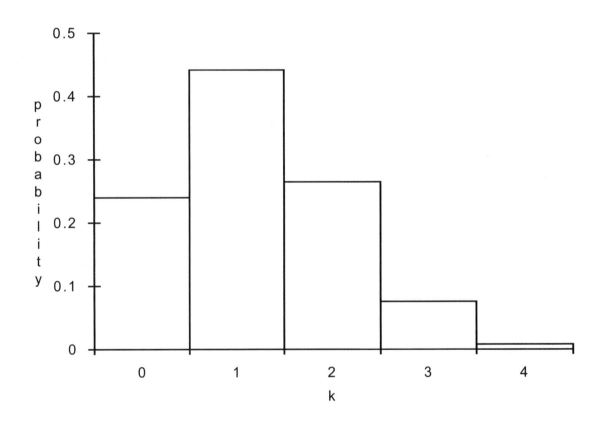

BINOMIAL DISTRIBUTION B(4, .3)

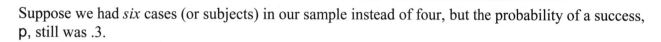

EXERCISES FOR CHAPTER 9

Suppose we had *six* cases (or subjects) in our sample instead of four, but the probability of a success, p, still was .3.

1. What would be the probability of getting *exactly six* successes? I.e., P(k = 6) =?

2. P(k = 5) is ?

3. P(*Exactly four* successes) = P(k = 4) = ?

4. Which is more impressive evidence that the treatment worked, i.e., that the treatment *raised* the success rate *above* .3
    A) *four* successes in a sample of size four, or
    B) *six* successes in a sample of size six?

5. What's the probability of getting four failures, *then* two successes, *in that order*?

6. What's the probability of getting 1 success, *then* two failures, *then* 1 success, *then* two failures?

7. What's the probability of getting *5 or more* successes?

8. What's the probability of getting *4 or more* successes?

Suppose 40% of a group of students are female.

Five are picked at random, with replacement.

What's the probability of picking...

9. ...*no* females?

10. ...*exactly one* female?

11. ...*exactly 2* females

12. ...*at least* three males? (two or fewer females?)

13. ...the *first two* females, *then* three males?

Suppose 60% of the people in a large population support Jones, and a random sample of size 4 is picked from the population (with replacement). Let k represent the number of people in the sample who support Jones. (Note that we know that p, the population *proportion* is .6)

14. What is the probability that k = 0, i.e. that *none* of the four people picked support Jones?
      A) .0256 B) .1296 C) .1536 D) .3456 E) .5

15. What is the probability that k = 1?
      A) .0256 B) .1296 C) .1536 D) .3456 E) .5

16. What is the probability that k = 2?
      A) .0256 B) .1296 C) .1536 D) .3456 E) .5

17. What is the probability that k = 3?
      A) .0256 B) .1296 C) .1536 D) .3456 E) .5

18. What is the probability that k = 4, i.e. that *all* of the four
      people picked support Jones?
      A) .0256 B) .1296 C) .1536 D) .3456 E) .5

19. What is the probability that k is 3 *or* 4?
      A) .1792 B) .4752 C) .1552 D) .4992 E) .5

20. What is the probability that the *first three* people picked all support Jones and *then* the fourth person picked does not support Jones, *in that exact order*?
      A) .3456 B) .1536 C) .0864 D) .0384

ANSWERS TO EXERCISES FOR CHAPTER 9

----

1. .000729 or about .001

    $$p = .3, \quad 1 - p = .7, \quad n = 6, \quad k = 6, \quad n - k = 0$$

    Using the binomial table, we see that there's 1 way to get exactly six successes in six tries, so the probability is
    $$(1)(.3)^6(.7)^0 = (1)(.000729)(1) = .000729$$

2. .010206 or about .010

    Same as above, but $k = 5$, so $n - k = 6 - 5 = 1$
    Using the binomial table, we see that there are *6* ways to get exactly five successes in six tries, so the probability is
    $$(6)(.3)^5(.7)^1 = (6)(.00243)(.7) = .010206$$

3. .059535 or .060

    Same as above, but $k = 4$, so $n - k = 6 - 4 = 2$
    Using the binomial table we see that there are *15* ways to get exactly four successes in 6 trials, so the probability is
    $$(15)(.3)^4(.7)^2 = (15)(.0081)(.49) = .059535$$

4. B) is correct, because B) is much *less likely to occur by chance.*

5. .021609 or about .022, which is $(.7)^4(.3)^2$

6. .021609, the same as the previous answer.

    Any path with 4 failures and two successes   will have the same probability, i.e.,

    $$(.3)(.7)^2(.3)(.7)^2 = (.7)^4(.3)^2$$

7. .010935 or about .011

    $$\text{P(5 or more successes)} = \text{P(5 successes)} + \text{P(6)}$$
    $$= .010206 + .000729 = .010935$$

8. .070285 or about .070

    $$\text{P(4 or more successes)} = .059535 + .010935 = .070470$$

---

9. .07776 or .078   The probability you *won't* pick a female is $1 - .4 = .6$, and

$(.6)^5$ is .07776

10. .2592 or .259   There are 5 ways to pick *one* female.

$5(.4)^1(.6)^4 = .2592$

11. .3456 or .346 $10(.4)^2(.6)^3 = .3456$

12. .68256 or .683   .07776 + .2592 + .3456 (See answers to 9, 10, 11)

13. .03456 $(.4)^2(.6)^3$

---

14. A $1(.6)^0(.4)^4 = .0256$

15. C $4(.6)^1(.4)^3 = .1536$

16. D $6(.6)^2(.4)^2 = .3456$

17. D $4(.6)^3(.4)^1 = .3456$

18. B $1(.6)^4(.4)^0 = .1296$

19. B   .3456 + .1296 = .4752

20. C $(.6)(.6)(.6)(.4)$

Draw one path through a tree, with 3 successes, then one failure

---

REVIEW EXERCISES FOR CHAPTERS 8 & 9

TRIALS by JURY

Suppose each of 12 jurors was polled independently, secretly and separately (instead of the actual process of *deliberating*). Suppose the probability that each juror found the defendant guilty is .9.

A1. What is the probability of a *unanimous* vote of *guilty* in that situation?

A2. What is the probability of a *unanimous* vote of *not guilty* in that situation?
(HINT: Your calculator may choke on this! Try computing it for 2 jurors, then 3 jurors, etc., and you'll see the obvious pattern.)

A3. Would the situation described above constitute a set of Bernoulli trials?

A4. Would you expect the *usual* procedure, in which people meet and try to influence each other constitute a set of Bernoulli trials?

A5. If you knew that each juror had .9 probability of voting guilty, and the usual procedure was followed, could you compute the probability that all 12 jurors would vote guilty?

JAMMIN'

On a saxophone, you can only play *one* note at a time. Suppose that in a certain place in a tune, the probability that a saxophonist plays the note 'C' is .4, and the probability that she plays 'G' is .3.

A6. Based on the info above, what is P(C & G)?

A7. Are the events 'C' and 'G' mutually exclusive?

A8. Are the events 'C' and 'G' independent?

A9. Based on the info above, what is P(C or G)?

PICKIN' AT RANDOM

On a guitar, you can play up to six notes at a time (But *please,* take *lessons* first!). Suppose that in a certain place in a tune, the probability that a guitarist plays the note 'C' is .4, and the probability that she plays 'G' is .3. The probability that she plays a 'G' *given that* she plays a 'C' is .2.

A10. Based on the info above, what is P(C & G)?

A11. Are the events 'C' and 'G' mutually exclusive?

A12. Are the events 'C' and 'G' independent?

A13. Based on the info above, what is P(C or G)?

VIVA--A---AH...., LAS VEGAS! *   (©Doc Pomus, 1961?)

A♣	2♣	3♣	4♣	5♣	6♣	7♣	8♣	9♣	10♣	J♣	Q♣	K♣
A♦	2♦	3♦	4♦	5♦	6♦	7♦	8♦	9♦	10♦	J♦	Q♦	K♦
A♥	2♥	3♥	4♥	5♥	6♥	7♥	8♥	9♥	10♥	J♥	Q♥	K♥
A♠	2♠	3♠	4♠	5♠	6♠	7♠	8♠	9♠	10♠	J♠	Q♠	K♠

In the game Blackjack you are dealt cards and you try to make the total of the cards you have been dealt add up to 21 (or as close as possible without exceeding 21).

There are four suits of cards, with 13 cards per suit. The sample space is illustrated above.

B1. How many possible outcomes are there in one pick of a card?

B2. If you have a 6 and a 9, the current total of your cards is 15. What is the probability that the *next card* you are dealt will be a 6, giving you a winning total of 21?
HINT: How many cards are left? How many are sixes?

B3. If you have a 6 and a 9, the current total of your cards is 15. What is the probability that the next card you are dealt will be a 5, giving you a total of (exactly) 20?

B4. Suppose you have a 6 and a 9, and suppose in the current situation, you need a total of 20 *or* 21 to win. What is the probability that the next card you are dealt will give you a total of 20 *or* 21?

B5. Suppose you have a 6 and a 5. If your next card is a ten, Jack, Queen, or King (Denoted '10', 'J', 'Q', 'K' above in the sample space) your total will be 21.
What is the probability that the next card you are dealt will give you a total of 21?

B6. Suppose you have a 6 and a 5. If your next card is a ten, Jack, Queen, or King (Denoted '10', 'J', 'Q', 'K' above in the sample space) your total will be 21.
Suppose that you (like the *Rain Man* character in the movie) have a great memory for cards, and you have noticed that 20 cards have already been dealt (including your two) and *none* of them was a ten, Jack, Queen or King. I.e. *all* of those cards are still in play, but only 32 cards are left. What is the probability that the next card you are dealt will give you a total of 21?

* If you find yourself humming the old Elvis Presley song "*Viva Las Vegas*", you might enjoy the haunting, slow version by Shawn Colvin on the CD "A Tribute to Doc Pomus".

ANSWERS TO REVIEW EXERCISES FOR CHAPTERS 8 & 9

TRIALS by JURY

A1. $(.9)^{12}$ = .2824295.   It's ok to multiply because the opinions are all *independent*.

A2. $(.1)^{12}$ = .000000000001   P(not guilty) = 1 -.9 = .1 in each case.

A3. Yes, there are two possible results, the probabilities are all .9, and they're independent.

A4. No, jurors influence each other, so one juror's guilty verdict can influence others, making them less likely to find the defendant not guilty. This makes the jurors decisions *not* independent of each other.

A5. No. You can't just multiply the probabilities when trials are not independent.

JAMMIN'

A6. 0. 'C' and 'G' can't both occur, because only *one* note can be the note played next.

A7. Yes

A8. No.   P(C) is .4   P(C|G) is 0.

A9. .7   We can just add .4 and .3, because the events are *mutually exclusive*.

PICKIN' AT RANDOM

A10. .08 = (.4)(.2) = P(C)P(G|C)   Using the multiplication rule

A11. No, you can play *both* notes next.

A12. No.   P(G) = .3, but P(G|C) = only .2.

A13. .62   (.4) + (.3) - (.08)   Using the addition rule

VIVA--A---AH...., LAS VEGAS!   *(©Doc Pomus, 1961?)*

B1. 52

B2. .06 = 3/50   You have two cards, so there are 50 left in the deck. 3 are sixes.

B3. .08 = 4/50   4 cards in the deck are 5's

B4. .14 = .06 + .08   You can add because the events are mutually exclusive--
                           if you get 20 you didn't get 21)

B5. .32 = 16/50   There are four tens, four Jacks, four Queens, and four Kings
                           among the 50 cards left in the deck.

B6. .5 = 16/32   There are four tens, four Jacks, four Queens, and four Kings
                           among the *32* cards left in the deck.

CHAPTER 10

DESCRIBING PROBABILITY DISTRIBUTIONS

10.1 COMPUTING μ_X AND σ_X FOR ANY RANDOM VARIABLE X

Random variables are most often used to describe *populations* or *events*. For example the random variable X described by the probability distribution below could represent someone's opinion about a population or someone's estimate of the events that might occur when a game of chance is played. The Greek letters μ and σ are used to denote the mean and standard deviation of a random variable, and these quantities are called *parameters* of the random variable (or of the probability distribution that specifies the random variable).

COMPUTING μ_X

TABLE 1: **Probability distribution** for X showing computation of μ_X

X_i	p_i	$X_i p_i$
20	.1	2
40	.2	8
60	.3	18
80	.4	32

$\sqrt{}$ 1.0 $\mu_X = 60$

The different possible scores of the random variable are listed in the first column, and the probability for each score in the second column. The subscript 'i' is used to denote that there are several values possible for both X and for p.

Here are two situations that could be represented by the distribution in Table 1:

"Zack thinks that 10% of the people in his town have incomes of about $20,000, 20% have incomes of 40,000, 30% make $60,000 and 40% make $80,000."

"Bo invests in a risky scheme proposed by his financial advisor, and estimates that for each share of $50 he buys, he has a .1 chance to end up with only $20, a .2 chance to earn $40, a .3 chance to earn $60 and a .4 chance to earn $80."

Zack has an *opinion* about a *population;* Bo has *estimates* of the value of *events* and how likely the events are. The mean of the random variable X, or μ_X, also referred to as the **expected value** of X, or E(X), tells us the *typical* value of X. The computation of μ_X is illustrated in the third column of Table 1; the value is 60. We'd say the "average income in the town," in Zack's case is $60,000, and "the expected gain from the investment" in Bo's case is $60 for each $50 invested.

This formula summarizes the computation. It is the only general formula that works for *all* random variables.

> **(10.1.1)   For *any* random variable X, the *mean*,**
> **or *expected value* of X is**
>
> $$\mu_X = E(X) = \Sigma X_i p_i$$

COMPUTING σ_X

The standard deviation of a random variable indicates how far a typical score is from the mean. It is the most common measure of the *spread* or *dispersion* of the variable.

TABLE 2: Computation of σ

X_i	p_i	$X_i - \mu_X$	$(X_i - \mu_X)^2$	$(X_i - \mu_X)^2 p_i$
20	.1	-40	1600	160
40	.2	-20	400	80
60	.3	0	0	0
80	.4	20	400	160

$$1.0 \qquad \text{Variance} \quad = \quad \Sigma (X_i - \mu_X)^2 p_i = \sigma^2 = 400$$

$$\text{Standard Deviation} = \qquad \sigma = \sqrt{\sigma^2} = \sqrt{400} = 20$$

The computation of σ, the standard deviation of the random variable X is shown in Table 2. The quantity σ^2 is referred to as the *variance* of X, and the positive square root of the variance is σ.

Zack could say "The income of a typical person in the town is about $20,000 away from the mean income."

Bo could say he expects to *average* $60 for every $50 invested, but there's *risk* involved, because the actual amount earned is going to typically be about $20 away from the average. Note that the interpretation of σ in the case of gambles or investments (is there a difference?) is that it measures the *risk*.

Here's the general formula for computing the standard deviation:

> **(10.1.2)**   **For *any* random variable X, the *standard deviation* of X is**
>
> $$\sigma_X = \sqrt{\Sigma(X_i - \mu_X)^2 \, p_i}$$

BOX MODELS

Sometimes it's helpful to create a picture of a random variable in a way that makes it easy to see the probabilities for each score. Urn and box models have been used in this way for centuries.

> **(10.1.3)**   **A box model (or urn model) is a representation of a random variable as a container with tickets in it, such that:**
>
> - **The tickets have on them the *possible scores* of the variable.**
>
> - **The *proportion* of tickets with each score is equal to the *probability* of that score.**

Here's a box model for the variable X in Table 1:

Figure 1:   BOX MODEL FOR X

    20   40   40   60   60   60   80   80   80   80

We put *one* ticket in the box with "20" on it and *four* tickets with "80". Why? So that the *proportion* of 20's comes out to be .1 and the *proportion* of 80's is .4. A little experimentation will show that it is not hard to create a box model for any random variable from its probability distribution.

> **(10.1.4)**   **The mean and standard deviation of the values on the tickets in a box model always match the mean and standard deviation of the random variable it is based on.**

PRACTICE: Check that the mean of the tickets in the box above is 60 and the standard deviation is 20.

10.2 COMPUTING μ_X AND σ_X FOR A "0,1" VARIABLE X

The *general* formulas (10.1.1) and (10.1.2) will always allow you to compute the mean and standard deviation for *any* probability distribution. However, for some specific kinds of probability distributions, it's a lot faster to use *shortcut formulas*. Here are the shortcut formulas to use when the probability distribution is a "0,1" distribution:

> **(10.2.1)   If X is a random variable with two possible scores, 0 and 1, and the probability of a 1 (representing "success") is p, then**
>
> $$\mu_X = E(X) = p$$
>
> $$\sigma_X = \sqrt{p(1-p)}$$

Variables like this, called *dichotomous* variables, describe situations in which there are exactly two possible categories. One category is traditionally designated a "success" and assigned a score of 1. the other category is labeled "failure" and assigned a score of 0. "p" is always the probability of a 1, or "success". If the random variable describes the result of random sampling from a population, p is the proportion of 1's, or the proportion of successes in the population. We'll refer to these variables as *"0,1" random variables*.

EXAMPLE

Keanu flips a coin once. He will be paid \$1 if the coin comes up "heads" and \$0 if the coin comes up "tails". Let X denote how much he earns. What Can You Conclude? (WCYC?)

ANSWER

X is a dichotomous random variable with two possible values 0 and 1.
The mean, or expected value of X tells us how much Keanu expects to make.
The mean of X is .5, because P(1) = .5. (or, \$.50 in this case)
The standard deviation of X, σ_X, is $\sqrt{(.5)(1-.5)} = \sqrt{.25} = .5$

10.3   THE MEAN AND STANDARD DEVIATION OF A BINOMIAL SAMPLING DISTRIBUTION

COMPUTATION

The following formula will allow you to quickly compute the mean and standard deviation of any binomial distribution. However, a binomial distribution is a sampling distribution, and for most students, the *interpretation* of the mean and standard deviation of a sampling distribution (to be covered in the next section) is more difficult than the *computation*.

> **(10.3.1)** **If k is a random variable with the binomial distribution B(n, p), then**
>
> $$\mu_k = E(k) = np$$
> $$\sigma_k = SE_k = \sqrt{np(1-p)}$$

The SE of k is the *standard error* of the statistic k. It tells us how far away k usually is from its expected value.

B(n, p) is the sampling distribution for the sum of n Bernoulli Trials. For each independent Bernoulli trial, the probability of a 1 is p. k is the statistic "the sum", or "the count". It's just the number of 1's that occurred in n tries.

Many events in our world are Bernoulli trials! *Any* situation involving *independent* events that may either succeed or fail, or *any* variable that divides cases into two groups can be represented as a Bernoulli trial.

EXAMPLE

Keanu plays the game described above 100 times.
Describe the total amount he can expect to end up winning after 100 plays.

ANSWER

Because each play is a Bernoulli trial with p = .5, the total amount is the sum of 100 Bernoulli trials. This sum, k, has the binomial distribution B(n, p), or B(100, .5) in this case. E(k) = np = (100)(.5) = 50, so we expect his winnings to typically be about $50.

However

$$\sigma_k = \sqrt{np(1-p)} = \sqrt{(100)(.5)(.5)} = \sqrt{25} = 5$$

so we expect the actual amount won typically to be about $5 away from the expected value of $50.

CHANGING THE SAMPLE SIZE

> **(10.3.2)** **Suppose you change n, the number of trials in a binomial distribution, by multiplying n by some factor f.**
>
> - μ_k, **the mean of the binomial distribution,**
>   **will be *multiplied* by f.**
> - σ_k, **the standard deviation,**
>   **will be multiplied by the *square root* of f.**

EXAMPLE

Suppose we increase the sample size in the previous example by multiplying it by 4. That is, we consider B(400, .5) instead of B(100, .5). How should this affect the mean and SD of the distribution?

ANSWER

(10.3.2) says the mean of the new distribution should be 4 times the mean of the old distribution, or (4)($50) = $200

(10.3.2.) says that multiplying the sample size by 4 should cause the standard deviation to be multiplied by the square root of 4, or 2. So the SD of the new distribution should be (2)($5) = $10.

EXERCISES FOR CHAPTER 10, SECTIONS 10.1 - 10.3

X_i	p_i
0	.1
6	.4
10	.4
16	.1
	1.0

1. The mean of the random variable X above is...

2. The SD of X is...

3. Create an appropriate box model to describe X.

Mr. Zane thinks that 10% of the people in the population support Prop. 99. Assuming He's right...

4. What is the mean of the population (If a "1'" represents a person who supports Prop.99)

5. What's the SD of the population?

6. Create a box model to describe the population.

Mr. Zane draws a sample of size 900 from the population.

7. How many Prop 99 supporters should he expect to find in his sample?

8. About how far off will his sample sum (the number of "successes" in his sample) typically be?

---

9. A binomial distribution has a SD of 33 when the sample size is 100. How big would the SD be if you increased the sample size to 900?

Suppose that the proportion of the voters in a population who support Jones is .20, and a random sample of size 400 is picked from the population (with replacement). Let k represent the number of people in the sample who support Jones.

As usual, designate a voter who supports Jones with a "1" and a voter who doesn't support Jones with a "0".

NOTE: QUESTIONS 10 - 12 REFER TO THE *POPULATION* OF 1's and 0's

10. What is the mean of the *population* (all the voters) in this case?
        A) .40   B) .20   C) .10   D) .50   E) .04

11. What is the standard deviation of the *population* in this case?
        A) .40   B) .20   C) .10   D) .50   E) .04

12. The shape of the distribution of scores *in the population* is
        A) symmetrical, but not approximately normal
        B) symmetrical and approximately normal
        C) neither symmetrical nor approximately normal

NOTE: QUESTIONS 13 -16 REFER TO THE *SAMPLING DISTRIBUTION* OF k

13. How many voters who support Jones would we expect to find in a sample of size 400?
    What is the value of μ_k, the expected value of k?
    What is the mean of the *sampling distribution* of k?
        A) 80   B) 90   C) 10   D) 20   E) 320

14. What is the standard error of k, σ_k ?
    What is the standard deviation of the *sampling distribution* of k?
        A) 8   B) 16   C) 32   D) 4   E) 1

15. What is the shape of the *sampling distribution* of k?
        A) neither binomial nor approximately normal
        B) binomial and approximately normal
        C) binomial, but not approximately normal
        D) cannot be determined

16. Estimate the probability that k is less than or equal to 72.
        A) .0256   B) .1296   C) .1587   D) .3456   E) .5

TABLE 1:

$$\underline{X}\ \underline{p}$$
2 .6
7 .2
12 .2

17. The mean of the random variable X described in TABLE 1 is
      A) 3   B) 7   C) 6   D) 5   E) 8

18. The standard deviation of the random variable X is
      A) 4   B) 1   C) 2   D) 3   E) 6

----

19. A binomial distribution has a standard deviation of 16 when the sample size is 100.
How big will the standard deviation be if you increase the sample size to 400?
    Note: This question is about k, the sample sum, not the sample proportion!
(This question could have been worded: "The standard error of k is 16 when n = 100.
What will the standard error of k be if n is increased to 400?")]
      A) 64   B) 4   C) 16   D) 1   E) 32

ANSWERS TO EXERCISES FOR CHAPTER 10.1 - 10.3

1. 8

2. 4

3.

0	6	6	6	6	10	10	10	10	16

4. .1

5. .3

6.

| 0 | 0 | 0 | 0 | 0 | 0 | 0 | 0 | 0 | 1 |

7. 90 $\mu_k = np = (900)(.10) = 90$

8. 9 $\sigma_k = \sqrt{np(1-p)} = \sqrt{(900)(.1)(.9)} = \sqrt{81} = 9$

9. 99   The sample size, n, goes from 100 to 900, so n is multiplied by 9.

σ_k will be multiplied by $\sqrt{9}$, or 3.   (3)(33) = 99

---

10. B

11. A

12. C

13. A

14. A

15. B

16. C

---

17. D

18. A

---

19. E

10.4 INTERPRETING THE MEAN AND SD OF A SAMPLING DISTRIBUTION

THE MEAN OF A POPULATION vs THE MEAN OF A SAMPLING DISTRIBUTION

The notation "μ_X" implies automatically that a whole population has been measured on the variable X, and the mean of the entire population has been computed. "μ_X" is called a *parameter* of the population, i.e. a statistic that has been computed for *all* cases, and hence describes the *entire* population.

Suppose you pick a sample of size n from a population, and compute some statistic for that sample. The *one* value of the statistic that you get from your *single* sample can be thought of as coming from a huge distribution of *all possible* values of the statistic for *all possible* samples that might have been picked. Recall that this more complicated distribution is called the *sampling distribution* for the statistic.

Soon we'll be doing inferential statistics, in which the population is unknown, and all we have to go on is one sample from the population. We'll try to draw meaningful, realistic estimates about the whole population from the single sample we picked at random. The *sampling distribution* of the statistic is the fundamental distribution involved when we try to make inferences about an entire population from a sample.

The *mean of the sampling distribution* for a statistic is also called "the *expected value* of the statistic." It tells you the *value of the statistic* that you'd *expect* to get from a typical sample selected at random. For any statistic, the *expected value* of the statistic is usually designated

$$\text{"E(statistic)" or "}\mu_{\text{statistic}}\text{",}$$

where the *name* of the particular statistic being used is filled in for the word "statistic". Here are some examples of the use of this notation:

μ_k or E(k)   denotes the expected value of k, the sample *count*, or sample *sum* for a 0,1 variable.
It's the "mean of the sampling distribution of k".

$\mu_{\hat{p}}$ or E($\hat{p}$)   denotes the expected value of the sample *proportion*, $\hat{p}$, k/n.
It's the "mean of the sampling distribution of $\hat{p}$".

$\mu_{\overline{X}}$ or E($\overline{X}$)   denotes the expected value of the sample *mean*, $\overline{X}$, $\Sigma X/n$.
It's the "mean of the sampling distribution of $\overline{X}$".

None of these is conceptually the same as μ_X, the mean of the *scores in the population*!

THE SD OF A POPULATION vs THE SD OF A SAMPLING DISTRIBUTION

The notation " σ_X " implies automatically that a whole population has been measured on the variable X, and the *standard deviation* of the entire population has been computed. " σ_X " is also called a **parameter** of the population, i.e. a statistic that has been computed for *all* cases, and hence describes the *entire* population.

The **standard deviation of the sampling distribution** for a statistic is also called "the **standard error** of the statistic". It tells you the *size of the error of the statistic* that you'd *expect* to get from a typical sample selected at random. The error of a statistic for a particuar sample tells you how far the statistic is from its expected value. For any specific statistic, the *standard error* of the statistic is usually designated

$$\text{"SE(statistic)" or "}\sigma_{statistic}\text{",}$$

where the name of the particular statistic being used is filled in for the word "statistic".

σ_k or SE(k)   denotes the *standard error* of k, the sample *count*, or sample *sum* for a 0,1 variable.

                   It's the "standard deviation of the sampling distribution of k".

$\sigma_{\hat{p}}$ or SE($\hat{p}$)   denotes the *standard error* of the sample *proportion*, $\hat{p}$, k/n.

                   It's the "standard deviation of the sampling distribution of $\hat{p}$".

$\sigma_{\overline{X}}$ or SE($\overline{X}$) denotes the *standard error* of the sample *mean*, $\overline{X}$, $\Sigma X/n$.

                   It's the "standard deviation of the sampling distribution of $\overline{X}$".

None of these is conceptually the same as σ_X, the standard deviation of all the *scores in the population*!

THE CHANCE ERROR OF A SAMPLE STATISTIC vs STANDARD ERROR

> **(10.4.1)**   Given *one* specific sample from a population, the *chance error* of the statistic *for that sample*, (also called *sampling error*) is
>
>   **(the value of the statistic) - (the expected value of the statistic)**

EXAMPLE

Suppose the value of k for a sample you have picked is 47, but the expected value of k is 53. The chance error or sampling error for k in this case is -6, because

(the value of k for the sample) - (the expected value of k) = 47 - 53 = -6

Note the obvious interpretation: Your sample sum, k, was 6 *lower* than expected.

(10.4.2) The *standard error* of any statistic

- **is the standard deviation of the *sampling distribution* for that statistic.**

- **always indicates the *typical size* of the chance error of the statistic (that you'd expect to find in a sample picked at random from the population.)**

EXAMPLE

Suppose the expected value of $\hat{p}$ is .60 and the SE of $\hat{p}$ is .04. You pick a sample and for your sample $\hat{p}$ = .48.

      A) What's the chance error of $\hat{p}$ for your sample?

      B) How does that compare to the SE of $\hat{p}$?

ANSWER

      A) -.12 = .48 - .60   The sample proportion was .12 *less than* expected.
      B) The SE was .04, which tells us we expect a typical sample proportion to be off by .04, (or "in error" by about .4). Our sample showed *more* error than expected; actually *three times* as much error as we would have expected, since $|-.12|$ = *three times* (.04).

10.5 THE NORMAL APPROXIMATION TO A BINOMIAL DISTRIBUTION

Imagine trying to compute the probability that k is greater than 80 in a sample of size 100. Using the binomial formula, you'd have to compute $P(k = 81)$, $P(k = 82)$, etc, up to $P(k = 100)$. Then you'd add all those probabilities to get $P(k > 80)$.

Happily, there's a much easier way to get very accurate estimates of probabilities like this, because when n is fairly large, binomial distributions have shapes very close to normal distributions, and cumulative probabilities which can be estimated using the cumulative standard normal probabilities in the z-table.

Many *sampling distributions* have shapes that are approximately normal, and *cumulative* distributions that are approximately *cumulative* normal. In fact the most common use of the standard normal table is to provide approximate percentile ranks (or cumulative probabilities) for sampling distributions, such as binomial distributions. That's why normal approximations were stressed previously in Chapter 7.

(10.5.1) When n is large (30 or more) the binomial distribution B(n,p)

- **has a *shape* that is approximately normal (and the *cumulative* binomial has approximately the *cumulative* normal shape)**

- **may be *approximated* by a normal distribution with mean = np**
  standard deviation = $\sqrt{np(1-p)}$

So if the sample is reasonably large, questions about percentile ranks of the sampling distribution of k can be answered using normal approximations.

EXAMPLE
Suppose p = .9 and n = 400.
  A) Describe and sketch the population.
  B) Describe and sketch the sampling distribution of k, the number of successes in a sample.
  C) Suppose you pick a sample of size 400 at random. Estimate the probability that k is greater than 369 in your sample.

ANSWER
  A) Since p was specified we know the population consists of 1's (representing "success") and 0's (representing "failure").
    the proportion of 1's is .9, so the proportion of 0's is .1
    μ, the mean of the population is .9
    σ, the standard deviation of the population is .3
    (because for a 0,1 pop, $\sigma = \sqrt{p(1-p)} = \sqrt{(.9)(.1)} = \sqrt{.09} = .3$

SKETCH OF THE *POPULATION*:

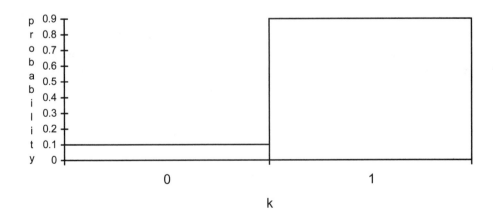

0,1 Population   p = .9

B) k has a binomial distribution, B(n,p). In this case it's B(400,.9)
This distribution is approximately normal, with a mean of 360 and a SD of 6.

$$\mu_k = np = (400)(.9) = 360$$

$$\sigma_k = \sqrt{np(1-p)} = \sqrt{(400)(.1)(.9)} = \sqrt{36} = 6$$

SKETCH OF THE *SAMPLING DISTRIBUTION* OF k:

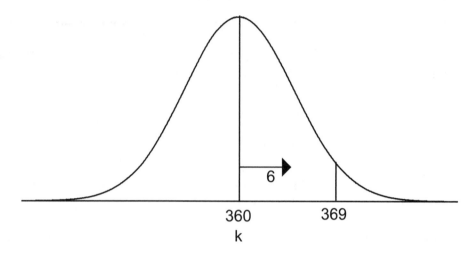

C) .0668

We want the probability of getting a k value greater than 369 in the *sampling distribution* of k.
This distribution which is approximately normal, with a mean of 360 and a SD of 6. First we
"standardize" the value we're interested in, 369, as follows (the value of k we got from our sample
is designated "obtained k", or "sample k")

$$\text{standardized k} = \frac{\text{"obtained k"} - \mu_k}{\sigma_k} = \frac{369 - 360}{6} = 1.5$$

Our sample k is 1.5 standard deviations above the typical k value of 360 in the sampling
distribution for k. Using the standard normal table, we see that the probability of getting a z score
less than or equal to 1.5 is .9332, so the probability of getting a z score greater than 1.5 is .0668.
(The easiest way to obtain this is just to look up *-1.5* in the z table.)

EXERCISES FOR CHAPTER 10, SECTIONS 10.4 - 10.5

----

1. Joe says "the SD of the *population* in the previous example in section 10.5 was .3, and the SD of the *sampling distribution* was 6. How can there be two *different standard deviations* in the same example?" You'd reply...

Suppose you flip a coin that you believe to be fair 400 times. You count the number of heads.

2. Describe the 'population'. What are μ and σ for the population you are 'sampling' from.

3. What statistic is involved? Describe its sampling distribution.

4. How many heads do you expect to get? I.e., what do you expect k to be, typically?

5. About how far from that count will a typical sample be?

Suppose you actually obtain 231 heads.

6. What's the *chance error* for your "sample"?

7. What's the probability of getting that many heads just by chance? I.e., how likely is k to be 231 or more?

Fast Eddie agrees to pay you for a job with a gamble. You'll roll a fair die 720 times. You'll be paid $1 each time a six comes up.

8. The approach you'll use in answering questions about this situation is called...

9. Describe the population. What are μ and σ for this population.

10. What statistic is involved? Describe its sampling distribution.

11. How much do you expect to win? I.e., what do you expect k to be, typically?

12. About how far from that count will a typical "sample" of 720 rolls be?

Suppose you obtain 148 sixes after 720 rolls.

13. What's the chance error for your "sample"?

14. What's the probability of obtaining a count that high just by luck? I.e., how likely is k to be as high as 148?

15. If Fast Eddie knows about statistics, should he be suspicious of these results? I.e., should he suspect that you've used a die in which P(six) is greater than 1/6?

REVIEW QUESTIONS

Compute the mean and SD of this probability distribution:

X	p
0	.125
4	.75
8	.125

16. $\mu_X =$

17. $\sigma_X =$

Compute the mean and SD of this probability distribution:

X	p
0	.3
2	.1
5	.1
7	.1
10	.1
12	.3

18. $\mu_X =$

19. $\sigma_X =$

Compute the mean and SD of this probability distribution:

X	p
0	.36
1	.64

20. $\mu_X =$

21. $\sigma_X =$

Suppose the probability of success on each of three independent trials is .1.

22. Are these Bernoulli trials?

23. $P(k = 0)$ is ?   24. $P(k = 1)$ is ?   25. $P(k = 2)$ is ?   26. $P(k=3)$ is ?

27. What is the probability of two successes, *then* one failure?

28. $\mu_k =$

29. $\sigma_k =$

30. $P(k < 2) =$?

ANSWERS TO EXERCISES FOR SECTIONS 10.4 -10.5

---

1. You can compute the SD of any batch of numbers, or of any probability distribution.
   The population in this case is described by a probability distribution with two possible values 0, and
   1. The SD *of the population* tells us how far a typical score is from the population mean.
   The sampling distribution of k in the example has 401 possible values, from 0 to 400. It is a
   probability distribution (a binomial), so it, too, has a mean and SD. Its mean is 360. *Its* SD, called
   the SE of k, tells you how far a sample's k will typically be from 360, the expected value of k.

---

2. There are two scores: 1 (heads, or "success"), and 0 (tails or "failure")
     $P(1) = .5, \ P(0) = .5 \quad \mu = .5 \quad \sigma = .5$

3. k, because you *count* the number of heads. These are bernoulli trials, and k is the sum
   of 400 Bernoulli trials, so it has a binomial distribution with parameters 400 and .5, i.e., it's
   B(400, .5). This binomial distribution has a mean of 200 and a SD of 10, and it's approximately
   normal in shape.

4. 200

5. 10

6. 31 $k - E(k) \ = \ 231 - 200 = 31$

7. .001 (Estimated)   std score = $(231 - 200)/10 \ = \ 3.1 \quad P(z > 3.1) = .001$ from z table.

----

8. Rational (classical, logical). You need to assume the six sides of a die are equally likely.

9. 1's and 0's. $P(1) = 1/6$ $P(0) = 5/6$ $\mu = 1/6 = .167$ $\sigma = .373$

10. k, because you're adding up the successes.
    It has a binomial distribution with $n = 720$ and $p = .167$, i.e., it's B(720, .167)
    Its mean is 120 and its SD, the SE of k, is

$$\sigma_k = \sqrt{np(1-p)} = \sqrt{(720)(1/6)(5/6)} = \sqrt{100} = 10$$

    It is approximately normal in shape.

11. $120

12. $10

13. +28

14. .0026   std score $= (148 - 120)/10 = 2.8$ $P(z > 2.8) = .0026$

15. Yes, using the usual criteria. *Either* you cheated *or* you were lucky.
    The probability of being *this* lucky is .0026.
    Since it's *un*likely you got $148 just by luck, it's *more likely* that it wasn't just by luck. i.e. that
    cheating might have been involved.

ANSWERS TO REVIEW QUESTIONS

16. 4

17. 2

18. 6

19. 5

20. .64

21. .48

22. Yes, you're dealing with "success" (presumably, versus "failure"), trials are independent,
    and all trials have the same probability of a success.

23. .729

24. .243

25. .027

26. .001

27. .009 $= (.1)^2(.9)^1$

28. .3

29. .52

30. .972 $= .729 + .243$

10.6 REVIEW OF CHAPTERS 9 AND 10

PROBABILITY DISTRIBUTIONS IN GENERAL

The general notion of a probability distribution was defined as a set of values along with a probability that each value occurs. Formulas were provided for finding the mean and standard deviation of any probability distribution: (9.1, 10.1)

GENERAL FORMULAS FOR *ALL* PROBABILITY DISTRIBUTIONS

For *any* random variable X, the *mean*, or *expected value* of X is

$$\mu_X = E(X) = \Sigma X_i p_i$$

For *any* random variable X, the standard deviation of X is

$$\sigma_X = \sqrt{\Sigma(X_i - \mu_X)^2 p_i}$$

These formulas will work for *any* probability distribution, but they are not always the *easiest* formulas to use. For two special cases, shortcut formulas were provided. These special cases were "0,1" distributions and binomial distributions.

FIRST SPECIAL CASE: "0,1" DISTRIBUTIONS

These "0,1" distributions come up often; every time we are describing a population using a nominal scale variable with two possible categories. The variable is called "dichotomous". Examples of scores on such variables: "living vs. dead," "heads vs. tails'", "male vs. female", "treated vs. not treated', "for vs. against," etc.

To make it clearer how statistics are used in these situations, one category is traditionally labeled "success" and the other "failure", and we think of the population as comprised of 1's (successes) and 0's (failures).

There is only one important parameter of a population like these: **p**, the proportion of 1's in the population. (p is also the population "mean", if you consider that adding up all the 0's and 1's and dividing by N, the population size, will give you p, the proportion of 1's. For simple "0,1" populations, it's not necessary to use the general formula above to compute the population mean and standard deviation. This shortcut is quicker:

SHORTCUT FORMULAS FOR *"0,1"* DISTRIBUTIONS

If X is a random variable with two possible scores, 0 and 1, and the probability of a 1 is p, then

$$\mu_X = E(X) = p \qquad \text{and} \qquad \sigma_X = \sqrt{p(1-p)}$$

SECOND SPECIAL CASE: BINOMIAL DISTRIBUTIONS

Suppose you draw a sample of size *n, with replacement,* from a "0,1" distribution whose   . proportion (of 1's) is *p*. You count up *k*, the number of 1's (successes) in your sample.
The statistic you have computed, k, is the sample sum when the sample has been drawn from a 0,1, population. This statistic, k, also called the *count*, is used so often that its sampling distribution has its own abbreviation, "*B(n,p)*", the "*binomial distribution with parameters n and p*"
Examples of typical references to the statistic k are "the number of people in our sample who support Smith," "the number of patients who improved," "the number of heads in 400 coin flips." In Chapter 9, we showed how to compute B(n,p) using the binomial formula. (Computing B(n,p) requires computing n+1 probabilities, one for each possible value of k, where k ranges from 0 to n) In Chapter 10.3 these shortcut formulas were given, to allow you to compute the mean and standard deviation of a binomial distribution quickly:

SHORTCUT FORMULAS FOR *BINOMIAL* DISTRIBUTIONS

If k is a random variable with the binomial distribution B(n, p), then

$$\mu_k = E(k) = np \quad \text{and} \quad \sigma_k = SE_k = \sqrt{np(1-p)}$$

A BINOMIAL DISTRIBUTION IS A SAMPLING DISTRIBUTION FOR k

The binomial distribution is our first *sampling distribution*. It is a probability distribution, but the probabilities it provides are *probabilities for values of a statistic*, k. Each sampling distribution has a mean and standard deviation like any other probability distribution, but the interpretation is different. The interpretation of μ and σ for sampling distributions is covered in 10.4:

The **mean of a sampling distribution** for a statistic, also called the **expected value** of the statistic, tells you the typical value of the statistic you'd expect to get if you picked a sample at random and computed the statistic for that sample.

The **standard deviation of a sampling distribution** for a statistic, also called the **standard error (SE)** of the statistic tells you how far from the expected value a typical sample statistic will be. The difference between the statistic for one particular sample and the expected value is called the chance error. The SE is also the typical size of the chance error.

So μ_k , the mean of the a binomial sampling distribution, is also the *expected value of k, or E(k)*, and it tells us "the value of k for a typical sample."

And σ_k , the standard deviation of a binomial sampling distribution, is also the *standard error of k, or SE_k* , and it tells us "how far k is from μ_k in a typical sample."

BINOMIAL DISTRIBUTIONS ARE APPROXIMATELY NORMAL FOR LARGE n

When n is 30 or more B(n,p) has an approximately normal shape. This allows us to use the standard normal distribution to approximate probabilities for binomial distributions. (10.5) So we can use the z distribution to estimate probabilities like "the probability of obtaining *k* or more successes in a sample of size *n* from a population in which the proportion of successes is *p*," for any possible values of k, n, and p, as long as n is 30 or more.

CHAPTER 11

INFERENCE ABOUT PROPORTIONS

11.1 THE SAMPLING DISTRIBUTION OF $\hat{p}$

Previously we defined k as the number of successes in a sample picked from a 0,1 population. When we actually pick a sample from a 0,1 population, we're more likely to describe our sample using the statistic '*sample proportion*' or '*sample percent*' than the count, k.

(11.1.1) $\hat{p}$ = k/n denotes the sample proportion.

**The "^" signifies that it is an "estimate of" p,
the population proportion.**

If Smith finds *50* successes in a sample of size *200*, and Jones finds *8* successes in a sample of size *32*, $\hat{p}$ in *both* cases is .25, and reporting $\hat{p}$ calls attention to this similarity better than reporting the k values of 50 and 8. In both cases the best estimate of the population proportion, p, based on the samples would be .25.

Of course, the sampling distribution for $\hat{p}$ will always have the same shape and the same probabilities as the sampling distribution for k, which is B(n,p). The values will just be *rescaled* because each $\hat{p}$ value is a possible k value divided by n. The possible values of $\hat{p}$ always range from 0 (which is 0/n) to 1 (which is n/n).

**(11.1.2) Assume that we compute the statistic $\hat{p}$ for a sample
of size n from a population with proportion equal to p.**

The *sampling distribution* of $\hat{p}$ can be described as follows:

- **Its *mean* is called the 'Expected Value of $\hat{p}$' , or $\mu_{\hat{p}}$, and**

$$\mu_{\hat{p}} = p$$

- **Its *standard deviation* is called the 'Standard Error of $\hat{p}$'**

or $\sigma_{\hat{p}}$. $$\sigma_{\hat{p}} = \sqrt{\frac{p(1-p)}{n}}$$

- **Its *shape* is *binomial*. (The same as the *shape* of B(n, p).)**

EXAMPLE

Suppose n equals 100 and p is .9. Describe the sampling distribution of the sample proportion.

ANSWER

The sampling distribution of $\hat{p}$ will be binomial in shape, with a mean of .9 and a standard deviation of

$$\sigma_{\hat{p}} \;=\; \sqrt{\frac{.9(1.0 - .9)}{100}} \;=\; .03$$

11.2   *THE NORMAL APPROXIMATION TO THE SAMPLING DISTRIBUTION OF $\hat{p}$*

Since $\hat{p}$ has a sampling distribution identical in shape to the sampling distribution of k, *normal approximations* can be used when n is 30 or more, just as with k. Typical questions requiring the use of the normal approximation look like this:

"If a sample of size n is drawn from a population in which the proportion of successes is known to be *p*, estimate the probability that the sample proportion is greater than or equal to $\hat{p}$."

(11.2.1)   When n is 30 or more, the *sampling distribution* of $\hat{p}$, the sample proportion, is approximately normal.

EXAMPLE:
Suppose a sample of size 100 is drawn from a population in which the proportion of successes is .9.

A) Sketch the population and sketch the sampling distribution of $\hat{p}$.

ANSWER:

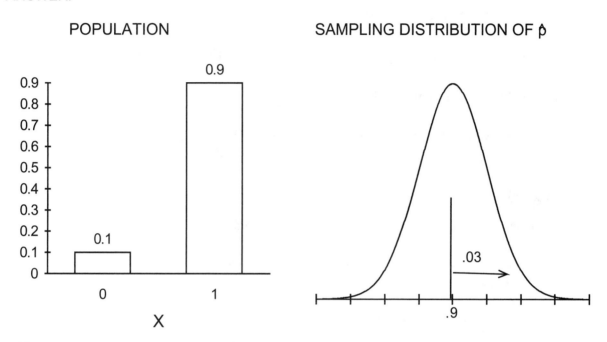

B) Do the population distribution and the sampling distribution have the same shape?

ANSWER: No.
> The population only has two possible scores, 0 and 1. It is negatively skewed,
> Its shape is *not* approximately normal!
> The sampling distribution has 101 possible scores: 0, 0.01, 0.02, etc.
> The shape of the *sampling distribution* is exactly binomial, and it also *is* approximately normal.

C) Estimate the probability that the sample proportion, $\hat{p}$, is less than or equal to .84

ANSWER: .0228

> From the example above, the mean of the sampling distribution is .9 and its standard deviation is .03. Its shape will be approximately normal, because the sample size is large.

> So we need the probability of obtaining a value less than or equal to .84 in an approximately normal distribution with a mean of .9 and a SD of .03.

> We standardize the value .84: standard score = (.84 - .9)/.03 = -2

> We then look up -2 in the standard normal table and find that the probability of a **z** score less than or equal to -2 is .0228.

EXERCISES FOR CHAPTER 11, SECTIONS 11.1 - 11.2

---

n = 100

Suppose you flip a fair coin 100 times, and you compute $\hat{p}$, the proportion of heads..

1. Describe the sampling distribution of $\hat{p}$.

2. What's the probability that $\hat{p}$ is less than or equal to .51?

3. What's the probability that $\hat{p}$ is less than or equal to .49?

4. What's the probability that $\hat{p}$ is between .49 and .51?

n = 10,000

5-8   Repeat questions 1-4, but assume that the coin was flipped 10,000 times.

Comparing the answers 5-8 with 1-4 shows how the *accuracy* of the sample proportion *increases* when n increases.

5. Describe the sampling distribution of $\hat{p}$.

6. What's the probability that $\hat{p}$ is less than or equal to .51?

7. What's the probability that $\hat{p}$ is less than or equal to .49?

8. What's the probability that $\hat{p}$ is between .49 and .51?

9. Does a sample size of 10,000 seem to result in *more accurate* estimates of the population proportion?

ANSWERS TO EXERCISES for SECTIONS 11.1 - 11.2

---

n = 100

1. Binomial and approximately normal in shape, with a mean of .5 and a standard deviation of .05.

$$\sigma_{\hat{p}} \;=\; \sqrt{p(1-p)/\ n} = \sqrt{(.5)(1-.5)/\ 100} = \sqrt{.0025} = .05$$

2. .5793

$$(.51 - .5)/.05 \;=\; .2 \quad P(z < .2) = .5793$$

3. .4207

$$(.49 - .5)/.05 \;=\; -.2 \quad P(z < -.2) = .4207$$

4. .1586

$$P(z \text{ is between } -.2 \text{ and } .2) \;=\; P(z \text{ is less than } .2) - P(z \text{ is less than } -.2)$$

$$.5793 - .4207 \;=\; .1586$$

n = 10,000

5. Binomial and approximately normal in shape, with a mean of .5 and a standard deviation of .005.

$$\sigma_{\hat{p}} \;=\; \sqrt{p(1-p)/\ n} = \sqrt{(.5)(1-.5)/\ 10,000} = \sqrt{.000025} = .005$$

6. .9772

$$(.51 - .5)/.005 \;=\; 2 \quad P(z < 2) = .9772$$

7. .0228

$$(.49 - .5)/.005 \;=\; -2 \quad P(z < -2) = .0228$$

8. .9544

$$P(z \text{ is between } -2 \text{ and } 2) \;=\; P(z \text{ is less than } 2) - P(z \text{ is less than } -2)$$
$$.9772 - .0228 \;=\; .9544$$

9. Yes.

When n = 100 the probability that $\hat{p}$ is within .01 of the correct population proportion (.5) is only .1586. (From question 4 above)

However, when n = 10,000, the probability that $\hat{p}$ is within .01 of the correct value of .5 is .9544. (From Question 9 above) So the *larger* sample is much more likely to produce an *accurate* estimate.

11.3   CONFIDENCE INTERVAL ESTIMATES FOR p, THE POPULATION PROPORTION

INFERENCE ABOUT POPULATIONS BASED ON SAMPLES

You've learned how to estimate what the sampling distribution for a statistic will look like, *given* information about the population. For example, if you are told that the proportion of successes, p, is .2 in the *population*, and the sample size, n, is 100, you can conclude: The *sampling distribution* of the sample proportion, $\hat{p}$, is approximately normal, with a mean of .2 and a SD of .04. That's *exactly* what the sampling distribution is like, assuming the description of the population is correct.

As you may have expected, in most interesting applications, the population proportion is *not known* in advance; so we *cannot* know the sampling distribution exactly. Because we usually *don't* know any parameters of the population in advance, they must be estimated from sample data. The branch of statistics that deals with such estimates is *inferential* statistics.

(11.3.1)   *Inferential statistics* **is the branch of statistics which describes techniques for drawing conclusions (or,** *inferences***) about an entire** *population***, based on data obtained from a random** *sample***.**

The two common types of inferences about populations are
- ***estimates* of population parameters, which include**
  - **-- point estimates of population parameters**
  - **-- confidence interval estimates of population parameters**
- ***tests of hypotheses* about population parameters**

We'll cover our first examples of point estimates and confidence interval estimates in this section, and our first hypothesis tests later in section 11.4. The statistic used will be a simple one, $\hat{p}$, the sample proportion. (It can help you to develop the correct intuitions if you keep in mind that $\hat{p}$, which is k/n, is just the *mean* of a sample picked from a 0,1 population. Many techniques that work for $\hat{p}$ will later turn out to work for the sample mean, $\overline{X}$, as well.)

POINT ESTIMATES

Your intuitions would get you off to a good start in doing inferential statistics! For example, most students would agree that a rule like, "To estimate a population parameter, use the corresponding sample statistic," makes intuitive sense. And this rule *works* for the common statistics $\overline{X}$, $\hat{p}$, and sample percent. (We'll abbreviate sample percent "pct", or "%" and use "PCT" in upper case letters to designate population percent when it's necessary to distinguish them.)

> **(11.3.2)** A *point estimate* of a population parameter is the single number, computed from sample data, intended to predict or estimate the parameter.
>
> - **The best point estimate of μ, the population mean, is $\overline{X}$, the sample mean.**
>
> - **The best point estimate of p, the population proportion, is $\hat{p}$, the sample proportion.**
>
> - **The best point estimate of the population percent is the sample percent.**

However, the best point estimate of σ, the population standard deviation is *not* the SD of the sample. We'll show how to estimate σ accurately in the next chapter.

UNBIASED ESTIMATES

You would want a point estimate to have this quality: The typical, or average, value of the point estimate should be the same as the value of the parameter you're trying to estimate. Point estimates with this property are called *unbiased*.

> **(11.3.3)** A sample statistic is called an *unbiased* point estimate of a population parameter...
>
> - **if the *expected value* of the statistic is equal to the parameter.**
>
> - **if the *mean of the sampling distribution* of the statistic is equal to the parameter.**

The sample proportion, $\hat{p}$, for example, is unbiased. Suppose the population proportion is .2 in a population of size 1,000,000. There are *very many* possible samples of size 10! The value of $\hat{p}$ for some of these samples is 1.0, and if we were to pick *those* samples, our point estimate of p would be 1.0, i.e., we'd *overestimate* p considerably. Other samples with a $\hat{p}$ of 0 would lead us to *underestimate* p. But overall, the *average* of all $\hat{p}$ values for all possible samples is exactly p. The formula for the *expected value* of $\hat{p}$ assures us of this:

$$\text{Expected Value of } \hat{p} = \mu_{\hat{p}} = p$$

$\hat{p}$ is an *unbiased* point estimate of p. Similarly $\overline{X}$ is an *unbiased* point estimate of μ, and the sample percent is an *unbiased* point estimate of the population percent.

CONFIDENCE INTERVAL ESTIMATES

Suppose you find 1 success in a random sample of size 5, and Dr. Zell, another researcher finds 200 successes in a sample of size 1,000. Both of you would come up with the same point estimate, .2, for p, the population proportion. The point estimate itself does not convey anything about the *accuracy* of the estimate being made. You know Dr. Zell, who measured *995* more cases than you did, should be entitled to *more confidence* in her estimate! Someone who wanted to really make use of *all* the information in the sample would want to give an estimate of the population proportion along with some information about the *accuracy* of the estimate, which clearly would depend on the sample size.

The right way to do this is to give a confidence interval estimate, rather than a point estimate. Confidence interval estimates are trickier to compute and to understand, but they give much more meaningful information.

(11.3.4) A 99% confidence interval estimate for a population parameter consists of a lower limit (LL) and an upper limit (UL), usually written,

" LL - UL " or " LL → UL "

computed from sample data in a way that guarantees the following probability statement:

"The probability that the interval LL - UL contains the correct value of the population parameter is at least .99"

99% was used as the "confidence level" because it's the most common one. Any level of confidence under 100% can be set.

If you keep the typical estimation situation in mind, you'll never fall prey to a common misinterpretation. **Someone about to make a confidence interval estimate for some population parameter has just picked *one* sample from *one* single population.** The population parameter *doesn't vary*; it *isn't* a random variable. The '.99' probability refers to the probability that we pick a *'good'* sample, one that leads us to compute a confidence interval that contains the (*one, single*) actual population parameter.

Sometimes people ask, "Isn't there some *better* technique (better than confidence intervals), one that would give *100%* confidence?" The possibility, even remote, of being *wrong* about the population parameter bothers people, understandably, in cases where "success" may mean "the patient lived, or recovered from an illness".

The answer is "*No!*" Confidence interval techniques use *all* the information from a sample; there's no way to get more confidence without taking a larger sample. And there's *never* a way to get 100% confidence about any population parameter without measuring the entire population! (In which case you're *not* really "sampling" or doing inferential statistics anymore.) So, getting at the (approximate) truth about a whole population from a sample is *challenging*; and the techniques of inferential statistics are the *strongest known* techniques for doing this!

COMPUTING CONFIDENCE INTERVAL ESTIMATES FOR p

Here's how to compute a confidence interval estimate for the population proportion from a sample:

(11.3.5) If $\hat{p}$ is the sample proportion for a sample of size n, then a confidence interval estimate for p, the population proportion, is

$$\hat{p} \pm z \,(\text{ estimated } \sigma_{\hat{p}})$$

Where estimated $\sigma_{\hat{p}} = \sqrt{\hat{p}(1-\hat{p})/\ n}$

and z is the value in the standard normal distribution such that the probability between -z and +z is equal to the confidence level.

The term "estimated $\sigma_{\hat{p}}$" designates the *estimated standard error* of $\hat{p}$. Note that the *estimated* SE of $\hat{p}$ is computed the same way the SE of $\hat{p}$ would be, except that $\hat{p}$ is used in the formula instead of p. If we *knew* p we could *compute* the SE of $\hat{p}$ *exactly*. Since we don't know p, we must *estimate* the standard error of $\hat{p}$.

This is a little paradoxical and unintuitive at first! It's called a ***bootstrapping technique***, because it seems to be "magical" like "lifting oneself up by one's bootstraps". You *use* the sample proportion, $\hat{p}$, to *estimate* the standard error of the sample proportion, $\hat{p}$. It seems paradoxical to use a value to estimate the accuracy of that same value, but the procedure can be proved mathematically to work perfectly.

You don't need to compute the correct z value each time you compute a confidence interval. The appropriate z values for the common confidence levels are included in a separate box under the heading "Commonly Used z-Table Values" included with the standard normal table. These values are also often referred to as "two tailed" z values.

EXAMPLE
Suppose you found 90 successes in a random sample of size 100.
Create a 95% Confidence Interval Estimate for p, the population proportion.

ANSWER

$n = 100$ and $k = 90$, so $\hat{p} = k/n = .9$ for the sample.

estimated $\sigma_{\hat{p}} = \sqrt{\hat{p}(1-\hat{p})/\ n} = \sqrt{.9(1-.9)/\ 100} = .03$

$z = 1.96$ for a 95% confidence interval estimate.

95% CI (Confidence Interval) Estimate for p =

$\hat{p} \pm z\ (\text{estimated } \sigma_{\hat{p}}) = .9 \pm (1.96)(.03) = .9 \pm .0588$, or

.8412 - .9588

EXERCISES FOR CHAPTER 11, SECTION 11.3

PRACTICE *COMPUTING* SE$_{\hat{p}}$ WHEN p IS *KNOWN*

In each Question below, substitute the values of p, n, and $\hat{p}$ into this question:

"Given that the population proportion is (p) and the sample size is (n) , **compute** $\sigma_{\hat{p}}$ and **estimate** the probability that the sample proportion is greater than ($\hat{p}$)."

QUESTION	DATA: (p)	(n)	($\hat{p}$)	ANSWERS: $\sigma_{\hat{p}}$	est P($\hat{p}$ > X)	
1.	.1	100	.13	.030	.1587	P(z > 1.0)
2.	.1	400	.13	.015	.0228	P(z > 2.0)
3.	.1	900	.13	.010	.0013	P(z > 3.0)
4.	.1	900	.11	.010	.1587	P(z > 1.0)
5.	.9	100	.75	.030	>.9999	P(z > -5)!
6.	.2	100	.30	.040	.0062	P(z > 2.5)
7.	.2	10,000	.22	.004	<.0002	P(z > 5)!

PRACTICE *ESTIMATING* $\sigma_{\hat{p}}$ AND p, WHEN p IS *UNKNOWN*

Given k successes in a sample of size n. **Estimate** the standard error of $\hat{p}$, the sample proportion, and create a 90% confidence interval **estimate** for p, the population proportion.

QUESTION	DATA: (k)	(n)	ANSWERS: est $\sigma_{\hat{p}}$	90% C.I. est for p
8.	10	100	.030	$.1 \pm .0495$
9.	40	400	.015	$.1 \pm .0248$
10.	90	900	.010	$.1 \pm .0165$
11.	20	100	.040	$.2 \pm .066$
12.	2000	10,000	.0040	$.2 \pm .0066$

13. Do all 90% confidence intervals have the same width?

    ANSWER: No

14. Do all 90% confidence intervals for the *same sample size* have the same width?

    ANSWER: No, compare the answers to Question 8 and Question 11.

11.4 TESTING A HYPOTHESIS ABOUT p, THE POPULATION PROPORTION

HYPOTHESES ABOUT POPULATIONS

People get hunches or opinions about *populations* frequently, even if they have never been exposed to statistics and probability. Someone once told me to "watch out for people who drive red Dodges, they all drive like maniacs." She had a hunch about the *population* of drivers of red Dodges. People make statements like "the public will go for family films, if they'd just release more of them," "Super Slick makes engines last longer," and "four out of five people prefer Diet Coke". These statements are made with confidence, and they're about very large populations.

Theories created by researchers in the social, physical, biological and medical sciences, as well as the fields of education, engineering, business and even law, make predictions about populations. Recall that a population may be any set of things, individuals or events. Theories that make correct predictions about populations earn *credibility* and *acceptance*.

Since the 1800s a set of techniques has evolved for testing predictions or opinions about *populations*, based on simple random *samples* from those populations. This set of procedures is accepted worldwide; it is used everywhere scientific research is done. It provides one clear set of criteria for proving that certain opinions about populations are right or wrong. The procedures are referred to as *hypothesis tests* or *significance tests*.

There are a few *nice* things about hypothesis tests that should be kept in mind, perhaps to provide motivation if the going gets rough:

> The hypothesis tests learned in elementary statistics are the same ones that can actually be used in practice. They are "state of the art," for dealing with the basic questions about typical sets of data. The same tests you'll be learning about appear in doctoral dissertations, research publications, licensing exams, etc.

> The hypothesis tests are all similar. There's a general kind of reasoning in hypothesis testing that you get used to.

> These techniques are *extremely general*! You can apply them to almost any area that your imagination and curiosity might lead you to. Recall how many different examples of nominal, ordinal and interval scale variables there are. Once you learn a hypothesis testing technique, you can use it on *any variable* that has been measured on the same type of scale.

> People do intuitive "hypothesis tests" all the time without analyzing what they're doing. Learning how to do them "by the book" when necessary can help you understand and appreciate the "built in" inference techniques that seem to be guaranteed by our human genes.

Hypothesis tests are part of *inferential* statistics because they involve picking a sample and then using the information from the sample to make an *inference* about the whole population.

NULL AND ALTERNATE HYPOTHESES

An opinion about a population can always be translated into a statement about a population parameter. Suppose you want to prove that some statement is true, and the statement is about a population. It's helpful (and traditional) to imagine what someone might believe *before* you have convinced them you're right. You might imagine a "devil's advocate", or "skeptic" to whom you want to present evidence so convincing that your point is made beyond a doubt. The skeptic's opinion about the population is called the ***null hypothesis***, denoted H_0. The statement describing your opinion about the population is called the ***alternate hypothesis***, and is denoted H_1.

The thing about hypothesis tests that most students find surprising and unintuitive at first is that hypothesis tests always proceed by assuming ("for argument's sake") that the null hypothesis is true! Every hypothesis test refers to a specific sampling distribution, and that sampling distribution is *always* based on the *null* hypothesis.

Numerous examples will be presented to make these statements clear. The examples will all be presented in a structured, organized format, designed to assure that readers will be able to understand *why* the steps of a hypothesis test are carried out, and *why* the conclusions make sense.

Understanding hypothesis testing takes patience and work. The last several chapters have focussed on sampling distributions and the estimation of probabilities, because those are the topics required to *understand* hypothesis tests.

There is a tendency for elementary texts to slip into a "cookbook" approach when presenting hypothesis testing. Often a formula is given for computing a "z value", and the reader is told where to find the significance level. In my opinion insufficient attention is given to the *reasoning* involved, including how and why the sampling distribution is estimated, how the sampling distribution is used, what the "z value" is really estimating, etc.

Using the structured approach presented below is more work at first, compared to just plugging some scores into a formula. It will be worth the additional effort if you end up being able to explain what you're doing, and why it makes sense to do it!

EXAMPLE

Suppose Mark Anthony (a *real* professional "mentalist"!) claims that he can control coins as they flip through the air, and cause them to come up heads more often than expected. We agree to flip a coin 100 times to test his powers. The coin comes up heads 65 times.
Is this convincing evidence that his powers had an effect, or was it just due to chance?

The outline on the following page includes all the computations to carry out the appropriate hypothesis test in this case.

HYPOTHESIS TEST FOR A POPULATION PROPORTION

POPULATION: All coin flips that Mark tries to influence to come up heads

VARIABLE: Whether the coin comes up heads (1) or tails (0)

H$_0$: $p = .5$ This is the skeptical position: There's no effect, the proportion of heads
will be just what you'd expect by chance.

H$_1$: $p > .5$ This is what Mark is trying to prove.

SAMPLE SIZE: $n = 100$

OBSERVED SAMPLE STATISTIC:
$\hat{p}$, the sample proportion $= k/n = 65/100 = .65$

ASSUMING H$_0$ IS TRUE...

POPULATION DISTRIBUTION:
$0,1$ with $P(1) = p = .5$

SAMPLING DISTRIBUTION:
Binomial in shape, also approximately normal because $n > 30$

$\mu_{\hat{p}} = .5$

$\sigma_{\hat{p}} = SE_{\hat{p}} = \sqrt{p(1-p)/\ n} = \sqrt{(.5)(1-.5)/\ 100} = \sqrt{.0025} = .05$

This is the sampling distribution of $\hat{p}$, given that $p = .5, n = 100$

OBSERVED TEST STATISTIC:

$$\text{Standardized } \hat{p} = \frac{\text{observed } \hat{p} - \mu_{\hat{p}}}{\sigma_{\hat{p}}} = \frac{.65 - .5}{.05} = 3.0$$

The observed test statistic is always a rescaled version of the sample statistic
that we'll use to estimate a probability. In this case we standardize $\hat{p}$ so that
we can use the z distribution to find the probability of getting a sample
proportion as high as .65 by chance. This probablility is "*p*", the "obtained significance
level." If *p* is less than .01, we *reject* the null hypothesis.

OBSERVED SIGNIFICANCE LEVEL: $P(z \geq 3.0) =$ "*p*" $= .0013$

The probability of getting a proportion as high as .65, if the null hypothesis is true is .0013.

CONCLUSION: We can reject the null hypothesis at the .01 level of significance,
because *p* < .01

We'll assume that .01, often called an "alpha level," or "significance level," is the cutoff to use for significance, unless otherwise specified. We'll reject the null hypothesis if $p < .01$

Here's how the reasoning outlined above might be expressed informally by Mark to a skeptic:

"You think I can't control the coin, and that the probability it will come up heads is .5. Assume *you* are right. If you are, the sampling distribution for the sample proportion should be approximately normal, with a mean of .5 and a standard deviation of .05."

"I flipped the coin and got 65 heads in 100 tries, for a sample proportion of .65. That's *much higher* than you'd expect by chance. In fact, the probability (p) of getting a sample proportion that high *just by luck* is .0013."

"Either I was just *lucky*, or I was really having an *effect* on the coin. The chance of getting as much success as I did by luck is so low (*less than .01*), you have to agree; you seem to be *wrong*, and I seem to be *right*!"

Note that the probability .0013 was arrived at by referring to the *sampling distribution* of the statistic, after assuming that the null hypothesis was true.

EXERCISES FOR CHAPTER 11, SECTION 11.4

The following exercises will help you get familiar with the computations and the reasoning involved in hypothesis tests about the population proportion. Note that even though the entire outline above is not explicitly mentioned, the reasoning does require all the steps in the outline.

AL'S FREE THROWS

Suppose it is well known that Al makes 80% of his free throws. His coach is convinced that if Al will shoot underhand like Rick Barry used to, Al will make a higher proportion of his shots. The coach convinces Al to try shooting underhand, and Al makes 344 shots in 400 attempts. Assume that the 400 shots represent a random sample.

Assume that Al represents the skeptic, and the Coach is the "researcher" trying to prove something new.

1. State the null hypothesis that would be used in this case.

2. Assume that Al is right. The distribution of scores in the population would then be _____ in shape, with a mean of ___ and a standard deviation of ____ .

3. The sampling distribution of $\hat{p}$ will be _____ in shape, with a mean of ____ and a standard deviation of _____.

4. What proportion of his underhand shots would Al expect to make?

5. How big would he expect the chance error of $\hat{p}$ to be?

6. What was $\hat{p}$ for Al's sample?

7. What was the *chance error* of $\hat{p}$ for Al's sample?

8. If Al is right about the population proportion, what is the probability that $\hat{p}$ would be .86 or more just by chance?

9. Can you reject the null hypothesis at the .01 significance level?

10. Describe the population used in this example precisely.

JONES' TALK I: n = 36

Mr. Jones knows that over many years the proportion of students who graduate within 4 years is .64. He picks 36 students at random and gives them a motivational talk. 27 of the students in his sample graduate within 4 years. Conduct the usual hypothesis test.

11. State the null hypothesis that would be used in this case.

12. Assume that the null hypothesis is right. The distribution of scores in the population would then be _____ in shape, with a mean of ____ and a standard deviation of ____ .

13. The sampling distribution of $\hat{p}$ will be _____ in shape, with a mean of ____ and a standard deviation of _____.

14. What was $\hat{p}$ for Mr. Jones' sample?

15. What was the chance error of $\hat{p}$ for Mr. Jones?

16. "*p*" is the probability of getting a graduation rate of 27/36 or more just by chance. What is the value of *p*?

17. Can Mr. Jones reject the null hypothesis at the .01 significance level?

18. Describe the population used in this example precisely.

JONES' TALK II: n = 144

Mr. Jones knows that over many years the proportion of students who graduate within 4 years is .64. He picks 144 students at random and gives them a motivational talk. 108 of the students in his sample graduate within 4 years. Conduct the usual hypothesis test.

19. The sampling distribution of $\hat{p}$ in this case will be _____ in shape, with a mean of ____ and a standard deviation of _____.

20. What was $\hat{p}$ for Mr. Jones' sample?

21. What was the chance error of $\hat{p}$ for Mr. Jones'?

22. "*p*" is the probability of getting a graduation rate of 108/144 just by chance. What is the value of *p*?

23. Can Mr. Jones reject the null hypothesis at the .01 significance level?

24. How did increasing the sample size from 36 to 144 affect this hypothesis test?

---

25. Suppose a population can be correctly described as follows: "p=.4".
    Which of the following is *not* a statement that you can conclude?
    A) The population is a '0,1' population
    B) The population is approximately normal.
    C) The probability of a 'success' or '1' is .4.
    D) The probability of a 'failure' or '0' is .6.
    E) *Every one* of the statements above *can* be concluded.

---

26. Suppose that several confidence intervals (with different confidence levels)
    are created from the same population, using samples of the same size, 400.
    Which kind of confidence interval would you expect to be *narrowest*?
    A) a 90% confidence interval
    B) a 99.9% confidence interval
    C) a 99% confidence interval

---

27. Suppose that several confidence intervals (with different confidence levels)
    are created from the same population, each using a confidence level of 99%.
    Which kind of confidence interval would you expect to be *narrowest*?
    A) one based on a sample of size 10
    B) one based on a sample of size 100
    C) one based on a sample of size 1000

---

28. Suppose the population we're concerned with is the set of all students in our class.
    Which of the following distributions would have the *smallest* standard deviation.
    A) the distribution of scores in the population
    B) the sampling distribution of $\hat{p}$ for samples of size 10
    C) the sampling distribution of $\hat{p}$ for samples of size 100

---

29. The sampling distribution of $\hat{p}$ for samples of size 20 describes all possible _____
    and their probabilities.
    A) values of the population proportion, p
    B) values of the sample proportion, $\hat{p}$, for all possible samples of size 20
    C) values of $\hat{p}$ for all samples of all possible sizes
    D) scores in the population
    E) scores in a sample

ANSWERS TO EXERCISES FOR SECTION 11.4

AL'S FREE THROWS

1. The proportion of all underhand shots that Al will ever make is .8; i.e. $p = .8$

2. Negatively skewed, with a mean of .8 and a SD of .4

3. Binomial (and approximately normal), .8, .02

4. .8

5. .02

6. .86 $\hat{p} = k/n = 344/400$

7. .06   **CE** of $\hat{p} = \hat{p} - E(\hat{p}) = .86 - .80 = .06$
    The **CE** of any statistic is
      (the observed value of the statistic) - (the expected value of the statistic)

8. .0013   Because the test statistic is $(.86 - .80)/.02 = 3.0$, and $P(z \geq 3.0) = .0013$

9. Yes, $p < .01$

10. The set of all underhand free throws made by Al.

AL'S FREE THROWS : OUTLINE FORMAT

For reference, here's how the exercises above would look set up in the complete outline format for a hypothesis test.

HYPOTHESIS TEST FOR A POPULATION PROPORTION

POPULATION: All *underhand* free throws that Al ever makes
                  This is the population the sample was drawn from!

VARIABLE: Whether the free throw succeeds (1) or fails (0)

H_0: $p = .8$ This is the skeptical position: There's no improvement, the
               proportion he makes is just what it used to be the old way.
H_1: $p > .8$ This is what the Coach is trying to prove.

SAMPLE SIZE: $n = 400$

OBSERVED SAMPLE STATISTIC:
   $\hat{p}$, the sample proportion $= k/n = 344/400 = .86$

ASSUMING H_0 IS TRUE...
  POPULATION DISTRIBUTION:
     $0,1$ with $P(1) = p = .8$
  SAMPLING DISTRIBUTION:
     Binomial in shape, also approximately normal because $n > 30$
     $\mu_{\hat{p}} = .8$
     $\sigma_{\hat{p}} = SE_{\hat{p}} = \sqrt{p(1-p)/\ n} = \sqrt{(.8)(1-.8)/\ 400} = \sqrt{.004} = .02$
        This is the *sampling distribution* of $\hat{p}$, given $p = .8$, $n = 400$

OBSERVED TEST STATISTIC:
$$\text{Standardized } \hat{p} = \frac{\text{observed } \hat{p} - \mu_{\hat{p}}}{\sigma_{\hat{p}}} = \frac{.86 - .8}{.02} = 3.0$$

The observed test statistic is always a rescaled version of the sample statistic that we'll use to estimate a probability. In this case we standardize $\hat{p}$ so that we can use the z distribution to find the probability of getting a sample proportion as high as .86 by chance.

  OBSERVED SIGNIFICANCE LEVEL: $P(z \geq 3.0) = "p" = .0013$
     The probability of getting a proportion as high as .86,
     if the null hypothesis is true, is .0013.
  CONCLUSION: We can reject the null hypothesis at the .01 level of significance,
        because $p < .01$

JONES' TALK I: n = 36

11. Among the students who got the motivational talk the proportion of students who graduate within 4 years is .64 (the same as it has been in the past for students who *don't* get the talk)

12. Negatively skewed, .64, .48

SKETCH OF POPULATION

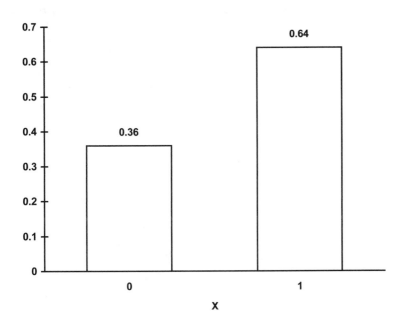

13. Binomial (and approximately normal), .64, .08

SKETCH OF SAMPLING DISTRIBUTION OF p̂

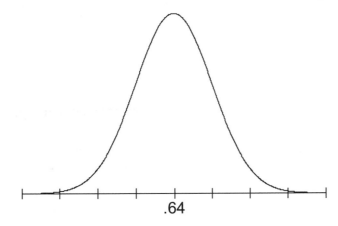

14. $\hat{p} = 27/36 = .75$

15. .11   (.75 - .64)

16. .0838   (.75 - .64)/.08 = 1.375; P(z ≥ 1.38) = .0838

17. No, *p* is not < .01

18. The set of all students at the school the sample was drawn from, *assuming* they were *all* given the motivational talk(!)

JONES' TALK II: n = 144

19. Binomial (and approximately normal),   .64,   .04

20. $\hat{p} = 108/144 = .75$

21. .11   (.75 - .64)

22. .0030   (.75 - .64)/.04 = 2.75; P(z ≥ 2.75) = .0030

23. Yes, *p* is < .01

24. When n was changed from 36 to 144, (i.e., n was multiplied by 4) the SE of the proportion was divided by 2; it went from .08 to .04. $\hat{p}$ was .75 in both cases, so the test statistic got twice as large. This caused *p* to drop dramatically. Intuitively, the *larger* sample makes it *less likely* that the difference between .75 and .64 was just due to *chance*.

25. B

26. A

27. C

28. C *Larger* sample sizes result in *smaller* standard errors, and *narrower* confidence intervals.

29. B

REVIEW QUESTIONS for CHAPTERS 8 - 11

Suppose the proportion of patients that will recover if they are given Dr. Vedder's new treatment is .64. Dr. Vedder treats a random sample of 256 patients from the population.

As usual, do all computations as if sampling were done with replacement. Let "1" denote patient who recovers; and let "0" denote a patient who does not recover.

R1. What is the mean of the population
          A) .48   B) .64   C) .36   D) .04   E) .03

R2. What is the standard deviation of the population?
          A) .48   B) .64   C) .36   D) .04   E) .03

R3. What is the mean of the *sampling distribution* of the statistic "sample proportion" for samples of size 256 from this population?
     What is the *expected value* of the sample proportion?
          A) .48   B) .64   C) .36   D) .04   E) .03

R4. What is the standard deviation of the sampling distribution of the statistic "sample proportion?"
     What is the standard error of the sample proportion?
     How much "in error" will a typical sample proportion be?
          A) .48   B) .64   C) .36   D) .04   E) .03

R5. Estimate the probability that the sample proportion is greater than .73 just by chance.
          A) .9772   B) .0228   C) .9332   D) .0668   E) .0013

Suppose that the proportion of consumers who prefer Snapple (a drink) to its main competitor is well known and generally accepted to be .4.

Ms. Alton develops a new version of Snapple, called "New Snapple" and tests a random sample of 600 consumers to try to prove that the proportion of consumers who would prefer New Snapple is greater than .4.

270 of the consumers in the sample prefer New Snapple to the competitor.

Assume that we designate a consumer in the population who prefers New Snapple as a "success", with a score of 1.

A hypothesis test is conducted with the following null and alternate hypotheses:

NULL HYPOTHESIS:
   H_0 : $p = .4$ "The proportion of consumers in the population who prefer New Snapple is .4"
          (The same as it was for original Snapple)
ALTERNATE HYPOTHESIS:
   H_1 : $p > .4$ "The proportion of consumers in the population who prefer New Snapple is *greater than .4*"

QUESTIONS ABOUT THE *POPULATION* (ASSUMING H_0 IS TRUE)

R6. If the null hypothesis is true, μ, the mean of the *population* is
        A) .16   B) .04   C) .02   D) .4   E) .49

R7. If the null hypothesis is true, σ, the standard deviation of the *population* is
        A) .16   B) .6   C) .02   D) .4   E) .49

R8. If the null hypothesis is true, the shape of the *population* is
        A) approximately normal   B) symmetrical, but not approximately normal
        C) skewed   D) none of the above

QUESTIONS ABOUT THE *SAMPLING DISTRIBUTION* OF $\hat{p}$ (ASSUMING H_0 IS TRUE)

R9. If the null hypothesis is true, $E(\hat{p})$, the *expected value* of the sample proportion, is
        A) .16   B) .04   C) .02   D) .4   E) .49

R10. If the null hypothesis is true, $\sigma_{\hat{p}}$, the *standard error* of the sample proportion, is
        A) .16   B) .04   C) .02   D) .0004   E) .49

R11. If the null hypothesis is true, the shape of the *sampling distribution* of proportion is
        A) approximately normal   B) symmetrical, but not approximately normal
        C) skewed   D) none of the above

R12. What is the value of $\hat{p}$, the sample proportion, for the sample described above?
        A) .4   B) .04   C) .49   D) .45   E) .6

R13. Does the value of $\hat{p}$ support the alternate hypothesis, H_1?
        A) Yes, because $\hat{p}$ is greater than .4
        B) No, because $\hat{p}$ is greater than .4
        C) Yes, because $\hat{p}$ is less than .4
        D) No, because $\hat{p}$ is less than .4

R14. If the null hypothesis is true, what is the probability of obtaining a sample proportion as high as the one in this sample? (i.e. greater than or equal to the observed $\hat{p}$ in this sample)
        A) .0668   B) .0228   C) .0013   D) .01   E) .0062

R15. Ms. Alton can "reject the null hypothesis" if the probability in Question 20 is less than .01. Can she reject the null hypothesis?
        A) Yes   B) No

Suppose you find 360 "successes" or 1's in a random sample of size 600 picked from a large population.

R16. Your best estimate of the population proportion is

        A) .49   B) .6   C) .0001   D) .01   E) .24

R17. Your best estimate of the standard error of the sample proportion for samples of size 600 is

        A) .02   B) .6   C) .0001   D) .01   E) .24

R18. The 99% confidence interval estimate for the population proportion based on this sample is

        A) .5742 - .6258
        B) .597 - .603
        C) .599 - .601
        D) .5484 - .6516
        E) .5873 - .6127

Suppose Boston's probability of winning is .6 in any game, no matter who the opponent is. As usual, let "success" or a "1" designate "Boston wins", and assume games played are a random sample from the set of all possible games. Suppose Boston plays 5 games against New York.

R19. What's the probability that New York wins the *first two* games, *then* Boston wins the last three games?

        A) .33696   B) .3910   C) .2592   D) .03456   E) .07776

R20. What's the probability that Boston wins (exactly) 4 of the 5 games?

        A) .33696   B) .3910   C) .2592   D) .05184   E) .07776

R21. What's the probability that Boston wins 4 or more of the five games?

        A) .33696   B) .3910   C) .2592   D) .05184   E) .07776

R22. The best description of the *sampling description of k*, the number of successes in this case is

        _____ in shape, with a mean of ____ (Note that n, the number of games sampled, is 5)
        A) approximately normal, 3   B) binomial, .6
        C) binomial, .4   D) approximately normal, .6
        E) binomial, 3

Suppose Boston plays 60 games in the season and its probability of winning each game is .6.

R23. How many of the 60 games should we expect Boston to win in the season?

        A) 60   B) 30   C) 36   D) 24   E) 48

R24. Estimate the probability that Boston wins *fewer than 30* games of the 60 played in the season. I.e., Estimate the probability that k, the number of wins, is *29 or less*.

        A) .0228   B) .0322   C) .9678   D) .9332   E) .0668

There are five people in a pool of candidates.

Two of the candidates are Female and three are Male.

Two will be picked at random *without replacement*; i.e. we'll end up with two different candidates that have been picked, and three that haven't.

Let "F1" represent the event "a Female is picked on the first pick"

Let "F2" represent the event "a Female is picked on the second pick"

R25. P(F2) =   A) 0   B) .2   C) .1   D) .25   E) .4

R26. P(F2|F1) =   A) 0   B) .2   C) .1   D) .25   E) .4

R27. P(F1 and F2) =   A) .05   B) .16   C) .1   D) .04   E) 0

R28. The event F1 and the event F2 are

        A) independent but not mutually exclusive

        B) mutually exclusive, but not independent

        C) mutually exclusive and independent

        D) neither mutually exclusive nor independent.

R29. The variable "the total number of females picked to be in our sample in the two picks" is a random variable whose probability distribution is

        A) binomial   B) approximately normal   C) neither of the above

---

TABLE 1

X	p
0	.3
1	.4
5	.1
10	.1
11	.1

R30. The mean of the variable X in Table 1 is

        A) 5   B) 3   C) 6   D) 1   E) 2

R31. The standard deviation of X is

        A) 4   B) 2   C) 1   D) 8   E) 6

R32. Which distribution would you inspect to estimate the probability that the *sample proportion* was greater than .4?

        A) the distribution of scores in the sample

        B) the distribution of scores in the population

        C) the sampling distribution of the sample proportion

---

R33. Suppose the standard error of the proportion is .036 when the sample size is 1600. What will the standard error be if the sample size is reduced to 16.

        A) .36   B) 3.6   C) .0036   D) .00036   E) .036

R34. Suppose the standard error of k, the sample count, is 10 when the sample size is 1600. What will the standard error be if the sample size is reduced to 16?

        A) 1000   B) 100   C) 10   D) 1   E) .1

R35. The standard error of $\hat{p}$

        A) is the standard deviation of the population

        B) tells exactly how far one particular sample proportion is from its expected value

        C) tells how far you'd expect a typical sample proportion to be from its expected value

        D) is the standard deviation of the scores in the sample

        E) more than one of the above is correct.

ANSWERS TO REVIEW QUESTIONS for CHAPTERS 8-11

R1. B

R2. A

R3. B

R4. E

R5. E $(.73 - .64)/.03 = 3$, and $P(z \geq 3) = .0013$

R6. D

R7. E

R8. C

R9. D

R10. C

R11. A

R12. D

R13. A

R14. E

R15. A

R16. B

R17. A

R18. D

R19. D

R20. C $5(.6)^4(.4)^1 = .2592$

R21. A $.2592 + .07776 = .33696$

R22. E

R23. C

R24. B $(29 - 36)/3.79 = -1.85$

R25. E

R26. D

R27. C

R28. D

R29. C

R30. B

R31. A

R32. C

R33. A   The sample size has been multiplied by .01. The SE of $\hat{p}$ will be *divided by* .1 (Because .1 is the *square root* of .01)

R34. D   The sample size has been multiplied by .01. The SE of k will be *multiplied by* .1 (Because .1 is the *square root* of .01)

R35. C

CHAPTER 12

INFERENCE ABOUT THE MEAN

12.1 INTRODUCTION

$\bar{X}$, the sample mean, is the most commonly used statistic, and probably the most intuitive inferential statistic: Picking a random sample of size n and computing $\bar{X}$ seems like a reasonable and obvious way to come up with a *point estimate* of μ, the population mean. And the obvious procedure is the correct one; there's no better way to estimate the population mean from a sample.

However, to produce *confidence interval* estimates for μ, or to *test hypotheses* about μ, we need to be able to describe the sampling distribution of the mean. The sampling distribution for $\bar{X}$, the sample mean, is more difficult to describe than the sampling distribution for $\hat{p}$, the sample proportion. This chapter will cover the same types of inferences as the previous chapter: point estimates, confidence interval estimates, and hypothesis tests. As was the case for $\hat{p}$, the *sampling distribution* will turn out to be the important one for inferential statistics. Much of the reasoning and terminology will be familiar, but some new procedures will be necessary because it is just more challenging to describe (and to approximate) sampling distributions for the mean.

12.2 THE SAMPLING DISTRIBUTION OF $\bar{X}$

As usual, we'll start by (unrealistically) assuming that we know all about the population. We'll see what conclusions can be drawn about the sampling distribution of $\bar{X}$ for a given population, known in advance.

Then, in later sections, we'll deal with the trickier task of estimating a sampling distribution of $\bar{X}$ *from sample data only*, when nothing is known in advance about the population.

Recall that the sampling distribution for any statistic indicates all possible values of the statistic and the probability that each value will occur in a random sample of size n.

(12.2.1) **The *sampling distribution of the mean* for samples of size n from the population, P, is the probability distribution for all possible values of $\bar{X}$.**

It indicates
   1) all possible values of $\bar{X}$
          (For samples of size n from P)
   2) the probability of each value of $\bar{X}$

The notation below *saves* so much time in the long run, it's definitely worth *committing to memory*, and the definitions are crucial for understanding inferential statistics!

REVIEW OF NOTATION AND DEFINITIONS

POPULATION PARAMETERS   (About one entire population, P)

μ_X , or μ the population mean (For the variable X)
The typical, or "average" score on the variable X
The most common measure of the location of P

σ_X, or σ the standard deviation of the population
How far a typical case's score is from the mean, μ
The size of the error you'd typically make if you used one score on X to estimate the population mean, μ
The size of the error you'd typically make if you used μ to estimate one case's score on X
The typical size of a deviation from the mean, X-μ

N   the number of cases in the population (or, its "size")

SAMPLE STATISTICS   (About *one* particular sample picked from the population P)

$\overline{X}$ the mean of the sample (For the variable X)

s_X , or s,   the standard deviation of the sample
or SD_X *How far a typical score in the sample is from the sample mean, $\overline{X}$*

n   the sample size, or number of cases in the sample

$CE(\overline{X})$ $\overline{X}$ - μ The *chance error* of the mean (for one sample)
For one particular sample, the difference between the sample mean, $\overline{X}$, and the population mean, μ
How far off you would have been if you had used this sample's mean, $\overline{X}$, to estimate μ, the mean of the whole population

PARAMETERS of the SAMPLING DISTRIBUTION of $\overline{X}$ (About *all possible* samples)

$\mu_{\overline{X}}$ or $E(\overline{X})$ the expected value of the sample mean
the mean of the sampling distribution of $\overline{X}$
The most typical value of $\overline{X}$ that will occur when you pick a sample of size n from the population

$\sigma_{\overline{X}}$ or $SE(\overline{X})$ the standard error of the sample mean
the standard deviation of the sampling distribution of $\overline{X}$
The typical size of the chance error of $\overline{X}$.
How far off you'll typically be, if you use $\overline{X}$ to estimate μ

The expected value of the sample mean and the standard error of the mean can be computed exactly, *if* we know the sample size and the mean and standard deviation of the population.

(12.2.2) MEAN AND SD OF THE SAMPLING DISTRIBUTION OF $\bar{X}$

For any variable, X, population, P, and sample size, n,

$$\mu_{\bar{X}} \text{ or } E(\bar{X}) = \mu$$
$$\sigma_{\bar{X}} \text{ or } SE(\bar{X}) = \sigma / \sqrt{n}$$

EXAMPLE

The mean of a population is 100 and its standard deviation is 10. A sample of size 16 is picked at random from the population. What do you expect the sample mean to be? How far from 100 do you expect the sample mean to typically be?

ANSWER

100, 2.5

The expected value of $\bar{X}$ is equal to μ, which is 100.

The standard error of $\bar{X}$ is $\sigma/\sqrt{n} = 10/\sqrt{16} = 2.5$

The rules in (12.2.2) allow us to compute the mean and SD of the sampling distribution of $\bar{X}$ exactly. The *shape* of the sampling distribution depends on the *shape* of the population when the sample size is small, but not when the sample size is large.

(12.2.3A) SHAPE OF THE SAMPLING DISTRIBUTION OF $\bar{X}$

- **If the shape of the distribution of scores in the population is *normal*, the shape of the sampling distribution of $\bar{X}$ is *normal*.**
- **If the shape of the distribution of scores in the population is *approximately normal*, the shape of the sampling distribution of $\bar{X}$ is *approximately normal*.**
- **If the shape of the population is *not* approximately normal then**
  if n is *small*, the shape of the sampling distribution is *unpredictable*.
  if n is *large*, the shape of the sampling distribution is *approximately normal*.

The most common applications of these rules can be summarized more succinctly:

(12.2.3B)   SHAPE OF THE SAMPLING DISTRIBUTION OF X̄

**If the population is *approximately normal*,
or the *sample size is large*, the sampling
distribution of X̄ will be approximately normal.**

Otherwise, the shape of the sampling distribution is unpredictable.

EXAMPLE 1 DESCRIBING THE SAMPLING DISTRIBUTION OF X̄ IF μ AND σ ARE KNOWN

Suppose it is **well known** that μ, the mean of all SAT scores is 500 and σ, the SD of all SAT scores is 100.

A) Describe the sampling distribution of X̄ for samples of size 16.

B) What is the probability of picking a sample of size 16 with a mean above 550?

ANSWER

A) The mean of the sampling distribution is 500 and its SD is 25. I.e., the expected value of X̄ is 500 and the standard error of X̄ is 25. The shape cannot be estimated, since we don't know the shape of the population.

B) Cannot be determined. We can't use the normal approximation, because we don't know the shape of the sampling distribution.

EXAMPLE 2

Suppose it is well known that the mean of all SAT scores is 500 and the SD of all SAT scores is 100, and the shape of the distribution of scores is *approximately normal*.

A) Describe the sampling distribution of X̄ for samples of size 16.

B) Estimate the probability of picking a sample of size 16 with a mean above 550.

ANSWER

A) Its mean is 500 and its SD is 25, and its shape is approximately normal. (Because the shape of the population was given as approximately normal)

B) .0228
We standardize the "obtained X̄" value of 550 within the sampling distribution, which has a mean of 500 and a SD of 25:
$$\frac{550-500}{25}=2.0$$

Then we look up -2.0 in the z table to and find the estimated probability .0228.

EXAMPLE 3

Suppose it is well known that the mean of all SAT scores is 500, the SD of all SAT scores is 100, and the distribution of SAT scores is *skewed*.

A) Describe the sampling distribution of X̄ for samples of size 400.

B) Estimate the probability of picking a sample of size 400 with a mean less than or equal to 485.

ANSWER
A) Its mean is 500 and its SD is 5, and its shape is approximately normal.
    (Because n is large.)
    Note that the population shape is unknown, which is OK when n is large.
B) .0013
    We standardize the "obtained $\overline{X}$" value of 485 within the sampling
    distribution, which has a mean of 500 and a SD of 5:
    $$\frac{485-500}{5}=-3.0$$
    And look up -3.0 in the z table to find the probability: .0013.

EXERCISES FOR CHAPTER 12, SECTIONS 12.1 - 12.2

----

n = 100
Suppose you draw a random sample of size 100 from a population with $\mu = 500$ and $\sigma = 200$.

1. Describe the sampling distribution of $\overline{X}$.

2. What's the probability that $\overline{X}$ is less than or equal to 515?

3. What's the probability that $\overline{X}$ is less than or equal to 485?

4. What's the probability that $\overline{X}$ is between 485 and 515?

n = 1600
5-8 : Repeat questions 1-4, but assume that the sample size was *1600*. Comparing the answers 5-8 with 1-4 shows how the accuracy of the sample mean *increases* when n increases. (and the *error* of the sample mean *decreases* as n increases)

9. Does a sample size of 1600 seem to result in more accurate estimates of the population mean?

ANSWERS TO THE PRECEDING EXERCISES

----

n = 100

1. Approximately normal in shape, with a mean of 500 and a standard deviation of 20

$$\mu_{\bar{X}} \text{ or } E(\bar{X}) = \mu = 500$$
$$\sigma_{\bar{X}} \text{ or } SE(\bar{X}) = \sigma/\sqrt{n} = 200/\sqrt{100} = 20$$

2. .7734 $(515 - 500)/20 = .75$ $P(z \le .75) = .7734$

3. .2266 $(485 - 500)/20 = -.75$ $P(z \le -.75) = .2266$

4. .5468 $P(z \text{ is between } -.75 \text{ and } .75) = P(z \le .75) - P(z \le -.75)$

$$.7734 - .2266 = .5468$$

----

n = 1600

5. Approximately normal in shape, with a mean of 500 and a standard deviation of 5.

$$\mu_{\bar{X}} \text{ or } E(\bar{X}) = \mu = 500$$
$$\sigma_{\bar{X}} \text{ or } SE(\bar{X}) = \sigma/\sqrt{n} = 200/\sqrt{1600} = 5$$

6. .9987 $(.515 - .500)/5 = 3$ $P(z \le 3) = .9987$

7. .0013 $(.485 - .500)/5 = 3$ $P(z \le -3) = .0013$

8. .9974 $P(z \text{ is between } -3 \text{ and } 3) = P(z \le 3) - P(z \le -3)$
$$.9987 - .0013 = .9974$$

9. Yes. When n = 100 the probability that $\bar{X}$ is within 15 of the correct value of μ is only .5468. However, when n = 1600, the probability that $\bar{X}$ is within 15 of the correct value of μ is .9974. That is, the probability that $\bar{X}$ is *close* to μ is much *higher* when n is 16 times *larger*.

12.3 *POINT ESTIMATES FOR* μ *AND* σ

Recall these definitions from the last chapter:

A *point estimate* of a population parameter is the single number, computed from sample data, intended to predict the population parameter.

A sample statistic is called an *unbiased* point estimate of a population parameter if...

- **the *expected value* of the statistic is equal to the parameter, that is..**

- **the *mean of the sampling distribution* of the statistic is equal to the parameter.**

As was previously mentioned, the rule "to estimate a population parameter, use the corresponding sample statistic," makes intuitive sense, and it often works. This rule *works* for the common statistics $\bar{X}$, $\hat{p}$, and the sample percent, but it *doesn't* work for σ. The best point estimate of σ, the population standard deviation, is *not* the SD of the sample.

(12.3.1) If a sample of size n is drawn from a population...

$\bar{X}$, the sample mean, is an *unbiased* point estimate of μ

$$\hat{\sigma}^2 = \frac{(\text{sample SS})}{n-1} \quad \text{is an } \textit{unbiased} \text{ point estimate of } \sigma^2$$

$$\hat{\sigma} = \sqrt{\frac{(\text{sample SS})}{n-1}} \quad \textit{is the } \textit{best estimate} \text{ of } \sigma$$

$$\hat{\sigma}_{\bar{X}} \text{ or EST SE}(\bar{X}) = \hat{\sigma}/\sqrt{n} \quad \textit{is the } \textit{best estimate} \text{ of } \sigma_{\bar{X}}$$

$\hat{\sigma}$ is called "sigma-hat". It is the **best estimate of** σ based on a sample. It is computed the same way as the sample standard deviation, except that you divide by n-1 instead of n. It is surprising to most students to find out that the *sample* SD is *not* the best estimate of the population standard deviation, σ.

Note that $\hat{\sigma}_{\overline{X}}$, the *estimated* SE of $\overline{X}$ is computed the same way the SE of $\overline{X}$ would be, except that $\hat{\sigma}$ is used in the formula instead of σ.

If we *knew* σ we could *compute* the SE of $\overline{X}$ exactly, using this formula:

$$\sigma_{\overline{X}} = \sigma \big/ \sqrt{n}$$

Since we don't know σ, we must *estimate* the SE of $\overline{X}$. This is another **bootstrapping technique,,** similar to the technique in the previous chapter. You use the sample data to compute $\hat{\sigma}$, and then use *that* to estimate the standard error of $\overline{X}$, with this formula:

$$\hat{\sigma}_{\overline{X}} = \hat{\sigma} \big/ \sqrt{n}$$

EXAMPLE

If the following set of scores is a random sample from a population, estimate
    A) the mean of the population
    B) the standard deviation of the population
    C) the standard error of the mean for samples of size 4. That is, estimate about how far $\overline{X}$, the sample mean, will typically be from μ, the population mean.

$$\frac{X}{\begin{array}{c} 2 \\ 2 \\ 8 \\ 8 \end{array}}$$

ANSWER
    A) 5
    B) 3.464   The SS is 36, so the best estimate of σ is

$$\hat{\sigma} = \sqrt{\frac{SS}{n-1}} = \sqrt{\frac{36}{3}} = 3.464$$

    C) 1.732 $\hat{\sigma}_{\overline{X}}$ or EST SE($\overline{X}$) $= \dfrac{\hat{\sigma}}{\sqrt{n}} = \dfrac{3.464}{\sqrt{4}} = 1.732$

12.4 CONFIDENCE INTERVAL ESTIMATES FOR μ

CONFIDENCE INTERVAL ESTIMATES IN GENERAL

Recall this definition from the previous chapter:

> **(12.4.1) A 99% confidence interval estimate for a population parameter consists of a lower limit (LL) and an upper limit (UL), usually written,**
>
> **" LL - UL " or " LL → UL "**
>
> **computed from sample data in a way that guarantees the following probability statement:**
>
> **"The probability that the interval LL - UL contains the correct value of the population parameter is at least .99"**

Confidence interval estimates for μ, the population mean are more challenging to compute than the confidence interval estimates for the population proportion covered in the previous chapter.

When we draw a sample and measure each case in the sample on an *interval scale* (numerical) variable, we need to estimate *both* the population *mean* and the population *standard deviation* from the sample data to compute a confidence interval. (Details will be provided below.)

There is more risk of error in this case, which causes us to need a new kind of sampling distribution, the *t distribution*.

Confidence intervals have this property, which will be clarified in examples below: The *higher* the confidence is, the *wider* the resulting confidence interval will be.

t DISTRIBUTIONS

The upcoming computation of confidence intervals for μ is going to require the use of a new family of sampling distributions, the set of **t distributions**.

TABLE 1: EXCERPT FROM THE t TABLE (Table A3 in the Appendix)

Two-tailed test (or confidence interval)		.01
One-tailed test	<u>df</u>	<u>.005</u>
	1	63.657
	2	9.925
	3	5.841
	4	4.604
	5	4.032
	6	3.707
	7	3.499
	8	3.355
	9	3.250
	10	3.169
	20	3.106
	30	2.750
	60	2.660
	120	2.617
	z	2.576

Table 1 shows some of the values from the t table that would be used to estimate 99% confidence intervals for μ. Note that there are two columns:

The left column indicates the degrees of freedom (abbreviated df). In inferences about one mean, μ, the relevant d.f. will always be n - 1.

The right column has two headings, one indicates .01, a ***two-tailed*** probability, and one indicates .005, a ***one-tailed*** probability.

FIGURE 1: ONE AND TWO TAILED PROBABILITIES

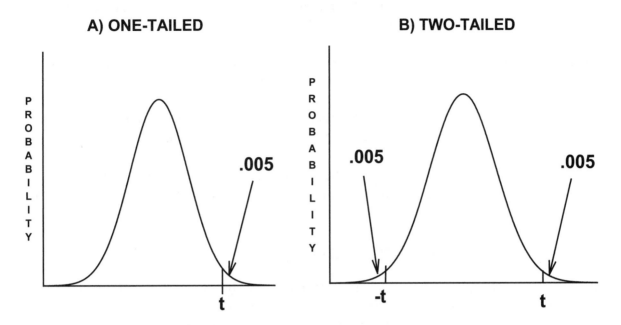

Confidence intervals usually use *two-tailed* probabilities. Figure 1B shows how the probability relates to the t values in the table. .005 of the probability is *below* -t and .005 is *above* +t, so the probability *between* -t and +t is .99. This is what we'll need later for a 99% confidence interval estimate. The following criteria tell when to use t distributions instead of z distributions for inference about the mean:

COMPARING THE z and t DISTRIBUTIONS

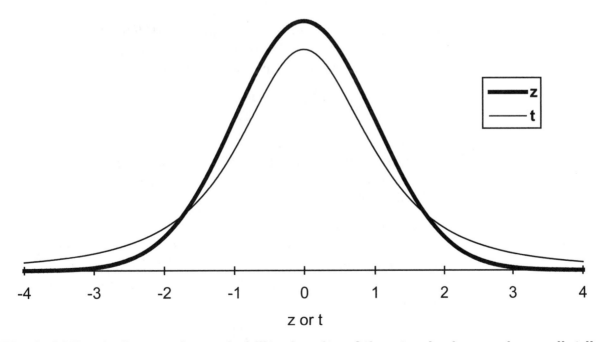

z or t

The bold line indicates the probability density of the standard normal, or z distribution.
The lighter line shows the probability density of the t distribution with 3 degrees of freedom.

The z distribution is of course *standard*. Each t distribution is also *standard*. These distributions always have a mean of zero and a standard deviation of 1.

For extreme values (lower than -1.72 or greater than +1.72) the t distribution has a higher probability density. Actually at the value of -4 or +4, the t distribution is several hundred times higher!

Because the t distributions have more probability "out in the tails", you are more likely to see extreme values occur in t distributions than in the standard normal. It follows that...

- It is *harder* to reject the null hypothesis when the t distribution must be used. You must obtain a more extreme value of the standardized sample mean in order to reject the null hypothesis

- Confidence intervals obtained using t values will generally be *wider*.

The t distribution is used when the population standard deviation was *estimated* from the sample data. That estimate may be in error, and t takes that error into account automatically. t is "less optimistic" about accuracy. The following examples should help make that clear.

ONE- TAILED PROBABILITIES

ASSUME FOR ALL EXAMPLES BELOW THAT df = 3 (I.E., refer to the *top row* in the t table)

EG 1. Which z score has at least .99 of the probability below it?
Which z score is the 99th percentile?
ANSWER: 2.33.   This is the lowest z score with a cumulative proportion of .99 or more.
NOTE: This z score, 2.33, appears in the "COMMONLY USED z-TABLE VALUES" table. It's the value you use for a *one tailed* z test, when alpha, the significance level is .01.

EG 2. Which z score has .01 or less of the probability *above it*?
ANSWER: 2.33

EG 3. Which z score has .01 or less of the probability *below it*?
ANSWER: -2.33   The z distribution is symmetrical. If the probability *above* 2.33 is known to be less than or equal to .01, then the probability below -2.33 will be the same.

EG 4. Which t score has .01 of the probability *above* it?
ANSWER: 4.541.   The one tailed t value is described in Figure B above the t values in your table. Note that the shaded region is labeled α (alpha) In this case we're asking "What positive t score corresponds to an alpha of .01"

EG 5. Which t score has .01 of the probability *below* it?
         ANSWER: -4.541.   The t distribution is symmetrical, with a mean of 0.
                  As with the z distribution, the t value that has .01 of the probability
                      below it is -1 times the t value with .01 of the probability above it.
                      (and vice versa)

TWO- TAILED PROBABILITIES

EG 6. Which is the z value such that the probability of obtaining a z-score between -z and +z is .99?
         ANSWER: 2.58   A z-score of -2.58 beats .005 of all z-scores.
                      A z-score of 2.58 is beaten by .005 of all z-scores.
                      All other z-scores (.99 of them altogether)
                          are *between* -2.58 and +2.58.
                      NOTE: This z score, 2.58, appears in the "COMMONLY USED z-
                          TABLE VALUES" table.
                          It's the value you use for a *two-tailed* z test, when alpha, the
                          significance level is .01, or for a **99% confidence interval.**

EG 7. Which is the t value such that the probability of obtaining a z-score between -z and +z is .99?
         ANSWER: 5.841   NOTE: This is the "two-tailed t critical value" for a probability of .01.
                          So *99%* of all t values lie between -5.841 and +5.841

(12.4.2) WHEN TO USE t INSTEAD OF z IN INFERENCES ABOUT μ

A) Whenever σ is *known*, and the population is *approximately normal*, use z.

    *If the distribution of scores in the population is approximately normal, and
σ, the population standard deviation is known, the z distribution is the correct
distribution to use in confidence interval estimates and hypothesis tests.*

B) Whenever σ is *estimated* and the population is *approximately normal*, use t.

    *If the distribution of scores in the population is approximately normal,
and σ, the population standard deviation is estimated from sample
data, the t distribution with n - 1 degrees of freedom is the correct distribution
to use in confidence interval estimates and hypothesis tests.*

C) When n is large, t is slightly more accurate, but you *can* use z!

    *No matter what shape the population has, when n is large (above 30)
the z distribution provides a good approximation, and is appropriate
to use in confidence interval estimates and hypothesis tests.*

To use the preceding criteria, it is often necessary to decide when a population can safely be considered approximately normal. These rules are commonly used:

(12.4.3)   WHEN TO ASSUME THE POPULATION IS APPROXIMATELY NORMAL

    A) If *long experience* with large samples from the population or similar populations has always indicated an approximately normal shape.

    B) If a sample drawn from the population has a *mode* near its *mean*, and is approximately *symmetrical*.

COMPUTING CONFIDENCE INTERVAL ESTIMATES FOR μ *(ANY SIZE SAMPLE)*

(12.4.4)   If $\bar{X}$ is the sample mean for a sample of size n from a population, P, then a 99% *confidence interval estimate for μ*, the population mean, is

    A) $\bar{X} \pm z\,(\,\sigma_{\bar{X}})$ If σ is *known* and P is approximately normal.

        $SE_{\bar{X}} = \sigma/\sqrt{n}$

        z is the value in the z distribution such that the probability between -z and +z is equal to 99%.

    B) $\bar{X} \pm t\,(\,\hat{\sigma}_{\bar{X}})$ If σ is *unknown* and P is approximately normal.

    C) $\bar{X} \pm t\,(\,\hat{\sigma}_{\bar{X}})$ If σ is *unknown* and n is large.

                (z can be used as an approximation for t)

        $\hat{\sigma}_{\bar{X}} = \hat{\sigma}/\sqrt{n}$ (*or*, $s/\sqrt{n}$ can be used because n is large)

        t is the value in the t distribution with n -1 d.f., such that the probability between -t and +t is equal to 99%.

Any other confidence level can be substituted for 99% in the above formula, as long as the appropriate t values are used.

EXAMPLE 1 CONFIDENCE INTERVAL ESTIMATE FOR μ (SMALL SAMPLE, σ UNKNOWN)

X	f
14	1
18	1
20	2
22	1
26	1

Given that this frequency distribution represents a random sample from a population,

A) Compute point estimates for μ, σ, and the SE of $\overline{X}$ for samples of size 6.
B) Compute a 99% confidence interval estimate for μ.

ANSWER

A) 20, 4, 1.63

$\overline{X} = 20$, the sample mean, is an unbiased point estimate of μ.

$$\hat{\sigma} = \sqrt{\frac{(\text{sample SS})}{n-1}} = \sqrt{\frac{80}{6-1}} = 4 \quad \text{is the best estimate of } \sigma$$

$$\hat{\sigma}_{\overline{X}} \text{ or EST SE}(\overline{X}) = \frac{\hat{\sigma}}{\sqrt{n}} = \frac{4}{\sqrt{6}} = 1.63 \quad \text{is the best estimate of } \sigma_{\overline{X}}$$

B) 20 ± 6.57 or $13.42 - 26.57$ or $(13.42, 26.57)$

$\overline{X} \pm t(\hat{\sigma}_{\overline{X}})$ can be used when σ is unknown and the *sample* is approximately normal.

(In this case the sample is symmetrical and has a mode equal to its mean, hence we can (tacitly) assume that the population is not likely to be far from normal in shape.)

$20 \pm (4.032)(1.63)$

$t = 4.032$ is used because d.f. $= 6 - 1 = 5$

20 ± 6.57

EXERCISES FOR SECTIONS 12.2 - 12.4

PRACTICE COMPUTING $\sigma_{\bar{X}}$ WHEN σ IS *KNOWN*   (Any sample size)

Given: The population mean is (μ), the population standard deviation is (σ) and the sample size is (n) , compute $\sigma_{\bar{X}}$, the standard error of the mean, and estimate the probability that the sample mean, $\bar{X}$, is greater than (C).
Assume the population is approximately normal.

QUESTION	*DATA:* (μ)	(σ)	(n)	(C)	*ANSWERS:* $\sigma_{\bar{X}}$	est P($\bar{X}$ > C)	
1.	80	32	4	84	16	.4013	P(z > .25)
2.	80	32	16	84	8	.3085	P(z > .50)
3.	80	32	64	84	4	.1587	P(z > 1.0)
4.	80	32	256	84	2	.0228	P(z > 2.0)
5.	80	8	64	84	1	<.0002	P(z > 4)!

PRACTICE *ESTIMATING* $\sigma_{\bar{X}}$ AND μ WHEN σ IS *UNKNOWN*

Given ($\bar{X}$), the mean of a sample of size (n), with sum of squares (SS), obtained from a population known to be **approximately normal**. Estimate the standard error of $\bar{X}$ (by computing $\hat{\sigma}_{\bar{X}}$) and create a 99% confidence interval estimate for μ, the population mean.

QUESTION	*DATA:* ($\bar{X}$)	(SS)	(n)	*ANSWERS:* $\hat{\sigma}_{\bar{X}}$	99% C.I. est for μ	t
6.	80	64	5	1.79	80 ± 8.24	4.604
7.	80	256	5	3.58	80 ± 16.48	4.604
8.	80	128	9	1.33	80 ± 4.46	3.355
9.	80	256	17	0.97	80 ± 2.83	2.921
10.	80	25600	1600	0.10	80 ± 0.26	2.576

11. Do all 99% confidence intervals for μ have the same width?
    ANSWER: No, different samples can lead to entirely different CI's

12. Do all 99% confidence intervals for the *same sample size* have the *same width*?
    ANSWER: No, width also depends on the sample sum of squares.

13. Usually, (but not always!) when the *sample SS* is larger, CI's are _____ ; and when *n* is larger
    CI's   are _____.   ANSWER: wider... narrower

12.5 TESTING A HYPOTHESIS ABOUT μ (SMALL SAMPLE)

NULL AND ALTERNATE HYPOTHESES ABOUT μ

"The president's approval rating went down last week." "Pork has less fat in it than it used to." "California students did better in math this year." "So-called 'smart drugs' have no effect." "Engineering majors earn more after graduation than drama majors." "Drama majors have more fun."

None of these statements necessarily represents the opinion of the writer! They're *opinions*, of a sort commonly voiced in the news, in conversations, etc. They're *generalizations*, and very many of *your* opinions are generalizations! One of the fringe benefits of learning about probability and statistics is that you tend to become more aware of how much automatic *inferring* and *generalizing* you carry on constantly, without ever analyzing the process. The quoted statements all implicitly refer to the *mean* of a population, and in each case someone has had some experience with a *sample*, leading to an opinion about a whole population. If you check off in your mind the numerous opinions that occur to you or that you express to others, many of them will involve opinions about population means. In this chapter you'll learn the "state of the art," the best rules that have evolved so far to *accurately* (and *justifiably*) generalize about the *mean* of a large group from a small sample.

In the previous chapter you saw examples in which opinions about the population *proportion* were translated into *hypotheses*. Hypotheses about μ, the population mean, will be handled in a similar way.

If you want to prove that some statement is true, and the statement is about a population mean, you'll need to imagine what someone might believe *before* you have convinced them you're right. You need to imagine a skeptic, to whom you want to present evidence *so convincing* that your point is made beyond a doubt. Recall that the *skeptic's* opinion about the population is called the **null hypothesis**, denoted H_0. The statement describing your opinion about the population, which you are trying to prove to be correct, is called the **alternate hypothesis**, and is denoted H_1.

We'll continue to present all hypothesis testing examples in an organized outline format. The goal is to have you understand *why* the steps of a hypothesis test are carried out, and *why* the conclusions make sense.

SMALL SAMPLE TESTS FOR μ

The test statistic used for small samples has a t-shaped distribution, not a z distribution, and the standard error of $\overline{X}$ used in the formula must be estimated from the sample. This makes 'small sample' tests for μ a little more complicated than tests for the population proportion.

In a **small sample** (n less than or equal to 30) hypothesis test for the population mean,

1) There must be some indication that the population is approximately normal in shape (Either similar populations must be well known to be approximately normal, or the sample itself must be roughly normal)

2) The test statistic to be used is the "standardized sample mean" or "obtained t":

$$\text{TEST STATISTIC: Standardized } \overline{X} = \text{"Obtained t"} = \frac{\overline{X} - \mu_0}{\hat{\sigma}_{\overline{X}}}$$

where the values of $\overline{X}$ and $\hat{\sigma}_{\overline{X}}$ are obtained from the sample data, and μ_0 is the value specified in the null hypothesis.

3) The *test statistic* has a *t* distribution, with n-1 degrees of freedom.

EXAMPLE 12.5.1   HYPOTHESIS TEST FOR μ (SMALL SAMPLE, σ UNKNOWN)

Suppose it is well known that the average student's performance on a memory task is 20, as measured on a widely used test. Dr. Mars believes that candy bar consumption will cause improved performance. A group of 10 experimental subjects picked at random are given candy bars, and they average 24 on the task. The SS (sum of squared deviations from the mean) for the 10 subjects is 81. The distribution of scores in the sample was approximately normal.

Is this convincing evidence that "the population of all candy bar eaters" has a mean above 20?

The outline that follows includes all the computations to carry out the appropriate hypothesis test in this case.

HYPOTHESIS TEST FOR A POPULATION MEAN   (Small Sample , σ unknown)

POPULATION: All students who are *given candy bars*.
(Note that we don't measure any others, there is *no control group* used here.)

VARIABLE: Performance on the memory task

H$_0$: $\mu = 20$ (This value of μ specified in the null hypothesis is referred to as μ_0.)
This is the skeptical position: There's no effect of candy bars, the mean of the group that had candy bars will be the same as it's always been in the past for other students.

H$_1$: $\mu > 20$ (This is what Dr. Mars is trying to prove.)

SAMPLE SIZE: $n = 10$

OBSERVED SAMPLE STATISTIC: $\overline{X}$, the sample mean $= 24$

ASSUMING H$_0$ IS TRUE...

POPULATION DISTRIBUTION:

Approximately normal, with a mean equal to $\mu_0 = 20$.
σ, the population standard deviation, is unknown, but it can be estimated:

$$\hat{\sigma} = \sqrt{\frac{SS}{n-1}} = \sqrt{\frac{81}{(10-1)}} = 3$$

SAMPLING DISTRIBUTION OF $\overline{X}$:

Approximately normal in shape

$\mu_{\overline{X}} = 20$ (Because the expected value of $\overline{X}$ is always μ_0 , which was given to be 20)

$\hat{\sigma}_{\overline{X}}$, the standard error of $\overline{X}$, is unknown, but it can be estimated:

$$\hat{\sigma}_{\overline{X}} = \frac{\hat{\sigma}}{\sqrt{n}} = \frac{3}{\sqrt{10}} = .948$$

OBSERVED TEST STATISTIC:

$$\text{Standardized } \overline{X} = \frac{(\text{Observed}\,\overline{X}) - \mu_0}{\hat{\sigma}_{\overline{X}}} = \frac{24 - 20}{.948} = 4.22$$

The observed test statistic is always a rescaled version of the sample statistic that we'll use to estimate a probability. In this case we standardize $\overline{X}$ so that we can use the t distribution to see if the probability of getting a sample mean as high as 24 is less than .01.

DISTRIBUTION OF TEST STATISTIC:
SHAPE: t-shaped, with n - 1 = 9 d.f.
             (It's t-shaped because an *estimate* of the standard error was used to compute it)
MEAN: 0
SD: 1

OBSERVED SIGNIFICANCE LEVEL:
The "obtained t" from our sample is 4.22
The t value with .01 of the probability above it is 2.821 (See table below)
The t value that cuts off .01 of the probability is referred to as the ".01 critical value."
The obtained t is *more extreme* (farther from 0) than the critical value, so *p*, the probability of getting a sample mean this high is *less than* .01.

CONCLUSION:
We can *reject* the null hypothesis at the .01 level of significance, because *p* < .01

t TABLE FOR .01 HYPOTHESIS TESTS AND 99% CONFIDENCE INTERVALS

The column in bold print includes **one-tailed** t values more commonly used in hypothesis testing. For example, if n is 10, then the appropriate df is 9, and the probability that t is greater than or equal to **2.821** is .01.

TABLE 2: EXCERPT FROM THE t TABLE

Two-tailed test (or confidence interval)		**.02**	.01
One-tailed test (typical hypothesis test)	df	**.01**	.005
	1	**31.821**	63.657
	2	**6.965**	9.925
	3	**4.541**	5.841
	4	**3.747**	4.604
	5	**3.365**	4.032
	6	**3.143**	3.707
	7	**2.998**	3.499
	8	**2.896**	3.355
	9	**2.821**	3.250
	10	**2.764**	3.169
	20	**2.528**	2.845
	30	**2.457**	2.750
	60	**2.390**	2.660
	120	**2.358**	2.617
	z	**2.326**	2.576

EXERCISES FOR SECTION 12.5

COMPUTATIONAL PRACTICE: HYPOTHESIS TESTS FOR μ, *SMALL SAMPLE*, WHEN σ IS *UNKNOWN*

Given ($\overline{X}$), the mean of a sample of size (n), with a sample sum of squares, (SS), obtained from a population known to be *approximately normal*. Estimate $\sigma_{\overline{X}}$, the standard error of $\overline{X}$, and test the hypothesis that μ is greater than 75.

QUESTION	DATA: $(\overline{X})$	(SS)	(n)	ANSWERS: $\hat{\sigma}_{\overline{X}}$	Standardized $\overline{X}$ ("obtained t")	Critical value of t	Reject H_0?
1.	80	64	5	1.79	2.79	3.747	No
2.	80	256	5	3.58	1.40	3.747	No
3.	80	128	9	1.33	3.76	2.896	Yes
4.	80	256	17	0.97	5.15	2.584	Yes
5.	80	25600	1600*	0.10	50 (!)	2.326*	Yes!

*1600 is not really a small sample, but the technique will work! Use the bottom row of your t table.

12.6 INFERENCE ABOUT μ BASED ON LARGE SAMPLES

THE STANDARD NORMAL APPROXIMATION

The previous small sample techniques, using σ and the t distribution, were fairly complicated. When the sample size is *large* (say, above 30) you *may* use the following shortcuts.

(12.6.1) CENTRAL LIMIT THEOREM

Given a population, P, with mean, μ, standard deviation σ, and *any shape*. Suppose a random sample of size n is drawn from P, such that n is greater than 30.

The sampling distribution of $\overline{X}$ will be approximately normal in shape.

$\mu_{\overline{X}}$, the *expected value* of $\overline{X}$, will be equal to μ

$\sigma_{\overline{X}}$, the *standard error* of $\overline{X}$, will be $\dfrac{\sigma}{\sqrt{n}}$

(12.6.2) APPROXIMATIONS USING THE CENTRAL LIMIT THEOREM

Given a population, P, with mean, μ , standard deviation σ, and *any shape*. Suppose a large random sample (n > 30) with mean $\bar{X}$ and standard deviation s is drawn from P.

- **The sampling distribution of $\bar{X}$ will be *approximately normal* in shape.**

- **The expected value of $\bar{X}$ will be *equal to* μ, and**

- **The standard error of $\bar{X}$, will be *approximately***

$$\hat{\sigma}_{\bar{x}} = \frac{\hat{\sigma}}{\sqrt{n}}$$

- **The sampling distribution of the test statistic:**

$$\frac{\bar{X} - \mu}{\hat{\sigma}/\sqrt{n}} = \frac{\bar{X} - \mu}{\hat{\sigma}_{\bar{x}}}$$

will be *approximately standard normal*.

The three differences allowed when the sample size is large are:

1) SD (or, s), the sample standard deviation, can be used to estimate σ.
    (I.e., computing $\hat{\sigma}$ is not required, and you can divide by n instead of n-1)

2) The standard normal distribution, or z distribution can be used to approximate
    the test statistic. (which actually has a t distribution with many degrees of
    freedom)

3) You don't need to know that the population is approximately normal
    (I.e., you don't need to have previous experience with the population, and
    you don't need to inspect the sample to see if it looks approximately
    normal.)

EXAMPLE 12.6.1 HYPOTHESIS TEST, LARGE SAMPLE

We'll consider the same example used in the previous section with a larger sample size and a few other adjustments. **Values and distributions that have been changed are in bold print**. (We'll multiply the sample size by 10 and the SS by 10, and we'll reduce $\bar{X}$ from 24 to 20.8. Note that 20.8 will still turn out to be *significantly* higher than 20.0!)

Suppose it is well known that the average student's performance on a memory task is 20, as measured on a widely used test. Dr. Mars believes that candy bar consumption will cause improved performance. A group of 101 experimental subjects picked at random are given candy bars, and they average 20.8 on the task. The SS (sum of squared deviations from the mean) for the 100 subjects is 810.

Note: Here, because of the large sample size, we *don't* need to know that the distribution of scores in the sample was approximately normal.

Is this convincing evidence that "the population of all candy bar eaters" has a mean above 20?

The outline below includes all the computations to carry out the appropriate hypothesis test in this case.

HYPOTHESIS TEST FOR A POPULATION MEAN (LARGE SAMPLE)

POPULATION: All students who are given candy bars.
(Note that we don't measure any others, there is no control group used here.)

VARIABLE: Performance on the memory task

H$_0$: $\mu = 20$ (This value of μ specified in the null hypothesis is referred to as μ_0.)
This is the skeptical position: There's no effect of candy bars, the mean of the group that had candy bars will be the same as it's always been in the past for other students.

H$_1$: $\mu > 20$ This is what Dr. Mars is trying to prove.

SAMPLE SIZE: n = **101**

OBSERVED SAMPLE STATISTIC: $\bar{X}$, the sample mean = 20.8

ASSUMING H_0 IS TRUE...

POPULATION DISTRIBUTION:

Approximately normal, with a mean equal to $\mu_0 = 20$.

σ, the population standard deviation, is unknown, but it can be estimated:

$$\hat{\sigma} = \sqrt{\frac{SS}{n-1}} = \sqrt{\frac{810}{100-1}} = 2.86$$

SAMPLING DISTRIBUTION OF $\overline{X}$:

Approximately normal in shape

$\mu_{\overline{X}} = 20$ (The expected value of $\overline{X}$ is always μ_0)

$\sigma_{\overline{X}}$, the standard error of $\overline{X}$, is unknown, but it can be estimated:

$$\hat{\sigma}_{\overline{X}} = \frac{\hat{\sigma}}{\sqrt{n}} = \frac{2.86}{\sqrt{100}} = .286$$

OBSERVED TEST STATISTIC:

$$\text{Standardized } \overline{X} = \frac{(\text{observed} \overline{X}) - \mu_0}{\hat{\sigma}_{\overline{X}}} = \frac{20.8 - 20}{.286} = 2.80$$

The observed test statistic is always a rescaled version of the sample statistic that we'll use to estimate a probability. In this case we standardize $\overline{X}$ so that we can use the **standard normal**, or **z** distribution to see if the probability of getting a sample mean as high as **20.8** is less than .01.

DISTRIBUTION OF TEST STATISTIC:

SHAPE: *approximately normal, or z-shaped*   (**Because n is large**)
MEAN: 0
SD: 1

OBSERVED SIGNIFICANCE LEVEL:
The "**obtained z**" from our sample is **2.81**
We can use the standard normal table to find "*p*", the probability of getting a z-score above 2.81. It's .0025.
So, we can estimate that the probability of getting a sample mean as high as 20.8 is .0025.

CONCLUSION:
We can *reject* the null hypothesis at the .01 level of significance, because **.0025 < .01**

SKETCH FOR EXAMPLE 12.6.1

It is very helpful to sketch the estimated sampling distribution for a hypothesis test. This distribution is *always* created assuming the *null* hypothesis to be true. Here's the appropriate sketch for the example above:

ESTIMATED SAMPLING DISTRIBUTION OF THE MEAN
ASSUMING H0 IS TRUE

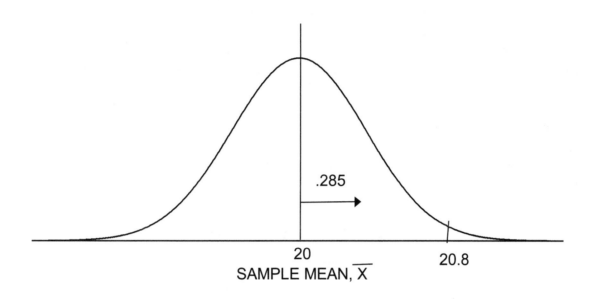

EXAMPLE 12.6.2   CONFIDENCE INTERVAL, LARGE SAMPLE

Use the data in the previous example 12.6.1 to create a 99% confidence interval estimate for μ.

The 99% CI estimate will be

$$\bar{X} \pm z(\hat{\sigma}_{\bar{X}})$$

$$20.8 \pm (2.58)(.285)$$

$$20.8 \pm .735, \text{ or } 20.06 - 21.54$$

The z value 2.58, is the two-tailed .01 value, which may be read from the bottom row of the t table, or from the table 'Commonly Used z Table Values'.

12.7 INFERENCE ABOUT μ WHEN σ IS KNOWN

All of the above inferential procedures assume that σ is *not* known at the time you are trying to draw inferences about μ. This is the most common situation, and it's usually taken for granted that σ is *unknown*, unless otherwise specified.

Occasionally situations do come up in which we have a very good idea what σ, the standard deviation of the population is, but we *still* need to make an inference about μ, which is *unknown*. This may occur when we are dealing with a long series of tests on batches of cases that are being measured under the same conditions. After a great deal of experience we may find that each batch has about the same standard deviation, and a similarly shaped distribution, but a different mean. We might conclude, "these batches are drawn from populations with different *means*, but the *standard deviations* of the populations seem to all be the same. It's not really necessary to estimate σ from one sample."

In such cases it isn't necessary to use the t distribution, because the error caused by *estimating* σ from a single sample is not present.

(12.7.1) INFERENCE ABOUT μ (When σ is KNOWN)

If either   1) n is large, or

2) the population is approximately normal,

the distribution of the test statistic

$$\frac{\overline{X} - \mu}{\sigma/\sqrt{n}} = \frac{\overline{X} - \mu}{\sigma_{\overline{X}}}$$

is approximately standard normal

This just says that you can use σ and the z distribution in doing hypothesis tests and computing confidence intervals.

EXAMPLE 12.7.1 HYPOTHESIS TEST, σ KNOWN

Suppose engineers at Honda know that the standard deviation of the variable "gas mileage" or "mpg" is *always close to 3.0* for Honda Civics, even though many experiments have been tried that increase or reduce the mean mileage. Also, the distribution of scores is always close to normal in shape. The mean mileage for the current model is known to be 35.0, but an independent inventor, "Bubba" claims that at his front lawn research center in Arkansas, he has developed a fuel injector modification that will *increase* mileage in Civics.

The engineers at Honda, always willing to experiment (The Honda Prelude *was* the first mass produced car with *4-wheel* steering!) test Bubba's design on 25 Civics drawn at random from the assembly line. The cars in the sample average 37 mpg.

A) Conduct the appropriate hypothesis test.

We'll show just the essentials in this case, which is fairly straightforward.

HYPOTHESIS TEST FOR A POPULATION MEAN (σ *KNOWN*)

POPULATION: All Honda Civics given Bubba's modification.
(Note that we don't measure any others, there is *no* control group used here.)

VARIABLE: mileage, or mpg

H$_0$: $\mu = 35$

(This value of μ specified in the null hypothesis is referred to as μ_0.)
This is the skeptical position: There's no effect of Bubba's new fuel injector, the mean mileage of the cars with Bubba's invention will be the same as it's always been in the past for other Civics.

H$_1$: $\mu > 35$ This is what Bubba is trying to prove.

SAMPLE SIZE: $n = 25$

OBSERVED SAMPLE STATISTIC: $\overline{X}$, the sample mean $= 37$

ASSUMING H$_0$ IS TRUE...

POPULATION DISTRIBUTION:

Approximately normal, with a mean equal to $\mu_0 = 35$.
σ, the population standard deviation, is **known to be 3**.

SAMPLING DISTRIBUTION OF $\overline{X}$:

Approximately normal in shape

$\mu_{\overline{X}} = 35$ (The expected value of $\overline{X}$ is μ_0)

$\sigma_{\overline{X}}$, the standard error of $\overline{X}$, is *known*, because σ is *known*. It is:

$$\sigma_{\overline{X}} \text{ or } SE(\overline{X}) = \frac{\sigma}{\sqrt{n}} = \frac{3}{\sqrt{25}} = .6$$

OBSERVED TEST STATISTIC:

$$\text{Standardized } \overline{X} = \frac{(\text{Observed } \overline{X}) - \mu_0}{\hat{\sigma}_{\overline{X}}} = \frac{37 - 35}{.6} = 3.33$$

The observed test statistic is always a rescaled version of the sample statistic that we'll use to estimate a probability. In this case we standardize $\overline{X}$ so that we can use the **standard normal**, or **z** distribution to see if the probability of getting a sample mean as high as 37 is less than .01.

DISTRIBUTION OF TEST STATISTIC:

SHAPE: *approximately normal, or z-shaped*
> **(Because the population is known to be approximately normal and σ was known, not estimated)**

MEAN: 0

SD: 1

OBSERVED SIGNIFICANCE LEVEL:

The **"obtained z"** from our sample is **3.33**

We can use the standard normal table to find "*p*", the probability of getting a z-score above 3.33. It's **.0004.**

So, we can estimate that the probability of getting a sample mean as high as 37 is .0004.

CONCLUSION:
We can *reject* the null hypothesis at the .01 level of significance, because **.0004** < .01

**ESTIMATED SAMPLING DISTRIBUTION OF THE MEAN
ASSUMING H0 IS TRUE**

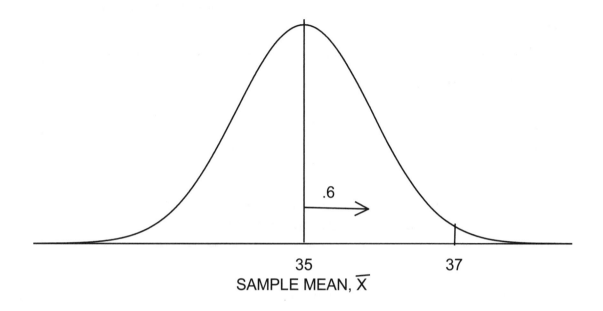

EXAMPLE 12.7.2 CONFIDENCE INTERVAL, σ KNOWN

Use the same data as in 12.7.1 to create a 99% confidence interval estimate for μ.

The 99% CI estimate will be

$$\bar{X} \pm z\,(\sigma_{\bar{X}})$$

$$37 \pm (2.58)(.6)$$

$$37 \pm 1.55, \text{ or } 35.45 - 38.55$$

12.8* THE SAMPLING DISTRIBUTION OF ΣX

Occasionally the **total, or sum** of scores in the sample, **ΣX,** is of more interest than the mean. There is a simple way to draw conclusions about the **sample sum,** also referred to as "the sum of draws".

(12.8.1) The sample sum, ΣX, is just n times $\bar{X}$, so

The expected value of the sum, $\mu_{\Sigma X} = n(\mu_{\bar{x}})$

The standard error of the sum, $\sigma_{\Sigma X} = n(\sigma_{\bar{x}})$

The sampling distribution of the sum has the same shape as the sampling distribution of $\bar{X}$

Or, the conclusions about the sum can be drawn *directly* from information about the population and the sample:

(12.8.2) If a sample of size n is drawn at random from a population, the sample sum, ΣX, will have an

expected value, or $\mu_{\Sigma X} = n\mu$

standard error, or $\sigma_{\Sigma X} = \sigma\sqrt{n}$

sampling distribution with a shape that is approximately normal *if either...*

- **the distribution of scores in the population is approximately normal, *or***

- **n is large**

EXAMPLE 12.8.1

Suppose each time you bet on a certain type of gamble, the average return on a bet of $100 dollars is $105, (i.e., you make $5 on the average) but the standard deviation of all such returns is also $105. Suppose that the odds remain the same no matter how much you bet.

A) If you bet 10,000 dollars on *one play*, what is your expected gain?
   What is the standard deviation of the amount you win?

ANSWER:
> 10,000 is 100 times $100, so you expect a return of $10,500
> (I.e., you'd expect to win $500, $5 for every hundred dollars bet)
>
> The standard deviation is **$10,500**! You have just raised the stakes 100 times higher, so both the expected value *and* the SD *of 1 play* are both 100 times greater.

B) Suppose instead you bet *100 separate times*, each time betting $100, with an expected return of $105 and a SD of $105.
   What would be the mean and SD of the *total* you end up with after 100 bets?

ANSWER:
$$\text{E(sum)} = n\mu = (100)(\$105) = \$10,500$$
$$\text{SE(sum)} = \sigma\sqrt{n} = (\$105)(10) = \boldsymbol{\$1,050}$$

C) In the second case, what's the probability that you end up losing money?

ANSWER:
> We need the probability of getting less than zero, in an approximately normal distribution with a mean of $10,500 and a SD of 1,050.
>
> We standardize $0 :
>
> $$\frac{0 - 10,500}{1,050} = -10$$
>
> and find that the probability that z is less than -10 is very close to zero, certainly less than .0001!

The second gamble may be described as 1/10 as *risky* as the first, because the SD of the total you end up with is only 1/10 as big.

12.9 SUMMARY

The hypothesis tests and confidence interval estimates covered above can be summarized in a short outline:

If σ is unknown:

Small sample

If the population is approximately normal in shape
use $\hat{\sigma}$ to estimate σ
the test statistic will have a t distribution with n-1 df

If the population is not approximately normal
inference about μ is not possible

Large sample

The population *does not* have to be approximately normal
use $\hat{\sigma}$ and the t distribution to be precise,
or
you can just use the sample SD and the z distribution as approximations

If σ is known:

Small sample

If the population is approximately normal in shape
It's not necessary to estimate σ.
Use the z distribution
If the population is not approximately normal
inference about μ is not possible

Large sample

The population can have *any* shape
It's not necessary to estimate σ.
Use the z distribution

EXERCISES FOR CHAPTER 12 SECTIONS 12.5 - 12.8

AL'S SCORING AVERAGE

Suppose it is well known that Al averages 12 points per game. His coach is convinced that if Al tries more outside shots, Al will average *more than* 12 points per game. The coach convinces Al to try shooting outside more, for 9 games. Al averages 16 points during the 9 games, and the SS (Sum of squared deviations from the mean) for the 9 games is 128. The distribution of scores among the 9 games in the sample is roughly symmetrical and "bunched" toward the center.
Assume (although this is questionable, of course) that the 9 games represent a random sample.
Assume that Al represents the skeptic, and the Coach is the "researcher" trying to prove something new.

1. State the null hypothesis that would be used in this case.

2. Assume that Al is right. The distribution of scores in the population would then be _____ in shape, with a mean of ____ and a standard deviation which can be estimated to be ____ .

3. The *sampling distribution* of $\bar{X}$ will be _____ in shape, with a mean of ____ and a standard deviation which can be estimated to be _____ .

4. How many points would Al expect to average for the 9 games? (I.e., what would he expect $\bar{X}$ to be for the 9 games in the "sample") _____

5. How big would he expect the chance error of $\bar{X}$ to be?

6. A) What was $\bar{X}$ for Al's sample? B). What was the chance error of $\bar{X}$ for Al's sample?

7. What is the "standardized sample mean" or "obtained t value" for the sample of 9 games?

8. What is the "t critical value"?

9. Can you reject the null hypothesis at the .01 significance level?

Suppose in the above example that the goal was to show that Al averages *less than* 12 points per game, and Al's average for the 9 games had been 8 (instead of 16).

10. A) What would be the obtained t value"
    B) What would be the "t critical value.
    C) Could we reject the null hypothesis?

JONES' MATH REVIEWS I: n = 16

Mr. Jones knows that over many years the mean Math SAT score of students who graduate from Irvine Remedial High School is 300, and the distribution is approximately normal. He picks 16 students at random and gives them a weekly math review session for six months before they take the SAT. His sample of 16 students average 330 on the Math SAT, and the SS for his sample is 24,000   Conduct the usual hypothesis test.

11. State the null hypothesis that would be used in this case.

12. Assume that the null hypothesis is right. The distribution of scores in the population would then be _____ in shape, with a mean of ___ and a standard deviation which can be *estimated* to be ____ .

13. The sampling distribution of $\bar{X}$ will be _____ in shape, with a mean of ____ and a standard deviation *estimated* to be _____.

14. What was $\bar{X}$ for Mr. Jones' sample?

15. What was the chance error of $\bar{X}$ for Mr. Jones' sample, assuming the null hypothesis is correct?

16. What is the "standardized sample mean" or "obtained t" value?

17. What is the t critical value?

18. Why do we refer to the t distribution in this case?

19. "*p*" is the probability of getting a sample mean SAT as high as 330 just by chance. What can you conclude about *p*?

20. Can Mr. Jones reject the null hypothesis at the .01 significance level?

21. Describe the population used in this example precisely.

JONES' MATH REVIEWS II: n = 100 (σ unknown)

Mr. Jones knows that over many years the mean Math SAT score of students who graduate from Irvine Remedial High School is 300. He picks 100 students at random and gives them a weekly math review session for six months before they take the SAT. His sample of 100 students average 308 on the Math SAT, and the SS for his sample is 160,000.   Conduct the usual hypothesis test.

22. State the null hypothesis that would be used in this case.

23. Assume that the null hypothesis is right. The distribution of scores in the population would then be _____ in shape, with a mean of ___ and a standard deviation which is about ____ .

24. The sampling distribution of $\bar{X}$ will be _____ in shape, with a mean of ____ and a standard deviation of about _____.

25. What was $\bar{X}$ for Mr. Jones' sample?

26. What was the chance error of $\bar{X}$ for Mr. Jones' sample?

27. What is the "standardized sample mean" or "obtained z" value?

28. "*p*" is the probability of getting a sample mean as high as 308 just by chance. Estimate the value of *p*.

29. Why do we use the z distribution in this case?

30. Can Mr. Jones reject the null hypothesis at the .01 significance level?

JONES' MATH REVIEWS III: n = 16 (σ known)

Mr. Jones knows that over many years the mean Math SAT score of students who graduate from Irvine Remedial High School is 300, and the distribution is *approximately normal*, and the *standard deviation is well known to be 100*.

He picks 16 students at random and gives them a weekly math review session for six months before they take the SAT. His sample of 16 students average 375 on the Math SAT. Conduct the usual hypothesis test.

31. State the null hypothesis that would be used in this case.

32. Assume that the null hypothesis is right. The distribution of scores in the population would then be _____ in shape, with a mean of ____ and a standard deviation which is ____ .

33. The sampling distribution of $\bar{X}$ will be _____ in shape, with a mean of ____ and a standard deviation of _____.

34. What was $\bar{X}$ for Mr. Jones' sample?

35. What was the chance error of $\bar{X}$ for Mr. Jones'?

36. What is the "standardized sample mean" or "obtained z" value?

37. "*p*" is the probability of getting a sample mean SAT as high as 375 just by chance. Estimate the value of *p*.

38. Why do we use the z distribution in this case?

39. Can Mr. Jones reject the null hypothesis at the .01 significance level?

----

40. Suppose that $\sigma_{\overline{X}}$ is 20. You can conclude that if you used _____ to estimate _____

the size of the error you'd make would typically be about 20.
     A) one case's score… the population mean.
     B) one case's score… the sample mean.
     C) the sample mean.. one case's score
     D) the sample mean.. the population mean.
     E) none of the above is correct

----

41. Suppose that you know that 'p=.2'. You can conclude that
     A) the sample being described is positively skewed.
     B) the population being described is positively skewed.
     C) the sample being described is negatively skewed.
     D) the population being described is negatively skewed.

----

42. The *sampling distribution* of the mean describes all _____ and their probabilities.
     A) scores in the population
     B) scores in the sample
     C) sample means for all possible populations
     D) sample means for all samples (of size n) from one population.
     E) none of the above is correct

----

43. Suppose that in a random sample of size 16, $\overline{X}$ is 32 and $\hat{\sigma}$ is 8. How big an *error* would
you expect to make, if you used $\overline{X}$, the sample mean to estimate μ, the population mean?
(I.e., about how *far off* will you be, if you estimate the population mean to be 32?)
     A) 0   B) 16   C) 2   D) 1   E) none of the above

JOB SATISFACTION?

Suppose that the mean job satisfaction rating of all employees at Company X is well known and generally accepted to be *equal to* 70. The rating have always had an approximately normal distribution. Dr. Alterior, an industrial psychologist suggests to the owners of Company X that they can *increase* the mean job satisfaction by establishing a 'flex time' policy. That is, Dr. Altville believes that putting employees on flex-time will cause the mean job satisfaction rating to become *greater than* 70.

Mr. Nullberg, the personnel manager, is skeptical about Dr. Alterior's claim. Mr. Nullberg thinks that even if a new flex-time policy is adopted, the mean job satisfaction rating of employees will remain equal to 70.

Dr. Alterior wants to convince the management that he is right, so she arranges to have a random sample of 5 employees chosen at random put on flex-time. These employees are polled after two months on flex-time. Their job satisfaction ratings are in the table below:

X
70
74
76
78
82

44. The alternate hypothesis that is appropriate in this case is H_1:
    A) The sample mean is equal to 70   D) The population mean is greater than 70
    B) The population mean is 70   E) The sample mean is greater than 70
    C) The population mean is greater than 75

QUESTIONS ABOUT THE *POPULATION* (ASSUMING H_0 IS TRUE)

45. If the null hypothesis is true, μ, the mean of the *population* is
    A) 1   B) .03   C) .01   D) 75   E) 70

46. Based on *sample data* we can *estimate* that σ, the standard deviation of the *population* is
    A) 1   B) 1.41   C) 4.47   D) 20   E) 2

QUESTIONS ABOUT THE *SAMPLING DISTRIBUTION OF* $\overline{X}$ (ASSUMING H_0 IS TRUE)

47. If the null hypothesis is true, $\mu_{\overline{X}}$, the *expected value* of the sample mean, is
    A) 1   B) .03   C) .01   D) 75   E) 70

48. Based on sample data we can estimate that $\sigma_{\overline{X}}$, the *standard error* of the sample mean,
    is approximately
    A) 1   B) 1.41   C) 4.47   D) 20   E) 2

49. Based on all information above, we can conclude that the shape of the *sampling distribution* of $\overline{X}$ is
    A) approximately normal   C) symmetrical, but not approximately normal
    B) skewed   D) none of the above

50. What is STD $\overline{X}$ the standardized sample mean?   (Sometimes called the 'Obtained t')
      A) 2.5   B) -2.0   C) 3.0   D) -3.0   E) -2.5

51. What is the appropriate *t critical value* in this case?
      A) 3.747   B) 4.604   C) 3.365   D) 4.032   E) 2.33

52. Can Mr. Altville reject the null hypothesis?
      A) Yes, because *p* seems to be less than .01   C) Yes, because *p* seems to be greater than .01
      B) No, because *p* seems to be less than .01   D) No, because *p* seems to be greater than .01

Suppose that these 5 scores represent *presidential approval ratings* obtained from a *random sample* of 5 voters from a population of 5 million voters. You may assume that the population is approximately normal.)

X
70
74
76
78
82

53. The best *point estimate* of the population mean, μ , based on this sample is ...
      A) 70   B) 72   C) 76   D) 78   E) 82

54. The best *point estimate* of the population standard deviation, σ, is...
      A) 42   B) 4.47   C) 1   D) 2.65   E) 2.00

55. The best estimate of $\sigma_{\overline{X}}$, the *standard error of the sample mean,* is...
      A) 42   B) 4.47   C) 1   D) 2.65   E) 2.00

56. If you use $\overline{X}$, the mean of *this sample*, to estimate μ, the mean of the entire population, how big an *error* would you expect to make, typically?
      A) 42   B) 4.47   C) 1   D) 2.65   E) 2.00

57. Create a 99% confidence interval estimate for the population mean, μ.
      A) 76 ± 4.604 D) 76 ± 9.208
      B) 76 ± 7.494 E) none of the above is correct
      C) 76 ± 8.064

58. Is it correct to state "the *probability* that the mean of the *entire population* of 5 million people lies within this confidence interval is .99." ?
      A) Yes   B) No   C) *Are you kidding?* You only sampled *one-millionth* of the population!

ANSWERS TO EXERCISES FOR CHAPTER 12 SECTIONS 12.5 - 12.8

AL'S SCORING AVERAGE

1. The mean points per game for all possible games Al plays while following the coach's advice (to shoot outside more) is 12.

2. Approximately normal (because the sample distribution was), with a mean of 12 and an unknown σ, which can be estimated to be

$$\hat{\sigma} = \sqrt{\frac{SS}{n-1}} = \sqrt{\frac{128}{9-1}} = 4$$

3. Approximately normal (because the population is), with a mean of 12 and a standard deviation, $SE(\overline{X})$ estimated to be

$$\hat{\sigma}_{\overline{X}} = \frac{\hat{\sigma}}{\sqrt{n}} = \frac{4}{\sqrt{9}} = 1.33$$

4. 12

5. about 1.33

6. A) 16   B) +4   It's $\overline{X} - \mu = 16 - 12$

7. 3.01

   The test statistic is the "obtained t" or "standardized sample mean" = (16 - 12)/1.33

8. 2.896 $p = .01$, df $= n - 1 = 9 - 1 = 8$

9. Yes, the obtained t is more extreme (further from zero) than the t critical value, so $p < .01$

---

10. A) *-3.01*

    The test statistic is the "obtained t" or "standardized sample mean" = (8 - 12)/1.33

   B) *-2.896*

    We just *negate* the t critical value in a *negative* test.

   C) *Yes*

    The obtained t is *more extreme* or *further from zero* than the t critical value.

AL'S SCORING AVERAGE : OUTLINE FORMAT

For reference, here's how the exercises above would look set up in the complete outline format for a hypothesis test.

HYPOTHESIS TEST FOR A POPULATION MEAN

POPULATION: All games played by Al in which he follows his coach's suggestion to "shoot outside more."
> Note that the population relevant to a hypothesis test is always the population that the *sample was actually drawn from*!

VARIABLE: The number of points Al scores in a game

H$_0$: $\mu = 12$ This is the skeptical position: There's no improvement; the mean number of points he scores is 12, just what it used to be the old way.

H$_1$: $\mu > 12$ This is what the Coach is trying to prove.

SAMPLE SIZE: $n = 9$

OBSERVED SAMPLE STATISTIC: $\overline{X}$, the sample mean $= 16$

ASSUMING H$_0$ IS TRUE... (and using sample data)

POPULATION DISTRIBUTION:
Approximately normal, mean $= 12$, SD approximately 4 (estimated from sample)

SAMPLING DISTRIBUTION:
Approximately normal, mean $= 12$, $\sigma_{\overline{X}} = $ approximately 1.33 (estimated from sample)

OBSERVED TEST STATISTIC:
$$\text{Standardized } \overline{X} = \frac{(\text{Observed } \overline{X}) - \mu_0}{\hat{\sigma}_{\overline{X}}} = \frac{16 - 12}{1.33} = 3.01$$

CRITICAL VALUE OF TEST STATISTIC
2.896 (The value of t, for 8 df., that has exactly .01 of the probability above it)

CONCLUSION:
We can reject the null hypothesis at the .01 level of significance, because "obtained t" is more extreme than "critical t", so *p* is less than .01.

JONES' MATH REVIEW I: *n = 16*

11. The mean SAT of students who get the reviews is 300 (the same as it has been in the past)

12. Approximately normal (The population is), mean of 300 , 40

$$\hat{\sigma} = \sqrt{\frac{SS}{n-1}} = \sqrt{\frac{24000}{16-1}} = 40$$

13. Approximately normal, mean of 300, standard deviation ($\sigma_{\overline{X}}$) about 10

$$\hat{\sigma}_{\overline{X}} = \frac{\hat{\sigma}}{\sqrt{n}} = \frac{40}{\sqrt{16}} = 10$$

14. 330

15. 30

16. 3.0   (330 - 300)/ 10

17. 2.602 $p = .01$, df $= 15$, one-tailed

18. When σ is *estimated* from the sample, as it was in this case, the test statistic has a *t-shaped* distribution, with n-1 df.

19. $p < .01$

20. Yes

21. The set of all students that at the school the sample was drawn from, if they were *all* given   the math review.

JONES' MATH REVIEW II: *n = 100, σ unknown*

22. The mean SAT of students who get the reviews is 300 (the same as it has been in the past)

23. *Unknown* (Note that the shape of the population is not given), mean of 300 , about 40

$$\text{Sample SD} = \sqrt{\frac{SS}{n}} = \sqrt{\frac{160000}{100}} = 40$$

24. Approximately normal, mean of 300, $\sigma_{\overline{X}}$ about 4

$$\hat{\sigma}_{\overline{X}} = \frac{\text{Sample SD}}{\sqrt{n}} = \frac{40}{\sqrt{100}} = 4$$

25. 308

26. 8

27. 2.0 $(308 - 300)/4$

28. about .0228   From z table $P(Z > 2.0) = .0228$

29. n, the sample size, is large (we could still use $\hat{\sigma}$ and t, which are slightly more accurate, but it is not necessary.

30. No, the probability of obtaining a value this extreme is about .0228.

     .0228 is not less than .01, so he can't reject at the .01 level.

JONES' MATH REVIEW III: n = 16, σ known

31. The mean SAT of students who get the reviews is 300 (the same as it has been in the past)

32. Approximately normal, 300, 100. (Note that this information is all *given* in this case)

33. Approximately normal, mean of 300, $\sigma_{\overline{X}}$ equal to 25 (exactly)

$$\sigma_{\overline{X}} = \frac{\sigma}{\sqrt{n}} = \frac{100}{\sqrt{16}} = 25$$

34. 375

35. 75

36. 3.0 $(375 - 300)/25$

37. about .0013   From the z table $P(Z > 3.0) = .0013$

38. σ is known in this case. It was not necessary to estimate σ.
    And the population is approximately normal, so even for small samples, the sampling distribution of $\overline{X}$ will be approximately normal in shape.

39. Yes, the probability of obtaining a value this extreme is about .0013.
    .0013 is less than .01, so he can reject at the .01 level.

----

40. D) the sample mean.. the population mean.

----

41. B) the population being described is positively skewed.
    There are only two scores, 0 and 1. 1 is less likely to occur.

----

42. D) sample means for all samples (of size n) from one population.

----

43. C) 2

JOB SATISFACTION?

44. D) The population mean is greater than 70

45. E) 70

46. C) 4.47

47. E) 70

48. E) 2

49. A) approximately normal

50. C) 3.0

51. A) 3.747

52. D) No, because p seems to be greater than .01

----

53. C) 76

54. B) 4.47

55. E) 2.00

56. E) 2.00

57. D) 76 ± 9.208

58. A) Yes

CHAPTER 13
THE LOGIC OF HYPOTHESIS TESTS

13.1 THE HYPOTHESES

Soon we'll be discussing more advanced kinds of hypothesis tests. It'll be much easier to understand the advanced tests if you keep the goals of *all* hypothesis tests in mind. Look over this brief chapter carefully and refer to it when necessary!

There is always one *null* hypothesis, H_0, which contains an *equal sign*.

The researcher usually wants to prove that the *alternate* hypothesis, H_1, is correct.

Both hypotheses are about the entire *population* (or populations)

A sample is always drawn from a population (or populations) in which it is *possible* for either H_0 or H_1 to be true.

We compute the *obtained value* of the statistic from the sample data.

> If the obtained value of the statistic *supports* H_1 we *proceed* -- otherwise we stop and state "We cannot reject H_0".

The *sampling distribution* is always estimated assuming that H_0 *is true*.

The value of the statistic obtained from the *sample* is compared with the *sampling distribution* of the statistic, and we estimate p, the *probability of obtaining a value as extreme (or 'as impressive')* as the actual obtained value, just by chance.

If p is *less* than alpha (usually .01) we say "We *can* reject H_0 at the (alpha) level of significance."

If p is *greater* than alpha, we say "We *cannot* reject H_0."

13.2   ERRORS

When a hypothesis test is performed, only the cases in the *sample* are actually measured; most cases in the population remain *unknown*.

Even after completing a hypothesis test, we can't be *sure* which of the two hypotheses is correct. So it is possible to follow the correct procedure and still come to an erroneous conclusion. Either the null hypothesis or the alternate hypothesis *may* be true, and we may either reject or fail to reject H_0, so there are four possible situations when any hypothesis test is conducted; two *correct* conclusions, and two possible *erroneous* conclusions.

If the *Null* Hypothesis, H_0, is true, and we...

...*reject* H_0 then we have made a <u>*TYPE I error*</u>

...*fail to reject* H_0 we have "correctly failed to reject"

If the *Alternate* Hypothesis, H_1, is true, and we...

...*reject* H_0 then we have "correctly rejected H_0"

...*fail to reject* H_0 we have made a <u>*TYPE II error.*</u>

13.3   SIGNIFICANCE LEVEL or ALPHA LEVEL (α)

Falsely claiming that you have proved something is considered the *worst* kind of error in scientific studies. In the terminology of hypothesis testing this amounts to 'rejecting H_0 when it is actually true' -- a Type I Error. The main goal of hypothesis testing is keeping the probability of a Type I Error *low*! *If* the null hypothesis is true, and you conduct a hypothesis in the usual way, rejecting H_0 just in case p is *less than* .01, then the probability that you will make a Type I Error is *less than* .01. In that case α is .01.

Note that alpha is *not* simply 'the probability of a Type I Error' (Though that statement appears in several introductory texts!) The precise probability related to alpha is this:

P(Type I Error | H_0 is true) < α or,

'The probability of a Type I Error, *given* that H_0 is true, is *less than* α'

We can also say

P(Correctly *failing to reject* H_0 | H_0 is true) $\geq$ 1 - α or,

'The probability of correctly failing to reject H_0, *given* that H_0 is true, is *at least* 1 - α'

13.4 BETA (β)

Suppose that H_1 is actually *true*. If you are the researcher, you hope that the sample you pick will reflect the population as a whole, and be convincing enough to let you *reject* H_0. If it isn't you'll make a Type II Error -- *failing to reject* H_0 when H_1 is *true*. (Of course you won't *know* you have made this error, because you won't know the whole population) *If* H_0 is false, then the probability of this kind of error is beta (β). Note that beta is *not* simply 'the probability of a Type II Error'.

P(Type II Error | H$_1$ is true) = β   or,

'The probability of a Type II Error, *given* that H$_1$ is true, is equal to β'

13.5 POWER

Correctly rejecting H_0 when H_1 is true is the *goal* of the researcher, who is trying to show that H_1 is correct. The probability of correctly rejecting H_0, if H_1 is *true*, is called the *power* of a hypothesis test.

P(Correctly rejecting H$_0$ | H$_1$ is true) = 1 - β = The *power* of the hypothesis test ,   or,

'The probability of rejecting H$_0$, *given* that H$_1$ is *true*, is equal to 1 - β'

Generally, the power of a test is *high* when n is *large* and when the standard error(s) are *small*.

13.6 SUMMARY

Table 13.6.1 summarizes the four possible situations which may occur after a hypothesis test has been conducted. Note that we must know about *two* things to decide whether an error occurred: The decision of the researcher and the state of the population that the hypotheses are about.

TABLE 13.6.1 SUMMARY OF DECISIONS AND ERRORS

	If H_1 is not true…	If H_1 is true…
… and you Reject H_0	TYPE I Error *If* H_0 is true, probability $< \alpha$	Correctly Reject H_0 *If* H_1 is true, probability = *power* = $1 - \beta$
… and you Fail to reject H_0	Correctly Fail to Reject *If* H_0 is true, probability $\geq 1 - \alpha$	Type II Error *If* H_1 is true… probability = β

EXERCISES FOR CHAPTER 13

----

1. Can you make a TYPE I error if the *alternate* hypothesis is true?

2. If the *alternate* hypothesis is true, what is the probability of making a Type I error?

3. If the *null* hypothesis is true, what is the probability of making a Type I error?

4. Can you make a TYPE II error if the *null* hypothesis is true?

5. If the *null* hypothesis is true, what is the probability of making a Type II error?

6. If the *alternate* hypothesis is true, what is the probability of making a Type II error?

7. If the *alternate* hypothesis is true, what is the probability of correctly rejecting the null hypothesis?

8. How will *increasing* the sample size affect the power of a hypothesis test?

ANSWERS TO EXERCISES FOR CHAPTER 13

1. No, because a Type I error requires two things:

The null hypothesis is true, and you reject the null hypothesis

2. 0

3. Less than α, (which usually means less than .01)

4. No, because a Type II error requires two things:

The alternate hypothesis is true, and you fail to reject the null hypothesis

5. 0

6. β

7. $1- \beta$, which is usually called the power of the statistical test.

8. Increasing n will always *increase* the power of a test.

CHAPTER 14

INFERENCE ABOUT DIFFERENCES

14.1 INTRODUCTION

THE PREVIOUS ONE-GROUP HYPOTHESIS TESTS

The techniques in the two previous chapters showed how to conduct hypothesis tests about the population proportion or the population mean for *one* population. Typical alternate hypotheses in such cases look like these:

$$\text{"p} > .4\text{"} \quad \text{or} \quad \text{"}\mu > 98.6\text{"}$$

These hypotheses each specify *one* population parameter (p or μ) and *one* specific value (".40", or "98.6" in the examples). We stated that the specific values often come from other, well known, populations, or from opinions expressed by people. For example, to inspire the alternate hypotheses above, we might have been given this information:

> "Bob thinks that .4 of the voters support Jones; but Jones thinks *more than* .4 of   the
> voters support him."
> "The average temperature is 98.6, but Dr. Smith thinks that people who are given a *new*
> drug will average *above* 98.6."

COMPARING TWO GROUPS

Very often hunches or opinions that are about *two groups* occur to people. We're referring to any opinion that describes a *comparison* between two groups, perhaps stating that one group is "better," or "worse," or merely "different" from another group. Here are examples:

> "Women liked Quayle *more than* men (liked Quayle)."
> "The proportion of women who liked Quayle is *greater than* the proportion of men
> who liked Quayle."
> "Drug A works much *better than* a Placebo"
> "Students who attend Mr. Jones reviews do a lot *better than* students who don't"
> "Amplifiers that get modified produce *more* watts of power than amplifiers that are not
> modified."
> "Smokers don't live *as long as* non-smokers"
> "Paranoid schizophrenics are *brighter than* most other people."

The earlier hypothesis tests, which required that we *know in advance* what value we expected from a group, (the value specified in the null hypothesis) would not help us to evaluate the opinions above.

The new tests which will be covered in this chapter *can* let us evaluate these hypotheses. These tests are called "two-group" or sometimes "two-sample", or "CASE 2" hypothesis tests.
Note that no specific numbers are mentioned in the informal hypotheses above! The exact proportion of more women who are supposed to like Quayle is not specified. *How many* watts of power the amplifiers produce is not stated.   Nor is the actual average life span of smokers or non-smokers. This is typical-- you can have a strong opinion about the *difference* between two groups, *without* knowing exactly where each group stands.

A NEW PARAMETER: $\mu_A - \mu_B$

Suppose you think that the mean of one group, say "Group A", is *greater than* the mean of some other group, "Group B". Your hunch is a belief about *two* groups, but it's a lot easier to deal with statistically if you phrase it in terms of *one* parameter:

(14.1.1) $\mu_A - \mu_B$ **, the difference between group means**
            is a parameter of *two* groups, A and B.

It denotes the *single value* obtained by computing
the mean of all cases in Group A, and
subtracting from it the mean of all cases
in Group B.

Your hunch is that "$\mu_A > \mu_B$", but it is better phrased as an alternate hypothesis this way:

H_1: $\mu_A - \mu_B > 0$, or "the difference between means is *greater than* 0"

The most obvious *skeptical* position is the corresponding null hypothesis:

H_0: $\mu_A - \mu_B = 0$, or "the difference between means is *equal to* 0"

USING A NEW STATISTIC: $\bar{X}_A - \bar{X}_B$

The way you'd test your hypothesis about the *difference* between these group means is fairly obvious:

1) You'd draw a random sample from Group A.
   This sample's mean, SD, and size will be designated: $\bar{X}_A$, SD_A and n_A, The subscript "A" indicates that they refer to Group A.

2) You'd draw another random sample, from Group B.
   This sample's mean, SD, and size will be designated: $\bar{X}_B$, SD_B and n_B.

3) You'd compute the "*obtained difference*" or "difference between sample means": $\bar{X}_A - \bar{X}_B$. Note that this statistic is *one* number, even though it's based on *two* groups. (You'd quickly check that this difference was *positive*, because it must be positive to support your alternate hypothesis!)

4) You'd estimate the *sampling distribution* for the difference, $\bar{X}_A - \bar{X}_B$ (assuming H_0 is true). You'd use the sampling distribution to estimate the "P" value, that tells, "how likely are we to obtain a difference as large as the obtained difference, if H_0 is true."

5) You'd be able to reject H_0 if $p < .01$.

These steps are the familiar ones for hypothesis tests! What is *new* is that since the hypotheses are about *two* groups, you need to deal with computations based on *two* samples. Also, estimating the *sampling distribution* for the difference is tricky, because this kind of estimate is affected by variation in *both* samples.

Either sample mean may be in error, and the difference between means, $\bar{X}_A - \bar{X}_B$, is going to be affected by *both* sources of error: the error in $\bar{X}_A$, *and* the error in $\bar{X}_B$. We'll see that these errors can be estimated and dealt with in a logical way, so conclusions about group differences can still be made with great confidence.

As usual, we'll first describe, in 14.2, what the sampling distribution of $\bar{X}_A - \bar{X}_B$ would look like for *known* groups A and B.

Then in later sections we'll show how to make the best inferences possible from two samples in the more realistic case, when *nothing* is known in advance about groups A and B.

14.2 THE SAMPLING DISTRIBUTION OF $\bar{X}_A - \bar{X}_B$

The sampling distribution of the difference between means can be easily described when the parameters of both groups are known, and both sample sizes are large, or both groups are approximately normal.

(14.2.1) CENTRAL LIMIT THEOREM

Suppose two random samples of sizes n_A and n_B are drawn from groups A and B. μ_A, σ_A, μ_B, and σ_B, the groups' means and standard deviations are all known.

The *sampling distribution* of the statistic $\bar{X}_A - \bar{X}_B$, the difference between sample means,

- Will be approximately normal if...
    both A and B are approximately normal, or if
    n_A and n_B are both large (> 30)

- Has a mean, denoted $\mu_{\bar{X}_A - \bar{X}_B}$, equal to $\mu_A - \mu_B$

    (This is also denoted "$E_{difference}$" or "Expected Value of the difference")

- Has a standard deviation, denoted $\sigma_{\bar{X}_A - \bar{X}_B}$ equal to

$$\sigma_{\bar{X}_A - \bar{X}_B} = SE_{difference} = \sqrt{(\sigma_{\bar{X}_A})^2 + (\sigma_{\bar{X}_B})^2} = \sqrt{\frac{\sigma^2_A}{n_A} + \frac{\sigma^2_B}{n_B}}$$

    (Also denoted "Standard Error of the difference")

EXAMPLE

Suppose you are given the following information about groups A and B:

$$\begin{array}{ll} \mu_A = 110 & \mu_B = 90 \\ \sigma_A = 60 & \sigma_B = 40 \\ n_A = 400 & n_B = 100 \end{array}$$

That is, a sample of size 400 is drawn from Group A, which has a mean known to be 110 and a standard deviation known to be 60. Another sample of size 100 is drawn from group B, which has a mean of 90 and a standard deviation of 40.

A) Describe the sampling distribution of $\bar{X}_A - \bar{X}_B$.

B) What is the probability that $\bar{X}_A - \bar{X}_B$ is greater than 30? Less than 7.5?

C) Suppose the actual samples have these means: $\bar{X}_A = 115$ $\bar{X}_B = 80$
    Compute *all three* chance errors that are relevant in this example.
    Is the chance error of $\bar{X}_A - \bar{X}_B$ *larger* or *smaller* than you would have expected?

ANSWERS
A) Approximately normal (because both sample sizes are over 30), with a mean of 20 and a standard deviation of 5.

The mean, $\mu_{\overline{X}_A - \overline{X}_B}$, or expected value of $\overline{X}_A - \overline{X}_B$ is $\mu_A - \mu_B = 110 - 90 = 20$

The standard deviation, $\sigma_{\overline{X}_A - \overline{X}_B}$, or standard error of $\overline{X}_A - \overline{X}_B$ is

$$\sigma_{\overline{X}_A - \overline{X}_B} = \sqrt{(\sigma_{\overline{X}_A})^2 + (\sigma_{\overline{X}_B})^2} = \sqrt{\frac{\sigma^2_A}{n_A} + \frac{\sigma^2_B}{n_B}} = \sqrt{\frac{(60)^2}{400} + \frac{(40)^2}{100}} = \sqrt{9 + 16} = 5$$

SKETCH: SAMPLING DISTRIBUTION OF THE DIFFERENCE, $\overline{X}_A - \overline{X}_B$

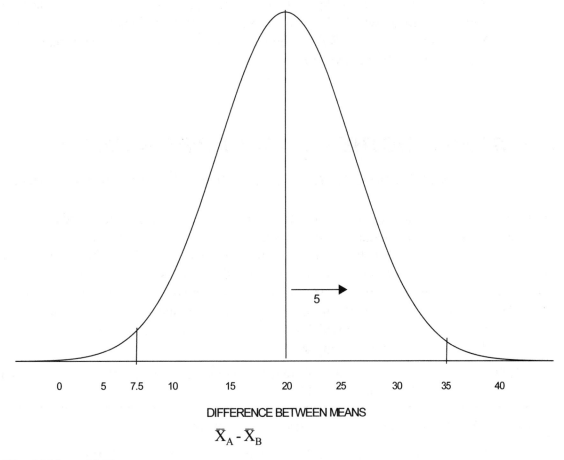

DIFFERENCE BETWEEN MEANS

$\overline{X}_A - \overline{X}_B$

B) .0228,   .0062

P(difference > 30) can be estimated using P(z > 2.0) = .0228, because
   Standardized difference =   (30 - 20)/5 = 2.0

P(difference < 7.5) can be estimated using P(z < -2.5) = .0062, because
   Standardized difference =   (7.5 - 20)/5 = -2.5

C) The chance error of $\overline{X}_A$ is +5, because $\overline{X}_A - \mu_A = 115 - 110 = +5$

  The chance error of $\overline{X}_B$ is -10, because $\overline{X}_B - \mu_B = 80 - 90 = -10$

  The "obtained" value of $\overline{X}_A - \overline{X}_B$ from the samples is $115 - 80 = 35$,
  and we know that the "expected" value is $\mu_A - \mu_B = 110 - 90 = 20$.

Therefore, the *chance error* of $\overline{X}_A - \overline{X}_B$ is

  (OBTAINED Difference) - (Expected difference) =

  $(\overline{X}_A - \overline{X}_B) - (\mu_A - \mu_B) = 35 - 20 = +15$

This *chance* error of $\overline{X}_A - \overline{X}_B$, (+15), is *three times larger* than the *standard* error of $\overline{X}_A - \overline{X}_B$ (which was 5, computed above), so it's much larger than you'd typically expect it to be.

We'd summarize these results informally this way:

  Sample A's mean was 5 *higher* than expected. (115 obtained vs. 110 expected)
  Sample B's mean was 10 *lower* than expected. (80 obtained vs. 90 expected)
  $\overline{X}_A - \overline{X}_B$, the *obtained difference* between the means, was 15 *greater* than expected (35 obtained vs. 20 expected)

14.3 TESTING HYPOTHESES ABOUT DIFFERENCES:
Large Independent Samples--- Two Group z-test

In testing hypotheses about population differences, we must *estimate* the standard error of the difference based on sample data. The formula is not difficult, but unfortunately the estimation *of* error *adds* error, and the test statistic may not have a nicely shaped distribution when the sample sizes are small. When both samples are large, however, the "standardized difference" has approximately a standard normal distribution, allowing the usual approximation to be used with confidence. In this section and the following one we cover statistics for *independent samples*— or '*between subjects' designs*, in which two separate, unrelated groups of cases are measured on the dependent variable and then compared.

Here's how the standard error of the difference is *estimated* from sample data (when each of the sample sizes is large, i.e. greater than 30)

(14.3.1) ESTIMATING $\sigma_{\overline{X}_A - \overline{X}_B}$, **the standard error of** $\overline{X}_A - \overline{X}_B$

When n_A **and** n_B **are both *large*,** $\sigma_{\overline{X}_A - \overline{X}_B}$ **may be *estimated* by computing**

$$\hat{\sigma}_{\overline{X}_A - \overline{X}_B} = \sqrt{(\hat{\sigma}_{\overline{X}_A})^2 + (\hat{\sigma}_{\overline{X}_B})^2} \approx \sqrt{\frac{(SD_A)^2}{n_A} + \frac{(SD_B)^2}{n_B}}$$

In other words, you just use the *sample* SD for each sample as if it were the *population* standard deviation in the formula for the standard error of the difference. (Compare 14.3.1 with 14.2.1)

EXAMPLE 1: *TESTING "WILD TULIP" (LARGE INDEPENDENT SAMPLE VERSION)*

Suppose the director of the new unrated film "Wild Tulip" and the producer disagree about the ending of the film. The producer believes that typical audience members who view the film "Wild Tulip" with a "happy ending" added will rate it higher (and enjoy it more) than viewers who see the film with the original "sad ending" created by the director. They show two different preview audiences different versions of the film, one with each ending.

The director agrees to release the film with the "happy" ending only if it tests significantly higher than the film with her original, "sad" ending.

(This example was made up before the novel and the film "The Player" were written, though the theme is similar!)

They obtain these data from random samples:

"Happy Ending ratings": $\bar{X}_A = 54.0$ $SD_A = 8.4$ $n_A = 49$

"Sad Ending ratings": $\bar{X}_B = 50.8$ $SD_B = 5.0$ $n_B = 100$

The hypothesis test will be presented here in the complete outline form.

Note that this kind of test may be used in *any* situation in which an independent variable divides the cases into two groups and the dependent variable is interval scale, as long as sample sizes are large (both must be at least greater than 30). We'll show how to deal with small samples in the next section.

HYPOTHESIS TEST: DIFFERENCE BETWEEN MEANS   (LARGE SAMPLES)

EXAMPLE 1: TESTING "WILD TULIP"

GROUPS: (A) *All possible viewers of the film with the "happy" ending.*

   (B) *All possible viewers of the film with the "sad" ending.*

SAMPLE SIZES: $n_A = 49$ $n_B = 100$

VARIABLE: *Preference for the film, as measured on a standard rating scale*

STATISTIC: *The difference between the mean of Group A and the mean of group B*

NULL HYPOTHESIS: $\mu_A - \mu_B = 0$.

ALTERNATE HYPOTHESIS $\mu_A - \mu_B > 0$ (or, "$\mu_A > \mu_B$ ")
(Because the burden of proof is on the producer here, who is trying to show that the "happy"
ending gets *higher* ratings, on the average)

DISTRIBUTION OF SCORES IN THE POPULATION: (Assuming H_0 is true): *unknown*
        No information was provided about the population means for the groups

OBSERVED VALUE OF THE STATISTIC BASED ON SAMPLE DATA:

   $\bar{X}_A = 54.0$ $\bar{X}_B = 50.8$,

   So the obtained difference, $\bar{X}_A - \bar{X}_B$ $= 54.0 - 50.8 = 3.2$

OBSERVED SDs OF THE SAMPLES: $SD_A = 8.4$ $SD_B = 5.0$

SAMPLING DISTRIBUTION OF THE DIFFERENCE, $\bar{X}_A - \bar{X}_B$
        (Assuming H_0 is true)

              SHAPE: *Approximately Normal*
                (Because the sample sizes are large)

              MEAN, $\mu_{\bar{X}_A - \bar{X}_B}$:   *0*

              (The *expected value of the difference*. It's 0 because the null hypothesis
              specified that the difference is 0)

              STANDARD DEVIATION, $\sigma_{\bar{X}_A - \bar{X}_B}$: *Estimated to be 1.3*

COMPUTATION:

EST $\sigma_{\bar{X}_A - \bar{X}_B}$ =

$$\hat{\sigma}_{\bar{X}_A - \bar{X}_B} = \sqrt{(\hat{\sigma}_{\bar{X}_A})^2 + (\hat{\sigma}_{\bar{X}_B})^2} = \sqrt{\frac{(SD_A)^2}{n_A} + \frac{(SD_B)^2}{n_B}} = \sqrt{\frac{(8.4)^2}{49} + \frac{(5.0)^2}{100}} = 1.3$$

SKETCH OF THE SAMPLING DISTRIBUTION OF THE DIFFERENCE, $\bar{X}_A$ - $\bar{X}_B$
(Assuming H_0 is true)

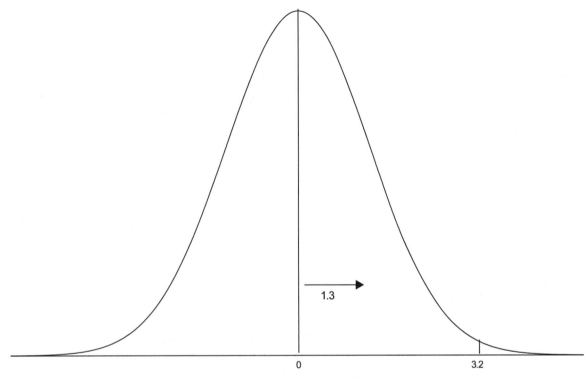

TEST STATISTIC: *2.46 ("obtained z")*

"obtained z" $= \dfrac{\text{(obtained difference)} - \text{(expected difference)}}{(\text{EST SE}_{\text{difference}})} = \dfrac{(\bar{X}_A - \bar{X}_B) - (0)}{(\hat{\sigma}_{\bar{X}_A - \bar{X}_B})}$

$= \dfrac{(54.0 - 50.8) - (0)}{1.3} = \dfrac{3.2}{1.3} = 2.46$

(Here, we have standardized the *obtained difference* between sample means, assuming it came from the sampling distribution of the difference between means sketched above)

OBSERVED SIGNIFICANCE LEVEL, P: *.0069*
Our alternate hypothesis specified ">", so "P" is
P(z > 2.46) = P(z < -2.46) = .0069

CAN WE REJECT THE NULL HYPOTHESIS AT THE .01 LEVEL? *Yes, because p < .01*

EXERCISES FOR CHAPTER 14, SECTIONS 14.1 - 14.3

---

1. Suppose the alternate hypothesis is:

> "The mean of Group A is *greater than* the mean of Group B."
>
> Samples of size 100 are drawn from each group.
>
>> Sample A, from Group A, has a mean of 340 and a SD of 50.
>>
>> Sample B has a mean of 430 and a SD of 20.
>
> Based on the data above, we
>
>> A) can reject the null hypothesis.
>>
>> B) cannot reject the null hypothesis.

Dr. Jones is trying to prove that *heavy* drinkers (Group A) score *lower* on the MAT, a memory test, than *light* drinker (Group B), on the average. She draws two samples of drinkers at random. (By the way, this is based on an actual study!)

Sample A consists of 36 *heavy* drinkers. The drinkers in Sample A average 110 on the MAT, with a SD of 48

Sample B consists of 49 *light* drinkers. The drinkers in Sample B average 141 on the MAT, with a SD of 42.

NOTE: You may assume that hypotheses about differences are stated in the usual order, i.e. "A - B", not "B - A".

2. The null hypothesis in this case states that the difference between the mean of ...

> A) Group A and the mean of Group B, in the population, is equal to 0
>
> B) Sample A and the mean of Sample B is equal to 0
>
> C) Group A and the mean of Group B, in the population, is greater than 0
>
> D) Sample A and the mean of Sample B is greater than 0
>
> E) None of the above is correct

3. The alternate hypothesis in this case states that the difference between the mean of ...(Use the answer choices from question 2)

4. Estimate $\sigma_{\overline{X}_A}$, the SE of the mean for Sample A in this case.

> A) 48   B) 8   C) 10   D) 6   E) 42

5. Estimate $\sigma_{\overline{X}_B}$, the SE of the mean for Sample B in this case.

> A) 48   B) 42   C) 10   D) 6   E) 8

6. Estimate $\sigma_{\overline{X}_A - \overline{X}_B}$, the SE of the *difference* between means in this case is...

> A) 48   B) 42   C) 10   D) 8   E) 6

7. Assuming that the null hypothesis is true, we'd expect the sampling distribution of *differences* in this case to be _____ in shape, with a mean of __ and a standard deviation of ____ .
   (Note that this question is asking about the *sampling* distribution.)
   - A) approximately normal, 0, 10
   - B) approximately normal, 31, 10
   - C) approximately normal, -31, 10
   - D) approximately normal, 0, 20
   - E) exactly normal, 0, 1

8. What standard score (or "z-score") corresponds to the *difference* between the mean of Sample A and the mean of Sample B in this case? I.e., what is "obtained z"?
   - A) 3.1   B) -3.1   C) 2.1   D) -2.1   E) -31

9. What is the "*p* value" ? I.e., what is the probability of obtaining a sample *difference* this extreme, assuming that the null hypothesis is true.
   - A) .9893   B) .9990   C) -.0179   D) .001   E) .0107

10. Can Dr. Jones reject the null hypothesis,(at the usual .01 level of significance) based on the value of *p*?
    - A) Yes, because *p* is greater than .01
    - B) Yes, because *p* is less than .01.
    - C) No, because *p* is less than .01
    - D) No, because *p* is greater than .01
    - E) None of the above is correct.

Dr. Brothers is trying to prove that high school juniors who *attend* her review class (Group A) score *higher* than high school juniors who *don't attend* her review class (Group B), on the average. She draws two samples of students at random.

Sample A, consisting of 100 students, is given her review class.
The students in Sample A average 526 on the SAT, with a SD of 48

Sample B, consisting of 144 students, is *not* given her review class.
The students in Sample B average 513 on the SAT, with a SD of 24.

NOTE: You may assume that hypotheses about differences are stated in the usual order, "A - B", not "B - A".

11. The null hypothesis in this case states that the difference between the mean of ...
    - A) Group A and the mean of Group B is greater than 0
    - B) Group A and the mean of Group B is equal to 0
    - C) Sample A and the mean of Sample B is greater than 0
    - D) Sample A and the mean of Sample B is equal to 0
    - E) None of the above is correct

12. The alternate hypothesis in this case states that the difference between the mean of ...
    (Use the answer choices from question 11)

13. The best estimate of $\sigma_{\overline{X}_A}$, the SE of the mean for Sample A in this case is...

        A) 4.8   B) 9.6   C) 2   D) 4   E) 5.2

14. The best estimate of $\sigma_{\overline{X}_B}$, the SE of the mean for Sample B in this case is...

        A) 4.8   B) 9.6   C) 2   D) 4   E) 5.2

15. The best estimate of $\sigma_{\overline{X}_A - \overline{X}_B}$, the SE of the *difference* between means in this case is...

        A) 9.6   B) 4.8   C) 4   D) 5.2   E) 10.4

16. Assuming that the null hypothesis is true, we'd expect the sampling distribution of *differences between means* in this case to be _____ in shape, with a mean of ___ and a standard deviation of ___ .   (Note that this question is asking about the *sampling* distribution.)

        A) exactly normal, 513, 5.2
        B) approximately normal, 526, 10.4
        C) exactly normal, 0, 5.2
        D) approximately normal, 0, 10.4
        E) approximately normal, 0, 5.2

17. What standard score (or "z-score") corresponds to the *difference* between the mean of Sample A and the mean of Sample B in this case?

        A) 2.5   B) 5.0   C) 1.25   D) -5   E) -5.2

18. What is the "*p*" ? I.e., what is the probability of obtaining a sample *difference* this extreme, assuming that the null hypothesis is true?

        A) .1056 B) .0228   C) .0013   D) .0062   E) .01

19. Can Dr. Brothers reject the null hypothesis, (at the usual .01 level of significance) based on the *p* value?

        A) Yes, because *p* is greater than .01
        B) Yes, because *p* is less than .01.
        C) No, because *p* is less than .01
        D) No, because *p* is greater than .01
        E) None of the above is correct.

Dr. Dristan is trying to prove that students with *allergies* (Group A) score *higher* on the
Math SAT than students without allergies (Group B), on the average.
She draws two samples at random:
Sample A consists of 49 students with allergies.
    The students in Sample A average 520 on the Math SAT, with a SD of 56
Sample B consists of 36 students without allergies.
    The students in Sample B average 480 on the Math SAT , with a SD of 90.
NOTE: You may assume that differences are computed in the usual order, i.e. "A - B", not "B - A".

20. The alternate hypothesis in this case states that the difference between the mean of ...
        A) Group A and the mean of Group B is equal to 0
        B) Sample A and the mean of Sample B is equal to 0
        C) Group A and the mean of Group B is greater than 0
        D) Sample A and the mean of Sample B is greater than 0
        E) None of the above is correct

21. The best estimate of $\sigma_{\overline{X}_A}$, the SE of the mean for *Sample A* in this case is.
        A) 15   B) 8   C) 17   D) 6   E) 10

22. The best estimate of $\sigma_{\overline{X}_A - \overline{X}_B}$, the SE of the *difference* between means in this case is...
        A) 15   B) 8   C) 17   D) 8   E) 6

23. Assuming that the null hypothesis is true, we'd expect the sampling distribution of *differences*
between means in this case to be ____ in shape, with a mean of ___ and a standard deviation
of ____.
(Note that this question is asking about the *sampling* distribution of differences between means)
        A) approximately normal, 0, 17
        B) approximately normal, 40, 10
        C) approximately normal, -40, 17
        D) approximately normal, 0, 10
        E) exactly normal, 0, 1

24. What standard score (or "z-score") corresponds to the *difference* between the mean of Sample A and the
mean of Sample B in this case?
        A) 0   B) -2.0   C) 2.0   D) -2.35   E) +2.35

25. What is the "*p* value" ? I.e., what is the probability of obtaining a sample mean this impressive,
assuming that the null hypothesis is true.
        A) .9772   B) .9906   C) -.0228   D) .0094   E) .0002
26. Can Dr. Dristan reject the null hypothesis,(at the usual .01 level of significance) based on the *p* value?
        A) Yes, because *p* is greater than .01
        B) Yes, because *p* is less than .01.
        C) No, because *p* is less than .01
        D) No, because *p* is greater than .01

ANSWERS TO EXERCISES FOR SECTIONS 14.1 - 14.3

---

1. B   The sample mean for A is *less than* the sample mean for B.
                  You're trying to prove that the population mean of A is *greater than* the mean of B.
                  The data do not support the hypothesis you're trying to prove!

---

2. A

3. E H_1 is "The mean of Group A is *less than* the mean of Group B"

4. B   For large samples such as this it isn't necessary to use $\hat{\sigma}$, we can just use the
                  sample SD in this formula:

$$\hat{\sigma}_{\overline{X}_A} = \text{EST SE}_A = \frac{SD_A}{\sqrt{n_A}} = \frac{48}{\sqrt{36}} = 8$$

5. D

$$\hat{\sigma}_{\overline{X}_B} = \text{EST SE}_B = \frac{SD_B}{\sqrt{n_B}} = \frac{42}{\sqrt{49}} = 6$$

6. C

$$\text{EST SE}_{\overline{X}_A - \overline{X}_B} = \hat{\sigma}_{\overline{X}_A - \overline{X}_B} = \sqrt{(\text{EST SE}_A)^2 + (\text{EST SE}_B)^2} = \sqrt{(8)^2 + (6)^2} = 10$$

7. A

8. B   "obtained z" or "standardized difference" =

$$\frac{\text{(obtained difference) - (expected difference)}}{(\text{EST SE}_{\text{difference}})} = \frac{(110 - 141) - (0)}{10} = -3.1$$

9. D $P(z < -3.1) = .0010$ (This can be read directly from the z table)

10. B

---

11. B

12. A

13. A   For large samples such as this it isn't necessary to use $\hat{\sigma}$, we can just use the
                  sample SD in this formula:

$$\hat{\sigma}_{\overline{X}_A} = \text{EST SE}_A = \frac{SD_A}{\sqrt{n_A}} = \frac{48}{\sqrt{100}} = 4.8$$

14. C

$$\hat{\sigma}_{\overline{X}_B} = \text{EST SE}_B = \frac{SD_B}{\sqrt{n_B}} = \frac{24}{\sqrt{144}} = 2$$

15. D

$$\text{ESTSE}_{\overline{X}_A - \overline{X}_B} = \hat{\sigma}_{\overline{X}_A - \overline{X}_B} = \sqrt{(\text{EST SE}_A)^2 + (\text{EST SE}_B)^2} = \sqrt{(4.8)^2 + (2)^2} = 5.2$$

16. E

17. A   "obtained z" or "standardized difference" =

$$\frac{(\text{obtained difference}) - (\text{expected difference})}{(\text{EST SE}_{\text{difference}})} = \frac{(526 - 513) - (0)}{5.2} = +2.5$$

18. D $P(z > +2.5) = P(z < -2.5) = p = .0062$

19. B
----
20. C

21. B   For large samples such as this it isn't necessary to use $\hat{\sigma}$, we can just use the sample SD in this formula:

$$\hat{\sigma}_{\overline{X}_A} = \text{EST SE}_A = \frac{\text{SD}_A}{\sqrt{n_A}} = \frac{56}{\sqrt{49}} = 8$$

22. C

$$\hat{\sigma}_{\overline{X}_B} = \text{EST SE}_B = \frac{\text{SD}_B}{\sqrt{n_B}} = \frac{90}{\sqrt{36}} = 15 \text{, so}$$

$$\text{EST SE}_{\overline{X}_A - \overline{X}_B} = \hat{\sigma}_{\overline{X}_A - \overline{X}_B} = \sqrt{(\text{EST SE}_A)^2 + (\text{EST SE}_B)^2} = \sqrt{(8)^2 + (15)^2} = 17$$

23. A

24. E   The "obtained z" or "standardized difference" =

$$\frac{(\text{obtained difference}) - (\text{expected difference})}{(\text{EST SE}_{\text{difference}})} = \frac{(520 - 480) - (0)}{17} = +2.35$$

25. D $P(z > +2.35) = P(z < -2.35) = p = .0094$

26. B

14.4 TESTING HYPOTHESES ABOUT DIFFERENCES:
Small Independent Samples-- Two Group t-test

ASSUMPTIONS FOR THE 'POOLED VARIANCES' METHOD

When performing a hypothesis test on the difference between means, if either the sample size for Sample A or for Sample B (or both) is less than 30, we must follow one of the procedures for the *small sample* case.

It's usually reasonable to assume that the *variances* of the two groups being compared are equal. This assumption allows better, stronger hypothesis tests to be made. It comes up so often it has a well-known name:

Homogeneity of Variance assumption: Groups A and B *must have variances that are equal*. I.e. , σ^2_A and σ^2_B must be equal. (So the *standard deviations*, σ_A and σ_B, must of course also be equal.)

A procedure which produces the correct result, even when an assumption is violated, is called **robust** against violations of the assumption. The usual hypothesis testing procedure is known to be *robust* against violations of the homogeneity of variance assumption, when the sample sizes are close to equal. If you keep the sample sizes close to each other, you'll come to the right conclusion, even if the population variances differ.

If you know that the two population variances seem to be *different* and you need to use sample sizes that are *different*, you should do a test using *separate variance estimates*. (This test is not covered here, but it is available in most statistical software packages)

The pooled variance t test (also called 'equal variances' t test) described below will parallel the preceding Section 14.3, with the following exceptions:

1) Groups A and B *must* both be *approximately normal.*

> This assumption seems troublesome at first. If we have only drawn a random *sample* from each group, how can we be sure both *entire* groups have distributions which are approximately normal? It is generally considered sufficient if either
> - the distribution of scores in each sample is not too far from normal, or
> - previous experience with the variable among similar populations and being has produced approximately normal distributions.

2) The standardized difference between means has *approximately* a *t distribution*, with df (degrees of freedom) equal to $n_A + n_B - 2$.

3) The standard error of the difference is estimated using a pooled estimate of the population variance, as follows:

$$\textbf{(14.4.1) 'POOLED VARIANCE' ESTIMATE FOR } \sigma_{\bar{X}_A - \bar{X}_B}$$

$$\hat{\sigma}_{\bar{X}_A - \bar{X}_B} = \sqrt{\frac{\hat{\sigma}^2_{POOLED}}{n_A} + \frac{\hat{\sigma}^2_{POOLED}}{n_B}} = \sqrt{(\hat{\sigma}^2_{POOLED})\left(\frac{1}{n_A} + \frac{1}{n_B}\right)}$$

$$\text{Where } \hat{\sigma}^2_{POOLED} = \frac{SS_A + SS_B}{n_A + n_B - 2}$$

$\hat{\sigma}^2$POOLED , the 'pooled variance estimate', is the way you estimate *one* variance by combining data from *two* samples. $\hat{\sigma}^2$POOLED .may seem complicated at first, but it makes sense! Remember, we're assuming that there's just *one* variance for *both* groups, A and B. If we tried to estimate this variance using only the sample from Group A, we'd divide SS_A by the degrees of freedom for Sample A, which is n_A-1. Similarly, if we tried to estimate this variance using the sample from Group B, we'd divide SS_B by the degrees of freedom for Sample B, which is n_B-1

$\hat{\sigma}^2$POOLED just *combines* both of these estimates into one—we combine the sum of squares by *adding* them, and we combine the degrees of freedom by *adding* them as well:

$$(n_A - 1) + (n_B - 1) = n_A + n_B - 2$$

The following example is adapted from Example 1 in Section 14.1 above, except here the sample sizes are *small*. Differences between this example and the previous one are in **bold** print.

EXAMPLE 1: *TESTING "WILD TULIP" (SMALL INDEPENDENT SAMPLE VERSION)*

Suppose the director of the new unrated film "Wild Tulip" and the producer disagree about the ending of the film. The producer believes that typical audience members who view the film "Wild Tulip" with a "happy ending" added will rate it higher (and enjoy it more) than viewers who see the film with the original "sad ending" created by the director. They show two different preview audiences different versions of the film, one with each ending.

The director agrees to release the film with the "happy" ending only if it tests significantly higher than the film with her original, "sad" ending.

They obtain these data from random samples:

"Happy Ending ratings": $\bar{X}_A = 131$ $SS_A = 3000$ $n_A = 8$

"Sad Ending ratings": $\bar{X}_B = 100$ $SS_B = 5640$ $n_B = 12$

We'll assume that ***distributions of these test scores are well known to be approximately normal.***

The hypothesis test will be presented below in the complete outline form.

Note that this kind of test may be used in *any* situation in which an independent variable divides the **case**s into two groups and the dependent variable is interval scale--so it is very widely used!.

HYPOTHESIS TEST: DIFFERENCE BETWEEN MEANS   (**SMALL** SAMPLES)

EXAMPLE 1: TESTING "WILD TULIP"

GROUPS: (A) *All possible viewers of the film with the "happy" ending.*

(B) *All possible viewers of the film with the "sad" ending.*

SAMPLE SIZES: $n_A = $ **8** $n_B = $ **12**

VARIABLE: *Preference for the film, as measured on a standard rating scale*

STATISTIC: *The difference between the mean of group A and the mean of group B*

NULL HYPOTHESIS: $\mu_A - \mu_B = 0$.

ALTERNATE HYPOTHESIS $\mu_A - \mu_B > 0$ (or, "$\mu_A > \mu_B$ ")
(Because the burden of proof is on the producer here, who is trying to show that the "happy" ending gets *higher* ratings, on the average)

DISTRIBUTION OF SCORES IN THE POPULATION : (Assuming H_0 is true):
Both groups are approximately normal
Neither group mean is known.

OBSERVED VALUE OF THE STATISTIC BASED ON SAMPLE DATA:

$\overline{X}_A = $ **131** $\overline{X}_B = $ **100** ,

So the obtained difference, $\overline{X}_A - \overline{X}_B$ = **131 - 100 = 31**

$SS_A = $ **3000** $SS_B = $ **5640**

(Use the formulas below to *estimate* the *SE of the difference*)

$$\hat{\sigma}^2{}_{POOLED} = \frac{SS_A + SS_B}{n_A + n_B - 2} = \frac{3000 + 5640}{8 + 12 - 2} = 480$$

$$\hat{\sigma}_{\overline{X}_A - \overline{X}_B} = \sqrt{\frac{\hat{\sigma}^2{}_{POOLED}}{n_A} + \frac{\hat{\sigma}^2{}_{POOLED}}{n_B}} = \sqrt{(\hat{\sigma}^2{}_{POOLED})\left(\frac{1}{n_A} + \frac{1}{n_B}\right)} =$$

$$\hat{\sigma}_{\overline{X}_A - \overline{X}_B} = \sqrt{(480)\left(\frac{1}{8} + \frac{1}{12}\right)} = 10$$

SKETCH OF THE SAMPLING DISTRIBUTION OF THE DIFFERENCE, $\overline{X}_A - \overline{X}_B$
(Assuming H_0 is true)

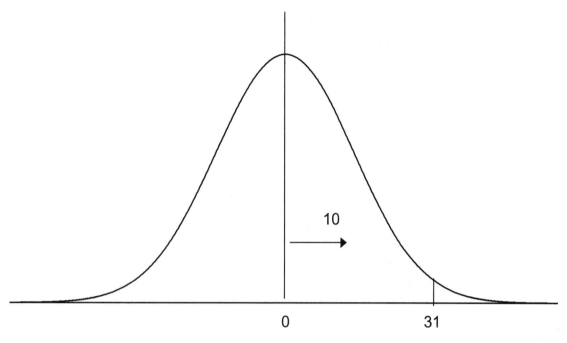

10

0   31

DIFFERENCE BETWEEN MEANS

TEST STATISTIC:

"obtained t" $= \dfrac{\text{(obtained difference)} - \text{(expected difference)}}{\hat{\sigma}_{\overline{X}_A - \overline{X}_B}} = \dfrac{(\overline{X}_A - \overline{X}_B) - (0)}{\hat{\sigma}_{\overline{X}_A - \overline{X}_B}}$

$= \dfrac{(131 - 100) - (0)}{10} = +3.1$

The standardized observed difference between sample means, assuming it came from the sampling distribution of the difference between means described in the previous question.

CRITICAL VALUE FOR t : *2.552*
(This is the positive one-tailed t value with a probability of .01. We use the positive value because the alternate hypothesis specified that the difference is *greater than* 0)

Degrees of freedom (df) for t: $n_A + n_B$ - 2

In this case n_A is 8 and n_B is 12 , so df $= 8 + 12 - 2 = 18$.

CAN WE REJECT THE NULL HYPOTHESIS AT THE .01 LEVEL?
Yes, because the obtained t value (+3.10) was more extreme than the critical value of t, (+2.552) so p is less than .01.

EXERCISES FOR CHAPTER 14, SECTION 14.4

---

1. Suppose the alternate hypothesis is: "The mean of Group A is greater than the mean of Pop. B."
Small samples of size *9* are drawn from each group. *Each group is approximately normal.*
   Sample A, from Group A, has a mean of 340 and a SD of 50.
   Sample B has a mean of 430 and a SD of 20.
  Based on the data above, we A) can reject the null hypothesis.   B) cannot reject the null hypothesis.

DR. JONES' DRINKING STUDY (SMALL SAMPLES)

Dr. Jones is trying to prove that *heavy* drinkers (Group A) score *lower* on the MAT, a memory test, than *light* drinker (Group B), on the average. She draws two samples of drinkers at random. (By the way, this is based on an actual study!)
Assume that each group is known to be approximately normal.

Sample A consists of 10 *heavy* drinkers. The drinkers in Sample A average 110 on the MAT. SS_A , the sample sum of squares for sample A is 2720.

Sample B consists of 20 *light* drinkers. The drinkers in Sample B average 125 on the MAT. SS_B , the sample sum of squares for sample B is 4000.

Assume that hypotheses about differences are stated in the usual order, i.e. "A - B", not "B - A".

2. The null hypothesis in this case states that the difference between the mean of ...
      A) Group A and the mean of Group B is equal to 0
      B) Sample A and the mean of Sample B is equal to 0
      C) Group A and the mean of Group B is less than 0
      D) Sample A and the mean of Sample B is less than 0
      E) None of the above is correct

3. The alternate hypothesis in this case states that the difference between the mean of ...
      (Use the answer choices from question 2)

4. The obtained difference (or sample difference) is...
      A) 15   B) -15   C) 10   D) 0   E) 42

5. The best pooled estimate of the population variance is...
      A) 48   B) 64   C) 10   D) 240   E) 80

6. The best estimate of the SE of the *difference* between means in this case is...
      A) 48   B) 42   C) 10   D) 8   E) 6

7. Assuming that the null hypothesis is true, we'd expect the sampling distribution of *differences* in this case to be _____ in shape, with a mean of ___ and a standard deviation estimated to be ___ .
(Note that this question is asking about the *sampling* distribution.)
      A) approximately normal, 0, 6
      B) approximately normal, 31, 6
      C) approximately normal, -31, 6
      D) approximately normal, 0, 15
      E) exactly normal, 0, 1

8. What standard score (or "t-score") corresponds to the *difference* between the mean of Sample A and the mean of Sample B in this case? I.e., what is "obtained t"?

   A) 3.1 B) -3.1 C) 2.5 D) -2.5 E) -31

9. How many degrees of freedom (df) are appropriate in this case?

   A) 8 B) 9 C) 16 D) 28 E) none of the above

10. What is the critical value for t? I.e., what is the value of *t* such that the probability of obtaining a t value more extreme is less than .01?

   A) -2.896 B) -2.821 C) -2.467 D) 3.355 E) 2.896

11. Can Dr. Jones reject the null hypothesis? (at the usual .01 level of significance)

   A) Yes, because *p* is greater than .01
   B) Yes, because *p* is less than .01.
   C) No, because *p* is less than .01
   D) No, because *p* is greater than .01
   E) None of the above is correct.

DR. BROTHERS' REVIEW (SMALL SAMPLES)

Dr. Brothers is trying to prove that high school juniors who *attend* her review class (Group A) score *higher* than high school juniors who *don't attend* her review class (Group B), on the average.

She draws two samples of students at random:
 Sample A, consisting of 25 students, is given her review class.
 The students in Sample A average 526.4 on the SAT, with $SS_A = 4000$

 Sample B, consisting of 16 students, is *not* given her review class.
 The students in Sample B average 510 on the SAT, with $SS_B = 2396$

NOTE: You may assume that differences are stated in the usual order: "A - B", not "B - A".

  Assume that each group is known to be approximately normal.

12. The null hypothesis in this case states that the difference between the mean of ...

   A) Group A and the mean of Group B is greater than 0
   B) Group A and the mean of Group B is equal to 0
   C) Sample A and the mean of Sample B is greater than 0
   D) Sample A and the mean of Sample B is equal to 0
   E) None of the above is correct

13. The alternate hypothesis in this case states that the difference between the mean of ...
   (Use the answer choices from the previous question)

14. The obtained difference (or sample difference) is...

   A) 16.4 B) -15 C) 10 D) 0 E) -16.4

15. The best *pooled* estimate of the population variance is...
      A) 48   B) 64   C) 164   D) 240   E) 80

16. The best estimate of the SE of the *difference* between means in this case is...
      A) 4.8   B) 4.1   C) 10   D) 8   E) 6

17. Assuming that the null hypothesis is true, we'd expect the sampling distribution of *differences between means* in this case to be _____ in shape, with a mean of ___ and a standard deviation of ____ . (Note that this question is asking about the *sampling* distribution.)
      A) exactly normal, 513, 5.2
      B) approximately normal, 526, 10.4
      C) exactly normal, 0, 5.2
      D) approximately normal, 0, 10.4
      E) approximately normal, 0, 4.1

18. What standard score (or "t-score") corresponds to the *difference* between the mean of Sample A and the mean of Sample B in this case?
      A) 2.5   B) -4.0   C) 1.25   D) -5   E) 4

19. How many degrees of freedom (df) are appropriate in this case?
      A) 41   B) 40   C) 39   D) 15   E) none of the above

20. What is the critical value for t? I.e., what is the value of t such that the probability of obtaining a t value more extreme is less than .01?
      A) 2.896   B) 2.821   C) 2.457   D) 2.423   E) 2.602

21. Can Dr. Brothers reject the null hypothesis? (at the usual .01 level of significance)
      A) Yes, because *p* is greater than .01
      B) Yes, because *p* is less than .01.
      C) No, because *p* is less than .01
      D) No, because *p* is greater than .01
      E) None of the above is correct.

DR. DRISTAN'S ALLERGY STUDY (SMALL SAMPLES)

Dr. Dristan is trying to prove that students with *allergies* (Group A) score *higher* on the Math SAT than students without allergies (Group B), on the average.

She draws two samples at random:
Sample A consists of 10 students with allergies.
    The students in Sample A average 560 on the Math SAT, with SS_A = 68,000
Sample B consists of 20 students without allergies.
    The students in Sample B average 500 on the Math SAT , with SS_B = 100,000

NOTE: You may assume that differences are computed in the usual order, i.e. "A - B", not "B - A".

    Assume that each group is known to be approximately normal.

22. The alternate hypothesis in this case states that the difference between the mean of ...
        A) Group A and the mean of Group B is equal to 0
        B) Sample A and the mean of Sample B is equal to 0
        C) Group A and the mean of Group B is greater than 0
        D) Sample A and the mean of Sample B is greater than 0
        E) None of the above is correct

23. The best pooled estimate of population variance in this case is.
        A) 30   B) 6,000   C) 400   D) 6   E) 10

24. The best estimate of the SE of the *difference* between means in this case is...
        A) 15   B) 40   C) 50   D) 8   E) 30

25. Assuming that the null hypothesis is true, we'd expect the sampling distribution of *differences* between means in this case to be _____ in shape, with a mean of ___ and a standard deviation of _____ .
(Note that this question is asking about the *sampling* distribution of differences between means)
        A) approximately normal, 60, 30
        B) approximately normal, 60, 10
        C) approximately normal, 0, 30
        D) approximately normal, 0, 10
        E) exactly normal, 0, 1

26. What standard score (or "t-score") corresponds to the *difference* between the mean of Sample A and the mean of Sample B in this case?
        A) 0   B) -2.0   C) 2.0   D) -2.35   E) +2.35

27. What is the critical value for t? I.e., what is the value of t such that the probability of obtaining a t value more extreme is less than .01?
        A) 2.896   B) 5.841   C) 4.541   D) 2.467   E) 2.602

28. Can Dr. Dristan reject the null hypothesis? (at the usual .01 level of significance)
        A) Yes, because p is greater than .01
        B) Yes, because p is less than .01.
        C) No, because p is less than .01
        D) No, because p is greater than .01
        E) None of the above is correct.

----

29. In the above examples, the sampling distribution for the difference was *approximately normal*, yet the test statistic used was "*obtained t*", not "obtained z" Why?"
        A) The *standardized sample difference* has an approximately t-shaped distribution *not* an approximately normal distribution.
           (Because two standard deviations are *estimated* in its computation)
        B) Carelessness!
        C) Why ask why?

ANSWERS TO EXERCISES FOR SECTION 14.4

----

1. B   The sample mean for A is *less than* the sample mean for B.
                 You're trying to prove that the population mean of A is *greater than* the mean of B.
                 The data do not support the hypothesis you're trying to prove!

DR JONES:

2. A

3. E H_1 is "The mean of Group A is *less than* the mean of Group B"

4. B

5. D $\hat{\sigma}^2{}_{\text{POOLED}} = \dfrac{SS_A + SS_B}{n_A + n_B - 2} = \dfrac{2720 + 4000}{10 + 20 - 2} = 240$

6. E $\text{EST } SE_{A\text{-}B} \text{ or } SE_{\text{difference}} =$

$$\hat{\sigma}_{\bar{X}_A - \bar{X}_B} = \sqrt{\dfrac{\hat{\sigma}^2{}_{\text{POOLED}}}{n_A} + \dfrac{\hat{\sigma}^2{}_{\text{POOLED}}}{n_B}} = \sqrt{(\hat{\sigma}^2{}_{\text{POOLED}})\left(\dfrac{1}{n_A} + \dfrac{1}{n_B}\right)} = \sqrt{(240)\left(\dfrac{1}{10} + \dfrac{1}{20}\right)} = 6$$

7. A

8. D   "obtained t" or "standardized difference" =

$$\frac{\text{(obtained difference)} - \text{(expected difference)}}{\text{(EST SE}_{\text{difference}})} = \frac{(-15-0)}{6} = -2.5$$

9. D $n_A = 10$ and $n_B = 20$, so df $= n_A + n_B - 2 = 28$

10. C   We use -2.467 because the alternate hypothesis specifies "less than"

11. B

DR BROTHERS

12. B

13. A

14. A

15. C $$\hat{\sigma}^2{}_{\text{POOLED}} = \frac{SS_A + SS_B}{n_A + n_B - 2} = \frac{2396 + 4000}{16 + 25 - 2} = 164$$

16. B

EST SE$_{\text{A-B}}$ or SE$_{\text{difference}}$ =

$$\hat{\sigma}_{\bar{X}_A - \bar{X}_B} = \sqrt{(\hat{\sigma}^2{}_{\text{POOLED}})\left(\frac{1}{n_A} + \frac{1}{n_B}\right)} = \sqrt{(164)\left(\frac{1}{16} + \frac{1}{25}\right)} = 4.1$$

17. E

18. E   "obtained t" or "standardized difference" =

$$\frac{\text{(obtained difference)} - \text{(expected difference)}}{\text{(EST SE}_{\text{difference}})} = \frac{(526.4 - 510) - (0)}{4.1} = +4.0$$

19. C $25 + 16 - 2 = 39$

20. C   39 df (Rounded *down* to 30), .01, one-tailed

21. B

DR DRISTAN:

22. C

23. B
$$\hat{\sigma}^2_{POOLED} = \frac{SS_A + SS_B}{n_A + n_B - 2} = \frac{68,000 + 100,000}{10 + 20 - 2} = 6000$$

24. E

EST SE_{A-B} or $SE_{difference}$ =

$$\hat{\sigma}_{\bar{X}_A - \bar{X}_B} = \sqrt{(\hat{\sigma}^2_{POOLED})\left(\frac{1}{n_A} + \frac{1}{n_B}\right)} = \sqrt{(6000)\left(\frac{1}{10} + \frac{1}{20}\right)} = 30$$

25. C

26. C

The "obtained t" or "standardized difference" =

$$\frac{(obtained\ difference) - (expected\ difference)}{(EST\ SE_{difference})} = \frac{(560 - 500)}{30} = +2..0$$

27. D   (df = 28)

28. D

---

29. A

14.5 TESTING HYPOTHESES ABOUT DIFFERENCES: DEPENDENT SAMPLES
(Repeated Measures Designs, 'Within subjects' Designs)

REPEATED MEASURES DESIGNS

Sections 14.3 and 14.4 covered small and large samples in which each case is in one group and is measured only once. There's another common situation in which we deal with two sets of scores and are interested in the difference, but the scores are generated by measuring each case *twice*.

The experimental designs typically are carried out this way:

1) Subjects are measured on the variable of interest before some treatment.
   (This is called a *pretest*)

2) Subjects are exposed to some treatment

3) Subjects are then measured again on the variable of interest.
   (This is called a *posttest*)

Each subject's difference between pretest and posttest scores is then computed, and the set of difference scores is analyzed statistically. For example, if the difference scores are all positive, you may argue that the treatment seems to cause an increase in the dependent variable. This specific design is often called a *pretest-posttest design*.

Sometimes each subject is measured only once, but before any assessment on the dependent variable, the subjects are 'matched' on some other possible variables to minimize confounding. In this case the matched pair of subjects is treated as if they constituted one case. One subject gets the treatment, and one doesn't. We subtract one score from the other to get a *difference score*. For example we may link Subject A and Subject B because they match on gender, age, severity of illness etc. and then give Subject A a drug and Subject B a placebo. Afterward we compute the difference between Subject A and Subject B's scores on the dependent variable 'Improvement'. Since the subjects were *matched*, the differences between their levels of improvement will show *less confounding* with the extraneous variables gender age, ethnicity, etc.

Designs like these are called *repeated measures designs* (because the measurements are repeated), *within subjects designs* (because the differences we see are caused by differences within the subjects, not between groups of different subjects) or most generally , *dependent samples designs*, because the first and second measurements are made on subjects who are either identical or matched.

Luckily, the statistical analysis of differences from repeated measures designs is simple! Once you have computed the differences, you can do a hypothesis test on the differences as if they were based on just one group of scores, using one-group techniques covered in the previous chapter (12.5 and 12.6)

EXAMPLE 1: "GOIN' TO THE CITY! ASSESSING A <u>CHANGE</u> IN HAPPINESS (Small n)

Suppose that Dr. Altoni is trying to show that people who move to New York from the Midwest generally are *less happy* after moving than those same people were *before* moving.

Dr. Altoni picks a random sample from a large group of people from the Midwest who plan to move to NY. Dr. Altoni measures their happiness *before* and *after* moving to New York. The results are summarized below, where the variable X_A represents is the movers' score on a Happiness Scale *before* moving and the variable X_B represents the same movers' scores *after* six months in New York. Suppose that the variable X is known to be approximately normal.

ID	X_A	X_B	D
Al	66	60	-6
Ben	60	54	-6
Cal	46	40	-6
Deb	52	38	-14

NOTE: $\overline{D}$ = -8 and the SS for D is 48.

The mean of the variable D, $\overline{D}$, is -8 and the SS for the variable D is 48. This is a *small sample*, so to estimate the population standard deviation σ, we must divide by n-1:

$$\hat{\sigma}_D = \sqrt{\frac{SS_D}{n-1}} = \sqrt{\frac{48}{4-1}} = 4$$

We use the estimate of the standard deviation of D to estimate the standard error of $\overline{D}$.

$$\hat{\sigma}_{\overline{D}} = \frac{\hat{\sigma}_D}{\sqrt{n}} = \frac{4}{\sqrt{4}} = 2$$

If the null hypothesis is true, we'd expect a typical difference to be 0, so we'd estimate that the sampling distribution of differences would have a mean of zero and a standard deviation of 2.

We *standardize* our obtained difference of -8:

$$\text{STD. } \overline{D} = \frac{\overline{D} - \mu_{\overline{D}}}{\hat{\sigma}_{\overline{D}}} = \frac{(-8) - (0)}{2} = -4$$

Using the t distribution, we find that the t critical value for 3 degrees of freedom is -4.541. We *cannot* reject the null hypothesis. We'd say "The obtained t value is closer to 0 than the t critical value is, so *p* is *not* less than .01, and we *can't reject* the null hypothesis."

EXAMPLE 2 *(Large n)*

Dr. Jones is trying to show that Drug A causes a *decrease* in cholesterol. She measures 100 subjects, then gives them all the drug treatment, then measures them again, after the drug has supposedly produced its effect. Dr Jones subtracts each subject's pretest score from the subject's posttest score to obtain a difference score, D. The mean of all the differences is -15 and the SD of all the differences is 60. Is this convincing evidence that there would be a population difference less than zero? That is can we reject the null hypothesis that the population difference is 0?

Answer: Yes.

We estimate the standard error of the differences to be

$$\hat{\sigma}_{\overline{D}} = \frac{SD_D}{\sqrt{n}} = \frac{60}{\sqrt{100}} = 6$$

We *obtained* a difference of -15 from our sample, and we would *expect* a difference of zero if the null hypothesis is true. Therefore the standardized difference is

$$STD.\ \overline{D} = \frac{\overline{D} - \mu_{\overline{D}}}{\hat{\sigma}_{\overline{D}}} = \frac{(-15) - (0)}{6} = -2..5$$

Using the normal approximation, we conclude that $p = .0062$, and we can reject the null hypothesis

EXERCISES FOR SECTION 14.5

COULD THIS BE PROZAC?

A researcher is trying to prove that depression gets reduced by a new treatment. She uses a *pretest-posttest* design. X_A represents the *pretest* depression scores for 4 subjects. X_B represents the *posttest* depression scores for *the same* 4 subjects, after they receive the new treatment. Assume that the variable X is approximately normal.

ID	X_A	X_B
Al	66	60
Ben	60	54
Cal	74	60
Deb	72	66

1. This type of design is also referred to as a _____ design. (read all answers)
   A) within subjects   B) repeated-measures
   C) dependent samples   D) all of the above are correct
   E) none of the above are correct

2. Suppose that the new treatment *works*; that is it *reduces* depression. If you compute the new variable, $D = X_B - X_A$ as usual in this case, would you expect the variable D to have a mean that is *greater than* zero or *less than* zero?
   A) *greater than* zero   B) *less than* zero

3. The alternate hypothesis is "The mean of all *differences* in the population is" (or "$\mu_{\overline{D}}$ is")
   A) less than zero   B) greater than zero   C) equal to zero

4. If the null hypothesis is true, what is $\mu_{\overline{D}}$?
   A) less than zero   B) greater than zero   C) equal to zero

5. What is $\overline{D}$ in this sample? What is the mean of all differences?
   A) 0   B) -8   C) -6   D) -4   E) 6

6. What is the best estimate of the standard error of the statistic $\overline{D}$ based on this sample? What is $\hat{\sigma}_{\overline{D}}$?
   A) 0   B) 2   C) 4   D) 6   E) 8

7. What is "STD $\overline{D}$"? (OR, "obtained t")
   What do you get when you standardize the mean of the sample differences?
   A) -6   B) -4   C) -3   D) -1.5   E) -1

8. What is the t critical value?
   A) -4.541   B) -5.841   C) -3.747   D) -4.604

9. Therefore, Dr. D ... the null hypothesis at the .01 significance level, because *p* is ...
   A) can reject, less than .01   C) can reject, greater than .01
   B) can't reject, less than .01   D) can't reject, greater than .01

PRACTICE MAKES PERFECT

X_A	X_B	$D = X_B - X_A$
502	505	+3
etc.	etc.	etc.

Suppose that 16 subjects are measured on the variable X (Say, a SAT test). Then they're given a treatment which is supposed to *increase* scores on the variable X.(An SAT review course) Then they're measured again on the variable X.(They *retake* the SAT.)

The format of the data obtained is described in TABLE 1 above. For each subject, we compute a difference, D, by subtracting the subject's second score from the subject's first score.

Suppose we're trying to prove that the mean of all *differences* in the *population* is greater than zero. That is, the alternate hypothesis is $H_1 : \mu_D > 0$

Suppose that the variable X is known to be approximately normal.

In a random sample of size **16** the mean of the differences, $\overline{D}$, is **6** and $\hat{\sigma}_D$ **is 8.0**.

10. The standard error of $\overline{D}$ in this situation is approximately…

(Or, $\hat{\sigma}_{\overline{D}}$ is equal to…)

A) 1   B) 2   C) 4

11. The standardized mean, STD $\overline{D}$, is

A) 2   B) 3   C) 4   E) 8

12. The t critical value is

A) 2.602   B) 2.584   C) 2.947   E) 2.921

13. Based *only on the information provided above*, we _____reject the null hypothesis in favor of this alternate hypothesis, because *p* is _____.

A) can reject, less than .01   C) can reject, greater than .01
B) can't reject, less than .01   D) can't reject, greater than .01

LESS THAN ZERO?

	X1 (PRETEST)	X2 (POSTTEST)	D (DIFFERENCE)
AL	34	30	-4
BO	21	13	-8
CAROL	10	6	-4
DEE	42	30	-12
ED	30	18	-12

H_0: $\mu_D = 0$ H_1: $\mu_D < 0$

14. Just by looking at the data format above, we can tell that this is an example of a _____
   A) repeated measures (or 'within subjects') design
   B) between groups design
   C) posttest only design

15. If the null hypothesis is true, what is $\mu_{\overline{D}}$?

   A) less than zero   B) greater than zero   C) equal to zero

16. What is $\overline{D}$ in this sample? What is the mean of all differences?
   A) 0   B) -8   C) -6   D) -4   E) -6

17. What is the best estimate of σ_D, the standard deviation of all the variable D, based on this sample? (Or, what is $\hat{\sigma}_D$?)
   A) 0   B) 2   C) 4   D) 1.79   E) 8

18. What is the best estimate of the standard error of the statistic $\overline{D}$ based on this sample? (Or, what is $\hat{\sigma}_{\overline{D}}$?)
   A) 0   B) 2   C) 4   D) 1.79   E) 8

19. What is "STD $\overline{D}$"? (OR, "obtained t")
   What do you get when you *standardize* the mean of the sample differences?
      A) -6   B) -4   C) -3.35   D) -1.5   E) -4.47

20. What is the t critical value?
      A) -4.541   B) -5.841   C) -3.747   D) -4.604   E) -3.365

21. Therefore, we ... the null hypothesis at the .01 significance level, because *p* is ...
   A) can reject, less than .01   C) can reject, greater than .01
   B) can't reject, less than .01   D) can't reject, greater than .01

REVERSAL OF OPINION?

Suppose Dr. Altville wants to assess the *change* in people's ratings of the President after the President's address. Dr Altville asks **64** voters to rate the President *twice*: once on the night *before* the President's speech (X_A), then again on the day *after* the President's speech (X_B). For each subject, the rating on the day after is subtracted from the rating on the day before, producing a *difference score*.($D = X_B - X_A$)

Dr. Altville is trying to prove that the mean difference in the population is **less than zero**.

Suppose the mean of the differences in the sample is $\overline{D} = -8$ and

the best estimate of the standard deviation of all differences is $\hat{\sigma}_D = 24$

22. The appropriate hypothesis test in this case is called a _____ test.
    A) between groups
    B) repeated measures or dependent samples
    C) factorial

23. Estimate the *standard error of the mean* (for the variable D), $\hat{\sigma}_{\overline{D}}$.
    A) 24   B) .612   C) 1   D) .375   E) 3

24. What is the *standardized sample mean (for the variable D)*
    A) -2.67   B) -2.33   C) -.67   D) -2.0   E) 2.67

25. Therefore, Dr. Altville ... the null hypothesis at the .01 significance level, because *p* is ...
    A) can reject, less than .01   C) can reject, greater than .01
    B) can't reject, less than .01   D) can't reject, greater than .01

ANSWERS TO EXERCISES FOR SECTION 14.5

COULD THIS BE PROZAC?

The same set of subjects is measured *twice* in this case. There's only one hypothesis test we've covered like this-- the "Dependent Samples t-test" in Section 14.5. (See 3-5 above for computations)

1. D

2. B

3. A

4. C

5. B

6. B

7. B

8. A

9. D

PRACTICE MAKES PERFECT

The same set of subjects is measured *twice* in this case. There's only one hypothesis test we've covered like this-- the "Dependent Samples t-test" in 14.5.

10. B

11. B

12. A

13 A

LESS THAN ZERO?

The same set of subjects is measured *twice* in this case.

14. A

15. C

16. B

17. C

18. D

19. E

20. C

21. A

The same set of subjects is measured *twice* in this case. There's only one hypothesis test we've covered like this-- the "Dependent Samples" in 14.5.

22. B   The voters give us their ratings *twice*.

23. E $$\hat{\sigma}_{\overline{D}} = \frac{\hat{\sigma}_D}{\sqrt{n}} = \frac{24}{\sqrt{64}} = 3$$

24. A $$\frac{-8 - 0}{3} = -2.67$$

25. A   Using the z table, we estimate that $p \approx .0028$

14.6* DIFFERENCES BETWEEN PROPORTIONS

THE SAMPLING DISTRIBUTION OF $\hat{p}_A - \hat{p}_B$

The sampling distribution of the *difference* between proportions can be easily described when the proportions of both groups are *known*:

(14.6.1) Suppose two random samples of sizes n_A and n_B are drawn from the "0,1" groups A and B.
p_A and p_B, the groups' proportions are known.

The sampling distribution of $\hat{p}_A - \hat{p}_B$, the *difference* between sample proportions,

1) will be approximately normal if n_A and n_B are both large (> 30)
2) Has a mean, denoted $\mu_{\hat{p}_A - \hat{p}_B}$, equal to $p_A - p_B$
    (Also denoted "$E_{difference}$" or "Expected difference)
3) Has a standard deviation, denoted $\sigma_{\hat{p}_A - \hat{p}_B}$, equal to

$$SE_{difference} = \sqrt{(\sigma_{p_A})^2 + (\sigma_{p_B})^2} = \sqrt{\frac{(p_A)(1 - p_A)}{n_A} + \frac{(p_B)(1 - p_B)}{n_B}}$$

(Also denoted "Standard Error of the difference")

EXAMPLE
Suppose you are given the following information about groups A and B:

$$p_A = .64 \qquad p_B = .80$$
$$n_A = 256 \qquad n_B = 100$$

That is, a sample of size 256 is drawn from group A, which has a proportion known to be .64. Another sample of size 100 is drawn from group B, which has a proportion of .8.

A) Describe the sampling distribution of $\hat{p}_A - \hat{p}_B$, the "difference between sample proportions".

B) What is the probability that $\hat{p}_A - \hat{p}_B$ is greater than 0?

C) What is the probability that $\hat{p}_A - \hat{p}_B$ is less than -.285?

D) Suppose the actual samples have these proportions: $\hat{p}_A = .54$ $\hat{p}_B = .85$

Compute *all three* chance errors that are relevant in this example.

Is the chance error of $\hat{p}_A - \hat{p}_B$ *larger* or *smaller* than you would have expected?

ANSWERS

A) Approximately normal (because both sample sizes are over 30), with a mean of -.16 and a standard deviation of .05.

The mean, $\mu_{\hat{p}_A - \hat{p}_B}$, or expected value of $\hat{p}_A - \hat{p}_B$ is $p_A - p_B = .64 - .8 = -.16$

The standard deviation, $\sigma_{\hat{p}_A - \hat{p}_B}$, or standard error of $\hat{p}_A - \hat{p}_B$ is

$$\sqrt{(\sigma_{\hat{p}_A})^2 + (\sigma_{\hat{p}_B})^2} = \sqrt{\frac{(p_A)(1-p_A)}{n_A} + \frac{(p_B)(1-p_B)}{n_B}} = \sqrt{\frac{(.64)(.36)}{256} + \frac{(.8)(.2)}{100}} = .05$$

SKETCH: SAMPLING DISTRIBUTION OF THE DIFFERENCE, $\hat{p}_A - \hat{p}_B$

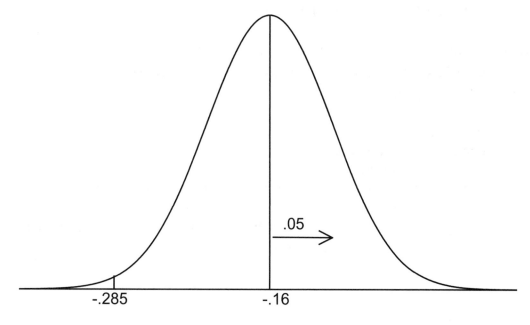

.05

-.285   -.16

DIFFERENCE BETWEEN SAMPLE PROPORTIONS

$\hat{p}_A - \hat{p}_B$

B) .0007

P(difference > 0) can be estimated using P(z > 3.2) = .0007, because

Standardized difference $= \dfrac{(0)-(-.16)}{.05} = 3.2$

C) P(difference < -.285) can be estimated using P(z < -2.5) = .0062, because

Standardized difference $= \dfrac{(-.285)-(-.16)}{.05} = -2.5$

D) The chance error of $\hat{p}_A$ is -.10, because $\hat{p}_A$ - p_A = .54 - .64 = -.10

The chance error of $\hat{p}_B$ is +.05, because $\hat{p}_B$ - p_B = .85 - .80 = +.05

The "obtained" value of $\hat{p}_A$ - $\hat{p}_B$ from the samples is .54 - .85 = -.31, and we know that the "expected" value is p_A - p_B = .64 - .80 = -.16.

Therefore, the *chance error* of $\hat{p}_A$ - $\hat{p}_B$ is

(OBTAINED Difference) - (EXPECTED Difference) =

($\hat{p}_A$ - $\hat{p}_B$) - (p_A - p_B) = -.31 - (-.16) = -.15

This *chance* error of $\hat{p}_A$ - $\hat{p}_B$, (-.15), is *negative,* and *three times greater in size* than the *standard* error of $\hat{p}_A$ - $\hat{p}_B$ (which was .05, computed above), so it's much larger (in size) than you'd typically expect it to be.

We'd summarize these results informally this way:

Sample A's proportion was .10 *lower* than expected. (.54 obtained vs. .64 expected)

Sample B's proportion was .05 *higher* than expected. (.85 obtained vs. .80 expected)

$\hat{p}_A$ - $\hat{p}_B$, the *obtained difference* between the proportions, was *negative,* and .15 *greater in size* than expected

TESTING HYPOTHESES ABOUT $p_A - p_B$ (LARGE SAMPLES)

In testing hypotheses about group differences in proportions, we must estimate the standard error of the difference based on sample data. As was the case for differences between means, the formula is not difficult, but the test statistic may not have a nicely shaped distribution when the sample sizes are small. When both samples are large, however, the "standardized difference between sample proportions" has approximately a standard normal distribution, allowing the usual approximation to be used with confidence.

Here's how the standard error of the difference between proportions is *estimated* from sample data (when sample sizes are large).

(14.6.2) ESTIMATING $\sigma_{\hat{p}_A - \hat{p}_B}$ **, the Standard Error of** $\hat{p}_A - \hat{p}_B$

When n_A **and** n_B **are *large*,** $\sigma_{\hat{p}_A - \hat{p}_B}$ **may be *estimated* by computing**

$$\sqrt{(\text{EST } \sigma_{\hat{p}_A})^2 + (\text{EST } \sigma_{\hat{p}_B})^2} = \sqrt{\frac{(\hat{p}_A)(1 - \hat{p}_A)}{n_A} + \frac{(\hat{p}_B)(1 - \hat{p}_B)}{n_B}}$$

In other words, you just use the sample proportion, $\hat{p}$, for each sample as if it were the group proportion, p.

EXAMPLE 1: *GENDER AND COMPUTER USE*
(From the optional supplementary text, *Statistics*, by FPP, *Example 3* on p.459)

Suppose you are trying to prove that the proportion of male students (Group A) who use computers on a regular basis is higher than the proportion of female students (Group B) who use computers on a regular basis.

You obtain these data from random samples:

Male Students: $\hat{p}_A = 107/200 = .535$ $\qquad n_A = 200$

Female Students: $\hat{p}_B = 132/300 = .44$ $\qquad n_B = 300$

I.e., 107 of the 200 males sampled used computers regularly, 132 of 300 females used computers regularly.

The hypothesis test will be presented here in the usual complete outline form.

HYPOTHESIS TEST: DIFFERENCE BETWEEN PROPORTIONS
(LARGE SAMPLES)

EXAMPLE 1: *GENDER AND COMPUTER USE*

GROUPS: (A) *Male students at a large university who agree to be polled*
             (B) *Female students at a large university who agree to be polled*

SAMPLE SIZES: $n_A = 200$ $n_B = 300$

VARIABLE: *Whether the student reports using computers regularly*
              (This will always be a nominal scale, dichotomous, variable. I.e., one
              with two categories, a "0, 1" variable)

A CASE WILL COUNT AS A SUCCESS, or "1",   IF

The student does use computers regularly

A CASE WILL COUNT AS A FAILURE, or "0",   IF

The student does not use computers regularly

STATISTIC: *The difference between the proportion of group A and the proportion of group B*

NULL HYPOTHESIS: $p_A - p_B = 0$.
              (We assume that people would expect *no* difference between
              proportions, before our study)

ALTERNATE HYPOTHESIS: $p_A - p_B > 0$ (or, "$p_A > p_B$")

DISTRIBUTION OF SCORES IN THE POPULATION: (Assuming H_0 is true): *unknown*
              (Nothing need be assumed about the groups except that they each make
              up a 0,1 population, and the *difference* between their proportions is 0)

OBSERVED VALUE OF THE STATISTIC BASED ON YOUR SAMPLES:

        $\hat{p}_A = .535$ $\hat{p}_B = .44$, *So the obtained difference,* $\hat{p}_A - \hat{p}_B = +.095$

SAMPLING DISTRIBUTION OF THE DIFFERENCE, $\hat{p}_A - \hat{p}_B$
(Assuming H_0 is true)

SHAPE: *Approximately Normal*
(Because the sample sizes are large)

MEAN, $\mu_{\hat{p}_A - \hat{p}_B}$: *0*

(The e*xpected value of the difference*. It's 0 because the null hypothesis specified that the difference is 0)

STANDARD DEVIATION, $\sigma_{\hat{p}_A - \hat{p}_B}$: *Estimated to be .045*

(We use the formulas below to estimate the *SE of the difference,)*

EST $\sigma_{\hat{p}_A - \hat{p}_B}$ = EST $SE_{\text{difference}}$ =

$$\sqrt{(EST\ \sigma_{\hat{p}_A})^2 + (EST\ \sigma_{\hat{p}_B})^2} = \sqrt{\frac{(\hat{p}_A)(1-\hat{p}_A)}{n_A} + \frac{(\hat{p}_B)(1-\hat{p}_B)}{n_B}} = \sqrt{\frac{(.535)(1-.535)}{200} + \frac{(.44)(1-.44)}{300}} = .045$$

SKETCH OF THE SAMPLING DISTRIBUTION OF THE DIFFERENCE, $\hat{p}_A - \hat{p}_B$
(Assuming H_0 is true)

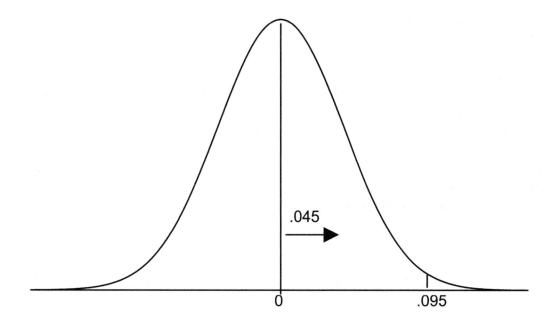

.045

0   .095

DIFFERENCE BETWEEN SAMPLE PROPORTIONS

TEST STATISTIC:

"obtained z" $= \dfrac{\text{(obtained difference)} - \text{(expected difference)}}{(\text{EST } SE_{\text{difference}})} = \dfrac{(\hat{p}_A - \hat{p}_B) - (0)}{(\text{EST } SE_{\text{difference}})}$

$$= \frac{(.535 - .44) - (0)}{.045} = \frac{.095}{.045} = +2.1$$

(We standardize the observed difference between sample proportions, assuming it came from the sampling distribution of the difference between proportions sketched above)

OBSERVED SIGNIFICANCE LEVEL: $p = .0179$

Our alternate hypothesis specified ">", so this is P(z > "obtained z") = P(z > 2.1)

CAN YOU REJECT THE NULL HYPOTHESIS AT THE .01 LEVEL?   *No*
("No", because *p* is *not* less than .01.)

EXAMPLE 2: *"WILD TULIP II" : TESTS USING PROPORTIONS*

Suppose the director of the new unrated film "Wild Tulip" and the producer disagree about the ending of the film. The producer believes that typical audience members who view the film "Wild Tulip" with a "happy ending" added will be *more likely to recommend it to others* than viewers who see the film with the original "sad ending" created by the director. They show two different preview audiences different versions of the film, one with each ending.

The director agrees to release the film with the "happy" ending only if a significantly higher proportion of test viewers who view the film with the "happy ending" report that they would recommend the film to others. (compared to the "sad ending".)

They obtain these data from random samples:

"Happy Ending ratings": $\hat{p}_A = 42/49 = .8571$ $n_A = 49, \ k_A = 42$

"Sad Ending ratings": $\hat{p}_B = 64/100 = .64$ $n_B = 100, \ k_B = 64$

The hypothesis test will be presented here in the complete outline form.

HYPOTHESIS TEST: DIFFERENCE BETWEEN PROPORTIONS
(LARGE SAMPLES)

EXAMPLE 2: *WILD TULIP II*

GROUPS: (A) *Preview viewers who see "Wild Tulip" with a happy ending*
          (B) *Preview viewers who see "Wild Tulip" with a sad ending*

SAMPLE SIZES: $n_A = 49$ $n_B = 100$

VARIABLE: *Whether the viewer states "I would recommend the film to others"*
          (This will always be a nominal scale, dichotomous, variable. I.e., one with two categories, a "0, 1" variable)

AN CASE WILL COUNT AS A SUCCESS, or "1", IF

      The viewer would recommend the film

AN CASE WILL COUNT AS A FAILURE, or "0", IF

      The viewer would not recommend the film

STATISTIC: *The difference between the proportion of group A and the proportion of group B*

NULL HYPOTHESIS: $p_A - p_B = 0.$

ALTERNATE HYPOTHESIS: $p_A - p_B > 0$ (or, "$p_A > p_B$ ")

DISTRIBUTION OF SCORES IN THE POPULATION: (Assuming H_0 is true): *unknown*
          (Nothing need be assumed about the groups in the population except that the *difference* between their proportions is 0)

OBSERVED VALUE OF THE STATISTIC BASED ON YOUR SAMPLES:

      $\hat{p}_A = .8571$ $\hat{p}_B = .64,$ *So the obtained difference,* $\hat{p}_A - \hat{p}_B = +.2171$

SAMPLING DISTRIBUTION OF THE DIFFERENCE, $\hat{p}_A - \hat{p}_B$
(Assuming H_0 is true)

SHAPE: *Approximately Normal*
(Because the sample sizes are large)

MEAN, $\mu_{\hat{p}_A - \hat{p}_B}$: *0*
(The e*xpected value of the difference.* It's 0 because the null hypothesis specified that the difference is 0)

STANDARD DEVIATION, $\sigma_{\hat{p}_A - \hat{p}_B}$: *Estimated to be .0693*
(We use the formulas below to estimate the *SE of the difference,*)

EST $\sigma_{\hat{p}_A - \hat{p}_B}$ = EST SE$_{\text{difference}}$ =

$$\sqrt{\frac{(\hat{p}_A)(1-\hat{p}_A)}{n_A} + \frac{(\hat{p}_B)(1-\hat{p}_B)}{n_B}} = \sqrt{\frac{(.8571)(1-.8571)}{49} + \frac{(.64)(1-.64)}{100}} = .0693$$

SKETCH OF THE SAMPLING DISTRIBUTION OF THE DIFFERENCE, $\hat{p}_A - \hat{p}_B$
(Assuming H_0 is true)

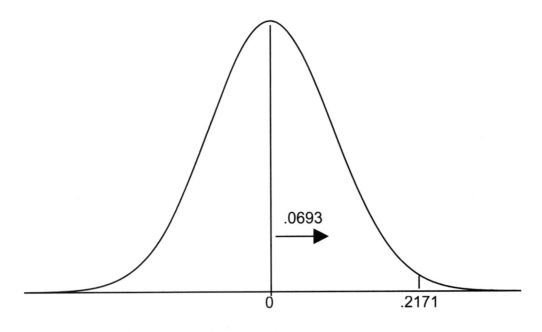

DIFFERENCE BETWEEN SAMPLE PROPORTIONS

TEST STATISTIC:

"obtained z "   =

$$\frac{(\text{obtained difference}) - (\text{expected difference})}{(\text{EST SE}_{\text{difference}})} = \frac{(\hat{p}_A - \hat{p}_B) - (0)}{(\text{EST SE}_{\text{difference}})}$$

$$= \frac{(.8571 - .64) - (0)}{.0693} = \frac{.2171}{.0693} = +3.13$$

(We standardize the observed difference between sample proportions, assuming it came from the sampling distribution of the difference between proportions sketched above)

OBSERVED SIGNIFICANCE LEVEL: p = *.0009*

Our alternate hypothesis specified ">", so this is   P(z > "obtained z") = P(z > 3.13)

CAN YOU REJECT THE NULL HYPOTHESIS AT THE .01 LEVEL?   *Yes*
("Yes", because p is less than .01.)

EXERCISES FOR SECTION 14.6

Dr. Lee thinks that a Clonidine Skin Patch (CSP Treatment) will help drinkers remain sober (i.e. abstain from alcohol), so that drinkers who receive the CSP Treatment (Group A) will have a *higher* rate of *maintaining sobriety* for 1 year than drinkers who receive a Placebo (Group B). He picks *two* samples at random to test his hypothesis.

Sample A consists of 64 drinkers who receive the CSP Treatment. The sobriety rate for this group is .36 (I.e. .36 is the proportion of this sample who maintain sobriety for 1 year)

Sample B consists of 256 drinkers receive a Placebo. The sobriety rate for this group is .20 (I.e. .20 of this sample maintain sobriety.)

1. The proportion to be considered, for each group, is the "proportion of subjects who maintain sobriety". The *null* hypothesis in this case states that the *difference* between the proportion in...
   A) Group A and the proportion in Group B is less than 0
   B) Group A and the proportion in Group B is 0
   C) Sample A and the proportion in Sample B is 0
   D) Group A and the proportion in Group B is greater than 0
   E) Sample A and the proportion in Sample B is less than 0

2. The alternate hypothesis in this case states that the *difference* between the proportion in...
   (Use the answer choices from the previous question.)

3. The best estimate of the standard error of proportion, σ_p or $SE_{\hat{p}}$ for Sample A is
   A) .025   B) .04   C) .06   D) .08   E) .10

4. The best estimate of σ_p (or $SE_{\hat{p}}$) for Sample B is
   A) .025   B) .04 C) .06   D) .08   E) .10

5. The best estimate of the standard error of the *difference* between proportions in this case is
   A) .0325   B) .05 C) .065   D) .08   E) .10

6. Assuming that the null hypothesis is true, we'd expect the sampling distribution (of the *difference* between proportions) in this case to be _____ in shape, with a mean of __ and a standard deviation of
   A) exactly normal, 0, .065
   B) approximately normal, 0, .0325
   C) approximately normal, .16, .065
   D) approximately normal, 0, .065
   E) exactly normal, 0, 1

7. What standard score (or z score) corresponds to the *difference* between sample proportions in this case?

      A) 2.46   B) -2.46   C) 5.12   D) -5.12   E) 0

8. What is the "P value" ? I.e. what is the probability of obtaining a *difference* between proportions this extreme just by chance, assuming that the null hypothesis is true?

      A) .0228   B) .01   C) .0069   D) .9931   E) less than .0003

9. Can Dr. Lee reject the null hypothesis, (at the usual ".01 level of significance") based on the *p* value?

      A) Yes, because *p* is greater than .01
      B) Yes, because *p* is less than .01
      C) No, because *p* is less than .01
      D) No, because *p* is greater than .01
      E) None of the above is correct

Ms. Waters thinks a series of motivational talks will help students remain in school long enough to graduate, so that students who *attend* the talks (Group A) will have a *lower* dropout rate than students who *do not attend* the talks (Group B). She picks two samples at random to test her hypothesis.

      Sample A consists of 64 students who *attend* the talks. The dropout rate for this group is .36 (I.e. the proportion of this sample who fail to graduate is .36)

      Sample B consists of 39 students who *do not attend* the talks. The dropout rate for this group is .52 (I.e. .52 of this sample fail to graduate.)

10. The proportion of interest in this case, for each group, is the "proportion of students who fail to graduate". The *null* hypothesis in this states that the *difference* between the proportion in...

      A) Group A and the proportion in Group B is 0
      B) Sample A and the proportion in Sample B is 0
      C) Group A and the proportion in Group B is greater than 0
      D) Sample A and the proportion in Sample B is less than 0
      E) Group A and the proportion in Group B is less than 0

11. The alternate hypothesis in this case states that the *difference* between the proportion in...
      (Use the answer choices from the previous question.)

12. The best estimate of $\sigma_{\hat{p}_A}$, the standard error of proportion for Sample A is

      A) .03 B) .04 C) .06 D) .08 E) .10

13. The best estimate of the standard error of proportion for Sample B is
      A) .03 B) .04 C) .06 D) .08 E) .10

14. The best estimate of the standard error of the *difference* between proportions in this case is
      A) .04 B) .05 C) .06 D) .08 E) .10

15. Assuming that the null hypothesis is true, we'd expect the sampling distribution
(of the *difference* between proportions) in this case to be _____ in shape,
with a mean of _____ and a standard deviation of ____.

        A) exactly normal, .36, .04
        B) approximately normal, 0, .10
        C) approximately normal, .20, .06
        D) approximately normal, 0, .05
        E) exactly normal, .36, .02

16. What standard score (or z score) corresponds to the *difference* between proportions
in this case?

        A) -1.6   B) 1.6   C) -3.2   D) 3.2   E) 0

17. What is *p*? I.e. what is the probability of obtaining a *difference* between proportions this extreme
just by chance, assuming that the null hypothesis is true?

        A) .0228 C) .9452 C) .0548 D) .0007 E) .9993

18. Can Ms. Waters reject the null hypothesis, (at the usual ".01 level of significance") based on the
value of *p*?

        A) Yes, because *p* is greater than .01
        B) Yes, because *p* is less than .01
        C) No, because *p* is less than .01
        D) No, because *p* is greater than .01
        E) None of the above is correct

Ms. Jones, a manager at a large computer store believes that running a "*48 hour burn in*" treatment on
all computers sold will *reduce the proportion* of computers which are returned for repairs after being sold.
To test her hunch she draws samples of computers to be sold, and produces these samples:

    Sample A consists of 96 computers that were all given the "burn in" treatment. The proportion
    returned for repairs in this group was .04 (I.e. .04 of this sample were returned)

    Sample B consists of 400 computers which were not given the "burn in" treatment. .10 of these
    400 computers were returned for repairs.

19. The proportion to be considered, for each group, is the "proportion of computers returned".
The *null* hypothesis in this case states that the *difference* between the proportion in...

        A) Group A and the proportion in Group B is less than 0
        B) Group A and the proportion in Group B is 0
        C) Sample A and the proportion in Sample B is 0
        D) Group A and the proportion in Group B is greater than 0
        E) Sample A and the proportion in Sample B is less than 0

20. The best estimate of $\sigma_{\hat{p}_A}$, the standard error of the proportion for Sample A is

        A) .02 B) .015 C) .04 D) .05 E) .03

21. The best estimate of $\sigma_{\hat{p}_B}$ is

         A) .02 B) .015 C) .04 D) .05 E) .03

22. The best estimate of the standard error of the *difference* between proportions in this case is

         A) .02 B) .025 C) .04 D) .05 E) .03

23. Assuming that the null hypothesis is true, we'd expect the sampling distribution (of the *difference* between proportions) in this case to be _____ in shape, with a mean of _____ and a standard deviation of _____.

         A) approximately normal, 0, .025
         B) approximately normal, .10, .05
         C) approximately normal, 0, .05
         D) exactly normal, 0, .01
         E) exactly normal, 0, .025

24. What standard score (or z score) corresponds to the *difference* between sample proportions in this case?

         A) 2.4 B) -2.4 C) 1.2 D) -1.2 E) 0

25. What is *p*? I.e. what is the probability of obtaining a *difference* between proportions this extreme just by chance, assuming that the null hypothesis is true?

         A) .9918 B) .1151 C) .0082 D) .8849 E) less than .0002

26. Can Ms. Jones reject the null hypothesis, (at the usual ".01 level of significance") based on the value of *p*?

         A) Yes, because *p* is greater than .01
         B) Yes, because *p* is less than .01
         C) No, because *p* is less than .01
         D) No, because *p* is greater than .01
         E) None of the above is correct

VOTER VARIATION (Population known)

Suppose that (unknown to Joe)
  the proportion of all Female voters ('Group A') in the population who support Jones is **.9**
  the proportion of all Male voters ('Group B') in the population who support Jones is **.4**

Joe picks random sample of voters from the population.
  the proportion of all Female voters ('Group A') in Joe's sample who support Jones is **.7**
  the proportion of all Male voters ('Group B') in Joe's sample who support Jones is **.5**

27.   The *population* difference is
        A) -.5   B) -.2   C) 0   D) .2   E) .5

28. The *sample* difference is
        A) -.5   B) -.2   C) 0   D) .2   E) .5

29. What would you have *expected* the sample difference to be?
        A) -.5   B) -.2   C) 0   D) .2   E) .5

30. What is the *chance error* of the difference for Joe's sample?
        A) -.5   B) -.3   C) 0   D) .3   E) .5

CHECKING THE CHIPS   *(Two large samples, using the proportion)*

Suppose Ms. Alton develops a new version of Lay's chips, called 'New Lay's' . She wants to try to prove that the **proportion** of consumers who prefer 'New Lays' chips to the competitors chips,' Chips Ahoy', is **greater than** the proportion of consumers who prefer 'Old Lays' to 'Chips Ahoy'.

She draws two samples of consumers at random:

Sample A consists of **100** consumers who are assigned at random to taste **New** Lay's, and state if they prefer New Lay's to Chips Ahoy.
The proportion of consumers in Sample A who prefer New Lays is **.80**.

Sample B consists of **233** consumers who are assigned at random to taste **Old** Lay's, and state if they prefer New Lay's to Chips Ahoy.
The proportion of consumers in Sample B who prefer New Lays is **.70**.

31. The alternate hypothesis is in this case is H_1:
The difference between _____ proportions is _____ .
      A) population ...*greater than* .10   D) population...*greater than* 0
      B) population... *equal to* 0   E) sample... *equal to* 0
      C) sample... *greater than* .10

32. If the null hypothesis is true, you'd expect the *sample difference* to typically be ...
      A) .10   B) 0   C) greater than 0   D) greater than .10

33. Using all of the information given, estimate the *standard error* of the difference for samples like the ones described above
      A) .02   B) .015   C) .025   D) .04   E) .05

34. The *standardized difference*, also referred to as "obtained z" or "the test statistic" is
      A) 3.33   B) 2.94   C) 4   D) 3   E) 2

35. Using the above information, we can estimate that P, the probability of obtaining a *sample difference* this high, just by chance, (if the null hypothesis is true) is
      A) .0016   B) .9984   C) .0228   D) .01   E) less than .0002

36. Therefore we... the null hypothesis at the .01 significance level, because *p* is ...
      A) can reject... less than .01   C) can reject... greater than .01
      B) can't reject... less than .01   D) can't reject... greater than .01

ANSWERS TO EXERCISES FOR SECTION 14.6

----

1. B

2. D

3. C

4. A

5. C

$$\text{EST } \sigma_{\hat{p}_A - \hat{p}_B} \quad = \quad \sigma_{\text{difference}} \text{ can be computed two equivalent ways.}$$

You can use the estimated standard errors from the two previous questions in this formula:

$$\sqrt{(\text{EST}\sigma_{\hat{p}_A})^2 + (\text{EST}\sigma_{\hat{p}_B})^2} = \sqrt{(.06)^2 + (.025)^2} = .065$$

or, you can use the sample proportions and sample sizes directly in this formula:

$$\sqrt{\frac{(\hat{p}_A)(1-\hat{p}_A)}{n_A} + \frac{(\hat{p}_B)(1-\hat{p}_B)}{n_B}} = \sqrt{\frac{(.36)(1-.36)}{64} + \frac{(.20)(1-.20)}{256}} = .065$$

6. D

7. A

$$\frac{(.36 - .20) - (0)}{.065} = \frac{.16}{.065} = 2.46$$

8. C

9. B

----

10. A

11. E

12. C

13. D

14. E

15. B

16. A

17. C

18. D

----

19. B

20. A

21. B

22. B

23. A

24. B

25. C

26. B

----

27. E   .5 = .9 - .4

28. D   .2 = .7 - .5

29. E   You'd expect the sample difference to typically be .5, because the population
                         difference is .5.

30. B -.3   .2 - .5
                         Joe got a difference of .2; he expected a difference of .5
                         the obtained difference is *.3 lower* than expected

----

31. D

32. B

33. E

34. E   (.8 - .7)/.05 = +2

35. C   The probability that z is greater than 2.0 is .0228

36. D   P is *greater than* .01

CHAPTER 15

INFERENCE ABOUT NOMINAL VARIABLES: χ^2

15.1 χ^2 HYPOTHESIS TESTS (ONE VARIABLE)

NOMINAL SCALE VARIABLES WITH MORE THAN TWO VALUES

We have previously covered the standard hypothesis test for a single population measured on one *dichotomous* nominal scale variable. Recall that a nominal scale variable divides a population into separate categories, and a *dichotomous* variable is one that divides the population into just *two* categories. We have referred to *dichotomous* variables as "0,1" variables.

A typical hypothesis about a "0,1" variable might be:

"The proportion of voters who favor Clinton is currently .35"

This hypothesis is really telling us about *two* proportions, the proportion who *favor* Clinton, and the proportion who *don't*, but it isn't necessary to specify the second proportion, since we know it must be .65. (This is a case we refer to as having *one degree of freedom*, since knowing *one* of the proportions determines the other. Only *one* of the two proportions is "free" to vary.)

Many nominal scale variables have *more than* two categories: E.g., eye color, blood type, ethnicity, marital status (divorced, widowed, etc.), state of residence, college major, brand of automobile, etc.. Hypotheses about these variables cannot be tested as if the variables were dichotomous. A new statistic χ^2 ("chi-square"), which has its own unique sampling distribution, is required.

For nominal scale variables, the typical null hypothesis about a population states, for each category, what the *proportion* of cases is for that category. So a one-population hypothesis about a nominal scale variable always specifies one proportion for each possible category.

Below are three examples of situations in which a one-variable (or "one population") χ^2 hypothesis test is appropriate. They illustrate the variety of questions that can be handled using the same hypothesis testing format. The numerical values are the same in each case, but the interpretation of the numbers, and the motives behind the tests are different.

EXAMPLE 1: THREE WAYS TO USE ONE-VARIABLE χ^2 TESTS

A) IS AN *OPINION* ABOUT A POPULATION CORRECT?

> Joe thinks 30% of the voters favor candidate A, 50% favor B, and 20% favor C.
> Bill disagrees with Joe. To settle their disagreement, they sample 60 voters at
> random, and find that 12 of the voters favor A, 42 favor B, and 6 favor C.

Although Joe's opinions are expressed in percentages (which is typical for opinion polls) the null
hypothesis can be easily formulated as a statement about population proportions:

$H_0 : p_A = .3, \ p_B = .5, \ p_C = .2$

H_1 : The null hypothesis is not correct.

Joe's opinion is the one we denote the null hypothesis because *it mentions specific values.*

B) IS A CERTAIN SAMPLE A *RANDOM* SAMPLE?

> 1,000 qualified families all apply for some desirable new subsidized housing. 60 of the
> families are to be chosen to get the new housing using a lottery. In their applications
> the families have identified themselves as being members of Group A, Group B or
> Group C (The "groups" might conceivably be based on ethnicity, national origin,
> religion, political party, etc). The proportions for the Groups A, B, and C were .3, .5,
> .2 respectively. Mr. Jones, who was in charge of the lottery, claims that his methods
> assure that the 60 families chosen were a random sample from the 1,000.   Of the 60
> families chosen, 12 were from Group A, 42 from Group B, and 6 from Group C. Ms.
> Smith claims that the lottery was not fair, and the 60 families were *not* a *random*
> sample from the 1,000 applicants.

In this case Mr. Jones' position corresponds to the null hypothesis (it specifies three proportions),
and Ms. Smith's position is the alternate hypothesis. Rejecting the null hypothesis in this case is
equivalent to saying " The sample is very unlikely to be a *random* sample from the specified
population."

C) IS A POPULATION *CHANGING*?

> The proportions of three species of fish in a certain lake in recent years *prior to this
> year* are well known to be .3, .5, and .2 for Species A, Species B and Species C,
> respectively. Ms. Bass, an environmentalist, believes that *this year* a chemical being
> dumped into the lake is affecting the ecology and changing the balance between these
> fish. Mr. Mercury, a spokesperson for Allied Chemical and Industrial Disposal, says
> that only harmless byproducts, which could not affect the fish, have been dumped. Ms.
> Bass collects 60 fish at random, and 12 are Species A, 42 are Species B, and 6 are
> Species C.

The null hypothesis in this case is about the population of fish *this year*, since that's the population
the sample was drawn from. The null hypothesis *uses* the proportions from past years and states
that those proportions *continue* to be correct this year. The null hypothesis in this case is stating
"there hasn't been a *change* in any of the proportions." Rejecting the null hypothesis is the same
as saying "the sample provides convincing evidence that the proportions have *changed* in the
population this year."

COMPUTING χ^2 (ONE VARIABLE)

FIGURE 1: One-variable χ^2 computation

	OBS	EXP p (From H_0)	EXP	OBS-EXP	(OBS-EXP)^2	$\frac{(OBS - EXP)^2}{EXP}$
A	12	.3	18	-6	36	2
B	42	.5	30	+12	144	4.8
C	6	.2	12	-6	36	3
	n = 60	1.0	60	0		χ^2 = 9.8

Figure 1 shows all the steps required to compute χ^2. The most foolproof and methodical way to carry out this computation is to arrange the computations in a series of labeled small tables (in this case columns with three entries) Each *cell*, or small box in a table tells you the value for one category. You can carry out (or check) the computations from left to right across the tables, one row at a time. For example, reading across the top row, we can quickly review: 'We obtained 12 A's in our sample versus 18 expected, so our sample had 6 fewer A's than expected.'

"OBS" abbreviates "observed frequencies". You will always be given the frequencies, or "counts" for each category. These tell you the number of cases in your sample in each category. The '12' in the table in this column indicates 12 of the 60 cases sampled were in Category A. I.e., those 12 cases' scores on the nominal scale variable were 'A'. The sum of this column is, of course, always n, the sample size.

"EXP p" abbreviates "expected proportion". The proportions expected are typically those stated in the null hypothesis for each category, and they will always be provided. In this case the expected proportion for Category A is .3, based on the null hypothesis. The sum of this column should always be 1.0.

"EXP" is the expected frequency, assuming that H_0 is true. For example, if n is 60, and the expected proportion for Category A is .3, we'd expect to get (.3)(60) = 18 A's in our sample.

"OBS - EXP" for each category, is the difference between the number you *got*, or 'obtained', in the sample, and the number you'd have *expected*, based on the null hypothesis. In our case we found 12 A's in our sample, but we expected 18 based on the null hypothesis. The -6 indicates that we got 6 *fewer* A's than expected. Note that the 'OBS - EXP' column is where you'd look if you wanted to describe or interpret discrepancies between the sample data and the population described in H_0. For example, referring to example C) above we might say 'Species A may have been harmed by chemicals being dumped, since Species A was *underrepresented* in our sample." This column should always sum to 0 if you have computed the expected frequencies and subtracted correctly.

"(OBS - EXP)^2" is obtained by squaring the previous column. This makes all the values positive, and emphasizes the effect of large differences.

"(OBS - EXP)^2 / EXP" requires that each entry in one column be *divided by* an earlier column, EXP. The effect is to *accentuate* differences obtained for low-frequency cells and *de-emphasize* differences found in high-frequency cells. χ^2 is computed by adding up all the entries in this column.

INTERPRETING χ^2

The χ^2 value obtained from the sample was 9.8. What does that number tell us? If we had obtained a value of 0, the interpretation would be easy-- the sample would have agreed perfectly with the null hypothesis. χ^2 is 0 *only* when the obtained frequencies in the sample agree exactly with the expected frequencies based on the null hypothesis. As you might expect, when the sample size is large, it is quite rare to obtain a χ^2 value exactly equal to 0, even when the null hypothesis is true.

It is probably clear from the computations above, the farther the *obtained* frequencies are from the *expected* frequencies, the *larger* χ^2 will be. *Large* values of χ^2 will always lead us to *reject* the null hypothesis, because they indicate large inconsistencies between the sample data and the predictions of the null hypothesis.

As usual, we must refer to the *sampling distribution* of a statistic to see whether the value is extreme enough to lead us to reject H_0. In the case of this new statistic there is no way to relate its distribution to one of the previous shapes (normal, or t-shaped). A new table of critical values is needed. Unfortunately, as with the t distributions, there is a different shaped distribution for every possible number of degrees of freedom. To find the appropriate degrees of freedom, subtract 1 from the *number of categories* (the number of possible scores on the variable, *not* the sample size).

(15.1.1) The number of degrees of freedom for a
             one variable χ^2 test is

             (the number of different categories) - 1

             If the tables are arranged as in the format
             above in FIGURE 1, this is equal to
             (the number of *rows* in each table) - 1

In our example there were three possible categories, A, B and C. There were three rows in each of the tables in Figure 1. So df = 3 - 1 = 2. The χ^2 table of Critical Values indicates that a value of 9.21 cuts off .01 of the probability. Since the obtained χ^2 for the sample was 9.8 which is *greater than* 9.21, we can reject H_0.

FIGURE 2: Sketch of the sampling distribution of χ^2 (df = 2)

.01

	9.21	9.8
	critical χ^2	obtained χ^2
	(from table)	(from sample)

EXAMPLE 2: CHECKING A DIE USING RATIONAL PROBABILITIES

"Amy accuses Bob of using a loaded (unfair) die. They roll the die sixty times, and obtain these sample data:"

Side of the die	Observed f
1	4
2	6
3	17
4	16
5	8
6	9

(EXAMPLE 2 is based on Example 1 in the text *STATISTICS* (FPP), 476-481.)

Rational probabilities dictate that the probability of each side should be 1/6, *if* the die is fair. The question is whether this die behaves according to rational probabilities.

The complete outline format will be used in presenting Example 2.

HYPOTHESIS TEST: χ^2 ONE VARIABLE

CHECKING A DIE

POPULATION: *All the possible rolls of one particular die.*

SAMPLE: *60 rolls of the die*
  The 60 rolls are assumed to be equivalent to a simple random sample, because rolls of a die are believed to be independent.

VARIABLE: *Which side of the die turned up?*
  This is a nominal scale variable for the purposes of this experiment)

STATISTIC: χ^2 *(Chi-square)*

HYPOTHESES:
  NULL HYPOTHESIS, H_0 :
   The die is fair.
   The proportion of rolls each side will turn up is 1/6, or about .167.

  ALTERNATE HYPOTHESIS, H_1 :
   The die is not fair.
   At least one side has a proportion not equal to 1/6.

DISTRIBUTION OF SCORES IN THE POPULATION (Assuming H_0 is true)
   Each of the possible scores, 1 through 6, occurs with the same probability, 1/6

OBSERVED VALUE OF THE STATISTIC IN THE SAMPLE: $\chi^2 = 14.2$
   (See FIGURE 3 below.)

SAMPLING DISTRIBUTION OF THE STATISTIC (Assuming H_0 is true):
   Approximately χ^2 with 5 degrees of freedom

  In this case the "sampling distribution of the statistic" is the sampling distribution of χ^2. This sampling distribution shows us all possible values of χ^2 that could occur, and how likely each value is to occur, if the null hypothesis is true.

OBSERVED SIGNIFICANCE LEVEL: $p > .01$
  We use the χ^2 table to approximate probabilities of the true sampling distribution. "Degrees of freedom" is equal to the (number of categories) -1. Using the table, with d.f. $= 6 - 1 = 5$, we see that 14.2 is less than the table value 15.09, so $p > .01$.

CAN YOU REJECT H_0 (At the .01 level of significance)? *No, p is not less than .01.*

FIGURE 3: χ^2 computation for EXAMPLE 2

	OBS	EXP p_i (From H_0)	EXP f	OBS-EXP	$(OBS-EXP)^2$	$\dfrac{(OBS - EXP)^2}{EXP}$
1	4	1/6	10	-6	36	3.6
2	6	1/6	10	-4	16	1.6
3	17	1/6	10	7	49	4.9
4	16	1/6	10	6	36	3.6
5	8	1/6	10	-2	4	.4
6	9	1/6	10	-1	1	.1
	n = 60	1.0	60	0		χ^2 = 14.2

ASSUMPTIONS BEHIND THE USE OF χ^2

1. The frequencies represent count data, with no case appearing in more than one cell in the table. I.e., each case must have been measured only once.

2. The cases' scores are independent of each other.

3. The expected frequency for each category is

       -- not less than 5 if d.f. is greater than 1

       -- not less than 10 if d.f. is equal to 1

4. If the d.f. equals 1, Yates' correction for continuity must be applied to the data.

YATES' CORRECTION FOR CONTINUITY

The χ^2 is continuous, but the data are discrete. When this situation arose in the case of the normal approximation, a 'correction for continuity' improved estimates. Yates' correction accomplishes the same improvement for count data, and it is *required* in the extreme case when there is only 1 degree of freedom. Note that this is equivalent to saying: "If the nominal scale variable is dichotomous (has only two categories), use Yates' correction." This rule will also hold when there are *two* variables in a χ^2 computation: In that case, if *both* variables are dichotomous, use Yates' correction.

CONTINUITY CORRECTION FOR χ^2

If there is only 1 degree of freedom in a χ^2 computation, the following *correction for continuity* must be performed on the observed frequencies to obtain a good fit with the sampling distribution in the χ^2 table:

For each observed frequency in the table:

      -- If the observed frequency is *greater* than the expected frequency, *subtract* .5 from the observed frequency.

      -- If the observed frequency is *less* than the expected frequency, *add* .5 to the observed frequency.

EXERCISES FOR CHAPTER 15.1 (ONE VARIABLE χ^2)

DR NULL'S "RANDOM" SAMPLE PART I

A population is well known to consist of 20% A's, 30% B's, 20% C's, and 30% D's.

A researcher, Dr. Null picks a "*random*" sample from this population and finds in her sample **7 A's, 18 B's, 13 C's and 12 D's.**

Dr. Alt claims that this was *not* a random sample from the population. Conduct the appropriate hypothesis test.

1. This type of hypothesis test is called a
  A) test of the difference between two proportions
  B) a two variable χ^2 test
  C) a one variable χ^2 test

2. How many C's would you have expected in the random sample?
  A) 13   B) 10   C) 8   D) 20

3. The χ^2 value obtained from the sample is
  A) 3   B) 6   C) 12   D) 1   E) 11.34

4. The χ^2 critical value is
  A) 9.21   B) 11.34   C) 13.28   D) 15.09

5. Can you reject? I.e., is this convincing evidence that this is *not* a random sample?
  A) Yes   B) No

DR NULL'S "RANDOM" SAMPLE   PART II

(Same as Part I, except for observed frequencies in bold print)

A population is well known to consist of 20% A's, 30% B's, 20% C's, and 30% D's.

A researcher, Dr. Null picks a "*random*" sample from this population and finds in her sample **28 A's, 72 B's, 52 C's and 48 D's.**

Dr. Alt claims that this was *not* a random sample from the population. Conduct the appropriate hypothesis test.

6. How many C's would you have expected in the sample?
          A) 40   B) 60   C) 52

7. The χ^2 value obtained from the sample is
          A) 3   B) 6   C) 12   D) 1   E) 11.34

8. The χ^2 critical value is
          A) 9.21   B) 11.34   C) 13.28   D) 15.09

9.   Can you reject? I.e., is this convincing evidence that this is *not* a random sample?
          A) Yes   B) No

10. The Part II data are like the Part I data except that
          A) all frequencies are 4 times larger
          B) the sample proportions are farther from the population proportions
          C) all frequencies have been increased by 14

DR NULL'S "RANDOM" SAMPLE   PART III

(Same as Part II, except for observed frequencies in bold print)

A population is well known to consist of 20% A's, 30% B's, 20% C's, and 30% D's.

A researcher, Dr. Null picks a "*random*" sample from this population and finds in her sample **4 A's, 21 B's, 16 C's and 9 D's.**

Dr. Alt claims that this was *not* a random sample from the population. Conduct the appropriate hypothesis test.

11. The χ^2 value obtained from the sample is
          A) 3   B) 6   C) 12   D) 1   E) 11.34

12. The χ^2 critical value is
          A) 9.21   B) 11.34   C) 13.28   D) 15.09

13. Can you reject the null hypothesis? I.e., is this convincing evidence that this is *not* a random sample?

>A) Yes   B) No

14. The Part III data are similar to Part I data except that
    A) all frequencies are 4 times larger
    B) the obtained sample proportions are farther from the expected sample proportions
    C) all frequencies have been increased by 14

Suppose that Washington's campaign manager says
>"You have *wide* support. I think that of the voters who support you...
>>.4 (or 40%) are Democrat
>>.4 are Republican, and
>>.2 (or 20%) are Independent"

Washington disagrees with his campaign manager.

They pick a random sample of voters who support Washington, and find that in their sample there are
>54 Democrats
>42 Republicans, and
>54 Independents

Perform the appropriate hypothesis test.

15. The alternate hypothesis in this case must correspond to
    >A) Washington's opinion as it applies to the population
    >B) Washington's opinion applied to the sample
    >C) The campaign manager's opinion applied to the population
    >D) The campaign manager's opinion applied to the sample

16. The χ² value obtained from the sample is
    >A) 9   B) 12   C) 7   D) 9.21   E) 25.2

17. The χ² critical value is
    >A) 6.64   B) 9.21   C) 11.34   D) 13.28   E) 12

18. Can the null hypothesis be rejected in this case?
    >(at the usual .01 level of significance)
    >>A) Yes B) No   C) Cannot be determined

ANSWERS TO EXERCISES FOR CHAPTER 15.1

PART I:

1. C

2. B

3. A

4. B   Because df = (# of categories - 1) = 4 - 1 = 3

5. B

FIGURE 1: The one-variable χ^2 computation for PART I   questions 1 - 5

	OBS	EXP p (From H_0)	EXP	OBS-EXP	(OBS-EXP)^2	$\frac{(OBS - EXP)^2}{EXP}$
A	7	.2	10	-3	9	.9
B	18	.3	15	+3	9	.6
C	13	.2	10	+3	9	.9
D	12	.3	15	-3	9	.6
	n = 50	1.0	50	0		χ^2 = 3.0

PART II:

6. A

7. C

8. B

9. A

10. A

FIGURE 2: The one-variable χ^2 computation for PART II   questions 6 - 10

	OBS		EXP p (From H_0)		EXP		OBS-EXP		(OBS-EXP)^2		$\dfrac{(OBS - EXP)^2}{EXP}$
A	28		.2		40		-12		144		3.6
B	72		.3		60		+12		144		2.4
C	52		.2		40		+12		144		3.6
D	48		.3		60		-12		144		2.4
	n = 200		1.0		200		0				χ^2 = 12.0

PART III:

11. C

12. B

13. A

14. B   (E.g. sample proportion of A's is 4/50 = .08 compared to .20 expected)

FIGURE 3: The one-variable χ^2 computation for PART III questions 11 - 14

	OBS		EXP p (From H_0)		EXP		OBS-EXP		(OBS-EXP)^2		$\dfrac{(OBS - EXP)^2}{EXP}$
A	4		.2		10		-6		36		3.6
B	21		.3		15		+6		36		2.4
C	16		.2		10		+6		36		3.6
D	9		.3		15		-6		36		2.4
	n = 50		1.0		50		0				χ^2 = 12.0

----

15. A

16. E

17. B

18. A

COMPUTATION: The one-variable χ^2 computation for questions 15 - 18

	OBS	EXP p (From H_0)	EXP	OBS-EXP	$(OBS-EXP)^2$	$\dfrac{(OBS - EXP)^2}{EXP}$
D	54	.4	60	-6	36	.6
R	42	.4	60	-18	324	5.4
I	54	.2	30	+24	576	19.2
	n =150	1.0	150	0		χ^2 = 25.2

15.2 χ^2 *HYPOTHESIS TESTS (TWO VARIABLES)*

RELATIONSHIPS BETWEEN TWO NOMINAL SCALE VARIABLES

The table below is referred to as a **contingency table** or **crosstabulation**. The six cells enclosed by a border constitute the *body* of the table. The body contains the table entries, which are all **frequencies**.

'GENDER' is called the *column variable* or *independent variable*, and 'CANDIDATE' is the *row*, or *dependent* variable, and 'F', 'M', 'Bush', etc are the possible **scores**.

The numbers in the rightmost column, '4', '8', and '12' are the **row totals** or *row marginals*; the numbers in the bottom row, '6' and '18' are the **column totals**. '24' in the bottom right corner is the *grand total* or simply the *total*, which indicates n, the number of cases measured.

Occasionally it is helpful to include row or column *proportions* in tables like this. These will be enclosed in parentheses (though there is no standard notation for this). In this table, '(.25)' is a *column* proportion. It indicates the proportion of all cases that were in the left column. 6/24, or .25, of all cases fall in the left column, and 18/24, or .75, fall in the right column. The **row proportions** are 1/6, 1/3 and 1/2 for the three candidates. Row proportions are put in parentheses, to the right of the row totals.

EXAMPLE 3

	GENDER:		
CANDIDATE:	F	M	
Bush	4	0	4 (1/6)
Perot	0	8	8 (1/3)
Clinton	2	10	12 (1/2)
	6	18	24
	(.25)	(.75)	

Crosstabulations are used to show relationships between nominal scale variables. In this case the independent variable is GENDER. Suppose the dependent variable CANDIDATE indicates voters' preference among possible candidates early on in a recent campaign.

There is a relationship between GENDER and CANDIDATE *in this table* if knowing a case's GENDER would enable you to better estimate the cases preferred CANDIDATE. The same test, applied to the whole population, would determine if a relationship exists between these variables in the whole population.

χ^2 is used to test hypotheses about relationships between nominal scale variables in the population. These tests are referred to as "Two-variable χ^2 tests" or "χ^2 tests of independence"

In this example the obvious null hypothesis is:
       H_0 : There is *no* relationship between GENDER and CANDIDATE in the population
The alternate hypothesis just states that the same variables *are* related:
       H_1 : There *is* a relationship between GENDER and CANDIDATE in the population

---

15.2.1 χ^2 HYPOTHESIS TESTS WITH TWO VARIABLES

If sample data are represented in a r x c contingency table (with r rows and c columns) , the null hypothesis

H_0: There is *no relationship* between the column variable and the row variable

May be tested by computing

Obtained $\chi^2 = \sum \dfrac{(\text{Observed } f - \text{Expected } f)^2}{(\text{Expected } f)}$

This statistic will have a sampling distribution which is approximately χ^2 , with (r - 1)(c - 1) degrees of freedom if...
- each cell has an Expected f of 1 or more
- the average Expected f for the table is 5 or more.

The computation required is similar to that in the one-variable case, except that several columns must be handled, and the expected values are harder to compute. Figure 4 shows the computations in sequence. Each step is explained below.

FIGURE 4: χ^2 computation for EXAMPLE 3

	OBS F	OBS M		
B	4	0	4 (1/6)	
P	0	8	8 (1/3)	
C	2	10	12 (1/2)	
	6	18	24	

	EXP F	EXP M	
B	1	3	4
P	2	6	8
C	3	9	12
	6	18	24

(OBS - EXP)	F	M
B	3	-3
P	-2	+2
C	-1	+1

(OBS-EXP)^2	F	M
B	9	9
P	4	4
C	1	1

$\dfrac{(\text{OBS - EXP})^2}{\text{EXP}}$	F	M
B	9	3
P	2	0.67
C	0.33	0.11

χ^2 = 15.11

OBS: This table contains the given sample data.

EXP: In the cells of this table are the EXPECTED frequencies, *if* the null hypothesis is true.
  To compute the EXP value for a cell, you refer to the OBS table, and you multiply the
    PROPORTION OF ALL CASES IN THE ROW by the COLUMN TOTAL (for the cell's
    column).

For example, 4 females preferred Bush, as indicated by the '4' in row 1, column 1 in the OBS table.
    We'd say the 'observed frequency' of Females who preferred Bush is 4.

To compute the corresponding *expected* frequency, which we'll denote *EXP*, we multiply '1/6' (The
    proportion for row 1) by 6 (the column total for column 1) and get '1'. '1' is put in the first row,
    first column of the EXP table. Similarly, for row 3, column 2, we multiply 1/2 by 18 to get 9,
    and put 9 in the third row, second column of the EXP table.

NOTE: There's a handy shortcut for this computation!

Expected Frequency for a cell = (Row Total)(Column Total)/ n

E.g., the expected frequency for Females who preferred Bush is

$$= (6)(4) / 24 = 1.0$$

The remaining three tables are created by performing the same computations as in the one-variable
    case, except the calculations are performed on each cell in the tables.

To compute X^2, we just add up all the cells in the last table.

EXAMPLE 4

The Public Health Service took a random sample of 2,237 Americans in 1962. They asked the
subjects' GENDER and HANDEDNESS (Right handed, Left handed, or Ambidextrous)

The results are shown in the table. Is this convincing evidence that GENDER and HANDEDNESS
are related in the entire population?

DATA FOR EXAMPLE 4:

HANDEDNESS:	GENDER: M	F
Right handed	934	1,070
Left handed	113	92
Ambidextrous	20	8

The appropriate hypothesis test is described in outline format below.

<u>HYPOTHESIS TEST</u>: χ^2 TWO VARIABLES

<u>GENDER AND HANDEDNESS</u>

POPULATION: *All people in the U.S. in 1962 aged 18 to 69.*

SAMPLE: *2,237 people sampled randomly from the above population.*

VARIABLES:
  COLUMN (independent) VARIABLE: *Gender*

  ROW (dependent) VARIABLE: *Handedness*
                      (This procedure always involves *two* nominal scale variables.)

STATISTIC: χ^2 , *Chi-square*

HYPOTHESES:

NULL HYPOTHESIS, H_0 : *Handedness is not related to gender.*
          I.e., people are equally likely to be right or left handed or ambidextrous, whether they are male
              or female.
          I.e., the *proportions* of people who fall into each possible category of "handedness" are the
              same for all men in the population as they are for all women in the population.

ALTERNATE HYPOTHESIS, H_1 : *Handedness is related to gender*
          I.e., people in the population are more (or less) likely to be right (or left) handed if they are male
          than if they are female..
          I.e., for at least one category of "handedness", the proportion of *men* who fall into that category
              is different from the percentage of *women* who fall into that category in
              the population.

DISTRIBUTION OF SCORES IN THE POPULATION (Assuming H_0 is true) :
  Any distribution of scores on the variable "handedness" is possible, BUT the probability
  distributions for men and women must be the same in the population.

OBSERVED VALUE OF THE STATISTIC IN THE SAMPLE: χ^2 = 12.41
    (See the computation in FIGURE 5 below.)

SAMPLING DISTRIBUTION OF THE STATISTIC :
  In this case the "sampling distribution of the statistic" is the sampling distribution of χ^2, with 2
  degrees of freedom. This sampling distribution shows us all possible values of χ^2 that could occur,
  and how likely each value is to occur, if the null hypothesis is true. It is asymmetrical, positively
  skewed.

OBSERVED SIGNIFICANCE LEVEL: *p < .01*

We use the χ^2 table to approximate probabilities of the true sampling distribution. "Degrees of freedom" is equal to:

(the number of columns - 1) (the number of rows - 1)

In this case, since there are 2 categories for the column variable and 3 for the row variable, this value is:

$$(2 - 1)(3 - 1) = 2$$

Using the χ^2 table, with df = 2, we see that 9.21 is the critical value for χ^2.

The obtained χ^2 value, 12.41, is greater than the critical value, 9.21, so *p* <.01.

CAN YOU REJECT H_0 ? (at the .01 significance level) :   *Yes, because p <.01*

FIGURE 5: χ^2 computation for EXAMPLE 4

OBS

	M	W		
R	934	1,070	2,004	(.896)
L	113	92	205	(.091)
A	20	8	28	(.013)
	1,067	1,170	2,237	

EXP

	M	W	
R	955.86	1048.1	2,004
L	97.78	107.2	205
A	13.36	14.6	28
	1,067	1,170	2,237

(OBS - EXP)

	M	W
R	-22	22
L	15	-15
A	7	-7

(OBS-EXP)^2

	M	W
R	484	484
L	225	225
A	49	49

$\dfrac{(OBS - EXP)^2}{EXP}$

	M	W
R	.50	.46
L	2.37	2.16
A	3.31	3.01

χ^2 = 11.81

REAL-WORLD EXAMPLE USING χ^2

Siegel, Shepard (1982)
Heroin "Overdose" Death: Contribution of Drug-Associated Environmental Cues, *Science,
216:23 April, 1982*

...Substantial tolerance generally develops to the effects of
opiates; the drug-experienced individual can survive a dose
many times greater than that which would kill the drug
inexperienced individual...

. . .

We suggest that drug "overdose" may frequently result
from a *failure of tolerance...*

. . .

The results of the study described below indicate that
heroin-induced mortality in heroin-experienced rats is
higher when the drug is injected in an environment *not*
previously associated with the drug than when it is injected
in the usual drug-administration environment.

(italics added)

Group	Number of Rats	Mortality (%)
ST	37	32.4%
DT	42	64.3%

[The author describes two groups of rats, each gradually exposed to increasing doses of heroin.
The rats in the ST (Similarly Treated) group are then given an overdose in a *simila*r
environment, and the DT (Differently treated) group are given an overdose in a *different*
environment, compared to the environment in which they usually get injected.]

Chi-square analysis indicates that ... mortality was significantly
higher in DT than in ST rats ($p<.001$).

PRACTICE QUESTIONS BASED ON THE Siegel (1982) STUDY ABOVE

1. *A Chi-square (χ^2) analysis is mentioned in this paragraph.*
   What is the independent variable, and what is the dependent variable?

2. *What level of measurement is being assumed for the independent variable? For the dependent variable? What possible values can each variable take?*

3. *What would the raw data for this part of the study look like? How would the raw data be summarized in a table? (Other than in the format presented in the article)*

4. *How many degrees of freedom are appropriate?*

5. *What critical value of χ^2 must have been used to establish that the obtained value was significant at the '.001 level', i.e., that 'p<0.001'?*

6. *What null hypothesis is being tested here?*

ANSWER TO 3: (Other answers will be discussed in class)

	ST	DT	
LIVED	25	15	39
DIED	12	27	40
	37	42	79

EXERCISES FOR CHAPTER 15, SECTION 15.2

---

1. In inferential statistics the most important distribution is the
      A) distribution of all scores in the population
      B) sampling distribution of the statistic being used

DOES A VOTER'S PREFERRED CANDIDATE DEPEND ON THE VOTER'S LOCATION ?

220 voters were randomly selected, 110 from a RURAL area, and 110 from an URBAN area. The voters were asked to choose their preferred candidate in an upcoming election. The contingency table below shows the results for each of the two locations (URBAN, RURAL) and each of four candidates (LEE, LOPEZ, KIM, ABDUL).

TABLE A

	LOCATION	
	URBAN	RURAL
LEE	60	40
LOPEZ	20	30
KIM	25	25
ABDUL	5	15

2. The number "20" in the first column, second row in the table above indicates that
      A) 20% of the urban voters support Lopez.
      B) 20% of the voters who support Lopez are urban.
      C) 20 % of all voters are urban supporters of Lopez.
      D) Altogether, 20 of the voters polled supported Lopez.
      E) 20 of the urban voters supported Lopez.

3. The typical null hypothesis in this type of situation is best expressed as...
      A) the mean for the urban voters is the same as the mean for the rural voters
      B) in this sample there is a relationship between location and candidate preference.
      C) in this sample there is no relationship between location and candidate preference.
      D) in the population there is a relationship between location and candidate preference.
      E) in the population there is no relationship between location and candidate preference.

4. The typical alternate hypothesis is...
      (Same choices as previous question)

5. How many variables are involved in the above study?
        A) 2   B) 6   C) 220   D) 110   E) 4

6. If the null hypothesis were true, how many urban voters would have been *expected* to vote for Lopez?
        A) 20   B) 10   C) 30   D) 25   E) 60

7. What value of χ^2 is obtained from the data in Table A?
　　　　A) 11.0　　B) 11.34　　C) 9.21　　D) 9.0　　E) 22

8. How many degrees of freedom (d.f.) are there in this table?
　　　　A) 4　　　B) 219　　　C) 218　　D) 3　　　E) 7

9. What is the appropriate "critical value" of χ^2, at the .01 significance level?
　　　　A) 13.28　B) 11.34　　C) .12　　D) .30　　E) 18.48

10. You _____ reject the null hypothesis in this case, because the obtained value of χ^2 _____ greater than the critical value.
　　　　A) can, is not
　　　　B) cannot, is
　　　　C) can, is
　　　　D) cannot, is not

GENDER AND CANDIDATE PREFERENCE

	GENDER	
	M	F
MUNOZ	20	55
LEE	35	40
MANN	0	15

The table above shows which of three candidates (MUNOZ, LEE, OR MANN) were preferred by voters in a random sample of 165 voters. The voters are separated by gender, and the null hypothesis is that there is no relationship between gender and candidate preference.

11. The sampling distribution of the statistic that you'll use to test this hypothesis is ____.
　　　　A) approximately t-shaped
　　　　B) exactly t-shaped
　　　　C) exactly z-shaped
　　　　D) approximately z-shaped
　　　　E) approximately Chi-squared χ^2 in shape

12. The number of degrees of freedom relevant in this case is
　　　　A) 6　　　B) 2　　　C) 5　　　D) 1
　　　　E) degrees of freedom are not relevant to the statistic being used.

13. The value of that statistic obtained from this sample is
　　　　A) 2　　　B) 15　　　C) 9　　　D) 0　　　E) 1

14. The critical value of the statistic is
　　　　A) 9.21　B) 15.09　C) 2.326　D) 2.576　E) 6.859

15. Can you reject the null hypothesis?
　　　　A) Yes　B) No

DOES DRUG X CAUSE A DIFFERENT PATTERN OF SIDE EFFECTS FROM "DRUG P" (PLACEBO)?

120 subjects were randomly chosen from a population of people with a serious illness. 24 of them were chosen at random and given DRUG X, while the remaining 96 received "DRUG P" (Actually a placebo).

Each subject was asked to report the main SIDE EFFECT experienced, if any.

The *contingency table* below shows the results for each of the two drugs (X, P) and each of four SIDE EFFECTS (HEADACHE, DIZZINESS, FATIGUE, or NONE).

TABLE A

	DRUG	
	X	P
HEADACHE	8	12
DIZZINESS	0	30
FATIGUE	4	6
NONE	12	48

16. The typical null hypothesis in this type of situation is best expressed as...
    A) in the population there is a relationship between DRUG and SIDE EFFECT.
    B) in the population there is no relationship between DRUG and SIDE EFFECT.
    C) in this sample there is a relationship between DRUG and SIDE EFFECT.
    D) in this sample there is no relationship between DRUG and SIDE EFFECT.
    E) the mean for the "DRUG X" subjects is the same as the mean for the "DRUG P" subjects

17. The typical *alternate* hypothesis is...
    (Same choices as previous question)

18. How many *scores* appear in the entire set of raw data in the above study?
    (*NOT* "How many different scores are *possible*?")
        A) 2   B) 6   C) 120   D) 60   E) 240

19. If the null hypothesis were true, how many subjects receiving Drug P would have been *expected* report Headaches?
        A) 20   B) 6   C) 12   D) 8   E) 16

20. What value of χ^2 is obtained from the data in Table A?
        A) 15.0 B) 7.5   C) 30.0 D) 3.25 E) 22

21. How many degrees of freedom (d.f.) are there in this table?
        A) 3   B) 6   C) 4   D) 119   E) 59

22. What is the appropriate "critical value" of X^2, at the .01 significance level?
      A) 13.28   B) 11.34   C) .12   D) .30   E) 18.48

23. You ____ reject the null hypothesis in this case at the .01 significance level, because the obtained value of χ^2 ____ greater than the critical value.
      A) cannot, is
      B) can, is
      C) cannot, is not
      D) can, is not

----

24. A Type I error occurs only if you *reject* the null hypothesis and it is actually *true*.
    If the alternate hypothesis is *actually true*, the probability of making a TYPE I ERROR is always
    (Assuming you perform a hypothesis test using the .01 level)
      A) between 0 and .01
      B) between .01 and 1.0
      C) exactly .01
      D) negative
      E) 0

DIAGNOSIS VS COUNTRY
Suppose in a study to test the relationship between DIAGNOSIS and COUNTRY, the following data are obtained from a random sample of patients from four different countries. Assume there are three possible psychiatric diagnoses: S (Schizophrenia), D (Depression), A (Anxiety Disorder). The row variable indicates the country. The data are represented as frequencies in the contingency table (or Crosstab) below:

		DIAGNOSIS		
		S	D	A
COUNTRY	USA	4	4	4
	KOREA	3	4	1
	JAPAN	0	4	0
	CANADA	0	2	2

25. The value of the statistic obtained from this sample is
      A) 18   B) 17.33   C) 8.33   D) 10.67   E) 24

26. The appropriate critical value for the statistic is
      A) 6.64 B) 13.28   C) 15.09 D) 16.81   E) 26.22

27. Can you reject the null hypothesis ?
      A) Yes   B) No

28. How many scores must appear in the raw data for this study?
      A) 28   B) 56   C) more than 56 D) 2 E) 7

TWINS

In a study of pairs of twins who were separated at birth, each twin is assessed with regard to primary PERSONALITY trait. (Assume there are three possible traits: A, B, or C.) The row variable indicates one of the twins' PERSONALITY and the column variable indicates the other twin's personality. The data are in the contingency table (or Crosstab).

TABLE 3:

		TWIN #2 PERSONALITY		
		A	B	C
TWIN #1	A	3	0	0
PERSONALITY	B	0	3	0
	C	0	0	3

29. The number of *scores* that appear in the raw data used to create Table 3 must be
　　　　A) 9　　B) 2　　C) 36　　D) 18　　E) 6

30. The value of the statistic obtained from this sample is　　A) 18　　B) 9　　C) 6　　D) 36　E) 12

31. The appropriate critical value for the statistic is　　　　A) 11.34　B) 13.28　C) 15.09　D) 18

32. Can you reject H_0 ?　　　　　　　　　　A) Yes　　B) No

DO "CITY A" AND "CITY B" HAVE THE SAME PATTERN OF CRIMES?

Assume that a suitable "random sample" of crimes are chosen from two cities during equivalent tim periods, to assess whether the percentages of each type of crime are the same for the two cities.   Th *contingency table* below shows the results for each of the two cities (A, B) and each of four types of crime (HOMICIDE, BURGLARY, ROBBERY, ASSAULT).

TABLE A

		CITY	
		A	B
CRIME	HOMICIDE	0	15
TYPE	BURGLARY	2	3
	ROBBERY	6	24
	ASSAULT	4	6

33. The typical null hypothesis in this type of situation is best expressed as...
　　　A) in the population there is a relationship between CITY and TYPE OF CRIME.
　　　B) in the population there is no relationship between CITY and TYPE OF CRIME.
　　　C) in this sample there is a relationship between CITY and TYPE OF CRIME.
　　　D) in this sample there is no relationship between CITY and TYPE OF CRIME.
　　　E) the mean for the "CITY A" is the same as the mean for the "CITY B"

34. The typical *alternate* hypothesis is...
　　　　(Same choices as previous question)

35. How many *scores* appear in the entire set of raw data in the above study?
    (*NOT* "How many different scores are *possible?*")
        A) 2   B) 6   C) 120   D) 60   E) 240

36. If the null hypothesis were true, how many HOMICIDES would have been expected in CITY A?
        A) 20   B) 6   C) 12   D) 3   E) 0

37. What value of χ^2 is obtained from the data in Table A?
        A) 15.0 B) 7.5   C) 28.8   D) 13.4   E) 22

38. How many degrees of freedom (d.f.) are there in this table?
        A) 3   B) 6   C) 4   D) 47   E) 59

39. What is the appropriate "critical value" of χ^2, at the .01 significance level?
        A) 9.27   B) 11.34 C) 13.282 D) 20.09 E) 6.64

40. You ____ reject the null hypothesis in this case at the .01 significance level, because the
    obtained value of χ^2 ____ greater than the critical value.
        A) cannot, is   B) can, is   C) cannot, is not   D) can, is not

----

50 Students are polled. They each indicate their GENDER (Female or Male) and their favorite color for
a certain product (Red, Green, or Blue) The results are displayed in the contingency table
(crosstabulation) below.

	F	M	
R	2	18	20
G	6	4	10
B	2	18	20
	10	40	50

41. If there were no relationship between gender and preferred color in the population, how many
    Male students in the sample would have been expected to prefer Green?.
        A) 2   B) 4   C) 8   D) 0   E) 16

42. The number of degrees of freedom (df) in this table is
        A) 1   B) 2   C) 3   D) 50   E) 49

43. The χ^2 value obtained from the sample is
        A) 9   B) 12.5   C) 8.75   D) 9.21   E) 5

44. The χ^2 critical value is
        A) 6.64   B) 9.21   C) 11.34   D) 13.28   E) 12

45. Can the null hypothesis be rejected in this case?
        (at the usual .01 level of significance)
        A) Yes   B) No   C) Cannot be determined

----

46. Two variable χ^2 tests are used to test for a relationship between...
        A) one nominal scale variable and one constant
        B) two nominal scale variables
        C) one nominal scale variable and one interval scale   variable
        D) two interval scale variables
        E) several different constant proportions

ANSWERS TO EXERCISES FOR SECTION 15.2

----

1. B!

2. E

3. E

4. D

5. A

6. D

7. A

8. D   (2-1)(4-1)

9. B

10. D
----
11. E

12. B   (2-1)(3-1)

13. B

14. A

15. A
----
16. B

17. A

18. E

19. E

20. A

21. A

22. B

23. B
----
24. E If the alternate hypothesis *is* true, the null hypothesis is *not* true.
     A Type I error can't occur unless the null hypothesis *is* true.
----
25. C   26. D   27. B   28. B
----
29. D   30. A   31. B   32. A
----
33. B

34. A

35. C

36. D

37. B

38. A

39. B

40. C
----
41. C

42. B

43. B

44. B

45. A

46. B

15.3 STRENGTH VERSUS SIGNIFICANCE: CRAMER'S V

SIGNIFICANCE DOES NOT IMPLY STRENGTH

If we perform a two variable χ^2 hypothesis test, and we reject the null hypothesis at the .01 significance level, we have found that the sample data provide *convincing* evidence that:

> There *is* a relationship between the independent variable and the dependent variable in the population.

In this case the data are called "*significant* at the .01 level." This sort of *statistical significance* is very specific in its interpretation, so it is different from the term significance commonly used synonymously with "important", "worthy of attention", etc.

Significance of the relationship does not imply that the relationship that exists in the population is necessarily *strong*, or *powerful* or *meaningful*. Rejecting H_0 only implies that *some* relationship (which might be a weak relationship) seems to exist in the population.

χ^2 measures the *significance* of a relationship between two nominal scale variables very well. Routinely, researchers all over the world compute the "obtained χ^2" value for a sample and reject H_0 if the obtained χ^2 is greater than the χ^2 critical value. However χ^2 does not provide a useful measure of the strength of a relationship.

MEASURING THE STRENGTH OF A RELATIONSHIP

A new statistic, Cramer's V, is generally accepted as a good measure of the strength of a relationship between two nominal scale variables. V ranges from 0 to +1.0, and is easily computed from χ^2, n, the number of rows (r) and the number of columns (c):

$$(15.3.1) \quad \text{Cramer's V} = \sqrt{\frac{\chi^2}{(n)(\text{Minimum of } r-1 \text{ or } c-1)}}$$

EXAMPLE 1

The three data sets in TABLE 1A, 1B and 1C below will show how differently χ^2 and Cramer's V are interpreted. In each case assume that there are two variables:

An independent column variable that indicates which treatment has been given.
  This variable has two possible scores: "Tx" (The actual treatment)and "P" (Placebo).
A dependent row variable that indicates the outcome of the treatment.
  This variable has two possible scores: "I" (Improved) and "N" (Not improved).

TABLE 1A: SIGNIFICANT, BUT NOT STRONG

	DATA (obtained frequencies)					Col. Proportions		
	Tx	P				Tx	P	
I	5,100	4,900	10,000		I	.51	.49	.50
N	4,900	5,100	10,000		N	.49	.51	.50
	10,000	10,000	20,000			1.00	1.00	1.00

$n = 20,000$ Obtained $\chi^2 = 8$ χ^2 Critical value $= 6.635$ Cramer's V $= .02$

Cramer's V COMPUTATION:

$$\text{Cramer's V} = \sqrt{\frac{\chi^2}{(n)(\text{Minimum of r-1 or c-1})}} = \sqrt{\frac{8}{(20,000)(2-1)}} = .02$$

In this case we'd say there was a subtle, or weak relationship between treatment and outcome. It is easy to see this by looking down each column, in the table of *column proportions* to the right of the DATA table.

Each column proportion is computed by dividing the cell frequency by the column total. For example, of the 10,000 subjects who were Treated (see col. 1), 5,100 Improved, so the column proportion for the Tx and I cell (the upper left cell) is 5,100/10,000 or .51.

Comparing the column proportions for the different columns makes it clear that in the sample, the treatment "worked" better than Placebo, but the effect of the treatment was subtle; the Improved proportion for the Treated subjects was .51 versus .49 for the Placebo subjects, and .50 for all subjects. The difference between the proportions that Improved is .51 - .49 = .02, so we'd say "In the sample, .02, or 2% more of the subjects who got the treatment Improved, compared to subjects given the Placebo".

However, even though the effect of the Treatment is subtle, we can be pretty sure that it exists in the whole population, not just in the sample. Our obtained χ^2 value is greater than the critical value, so we can reject the null hypothesis that there is no relationship between treatment and outcome in the population.

Note that we are able to reject because the sample size is so *large*. If we had the same subtle pattern of frequencies in a smaller sample (say 51 versus 49, or even 510 versus 490), we wouldn't be able to reject. When there's a weak relationship in the sample, you always need a large sample to be sure it didn't just occur by chance.

Cramer's V is *0* when there's *no* relationship and *1.0* when there's a *perfect* relationship. In this case the Cramer's V value of .02 indicates a *weak* relationship between treatment and outcome.

TABLE 1B: STRONG, BUT NOT SIGNIFICANT

	DATA		
	Tx	P	
I	2	0	2
N	0	2	2
	2	2	4

	Col. Proportions		
	Tx	P	
I	1.0	0.0	.50
N	0.0	1.0	.50
	1.0	1.0	1.00

$n = 4$ $\chi^2 = 4$ χ^2 Critical value $= 6.64$ Cramer's V $= 1.0$

Cramer's V COMPUTATION:

$$\text{Cramer's V} = \sqrt{\frac{\chi^2}{(n)(\text{Minimum of r - 1 or c - 1})}} = \sqrt{\frac{4}{(4)(2-1)}} = 1.0$$

The table of column proportions in this case shows that the treatment has a perfect success rate; all of the Treated subjects improved and none of the Placebo subjects improved. This is a *perfect* relationship, and Cramer's V is 1.0. It is the *strongest possible* relationship for two dichotomous variables when n = 4.

Yet these data are not *statistically* significant. We cannot reject H_0, because the obtained χ^2 value of 4 is less than the critical value. This is a somewhat paradoxical situation: The *sample* data show the strongest possible relationship, and yet we cannot conclude that there exists any relationship at all in the *population*. The problem is in n, the sample size. A sample of size 4 is too strongly affected by chance to allow any conclusion to be made with confidence about a whole population. Recall that none of the hypothesis testing techniques place any limit on population size. It would be surprising if you could reject a hypothesis about a population of several billion cases by picking only 4 at random and measuring them!

TABLE 1C: STRONG AND SIGNIFICANT

	DATA		
	Tx	P	
I	4	0	4
N	0	4	4
	4	4	8

	Col. Proportions		
	Tx	P	
I	1.0	0.0	.50
N	0.0	1.0	.50
	1.0	1.0	1.00

$n = 8$ $\chi^2 = 8$ Cramer's V $= 1.0$

Cramer's V COMPUTATION:

$$\text{Cramer's V} = \sqrt{\frac{\chi^2}{(n)(\text{Minimum of r - 1 or c - 1})}} = \sqrt{\frac{8}{(8)(2-1)}} = 1.0$$

Table 1C is just like 1B except all the cell frequencies have been doubled. Again Cramer's V is 1.0, because this is still a *perfect* relationship. Cramer's V is *not affected* by a uniform rescaling of all the frequencies. If the proportions stay the same, Cramer's V will be the same.

However, χ^2 *does* change as the frequencies increase. Doubling all the frequencies will *double* χ^2, in this case from 4 to 8. Now we *can* reject H_0! The *larger* sample size of 8 *is* sufficient to allow us to conclude that there *does* seem to be a relationship between treatment and outcome in the entire population.

15.4 TRIVARIATE TABLES: CONTROLLING FOR A VARIABLE

CONTROL VARIABLES

Suppose we perform a two variable χ^2 hypothesis test, and we reject the null hypothesis at the .01 significance level. We have found that the sample data provide *convincing* evidence that there is a relationship between the independent and dependent variables in the population. The relationship is not necessarily *causal!* A common *error* made by statistical beginners is to assume that every relationship that exists between two variables must be causal.

TIP: *CORRELATION IS NOT CAUSATION!*

The existence of a *relationship* (or correlation) between variables *does not imply* that the independent variable *'causes'* the dependent variable.

Suppose that we suspect that a relationship between two nominal scale variables may really be due to a third variable which is *confounded* with the independent variable. The procedure we use to investigate this is called *controlling for* the confounding variable, and that variable is then called the *'control variable'* or the 'variable controlled for'. We simply create a *trivariate* table, using the control variable to divide all the subjects into groups first, then creating one bivariate table for each group of subjects. If the relationship between the independent variable and the dependent variable is noticeably weaker in each of the tables that result when we control for the control variable, we conclude that the original relationship may be spurious. The following example is based on hypothetical data, but it dramatically illustrates how misleading bivariate tables can be!

EXAMPLE 1*

Suppose that at HUPD (The Hypothetical University of Possible Discrimination) careful records are kept regarding applicants' ethnicity.

TABLE 15.4.1

(A) DATA

		ETHNICITY Maj.	Min.
ADMISSION STATUS	Admitted	220	30
	Not	180	50

(B) Column Proportions

	ETHNICITY Maj.	Min.
Admitted	.55	.375
Not	.45	.625

$n = 480$ $\chi^2 = 8.181$ $p < .01$ Cramer's V $= .131$

Suppose the results of a random sample of 480 students are displayed in the table above.

1. *Is there a relationship between ethnicity and admission in the data presented above?*

    Yes. It's weak (V $= .131$) but significant.

2. *Does there appear to be a relationship between ethnicity and admission in the population this sample came from?*

    Yes. $p < .01$, and we can reject the null hypothesis at the .01 level.

3. *55% of majority applicants were admitted. Only 37.5% of minority applicants were admitted. Can we conclude that the applicants ethnicity is causally related to their admission? Can we conclude that minority applicants were denied admission <u>because</u> they were minority applicants?*

    Not based on the data alone! This is a passive-observational study, not a true experiment. It is certainly *possible* that this is a causal relationship! But, there are likely to be other variables related to both admission and ethnicity that might have caused the pattern we see in the data.

TABLE 15.4.2 **TRIVARIATE ANALYSIS OF ADMISSION DATA**

SCHOOL THE STUDENT APPLIED TO

(A) ARTS

		ETHNICITY Maj.	Min.
ADMISSION STATUS	Admitted	200	20
	Not	100	10

(B) SCIENCES

	ETHNICITY Maj.	Min.
Admitted	20	10
Not	80	40

* The examples in this section are based on suggestions by UCI Professors Russ Dalton and Bernie Grofman.

Suppose TABLE 15.4.2 describes the trivariate analysis which results when we first divide the students into two groups based on the *school* they applied to within the university ('ARTS' or 'SCIENCES'). We then create a contingency table showing the relationship between ETHNICITY and ADMISSION for each group separately. This is called 'controlling for the effect of SCHOOL'.

4. *Within the ARTS School only, is there a relationship between ethnicity and admission?*

> No! Two-thirds of Majority applicants are admitted, and two-thirds of minority applicants
are admitted. χ² = 0 and Cramer's V = 0.

5. *Within the SCIENCES School only, is there a relationship between ethnicity and admission?*

> No! One-fifth of Majority applicants are admitted, and one-fifth of minority applicants are admitted. χ² = 0 and Cramer's V = 0.

6. <u>*Could*</u> *the relationship between ethnicity and admission be* <u>*spurious*</u>? *Why?*

> Yes. It disappears when we control for the variable SCHOOL. What *might* be occurring here is that most of the Minority applicants apply to the SCIENCES School, which is harder to get into.
> This *might* explain why the overall success rate of minority applicants is lower.

7. *Can we be* <u>*sure*</u> *that the disparity in admission rates is* <u>*not*</u> *caused by ethnicity?*

> No! Within each SCHOOL the proportions admitted are the same for minority and majority applicants. But it is *possible* that someone who wanted to systematically reduce the proportion of minority applicants admitted could set the admission rate *low* for the SCIENCES and *high* for the ARTS!

> The point is that statistical techniques can help us be *appropriately skeptical* about causality.

> We can more easily see the *possible* causes of relationships by controlling for confounded variables, but *proving* causality requires *experimental* designs, not the passive-observational ones such as the design in this example.

See exercises 31-35 below for another trivariate example.

EXERCISES FOR CHAPTER 15 (With REVIEW QUESTIONS)

For each of the 6 tables below answer A) through D). Try to come up with a rough estimate of the answer before computing. Computing column proportions will help you see the pattern of answers.

A) χ^2 = ?   B) Cramer's V = ?   C) χ^2 critical value = ?   D) Can you reject?

1.

	F	M	
A	5	0	5
B	0	10	10
C	5	0	5
	10	10	20

2.

	F	M	
A	4	1	5
B	2	8	10
C	4	1	5
	10	10	20

3.

	F	M	
A	3	2	5
B	4	6	10
C	3	2	5
	10	10	20

4.

	F	M	
A	2.5	2.5	5
B	5	5	10
C	2.5	2.5	5
	10	10	20

5.

	A	B	C	
F	5	0	5	10
M	0	10	0	10
	5	10	5	20

6.

	A	B	C	
F	5	0	0	5
M	0	10	5	15
	5	10	5	20

WHO KILLS WHOM?

In a study of convicts who committed homicides, the goal is to see whether GENDER (FEMALE or MALE) is related to TYPE OF VICTIM. Suppose TABLE 1 below shows a crosstabulation of data obtained randomly selected convicts are separated by the type of victim they killed. The row variable indicates the type of VICTIM a convict killed, and the column variable indicates the convict's GENDER.

TABLE 1: **NOTE: TOTALS are printed in the margins in bold print**

		GENDER		
		FEMALE	MALE	
TYPE OF	SPOUSE	24	12	**36**
VICTIM	ACQUAINTANCE	4	20	**24**
	STRANGER	0	24	**24**
		28	**56**	**84**

7. The number of *scores* that appear in the raw data used to create Table 1 must be
    A) 84   B) 2   C) 6   D) 288   E) 168

8. The value of χ^2 *obtained* from this sample is
    A) 15   B) 8.14   C) 13.28   D) 33.0   E) 9.21

9. The appropriate *critical value* of χ^2 is
    A) 16.29   B) 8.14   C) 13.28   D) 4.07   E) 9.21

10. Cramer's V is
    A) 2.38   B) 0   C) .627   D) 1.0   E) .393

11. Based on the above sample data we can say that the relationship between gender
    and type of victim in this sample seems to be _____?
    A) both statistically significant and fairly strong. B) statistically significant, but very weak.
    C) fairly strong, but not statistically significant   D) very weak, and not statistically significant.

FISH: THE TRUE STORY   (REVIEW: CHAPTER 11 TOPIC)

Al picks 576 fish at random from a certain population at random and finds that .36 of the fish contain excessive levels of Mercury.

12. Based on this sample, what is Al's best *point estimate* of the population proportion, p?
    A) .2304   B) .64   C) .36   D) .01   E) .02

13. Al would estimate the mean of the sampling distribution of $\hat{p}$ to be...
    A) .2304   B) .64   C) .36   D) .01   E) .02

14. Al would estimate the standard error of the sample proportion to be...
    A) .06   B) .64   C) .36   D) .01   E) .02

15. Compute a 95% CI estimate for p, the population proportion.
    A) $.36 \pm .0392$ or   .3208 - .3992   B) $.36 \pm .02$ or   .34 - .38
    C) $.36 \pm .196$ or   .164 - .556   D) $.36 \pm .0196$ or   .3404 - .3796
    E) $.36 \pm .05$ or   .31 - .41

DOES 'EMD' DECREASE ANXIETY?   (REVIEW: CHAPTER 12 TOPIC)

Suppose a new, controversial psychotherapy treatment, eye-movement desensitization (EMD) is being evaluated (It is! This e.g. is based on studies on 'EMD' in progress at this time.)

Dr Jones thinks that EMD treatment will have the effect of *lowering* peoples' anxiety levels. She conducts a two-sample hypothesis test, with a *treatment group*, Group A, and a *control group*, Group B, to try to show that the mean anxiety level of people who are given EMD treatment (Population A) is *lower than* the mean anxiety level for people who do not receive EMD treatment (Population B).

You may assume that both groups A and B are approximately normal and have equal variances.

She draws two samples of people at random:

  Sample A consists of **9** people who *are* given EMD treatment.
  The people in Sample A have an mean anxiety level of **160**,
        and $\hat{\sigma}$ for sample A is **22.5**.

  Sample B consists of **25** other people who *are not* given EMD treatment.
  The people in Sample B have an mean anxiety level of **191.25**,
        and $\hat{\sigma}$ for Sample B is **50**.

NOTE: You may assume that hypotheses about differences are stated in the usual order, i.e.
        "A - B", not "B - A".

16. The *alternate* hypothesis in this case states that the *difference* between the mean of ...
              A) Population A and the mean of Population B is greater than 0
              B) Population A and the mean of Population B is less than 0
              C) Sample A and the mean of Sample B is less than 0
              D) Sample A and the mean of Sample B is greater than 0
              E) None of the above is correct

17. The best estimate of the SE of the mean, $\sigma_{\overline{X}_A}$, for Sample A in this case is...
       A) 10.5   B) 7.5   C) 8   D) 12.5   E) 10

18. The best estimate of the SE of the *difference* between means , $\sigma_{\overline{X}_A - \overline{X}_B}$, in this case is...
       A) 10.5   B) 6   C) 8   D) 12.5   E) 10

19. Assuming that the null hypothesis is true, we'd expect the sampling distribution of *differences between means* in this case to be _____ in shape, with a mean of ___ and a standard deviation of ____ .

    A) exactly normal, 0, 10
    B) approximately normal, 0, 15
    C) exactly normal, 0, 15
    D) approximately normal, 0, 12.5
    E) approximately normal, 0, 10

20. What is the (obtained) difference between means in these samples?
    A) 31.25   B) -31.25   C) -2.5   D) 2.5   E) -3

21. What *standard score* corresponds to the *difference* between the mean of Sample A and the mean of Sample B in this case?
    A) 31.25   B) -31.25   C) -2.5   D) 2.5   E) -3

22. Can Dr. Jones reject the null hypothesis,(at the usual .01 level of significance) based on the P value?
    A) Yes, because P is greater than .01   C) Yes, because P is less than .01.
    B) No, because P is less than .01   D) No, because P is greater than .01

23. Suppose that, unknown to Dr. Jones, H_0 is actually true. Considering the answer to the previous question, you can conclude that the probability that Dr. Jones made a TYPE I error in this case is
    A) greater than .01 and less than 1.0
    B) 1.0
    C) 0
    D) less than .01

PARTY TIME!

Suppose the *proportions* of all voters who voted for candidates associated with one of the four major political parties (DEM, REP, LIB, COM -- this is a *hypothetical* country) in the last election are *known to be*

TABLE A: EXPECTED PROPORTIONS (Based on data from the last election)

POLITICAL PARTY	p
REP	.4
DEM	.3
LIB	.2
COM	.1

Ms. Tinker thinks that the proportions of voters who support the four political parties are *different this year*, and she decides to conduct the appropriate hypothesis test. In a random *sample* of 4,000 voters polled *this year*, she finds these frequencies of voters who support candidates of each of the four parties:

TABLE B: SAMPLE DATA

POLITICAL PARTY	f
REP	1590
DEM	1200
LIB	750
COM	460

24. The term 'DEM' represents a
    A) statistic   B) score   C) nominal variable   F) interval variable

25. To create the data summarized in TABLE B, _____ must have been measured on

_____ .

    A) 4000 cases,   4 variables
    B) 1 case,   4000 variables (Then the poor tired case *rested!*)
    C) 4 cases,   2 variables
    D) 4000 cases,   1 variable
    E) 4000 cases,   2 variables

26. This type of hypothesis test is called a
    A) a two variable χ^2 test
    B) a one variable χ^2 test
    C) test of the difference between two proportions

27. How many voters in the sample would you have *expected* to be in the 'COM' category?
    A) 1000   B) 4000   C) 400 D) 460   E) 100

28. The χ^2 value *obtained* from the sample is (approximately)
    A) 10.08   B) 12.09   C) 11.21   D) 9.21   E) 12.1875

29. The appropriate χ^2 *critical* value is (approximately)
    A) 9.2103   B) 13.2767   C) 11.3449   D) 15.09   E) 12.1875

30. Because the obtained χ^2 value is _____ than the critical value of χ^2 , you can conclude that P is _____ than .01. (Where P is the probability of obtaining a sample χ^2 value this high, if the null hypothesis were true.)
    A) greater, less
    B) less, greater

CONTROLLING FOR AGE (Based on Section 15.4)

Suppose this contingency table results when 250 Male and 250 Female voters are asked "Do you support the (political) Left or the Right?

TABLE A

		GENDER	
		F	M
POLITICAL	Left	80	170
PREFERENCE	Right	170	80

31. Is there a relationship between Gender and Political Preference in this sample?

CONTROLLING FOR AGE (Continued from previous page)

TABLE B   TRIVARIATE ANALYSIS OF VOTER DATA

AGE

(A) UNDER 30   (B) OVER 30
GENDER   GENDER

		F	M			F	M
POLITICAL	Left	40	160		Left	40	10
PREFERENCE	Right	10	40		Right	160	40

Suppose TABLE B above results when we control for age.

32. TABLE B is referred to as a _____ contingency table or crosstabulation.

33. Among the UNDER 30 voters, is there a relationship between GENDER and POLITICAL PREFERENCE?

34. Among the OVER 30 voters, is there a relationship between GENDER and POLITICAL PREFERENCE?

35. Informally summarize one conclusion that can be made from analyzing the data.

ANSWERS TO EXERCISES FOR CHAPTER 15

----

1. A) $\chi^2 = 20$ B) Cramer's V = 1.0   C) χ^2 critical value = 9.21   D) You can reject.

   Note that a *perfect* relationship can exist, even though not all column proportions are 0 or 1.0. The column proportions in the cells are *as far as possible* from the expected proportions.

2. A) $\chi^2 = 7.2$ B) Cramer's V = .6   C) χ^2 critical value = 9.21   D) You cannot reject.

   Here there's a *moderately strong* relationship, in a *small* sample, so we can't reject.

3. A) $\chi^2 = .8$ B) Cramer's V = .2   C) χ^2 critical value = 9.21   D) You cannot reject.

   This is a *weak* relationship.

4. A) χ² = 0!   B) Cramer's V = 0!   C) χ² critical value = 9.21   D) You cannot reject!

Absolutely *no* relationship exists between the column variable and the row variable in the sample. (Of course, you can't actually have frequencies of 2.5, but these were provided to show what a nonexistent relationship looks like-- it looks just like the *expected* table.) We'd say in this case "the data do not support the alternate hypothesis," since we are trying to prove that there *is* a relationship in the population, but there is *no* relationship in the sample.

5. A) χ² = 20   B) Cramer's V = 1.0   C) χ² critical value = 9.21   D) You can reject.

This is the same as Exercise 1., with the columns and rows *reversed.* It shows that χ² and Cramer's V are *symmetrical* statistics, they don't change when the independent and dependent variables are switched. The relationship "between X and Y" is always the same as the relationship "between Y and X."

6. A) χ² = 20   B) Cramer's V = 1.0   C) χ² critical value = 9.21   D) You can reject.

Why these values of χ² and Cramer's V are identical to those in the preceding question (Exercise 5) may not be obvious at first.

The sample sizes are both 20. If you compare the column proportions for the Obtained Table with the column proportions for the Expected Table, you'll see that in each case the *Obtained* proportions are '*as far as possible*' from the *Expected* proportions.

----

7. E   84 people are each measured on two variables: GENDER and TYPE OF VICTIM

8. D

9. E

10. C

11. A

----

12. C

13. C

14. E

15. A

----

16. B

17. B

18. D

19. D

20. B

21. C   (-31.5 - 0)/12.5 = -2.5

22. C   Your standardized sample mean was -2.5.
                If the *z distribution* was the one to use you could reject. (P would be .0062)
                But the sampling distribution of the standardized difference is a t distribution with 32
                degrees of freedom.
                The critical value of t is -2.457.
                The obtained t is *more* extreme than the critical t, so you can reject!

23. B
----
24. B

25. D

26. B

27. C

28. E

29. C   df. = 3

30. A
----
31. Yes

32. trivariate

33. No! 80% of younger females support the Left. *Same* for younger males.

34. No! 20% of older females support the Left. Same for older males.

35. The relationship between Gender and Political Preference seems to be spurious. It seems that
     younger people support the Left more, and in this sample, more younger people happened to be
     male.

CHAPTER 16

ONE WAY ANALYSIS OF VARIANCE

16.1 INTRODUCTION TO ANOVA

THE HYPOTHESES

Analysis of Variance (**ANOVA**) techniques are very widely useful. It has been estimated that 90% or more of all recent research articles published in psychology journals use ANOVA in some form. Another nice thing about these techniques is that they provide an *intuitive* set of concepts which help us see the connection between tests for "differences" between populations and tests about correlation between variables.

A one-way ANOVA hypothesis test is used when we are trying to show that

> A) some *nominal* scale independent variable is *related to* some dependent *interval* scale variable in the population.
>
> B) the *means* for *several different groups* of cases are *not* equal.

In one way ANOVA there is always exactly *one* variable that divides the population up into groups or categories, and *one* variable that is numerical. The null hypothesis always states that the means of all the groups are equal, and the alternate hypothesis always "disagrees":

(16.1.1) ONE WAY ANOVA HYPOTHESES
(in terms of group means)

H_0 : $\mu_1 = \mu_2 = ... = \mu_i = ... = \mu_k$

H_1 :   **At least two of the above means are *not* equal**

There can be *any number* of groups, which is what distinguishes ANOVA techniques from the simpler test for equality of *two* group means covered earlier. Note that we follow tradition in switching from *letter* subscripts ("μ_A, μ_B", etc.) to *numbered* subscripts ("μ_1, μ_2", etc.) when the number of groups is greater than two. The number of groups, which is also the number of possible scores on the nominal scale variable, is always designated "k". (Don't confuse this with the "k" covered earlier which designated "the number of successes in the sample". The context really will make it clear which is intended.) The letter "**i**" is traditionally used to designate the **independent variable** which determines which *group* an case is in, and "**X**" is used for the interval scale **dependent variable**.

> **(16.1.2) ONE WAY ANOVA HYPOTHESES**
> **(in terms of *variables*)**
>
> H_0 :   There is *no* relationship between i and X in the
>   population
>
> H_1:   There *is* a relationship between i and X in the
>   population

It will be easier for you to follow the logic of ANOVA if you relate the definitions to a specific example as you encounter them. EXAMPLE 1 will be used to represent a typical ANOVA hypothesis test throughout this chapter.

EXAMPLE 1: COLOR RATINGS

A market researcher presents six packages containing a product to six different "randomly chosen" consumers. Each consumer rates the package on a scale from 0 to 25. The packages are identical except two are red (Group 1), two are blue (Group 2) and two are green (Group 3).

The *ratings* obtained are:

Group 1: 0, 2   Group 1 mean, $\bar{X}_1 = (0 + 2)/2 \quad = 1$

Group 2: 20, 22   Group 2 mean, $\bar{X}_2 = (20 + 22)/2 = 21$

Group 3: 10, 12   Group 3 mean, $\bar{X}_3 = (10 + 12)/2 = 11$

The "Grand Mean", $\bar{X} = (0 + 2 + 20 + 22 + 10 + 12)/6 = 11$

The researcher is trying to establish that the ratings given to the different color packages will be different in the population, i.e., that "in the population, the mean ratings are not equal."

Now, the group means in the *sample* are clearly different: 1 vs. 21 vs. 11. However this may or may not be convincing evidence that a difference exists in the *population* between these groups.

FIGURE 1: "ANOVA" SKETCH OF X versus i

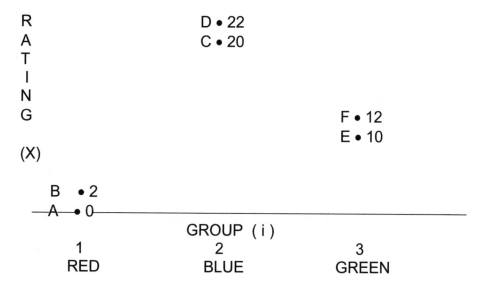

The 6 cases have been designated A through F. The score on X appears to the right of each point. In Figure 1 the independent variable, i, is *nominal* scale, so it just groups the cases into 3 groups. The sketch makes it clear that there is not much variation *within* groups, but there is considerable variation *between* groups.

BETWEEN GROUPS VARIATION

If there is *a lot* of variation *between* the group means in the sample, that will help us reject the null hypothesis, which states that there is *no* difference between group means in the population. In our sample, the group means are 1, 21 and 11. The "grand mean" or overall mean is 11.

Group 3's mean is *right at* the grand mean. Groups 1 and 2 both have means that are 10 units away from the grand mean. These *deviations* of the group means from the grand mean are squared and added to compute one number that summarizes the amount of variation between the different groups in the sample. (This is done for *each* of the six cases.)

(16.1.3)   SS$_{BETWEEN}$ or SS$_B$

Measures the amount of variation *between* the different group means. It describes the total amount of difference between all the groups. (In some texts it is referred to as SS$_{GROUP}$ or SS$_{EFFECT}$)

$$SS_{BETWEEN} = \sum(\overline{X}_i - \overline{X})^2$$

$\overline{X}_i$ is the mean of the ith group, $\overline{X}$ is the grand mean, and the sum is taken over all cases in the sample

---

If you didn't know which group a package is in, your best estimate of package's rating would be 11, the grand mean. If you know the package is blue, you'd *change* your estimate to 21, the group mean for blue packages. You are using information about the independent variable (Color) to better estimate the dependent variable (Rating). There's a general rule in cases like this that always applies: **The *more* you change your estimate by, the *stronger* the relationship is.**

WITHIN GROUP VARIATION

If there is very *little* variation *within* the groups in the sample, that will help us reject the null hypothesis. When scores are consistent, or similar, within *sample* groups, then each of the group means in the *sample* seems to be an accurate reflection of that group mean in the *population*.

In our sample, each of the six scores is 1 unit away from its group mean. For example, C, which is in Group 2, scored 20. The *mean* for Group 2 is 21, so C's *deviation* from its group mean is -1.

These deviations of all scores from their group means are squared and added to compute one number that summarizes the amount of variation within the different groups in the sample. (This is done for *each* of the six cases)

(16.1.4) SS_{WITHIN} or SS_W (Or 'SS_{ERROR}')

Measures the amount of variation *within* the different groups, i.e., how far the cases' scores on X are from their *group* means. In some texts it is referred to as SS_{ERROR}.

$$SS_{WITHIN} = \sum (X - \bar{X}_i)^2$$

$\bar{X}_i$ is the mean of the i_{th} group , and the sum is taken over all cases in the sample

---

MEAN SQUARES vs SUM OF SQUARES

We want to compute a ratio, called the "**F ratio**" which will give us one number that indicates *how convincing* the differences between sample means are. It will tell us whether the differences between sample means seem to be *due to chance* or *due to population differences* in group means.

$SS_{BETWEEN}$ and SS_{WITHIN} can't be used directly to compute a meaningful ratio, because the number of things that they summarize are not the same.

$SS_{BETWEEN}$ characterizes *differences* between *three* groups, but the overall mean $\bar{X}$ is used in these computations, and once $\bar{X}$ is computed only 2 of the differences are really "free" to vary.

SS_{WITHIN} characterizes *differences* between *six* cases and their *three* group means, but the three group means are used in these computations, and once the three group means are computed, only 3 of the differences are really 'free' to vary.

The number of differences that are 'free' to vary (that is, *not* determined by previous calculations) is called the 'degrees of freedom' or 'd.f.'. The total number of degrees of freedom is always n-1.

(16.1.5) In all One Way ANOVA computations the degrees of freedom for $SS_{BETWEEN}$ and SS_{WITHIN} are

$$d.f._{WITHIN} = n - k$$

$$d.f._{BETWEEN} = k - 1$$

k is the number of different categories in the independent variable. n represents the sample size

---

The SS values are divided by the appropriate degrees of freedom to take into account the number of differences that have contributed to the SS. The result is called the "**mean square**" or "mean squared difference (or just "MS"). It represents the average amount of variation *per degree of freedom*.

(16.1.6) MS, the 'mean squared deviation' is the average squared deviation *per degree of freedom*

In general, MS = SS/d.f.

In one way ANOVA computations, two MS values are computed:

$$MS_{BETWEEN} = \frac{SS_{BETWEEN}}{d.f_{BETWEEN}}$$

$$MS_{WITHIN} = \frac{SS_{WITHIN}}{d.f_{WITHIN}}$$

COMPUTING THE F RATIO

The obtained F ratio for a sample is the statistic that is used to test hypotheses in ANOVA. It is always computed by dividing the MS for some effect by the MS_{WITHIN}.

$$(16.1.7) \quad \text{Obtained F ratio} = \frac{MS_{BETWEEN}}{MS_{WITHIN}}$$

DATA REQUIREMENTS AND ASSUMPTIONS

In order for the hypothesis test in a one-way ANOVA to be meaningful the data must have been collected in a particular way, and the population sampled from must have certain properties:

ASSUMPTIONS ABOUT THE SAMPLE DATA

1. There is one nominal scale independent variable that divides the population into groups.

2. Each case in the sample appears in *only one* of the groups. (For example you couldn't run a study in which you asked each person to list their two favorite colors, and then use "favorite color" as the independent variable.

3. Each case in the sample was randomly sampled from some population.

4. There is one interval scale dependent variable.

ASSUMPTIONS ABOUT THE DISTRIBUTION OF SCORES IN THE POPULATION

5. Independence: Scores don't "influence each other." For example, if one person in the sample scores high, that doesn't make another person score high also.

6. Normality: Within each group in the population, the distribution of scores on the dependent variable are approximately normal.

7. Homogeneity of variance:

For each group in the population, the variance is the same as for each other group. (It is well known that minor violations of this assumption can be tolerated.)

EXAMPLE 1:   HYPOTHESIS TEST IN OUTLINE FORMAT

<u>ONE WAY ANOVA: COLOR RATINGS</u>

POPULATION: *All possible events in which a random consumer rates a product packaged in one of three colored packages.*

INDEPENDENT VARIABLE (i): *The color of the package*

        POSSIBLE VALUES: 1: *Red*
                                  2: *Blue*
                                  3: *Green*

DEPENDENT VARIABLE (X): *Rating given by a consumer to the packaging*
        POSSIBLE VALUES: *0 - 25*

SUM OF SQUARES COMPUTATION:

PARTITIONING OF THE SUM OF SQUARES

RAW DATA		SS TOTAL		SS BETWEEN GROUPS			SS WITHIN GROUPS		
i	X	$X-\bar{X}$	$(X-\bar{X})^2$	$\bar{X}_i$	$\bar{X}_i-\bar{X}$	$(\bar{X}_i-\bar{X})^2$	$\bar{X}_i$	$X-\bar{X}_i$	$(X-\bar{X}_i)^2$
1	0	-11	121	1	-10	100	1	-1	1
1	2	-9	81	1	-10	100	1	+1	1
2	20	+9	81	21	+10	100	21	-1	1
2	22	+11	121	21	+10	100	21	+1	1
3	10	-1	1	11	0	0	11	-1	1
3	12	+1	1	11	0	0	11	+1	1
		SS =	406	$SS_{BETWEEN}$ =		400	SS_{WITHIN}	=	6

$\text{d.f.}_{TOTAL} = n - 1 = 6 - 1 = 5$

$\text{d.f.}_{WITHIN} = n - k = 6 - 3 = 3$

$\text{d.f.}_{BETWEEN} = k - 1 = 3 - 1 = 2$

k is the number of different categories in the independent variable, in this case 3.

n, as usual represents the sample size, the total number of cases in all groups in the sample, in this case 6.

$MS_{WITHIN} = (SS_{WITHIN})/(d.f._{WITHIN}) = 6/3 = 2$

$MS_{BETWEEN} = (SS_{BETWEEN})/(d.f._{BETWEEN}) = 400/2 = 200$

OBTAINED VALUE FOR F $= (MS_{BETWEEN})/(MS_{WITHIN}) = 200/2 = 100$

CRITICAL VALUE FOR F: *30.81*

USING THE F TABLE:

We refer to *COLUMN 2*, because the "d.f._{BETWEEN}", also called the "NUMERATOR D.F.", is *2*.

We refer to *ROW 3*, because the "d.f._{WITHIN}", also called the "DENOMINATOR D.F.", is *3*.

The F critical value in column 2, row 3 is 30.81

CAN WE REJECT THE NULL HYPOTHESIS?
(That the groups all have equal means in the population)   *Yes*
Because the obtained F is *greater than* the critical value for F in the table, so *p* is *less than* .01.

There's a standard, convenient format for summarizing all of the crucial information in a set of ANOVA computations, referred to as an ANOVA Summary Table:

ANOVA SUMMARY TABLE

	SS	d.f.	MS	F ratio	F critical value
BETWEEN (Due to indep. vbl.)	400	2	200	100*	30.81
WITHIN (Due to error)	6	3	2		
TOTAL	406	5			

*Significant at .01 level

In the next chapter, we'll extend this format in a straightforward way, allowing three separate hypotheses to be tested in one table.

16.2 STRENGTH OF ASSOCIATION IN ANOVA: ω^2 and η^2

STRENGTH VS. STATISTICAL SIGNIFICANCE

The F ratio described above allows us to accurately check the *statistical significance* of a relationship between one nominal scale variable and one interval scale variable. More intuitively, it allows us to check whether 'a difference between group means found in the *sample* is impressive enough to convince us that some difference between group means exists in the *population* also.'

As usual, the test for significance involves assuming that there's *no* difference between groups in the population (the null hypothesis) and then trying to show that the differences between groups in the sample are very *impressive*, i.e., very *unlikely* to occur by chance.

Suppose that there actually does exist a *subtle* difference between groups in the population; say

$$\mu_1 = 100 \qquad \mu_2 = 99.99 \qquad \mu_3 = 100.01$$

In many circumstances we wouldn't be likely to be interested in such a minimal difference between groups. However with a powerful test using very large sample size, we might (correctly!) uncover this real, but mild, difference, and correctly *reject* the null hypothesis. In that case, the differences between group means are *statistically significant*, but not *strong*.

Suppose the group means represented depression levels found among groups of psychotherapy clients exposed to three different types of therapy (perhaps 'cognitive', 'dynamic', and 'medication'). Stating that 'depression levels are *significantly* related to the type of therapy' in this case is technically correct, but many readers would misunderstand that statement.

What would communicate better in this case is a measure of the *strength* of the relationship between groups, an indication, in practical terms, of how much this difference will *matter* to the population of clients. The statistic that measures strength in this case is ω^2 (omega squared). It's easy to interpret because it gives the *proportion* of variation in the dependent variable that can be explained by the independent variable. However, omega squared is presented here as an *inferential* statistic; it is the best estimate, for the *population*, of the proportion of variation due to the independent variable.

(16.2.1)   Omega-squared, ω^2

Measures the *strength* of association between one nominal scale variable, i, and one interval scale variable, X. It is the *best estimate* of the proportion of variation in X that is due to i in the population.

$$\omega^2 = \frac{SS_B - (df_B)MS_W}{SS_X + MS_W}$$

EXAMPLE

Referring back to the example in 16.1 above, which resulted in this ANOVA summary table:
(Values used to compute ω^2 are in bold print.)

ANOVA SUMMARY TABLE					
	SS	d.f.	MS	F ratio	F critical value
BETWEEN (Due to indep. vbl.)	**400**	**2**	200	100*	30.81
WITHIN (Due to error)	6	3	**2**		
TOTAL	**406**	5			

Omega squared is computed as follows:

$$\omega^2 = \frac{SS_B - (df_B)MS_W}{SS_X + MS_W} = \frac{400 - (2)2}{406 + 2} = \frac{396}{408} = .97$$

We see in this case that the relationship found is very strong.

INTERPRETING ω^2

In the example above we could state correctly, based on this result that, "Based on this sample, the best estimate of the percent of variation in preference due to color, in the population, is 97%."

Omega squared is only presented and discussed if the null hypothesis is rejected. In such cases it is always positive.

THE <u>SAMPLE</u> PROPORTION: η^2 (ETA-SQUARED)

Eta squared, η^2, is the proportion of variation in the *sample* that is due to the independent variable. It *does not* tell us what to expect in the population, and is merely a descriptive statistic about the sample. Surprisingly SPSS routinely provides values for eta squared but not omega squared! Be careful not to treat eta squared as a population estimate.

(16.2.2)   Eta-squared, η^2

Measures the *strength* of association in a *sample*.

$$\eta^2 = \frac{SS_B}{SS_X}$$

EXERCISES FOR CHAPTER 16

MULTIPLE CHOICE QUESTIONS

FIVE TREATMENTS COMPARED

Five different experimental treatments (A, B, C, D, E) are tried on three randomly assigned patients each. The numbers in the table below represent the "degree of success of the treatment" as measured on an interval scale variable. *NOTE: This format is not the usual raw data format. To save space the patients have been grouped based on their scores on the independent variable.*

TABLE 1:

TREATMENT

A	B	C	D	E
0	2	3	4	6
6	8	9	10	12
12	14	15	16	18

Perform the appropriate ANOVA on these data.

1. $SS_{BETWEEN}$, the sum of squares between groups, is
   A) 360   B) 60   C) 5   D) 120   E) 36

2. SS_{WITHIN}, the sum of squares within groups, is
   A) 360   B) 60   C) 5   D) 120   E) 36

3. $df_{BETWEEN}$, the degrees of freedom between groups, is
   A) 5   B) 4   C) 3   D) 12   E) 14

4. df_{WITHIN}, the degrees of freedom within groups, is
   A) 5   B) 3   C) 10   D) 15   E) 8

5. $MS_{BETWEEN}$, the mean squares between groups, is
   A) 36   B) 15   C) 12   D) 120   E) 30

6. MS_{WITHIN}, the mean squares within groups, is
   A) 36   B) 5   C) 12   D) 120   E) 30

7. The F ratio obtained from the data above is
   A) 5   B) 120   C) 30   D) .42   E) 36

8. The critical value of F in this case is
   A) 16.69   B) 5.64   C) 27.05   D) 28.71   E) 5.99

9. You conclude that you ____ reject the null hypothesis in this case, because *p* is ____ than .01.
   A) can, greater   B) cannot, less   C) cannot, greater   D) can, less than   E) can, equal to

---

MARKET RESEARCH

A market researcher has a new product rated by randomly selected consumers in each of four sections of the U.S. Raw data are presented below. *NOTE: This format is not the usual raw data format. To save space the consumers have been grouped based on their scores on the independent variable.*

TABLE 2   AREA

N	E	S	W
0	14	2	4
0	14	2	4
6	20	8	10
6	20	8	10

Numbers in the table show the ratings of the 16 consumers (four for each area)

Perform the appropriate ANOVA on these data.

10. $SS_{BETWEEN}$, the sum of squares between groups, is
     A) 232   B) 144   C) 464   D) 488   E) 121

11. SS_{WITHIN}, the sum of squares within groups, is
     A) 72   B) 144   C) 152   D) 464   E) 36

12. $df_{BETWEEN}$, the degrees of freedom between groups, is
     A) 2   B) 3   C) 4   D) 6   E) 8

13. df_{WITHIN}, the degrees of freedom within groups, is
     A) 12   B) 3   C) 4   D) 5   E) 8

14. $MS_{BETWEEN}$, the mean squares between groups, is
     A) 12   B) 6   C) 154.67   D) 77.33   E) 202.67

15. MS_{WITHIN}, the mean squares within groups, is
     A) 12   B) 18   C) 50.67   D) 24   E) 202.67

16. The F ratio obtained from the data above is
     A) 3   B) 4.3   C) 12.89   D) 16.88   E) 24

17. The critical value of F in this case is
     A) 16.69   B) 5.29   C) 27.05   D) 28.71   E) 5.95

18. You conclude that you ___ reject the null hypothesis in this case, because based on previous answers, *p* must be _____ .01.
     A) can, greater B) cannot, less C) cannot, greater D) can, less than   E) can, equal to

----

HOSPITAL SATISFACTION

An administrator is interested in testing the hypothesis that patient satisfaction is equal among three hospitals, which we'll Designate A, B and C. Suppose nine patients selected at random are randomly divided into three groups of three patients, and one set of three patients is sent to each of the three hospitals. Upon discharge from the hospital each patient rates their satisfaction with the care they received. Raw data obtained from the three hospitals are shown in Table 3:

TABLE 3   HOSPITAL

A	B	C
0	4	8
2	6	10
4	8	12

Numbers in the table show the ratings of the nine patients (three for each hospital) Perform the appropriate ANOVA on these data.

19. $SS_{BETWEEN}$, the sum of squares between groups, is
    A) 12   B) 16   C) 24   D) 96   E) 64

20. SS_{WITHIN}, the sum of squares within groups, is
    A) 12   B) 16   C) 24   D) 96   E) 64

21. $df_{BETWEEN}$, the degrees of freedom between groups, is
    A) 2   B) 3   C) 4   D) 6   E) 8

22. df_{WITHIN}, the degrees of freedom within groups, is
    A) 2   B) 3   C) 4   D) 6   E) 8

23. $MS_{BETWEEN}$, the mean squares between groups, is
    A) 3   B) 4   C) 48   D) 24   E) 96

24. MS_{WITHIN}, the mean squares within groups, is
    A) 3   B) 4   C) 48   D) 24   E) 96

25. The F ratio obtained from the data above is
    A) 3   B) 4   C) 6   D) 12   E) 24

26. The critical value of F in this case is
    A) 10.92   B) 13.27   C) 99.30   D) 99.33   E) 8.65

27. You conclude that you ___ reject the null hypothesis in this case, because p is ____ .01.
    A) can, greater   B) cannot, less   C) cannot, greater   D) can, less than   E) can, equal to

---

TASTE TEST

The three most popular brands of colas #1, #2, and #3, are compared in a taste test. Each is rated by three typical consumers chosen at random. The data obtained are shown in
TABLE 1 below, where i represents the brand of cola, and X is the rating. Perform a One Way ANOVA on these data to test the hypothesis that there is no difference in ratings among the three brands in the population.

TABLE 1

i	X
#1	4
#1	6
#1	8
#2	12
#2	14
#2	16
#3	8
#3	10
#3	12

Numbers in the table show the ratings of the nine consumers (three tasting each cola)

Perform the appropriate ANOVA on these data.

28. SS_{TOTAL}, the sum of squares for X is

        A) 30   B) 120   C) 6   D) 24   E) 36

29. $SS_{BETWEEN}$, the sum of squares between groups, is

        A) 30   B) 12   C) 6   D) 24   E) 96

30. SS_{WITHIN}, the sum of squares within groups, is

        A) 30   B) 12   C) 6   D) 24   E) 36

31. df_{WITHIN}, the degrees of freedom within groups, is

        A) 2   B) 3   C) 4   D) 6   E) 8

32. df$_{BETWEEN}$, the degrees of freedom between groups, is
        A) 2   B) 3   C) 4   D) 6   E) 8

33. MS$_{BETWEEN}$, the mean squares between groups, is
        A) 3   B) 1   C) 12   D) 16   E) 48

34. MS$_{WITHIN}$, the mean squares within groups, is
        A) 3   B) 4   C) 12   D) 16   E) 1

35. The F ratio obtained from the data above is
        A) 3   B) 4   C) 16   D) 12   E) 24

36. The critical value of F in this case is
        A) 10.92   B) 13.27   C) 99.30   D) 99.33   E) 8.65

37. You conclude that you ___ reject the null hypothesis in this case, because *p* is ____ .01.
        A) can, greater
        B) cannot, less
        C) cannot, greater
        D) can, less than
        E) can, equal to

----

38. You would use a One Way ANOVA if you were investigating the relationship between…
        A) Ethnicity and Gender
        B) Height and Weight
        C) Birth Order and Rank in Class
        D) Favorite Color and Level of Depression
        E) none of the above

----

39. The 'SSTOTAL' (Or, 'sum of squared deviations from the mean') for the variable X in a One Way ANOVA represents variation that
        A) is *definitely* due to the independent variable
        B) is *definitely* due to error
        C) is *definitely* due to the dependent variable
        D) *might* be due to the independent variable

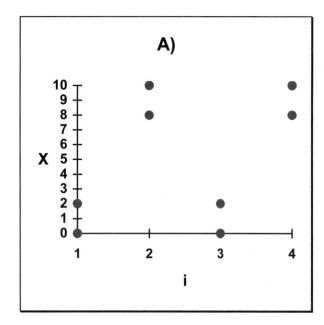

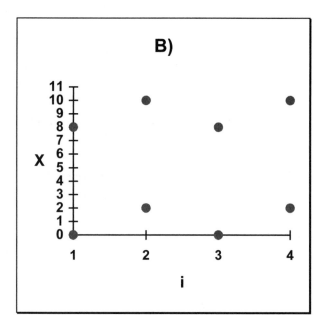

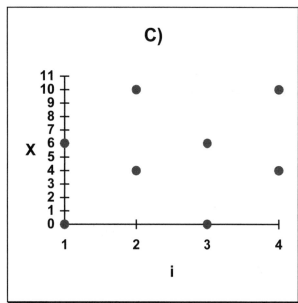

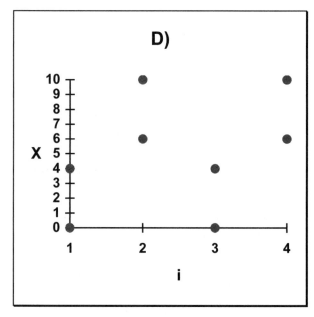

40. The graphs above show data for random samples of size 8 from a population.
Which graph above shows most variation due to *error*?
Which graph shows the most variation that *cannot* be explained by the independent variable i?
   A) A   B) B   C) C   D) D

41. Which graph above shows most variation that is due to the *independent variable*?
Which graph shows the most variation that *can* be explained by the independent variable?
   A) A   B) B   C) C   D) D

42. Which graph provides the *most convincing* evidence that there is a relationship between I
   and X in the population?   A) A   B) B   C) C   D) D

ANSWERS TO EXERCISES FOR CHAPTER 16

MULTIPLE CHOICE QUESTIONS

1. B	10. C	19. D	28. B
2. A	11. B	20. C	29. E
3. B	12. B	21. A	30. D
4. C	13. A	22. D	31. D
5. B	14. C	23. C	32. A
6. A	15. A	24. B	33. E
7. D	16. C	25. D	34. B
8. E	17. E	26. A	35. D
9. C	18. D	27. D	36. A
			37. D

----

38. D	39. D	40. B	41. A	42. A

COMPUTATION FOR THE EXERCISES ABOVE

If your answers matched the answers above you will not need to spend much time on the following section, which provides the details of all computations involved.

The format is that typically provided by a computer program. It provides examples of some of the compromises in notation that are made when a computer program does not assume that the printer which will be used can print out Greek letters, subscripts, etc.

Note the following substitutions which are used:

TEXTBOOKS	SOME COMPUTER PROGRAMS	
$\overline{X}$	M	(for "the mean")
$\overline{X}_i$	Mi	(the mean of the ith group)

EXAMPLE 1 from this chapter is also included to illustrate the new format with computations that will be familiar from the text above.

EXAMPLE 1: *COLOR RATINGS* (See section 16.1 above)

	DATA	SSX		SS BETWEEN			SS WITHIN		
i	X	X-M	( )2	Mi	Mi-M	( )2	Mi	X-Mi	( )2
1	0.0	-11.0	121.0	1.0	-10.0	100.0	1.0	-1.0	1.0
1	2.0	-9.0	81.0	1.0	-10.0	100.0	1.0	1.0	1.0
2	20.0	9.0	81.0	21.0	10.0	100.0	21.0	-1.0	1.0
2	22.0	11.0	121.0	21.0	10.0	100.0	21.0	1.0	1.0
3	10.0	-1.0	1.0	11.0	0.0	0.0	11.0	-1.0	1.0
3	12.0	1.0	1.0	11.0	0.0	0.0	11.0	1.0	1.0
12	66.0	0.0	406.0	66.0	0.0	400.0	66.0	0.0	6.0

COMPUTATION:

$$dfb = k-1 = (3 - 1) = 2$$
$$dfw = n-k = (6 - 3) = 3$$
$$MSB = SSB/dfb = 400.00/ 2 = 200.00$$
$$MSW = SSW/dfw = 6.00/ 3 = 2.00$$
$$F = MSB/MSW = 200.00/ 2.00 = 100.00$$

ANOVA SUMMARY TABLE:

SOURCE	SS	df	MS	F	Fcrit	REJECT?
BETWEEN	400.00	2	200.00	100.00	30.81	Yes
WITHIN	6.00	3	2.00			
TOTAL	406.00	5				

EXERCISES 1 - 9   *FIVE TREATMENTS COMPARED*

	DATA	SSX		SS BETWEEN			SS WITHIN		
i	X	X-M	( )2	Mi	Mi-M	( )2	Mi	X-Mi	( )2
1	0.0	-9.0	81.0	6.0	-3.0	9.0	6.0	-6.0	36.0
1	6.0	-3.0	9.0	6.0	-3.0	9.0	6.0	0.0	0.0
1	12.0	3.0	9.0	6.0	-3.0	9.0	6.0	6.0	36.0
2	2.0	-7.0	49.0	8.0	-1.0	1.0	8.0	-6.0	36.0
2	8.0	-1.0	1.0	8.0	-1.0	1.0	8.0	0.0	0.0
2	14.0	5.0	25.0	8.0	-1.0	1.0	8.0	6.0	36.0
3	3.0	-6.0	36.0	9.0	0.0	0.0	9.0	-6.0	36.0
3	9.0	0.0	0.0	9.0	0.0	0.0	9.0	0.0	0.0
3	15.0	6.0	36.0	9.0	0.0	0.0	9.0	6.0	36.0
4	4.0	-5.0	25.0	10.0	1.0	1.0	10.0	-6.0	36.0
4	10.0	1.0	1.0	10.0	1.0	1.0	10.0	0.0	0.0
4	16.0	7.0	49.0	10.0	1.0	1.0	10.0	6.0	36.0
5	6.0	-3.0	9.0	12.0	3.0	9.0	12.0	-6.0	36.0
5	12.0	3.0	9.0	12.0	3.0	9.0	12.0	0.0	0.0
5	18.0	9.0	81.0	12.0	3.0	9.0	12.0	6.0	36.0
45	135.0	0.0	420.0	135.0	0.0	60.0	135.0	0.0	360.0

COMPUTATION

```
dfb  =  k-1  =  ( 5 -   1)    =    4
dfw  =  n-k  =  (15 -   5)    =   10
MSB  =  SSB/dfb  =    60.00/ 4     =   15.00
MSW  =  SSW/dfw  =   360.00/10     =   36.00
F    =  MSB/MSW  =   15.00/ 36.00  =    0.42
```

ANOVA SUMMARY TABLE

SOURCE	SS	df	MS	F	Fcrit	REJECT?
BETWEEN	60.00	4	15.00	0.42	5.99	No
WITHIN	360.00	10	36.00			
TOTAL	420.00	14				

EXERCISES 10 - 18   *MARKET RESEARCH*

	DATA		SSX		SS BETWEEN			SS WITHIN		
i	X	X-M	( )2	Mi	Mi-M	( )2	Mi	X-Mi	( )2
1	0.0	-8.0	64.0	3.0	-5.0	25.0	3.0	-3.0	9.0
1	0.0	-8.0	64.0	3.0	-5.0	25.0	3.0	-3.0	9.0
1	6.0	-2.0	4.0	3.0	-5.0	25.0	3.0	3.0	9.0
1	6.0	-2.0	4.0	3.0	-5.0	25.0	3.0	3.0	9.0
2	14.0	6.0	36.0	17.0	9.0	81.0	17.0	-3.0	9.0
2	14.0	6.0	36.0	17.0	9.0	81.0	17.0	-3.0	9.0
2	20.0	12.0	144.0	17.0	9.0	81.0	17.0	3.0	9.0
2	20.0	12.0	144.0	17.0	9.0	81.0	17.0	3.0	9.0
3	2.0	-6.0	36.0	5.0	-3.0	9.0	5.0	-3.0	9.0
3	2.0	-6.0	36.0	5.0	-3.0	9.0	5.0	-3.0	9.0
3	8.0	0.0	0.0	5.0	-3.0	9.0	5.0	3.0	9.0
3	8.0	0.0	0.0	5.0	-3.0	9.0	5.0	3.0	9.0
4	4.0	-4.0	16.0	7.0	-1.0	1.0	7.0	-3.0	9.0
4	4.0	-4.0	16.0	7.0	-1.0	1.0	7.0	-3.0	9.0
4	10.0	2.0	4.0	7.0	-1.0	1.0	7.0	3.0	9.0
4	10.0	2.0	4.0	7.0	-1.0	1.0	7.0	3.0	9.0
40	128.0	0.0	608.0	128.0	0.0	464.0	128.0	0.0	144.0

COMPUTATION

```
dfb  =  k-1  =  ( 4 -   1)    =    3
dfw  =  n-k  =  (16 -   4)    =   12
MSB  =  SSB/dfb  =   464.00/ 3     =  154.67
MSW  =  SSW/dfw  =   144.00/12     =   12.00
F    =  MSB/MSW  =  154.67/ 12.00  =   12.89
```

ANOVA SUMMARY TABLE

SOURCE	SS	df	MS	F	Fcrit	REJECT?
BETWEEN	464.00	3	154.67	12.89	5.95	Yes
WITHIN	144.00	12	12.00			
TOTAL	608.00	15				

EXERCISES 19 - 27   *HOSPITAL SATISFACTION*

DATA		SSX			SS BETWEEN			SS WITHIN	
i	X	X-M	( )2	Mi	Mi-M	( )2	Mi	X-Mi	( )2
1	0.0	-6.0	36.0	2.0	-4.0	16.0	2.0	-2.0	4.0
1	2.0	-4.0	16.0	2.0	-4.0	16.0	2.0	0.0	0.0
1	4.0	-2.0	4.0	2.0	-4.0	16.0	2.0	2.0	4.0
2	4.0	-2.0	4.0	6.0	0.0	0.0	6.0	-2.0	4.0
2	6.0	0.0	0.0	6.0	0.0	0.0	6.0	0.0	0.0
2	8.0	2.0	4.0	6.0	0.0	0.0	6.0	2.0	4.0
3	8.0	2.0	4.0	10.0	4.0	16.0	10.0	-2.0	4.0
3	10.0	4.0	16.0	10.0	4.0	16.0	10.0	0.0	0.0
3	12.0	6.0	36.0	10.0	4.0	16.0	10.0	2.0	4.0
18	54.0	0.0	120.0	54.0	0.0	96.0	54.0	0.0	24.0

COMPUTATION

$$dfb = k-1 = (\ 3\ -\ 1) = 2$$
$$dfw = n-k = (\ 9\ -\ 3) = 6$$
$$MSB = SSB/dfb = 96.00/\ 2 = 48.00$$
$$MSW = SSW/dfw = 24.00/\ 6 = 4.00$$
$$F = MSB/MSW = 48.00/\ 4.00 = 12.00$$

ANOVA SUMMARY TABLE

SOURCE	SS	df	MS	F	Fcrit	REJECT?
BETWEEN	96.00	2	48.00	12.00	10.92	Yes
WITHIN	24.00	6	4.00			
TOTAL	120.00	8				

EXERCISES 28 - 37   *TASTE TEST*

DATA		SSX			SS BETWEEN			SSWITHIN	
n	X	X-M	( )2	Mi	Mi-M	( )2	Mi	X-Mi	( )2
1	4.0	-6.0	36.0	6.0	-4.0	16.0	6.0	-2.0	4.0
1	6.0	-4.0	16.0	6.0	-4.0	16.0	6.0	0.0	0.0
1	8.0	-2.0	4.0	6.0	-4.0	16.0	6.0	2.0	4.0
2	12.0	2.0	4.0	14.0	4.0	16.0	14.0	-2.0	4.0
2	14.0	4.0	16.0	14.0	4.0	16.0	14.0	0.0	0.0
2	16.0	6.0	36.0	14.0	4.0	16.0	14.0	2.0	4.0
3	8.0	-2.0	4.0	10.0	0.0	0.0	10.0	-2.0	4.0
3	10.0	0.0	0.0	10.0	0.0	0.0	10.0	0.0	0.0
3	12.0	2.0	4.0	10.0	0.0	0.0	10.0	2.0	4.0
21	92.0	0.0	120.0	90.0	0.0	96.0	90.0	0.0	24.0

COMPUTATION

$$dfb = k-1 = (\ 3\ -\ 1) = 2$$
$$dfw = n-k = (\ 9\ -\ 3) = 6$$
$$MSB = SSB/dfb = 96.00/\ 2 = 48.00$$
$$MSW = SSW/dfw = 24.00/\ 6 = 4.00$$
$$F = MSB/MSW = 48.00/\ 4.00 = 12.00$$

ANOVA SUMMARY TABLE

SOURCE	SS	df	MS	F	Fcrit	REJECT?
BETWEEN	96.00	2	48.00	12.00	10.92	Yes
WITHIN	24.00	6	4.00			
TOTAL	120.00	8				

CHAPTER 17

TWO WAY FACTORIAL ANALYSIS OF VARIANCE

17.1 INTRODUCTION

DATA REQUIREMENTS

Two Way ANOVA requires *two* independent nominal scale variables and *one* interval scale dependent variable. So it's the same as the One Way ANOVA, with one additional nominal independent variable. There are two formats commonly used for presenting the data. Here are examples of each:

TABLE 1A: TWO WAY ANOVA DATA   "TABLE" FORMAT

COLUMN TREATMENT

		PLACEBO	DRUG	
	PLACEBO	8, 10 $\overline{X}_{CELL} = 9$	6, 8 $\overline{X}_{CELL} = 7$	$\overline{X}_{ROW\,1} = 8$
ROW TREATMENT	DRUG	4, 6 $\overline{X}_{CELL} = 5$	18, 20 $\overline{X}_{CELL} = 19$	$\overline{X}_{ROW\,2} = 12$
		$\overline{X}_{COL1} = 7$	$\overline{X}_{COL\,2} = 13$	$\overline{X} = 10$

TABLE 1B: TWO WAY ANOVA DATA   "RAW DATA" FORMAT

	INDEPENDENT VARIABLES (NOMINAL SCALE)		DEPENDENT VARIABLE
CASE	ROW TREATMENT	COLUMN TREATMENT	SIDE EFFECTS $\underline{X}$
1	RP	CP	8
2	RP	CP	10
3	RP	CD	6
4	RP	CD	8
5	RD	CP	4
6	RD	CP	6
7	RD	CD	18
8	RD	CD	20

We'll use the data above in our first Two Way ANOVA example.

EXAMPLE 1: *TESTING FOR A DRUG INTERACTION*

Here's a very typical and intuitive example of the kind of situation in which Two Way ANOVA techniques are *needed*. Suppose a researcher at a drug company is checking *two* drugs for side effects, and for the existence of a drug interaction. We'll just refer to the two drugs as "the *row* drug" and "the *column* drug", so that it will be immediately obvious where they appear in TABLE 1A.

Each of 8 individuals chosen at random will be given two pills, one for each of the two drugs being assessed. Suppose each of the two pills may contain either a PLACEBO (denoted P) or the actual DRUG (denoted D). We'd say in this case, each of the two independent variables of interest has two possible *scores*, "P", for "placebo", indicating the individual received a pill with no active ingredient, and "D", indicating the individual received the actual drug. The two independent variables in cases like this are typically denoted "*row treatment*" (whether the individual got the row drug or the row placebo) and the "column treatment" (whether the individual got the column treatment or the column placebo).

THE TWO WAY FACTORIAL DESIGN

The procedure described above (dividing the 8 individuals into four groups of two individuals in which each individual receives two pills) guarantees that *each possible combination* of scores on the two independent variables are represented by a group of individuals. Each individual, after being exposed to *two treatments* (one for each independent variable) is measured on the *single* dependent variable "extent of side effects". This kind of experimental design, called a ***factorial design***, is common. The hypothetical data in TABLE 1 could have been obtained from such an experiment.

PICTURING DATA IN THE TABLE FORMAT (TABLE 1A)

The TABLE format helps you to see the effects more clearly. In TABLE 1A above, 24 scores which were obtained by 8 cases, each measured on 3 variables, are presented. The scores on the *dependent* variable (side effects) are grouped into "cells", or boxes, according to the cases' scores on the two *independent* variables, row treatment and column treatment.
If the cases or cases are people, they're referred to as *participants*.

The TABLE format lets you quickly identify the scores of all participants that were given a particular treatment. For example, four participants got the *column placebo,* and they scored 8, 10, 4 and 6 on the dependent variable (reading down the left column).

Four participants got the *row drug*, and they scored 4, 6, 18, 20 (reading across the lower row).

Two participants got both the row drug *and* the column drug, and they scored 18 and 20. These participants are in the same *cell*. Cells always contain the scores on the dependent variable for all participants that got the *same* treatment on *both* independent variables. Cell means for each cell, designated $\overline{X}_{CELL}$, are often included with the data. Cell means give you the best estimate of the scores in the population for cases given a particular *combination* of treatments. The cell mean of 19 in this case gives us an estimate of the extent of side effects that would be expected if all cases were given *both* drugs together.

THE RAW SCORE FORMAT (TABLE 1B)

This format is used in the SS computations required for ANOVA. There are four columns. The first column, *case* (or "participant") just provides an identification for the eight different cases in this sample. The term "case" is most common in current computer software. This column is optional, and *does not* represent a variable. The study is not *about* 'ID' numbers! The two independent variables will always have scores representing categories. These categories are sometimes represented by numbers: "Group 1, Group 2," etc., but these numbers are not meaningful, and they imply nothing about rank orderings or quantities.

17.2 THE "EFFECTS" OF THE INDEPENDENT VARIABLES

Two Way Analysis of Variance (Two Way ANOVA) is an extension of One Way ANOVA, in which there are *two* nominal scale independent variables instead of just one.

Each case's score on the dependent variable X is viewed as a sum of several effects:

(17.2.1) THE MODEL OF A SCORE

In a Two Way ANOVA, each case's score on the dependent variable X is expressed as the sum of the population mean, μ, and *four effects*:

$$X = \mu + \text{effect of row variable} + \text{effect of col. vbl.} + \text{effect of interaction} + \text{chance error}$$

This is referred to as the *model* of a score.

The variation (SS) and degrees of freedom (df) can each be partitioned into four parts:

$$SS_{TOTAL} = SS_{ROW} + SS_{COL} + SS_{INTERACTION} + SS_{ERROR}$$

$$df_{TOTAL} = df_{ROW} + df_{COL} + df_{INTERACTION} + df_{ERROR}$$

THE GOAL: EXPLAINING DEVIATIONS FROM THE MEAN

Suppose Joe is "Case 8" in the data set above. He scored 20 and the grand mean was 10. Joe's *deviation* from the mean is +10.

A goal of Two Way ANOVA is to be able to *explain* deviations like this +10, as much as possible, by referring to the *effects* of two independent variables, traditionally called the "*row*" variable and the "*column*" variable.

The *combined* effect of these two independent variables may be *stronger than you would have predicted* based on either one separately. This combined effect, called *interaction effect* must also be measured and considered.

The effect of chance *error*, or simply error, is just the name we put on the unexplained variation that is not due to any of the three effects above. It is measured by looking at the *within* cell variation.

So, for example, in a successful Two Way ANOVA, we'd want to be able to answer the question "*Why* did Joe score *10* units above the mean?" by analyzing that figure *+10*, and dividing it into *four* parts, each part due to one of the four effects above. The mathematics required to do this can be a little tedious, but it will seem easier and more intuitive if you try to keep this goal in mind.

There are *three steps* involved in a two way ANOVA, and *three* separate and independent hypothesis tests are performed.

STEP 1: TEST FOR MAIN EFFECTS OF THE ROW VARIABLE

The null hypothesis here is the same as it would be in a one way ANOVA: "There is no relationship between the *row* variable and the dependent variable." This hypothesis can be rejected when the *differences* between *row means* are extreme enough. The hypothesis is tested by computing a value of F equal to

$$F_{ROW} = \frac{MS_{BETWEEN\ ROWS}}{MS_{WITHIN}}$$

STEP 2: TEST FOR MAIN EFFECTS OF THE COLUMN VARIABLE

The null hypothesis is "there is no relationship between the *column* variable and the dependent variable." This hypothesis can be rejected when the *differences* between *column means* are extreme enough. The hypothesis is tested by computing a value of F equal to

$$F_{COLUMN} = \frac{MS_{BETWEEN\ COLUMNS}}{MS_{WITHIN}}$$

STEP 3: TEST FOR *INTERACTION* BETWEEN THE ROW AND COLUMN VARIABLES

The null hypothesis here can be stated informally: "If the *whole population* were measured, all the cell means will be just what you'd *expect*, based on *main effects* of the row and column variables." This "null" situation can be described as "there is no interaction between the two independent variables in the population.

The alternate hypothesis states that there *is* some interaction. **Interaction** exists when certain cells have means *different* from what you'd expect, based on row and column means. Our example below will show how the familiar concept of a "drug interaction" or "synergistic effect" corresponds exactly to *interaction* as it is measured in a two way ANOVA. (Synergistic effects are said to occur when the *combined* effect of two or more factors is greater or stronger than you'd expect, based on adding the individual effects of those factors.)

Hypotheses about this new interaction effect will be tested using an F ratio as usual. The only computations that are new are those which give the $SS_{INTERACTION}$ and $MS_{INTERACTION}$. The details of those computations will be provided below. Here is the F ratio used to test the significance of an interaction effect.

$$F_{INTERACTION} = \frac{MS_{INTERACTION}}{MS_{WITHIN}}$$

Note that in all three cases the MS (or "mean squares") for the *effect* (either "row effect", or "column effect" or "interaction effect") is in the *numerator*, and the denominator is always the MS *within* or MS *error*.

In each case, if the effect is very *strong*, the numerator will be a *high* value, and this will make F *high* and allow you to reject.

In each case, if there is a lot of random *error* or *within* cell variation, the denominator will be *large*, F will be *low*, and you are less likely to be able to reject.

Interaction is one of the most misunderstood, misused terms in statistics! It would be worth your time to memorize one of these brief definitions:

17.2.2 DEFINITIONS OF INTERACTION

Interaction exists when certain cells have means *different* from what you'd expect, based on row and column means.

Interaction exists when certain cell means cannot be predicted solely by using main effects.

Interaction exists when certain *combinations* of levels of independent variables produce surprisingly strong (or weak) effects.

17.3 UNDERSTANDING THE VARIATION DUE TO EACH EFFECT: INTUITIVE APPROACHES

A) SEEING THE FOUR SEPARATE EFFECTS ON CELL MEANS

TABLE 17.3.1: TWO WAY ANOVA DATA   ("TABLE" FORMAT)

	COLUMN TREATMENT		
	PLACEBO	DRUG	
PLACEBO	$\overline{X}_{CELL} = 9$	$\overline{X}_{CELL} = 7$	$\overline{X}_{ROW\,1} = 8$ (Effect = -2)
DRUG	$\overline{X}_{CELL} = 5$	$\overline{X}_{CELL} = 19$	$\overline{X}_{ROW\,2} = 12$ (Effect = +2)
	$\overline{X}_{COL1} = 7$ (Effect = -3)	$\overline{X}_{COL\,2} = 13$ (Effect = +3)	$\overline{X} = 10$

ROW TREATMENT (label at left of rows)

THE GRAND MEAN

$\overline{X}$, the grand mean, is 10. If the independent variables have *no* effect on the dependent variable, then all cell means will equal the grand mean. And if any of the cell means are *not* equal to the grand mean, then there is variation present which can be explained by the effects of the independent variables.

ROW EFFECTS

Suppose you find out that one participant in this study, Amy, received the *Row Placebo*. How does this information affect your estimate of Amy's score on the dependent variable? It *lowers* your estimate by 2 (From 10 to 8). We'll say "The effect of the Row Placebo is -2," because that's how information about this row affects your estimate. *Every cell* in the top row has a row effect of -2, and every cell in the bottom row has a row effect of +2.

COLUMN EFFECTS

Suppose you find out that one participant in this study, Ed, received the *Column Drug*. How does this information affect your estimate of Ed's score on the dependent variable? It *raises* your estimate by 3 (From 10 to 13). We'll say "The effect of the Column Drug is +3," because that's how information about this row affects your estimate. *Every cell* in the right column has a column effect of +3, and every cell in the left column has a column effect of -3.

Here are the original "observed" cell means we're trying to understand, along with the main effects described on the previous page:

"OBSERVED"
CELL MEANS

9	7
5	19

8 (Effect = -2)
12 (Effect = +2)
$\overline{X}$ = 10

7	13
(Effect = -3)	(Effect = +3)

It's easy to figure out what the **effect of the grand mean**, the **main effect of the row variable** and the **main effect of the column variable** must look like:

$\overline{X}$		+	"PURE" ROW EFFECTS		+	"PURE" COL EFFECTS		=	"EXPECTED" $\overline{X}$ + MAIN EFFECTS	
10	10		-2	-2		-3	+3		5	11
10	10		+2	+2		-3	+3		9	15

The $\overline{X}$ table shows what the cell means would be *if* they were affected *only* by the grand mean.

The "Pure" Row Effects table shows how each cell is affected by Row main effects.

The "Pure" Col Effects table shows how each cell is affected by Col main effects.

The "Expected" table above shows what you'd *expect* the pattern of cell means to be *if* there were *no interaction*, i.e., if the cell means were affected *only* by the grand mean and the two main effects, row and column.

The *difference* between the observed means and the expected means is the pattern of **interaction**:

"OBSERVED" CELL MEANS			-	"EXPECTED" $\overline{X}$ + MAIN EFFECTS			=	INTERACTION EFFECT		
9	7	8		5	11	8		+4	-4	0
5	19	12		9	15	12		-4	+4	0
7	13	10		7	13	10		0	0	0

VISUALIZING THE <u>COMBINATION</u> OF EFFECTS

Once the effects have been partitioned, the original cell means can be expressed as a *sum* of the effects that contribute to them.

"OBSERVED" CELL MEANS		=	$\overline{X}$		+	ROW EFFECTS		+	COL EFFECTS		+	INTERACTION EFFECTS	
9	7		10	10		-2	-2		-3	+3		+4	-4
5	19		10	10		+2	+2		-3	+3		-4	+4

B) PICTURING THE EFFECTS BY <u>GRAPHING</u> THE CELL MEANS

These data were presented and analyzed in TABLE 1 in section 17.1:

TABLE 1A: TWO WAY ANOVA DATA

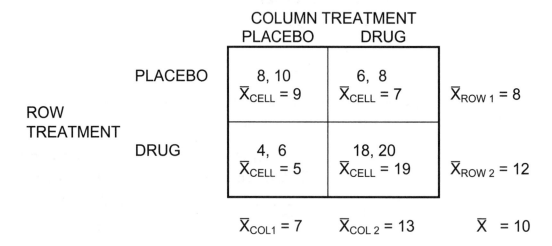

The figure below shows the usual way we'd graph the cell means to get a picture of the effects.

Each *line* in this graph represents one *row* of cell means.

    The *dashed* line shows the cell means for the Row Drug cells (the bottom row).
    The *solid* line shows the cell means for the Row Placebo cells (the top row).

The lines will be *parallel* if and only if there is *no* interaction.

    Here, the lines are clearly *not parallel*, showing that there *is* interaction.

FIG 17.3.1

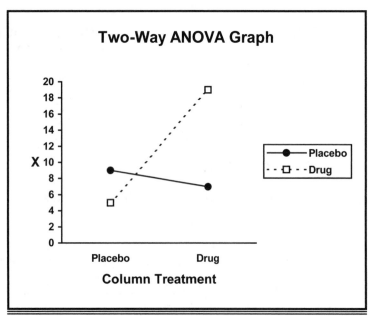

17.4 COMPUTATION OF THE VARIATION DUE TO EACH EFFECT

TABLE 17.4 A

DATA			SS$_{TOTAL}$			SS$_{WITHIN}$ or SS$_{ERROR}$		
R	C	X	$\overline{X}$	$X - \overline{X}$	$(X - \overline{X})^2$	$\overline{X}_{CELL}$	$X - \overline{X}_{CELL}$	$(X - \overline{X}_{CELL})^2$
RP	CP	8	10	-2	4	9	-1	1
RP	CP	10	10	0	0	9	+1	1
RP	CD	6	10	-4	16	7	-1	1
RP	CD	8	10	-2	4	7	+1	1
RD	CP	4	10	-6	36	5	-1	1
RD	CP	6	10	-4	16	5	+1	1
RD	CD	18	10	8	64	19	-1	1
RD	CD	20	10	10	100	19	+1	1
				√ 0	240		√ 0	8

Table 17.4 A shows the usual SS computation for X and the SS$_{WITHIN}$ computation, for the EXAMPLE 1 data. In Two Way ANOVA the *error* or *within* SS is computed using deviations from *cell means*, and it represents the variation within *cells*.

TABLE 17.4 B

DATA			SS$_{ROW}$			SS$_{COL}$		
R	C	X	$\overline{X}_{ROW}$	$\overline{X}_{ROW} - \overline{X}$	$(\overline{X}_{ROW} - \overline{X})^2$	$\overline{X}_{COL}$	$\overline{X}_{COL} - \overline{X}$	$(\overline{X}_{COL} - \overline{X})^2$
RP	CP	8	8	-2	4	7	-3	9
RP	CP	10	8	-2	4	7	-3	9
RP	CD	6	8	-2	4	13	+3	9
RP	CD	8	8	-2	4	13	+3	9
RD	CP	4	12	+2	4	7	-3	9
RD	CP	6	12	+2	4	7	-3	9
RD	CD	18	12	+2	4	13	+3	9
RD	CD	20	12	+2	4	13	+3	9
				√ 0	32		√ 0	72

The computations in TABLE 17.4 B are for the SS due to the main effects of the row variable and of the column variable. The SS$_{ROW}$ is the same value that would be obtained on a One Way ANOVA with the row variable as the independent variable. The TABLE 17.4 B computations are the same as the "between groups" computations in two One Way ANOVAs: One for the row variable, and one for the column variable.

The SS for the INTERACTION effect is computed by subtraction:

$$SS_{INTERACTION} = SS_{TOTAL} - SS_{ROW} - SS_{COL} - SS_{WITHIN}$$

$$= 240 - 32 - 72 - 8$$

$$= 128$$

The SS for INTERACTION is often referred to as "**R x C**" to indicate that *both* the case's row variable score *and* its column variable score are taken into account in determining the cell means which determine this SS.

17.5   THE ANOVA SUMMARY TABLE

COMPUTATION OF DEGREES OF FREEDOM (df)

To compute the MS, or "mean squared deviations," required for F ratios, we need the degrees of freedom for each effect. These formulas have been devised to count the number of values that can actually vary, taking into account the constraints of the data for an ANOVA.

$$df_{TOTAL} = n - 1$$

$$df_{ROW} = \text{Number of rows} - 1$$

$$df_{COL} = \text{Number of columns} - 1$$

$$df_{INTERACTION} = (df_{ROW})(df_{COL})$$

$$df_{ERROR} \text{ or } df_{WITHIN} = df_{TOTAL} - df_{ROW} - df_{COL} - df_{INTERACTION}$$

ANOVA SUMMARY TABLE

There is a standard format for reporting the results of a Two Way ANOVA. The SS computed above are used along with appropriate degrees of freedom to compute three F ratios.

SOURCE	SS	df	MS	F(Obtained)	F Critical Value
DRUG R (Row Vbl)	32	1	32	16 n.s.	21.20
DRUG C (Col Vbl)	72	1	72	36*	21.20
INTERACTION (R x C)	128	1	128	64*	21.20
ERROR (Within Cells)	8	4	2		
TOTAL	240	7			

$$* \, p < .01$$

The degrees of freedom were computed using the formulas above. 'n.s.' indicates 'not significant' MS values for all four effects (ROW, COL, INTERACTION, ERROR) are computed by dividing the SS by the df. E.g.:

$$MS_{ERROR} = SS_{ERROR} / df_{ERROR} = 8/4 = 2.$$

F ratios for ROW, COL and INTERACTION were computed by dividing the MS for each effect by MS_{ERROR}. For example,

$$F_{ROW} = MS_{ROW} / MS_{ERROR} = 32/2 = 16$$

F critical values are found in the F TABLE by looking in the *row* that corresponds to the *WITHIN (or ERROR) df* and the *column* that corresponds to the degrees of freedom for the effect being evaluated (Either "ROW" or "COL" or "INTERACTION"). In this case all critical F values are 21.20.

DATA REQUIREMENTS AND ASSUMPTIONS

In order for the hypothesis test in a two-way factorial ANOVA to be meaningful, the data must have been collected in a particular way, and the population sampled from must have certain properties:

ASSUMPTIONS ABOUT THE SAMPLE DATA

1. There are *two* nominal scale independent variables.

2. Each case in the sample appears in *only one* of the cells.

3. Each case in the sample was randomly sampled from some population.

4. There is *one* interval scale dependent variable.

ASSUMPTIONS ABOUT THE DISTRIBUTION OF SCORES IN THE POPULATION

5. Independence: Scores don't "influence each other". For example, if one person scores high, that doesn't make another person score high also.

6. Normality: Within each cell in the population, the distribution of scores on the dependent variable are approximately normal.

7. Homogeneity of variance:

For each cell in the population, the variance is the same as for each other cell. It is well known that minor violations of this assumption can be tolerated. ANOVA procedures are said to be fairly *robust* against violations of homogeneity of variance.

EXERCISES FOR CHAPTER 17

----

1. A Two Way ANOVA was performed on data which included scores for these variables
   Blood Type   Cholesterol Level
   Order of finish in a sprint   Gender

The independent variable(s) must have been _____ and the dependent variable(s) must have been _____.

EFFECTS OF ADS

TABLE 1:

(TV?) ROW	(RADIO?) COL	(SALES) X
N	N	10
N	N	13
N	N	16
N	Y	0
N	Y	3
N	Y	6
Y	N	4
Y	N	7
Y	N	10
Y	Y	18
Y	Y	21
Y	Y	24

12 retail stores in different cities are selected at random by a large national chain of stores to assess the effects of TV ads and radio ads on sales.

The stores are divided into four groups, with three stores in each group. For each group of stores, a different combination of TV and/or radio ads were run. A "Y" in the "TV" column indicates that TV ads were run for that store, and a "Y" in the "RADIO" column indicates that radio ads were run for that store. The third column shows the increase in sales for that store.

Conduct the appropriate ANOVA in this situation, and answer the following questions BASED ONLY ON THE INFORMATION IN TABLE 1.

2. SS_{TOTAL}, the total sum of squares for these data is...
   A) 12   B) 432   C) 108   D) 624   E) 1048

3. SS_{ROW} is A) 12   B) 432   C) 108   D) 624   E) 0

4. SS_{COL} is A) 12   B) 432   C) 108   D) 624   E) 0

5. $SS_{INTERACTION}$ is A) 12   B) 432   C) 108   D) 624   E) 0

6. The number of variables used in the above data is
    A) 1   B) 2   C) 3   D) 4   E) 12

7. The total degrees of freedom for Table 1 is
    A) 12   B) 11   C) 8   D) 3   E) 1

8. The number of *row* degrees of freedom is
    A) 12   B) 11   C) 8   D) 3   E) 1

9. The number of degrees of freedom for *interaction* is
    A) 12   B) 11   C) 8   D) 3   E) 1

10. The number of degrees of freedom for *within* cell variation (error) is
    A) 12   B) 11   C) 8   D) 3   E) 1

11. The "mean squares for rows", or MS_{ROW} is
    A) 9   B) 108   C) 12   D) 432   E) 1

12. MS_{COL} is
    A) 9   B) 108   C) 12   D) 432   E) 1

13. $MS_{INTERACTION}$ is
    A) 9   B) 108   C) 12   D) 432   E) 1

14. The obtained F ratio for the row variable (TV) is
    A) 48   B) 12   C) 1   D) 1.33   E) 108

15. The obtained F ratio for the effect of *interaction* is
    A) 48   B) 12   C) 1   D) 1.33   E) 108

16. The critical value of F appropriate for testing the above F ratios for significance is
    A) 34.12   B) 21.20   C) 5859   D) 13.74   E) 11.26

17. Three different null hypotheses are considered in cases such as this: ROW, COLUMN, and INTERACTION null hypotheses. Which of the three hypotheses *can be rejected* based on the data above?
    A) None of the three null hypotheses may be rejected.
    B) ROW and INTERACTION only   C) COL and INTERACTION only
    D) ROW and COL only   E) All three null hypotheses may be rejected.

DRUG EFFECTS: 12 PARTICIPANTS

TABLE 2A:

	P	D
D	0,3,6	14,17,20
P	2,5,8	4,7,10

TABLE 2B:

DRUG R ROW	DRUG C COL	EFFECT X
D	P	0
D	P	3
D	P	6
D	D	14
D	D	17
D	D	20
P	P	2
P	P	5
P	P	8
P	D	4
P	D	7
P	D	10

12 patients are selected at random. The patients are divided into four groups, with three patients in each group. For each group of patients, a different combination of two pills is administered daily. The first pill contains either DRUG R or a PLACEBO. The other pill contains either DRUG C or a PLACEBO. Conduct the appropriate ANOVA in this situation, and answer the following questions BASED ONLY ON THE INFORMATION IN TABLE 2.

18. How many variables are involved in the above data?
    A) 4   B) 12   C) 24   D) 2   E) 3

19. SS_{TOTAL}, the total sum of squares for these data is...
    A) 210   B) 420   C) 192   D) 108   E) 144

20. If you perform a one-way ANOVA using only the *row* variable as the independent variable and EFFECT as the dependent variable, the SS *between* groups is referred to as the "SS_{ROW}" For the data above the SS_{ROW} is
    A) 48   B) 192   C) 72   D) 108   E) 8

21. SS$_{COL}$ is   A) 48   B) 192   C) 72   D) 108   E) 8

22. If you subtract the SS due to effects of the row and column variables, and the SS due to error from the total SS, you are left with the SS due to *interaction* between the row and column variables. I.e.,

$$SS_{INTERACTION} = SStot - SS_{ROW} - SScol - SSwithin$$

   For the data in Table 2A, SS$_{INTERACTION}$ is
   A) 48   B) 192   C) 72   D) 108   E) 8

23. The number of *scores* involved in the raw data in this example must be
   A) 12   B) 24   C) 36   D) 48   E) 16

24. The total degrees of freedom for Table 2A is
   A) 12   B) 11   C) 7   D) 15   E) 1

25. The number of degrees of freedom for *within* cell variation (or "error") is
   A) 12   B) 11   C) 4   D) 8   E) 1

26. The "mean squares for rows," or MSrow is
   A) 48   B) 192   C) 72   D) 108   E) 8

27. MS$_{COL}$ is
   A) 48   B) 192   C) 72   D) 108   E) 8

28. MSwithin (or MSerror) is
   A) 48   B) 192   C) 72   D) 108   E) 9

29. The obtained F ratio for the row variable, DRUG R, is
   A) 12   B) 5.33   C) 48   D) 1.78   E) 21.33

30. The obtained F ratio for the effect of *interaction* is
   A) 12   B) 5.33   C) 48   D) 16   E) 21.33

31. The critical value of F appropriate for testing the above F ratios for significance is
   A) 10.56   B) 8.53   C) 8.68   D) 11.26   E) 21.20

32. Three different null hypotheses are considered in cases such as this: ROW, COLUMN, and INTERACTION null hypotheses. Which of the three hypotheses *can be rejected*?
   A) None of the three null hypotheses may be rejected.
   B) ROW and INTERACTION only
   C) COL and INTERACTION only
   D) ROW and COL only
   E) All three null hypotheses may be rejected.

DRUG EFFECTS: 8 PARTICIPANTS

TABLE 3:

DRUG R	DRUG C	EFFECT
ROW	COL	X
D	P	0
D	P	3
D	D	7
D	D	10
P	P	1
P	P	4
P	D	2
P	D	5

Eight patients are selected at random. The patients are divided into four groups, with two patients in each group. For each group of patients, a different combination of two pills is administered daily. The first pill contains either DRUG R or a PLACEBO. The other pill contains either DRUG C or a PLACEBO.

Conduct the appropriate ANOVA in this situation, and answer the following questions BASED ONLY ON THE INFORMATION IN TABLE 3.

33. SS_{TOTAL}, the total sum of squares for these data is...
    A) 76   B) 608   C) 152   D) 256   E) 144

34. If you perform a one-way ANOVA using only the *row* variable as the independent variable and EFFECT as the dependent variable, the SS *between* groups is referred to as the "SS_{ROW}"
    For the data above the SS_{ROW} is
    A) 8   B) 32   C) 18   D) 16   E) 36

35. SS_{COL} is A) 32   B) 8   C) 18   D) 16   E) 36

36. If you subtract the SS due to effects of the row and column variables, and the SS due to error from the total SS, you are left with the SS due to *interaction* between the row and column variables. I.e.,

$$SS_{INTERACTION} = SS_{tot} - SS_{ROW} - SS_{col} - SS_{within}$$

    For the data in Table 3, $SS_{INTERACTION}$ is
    A) 32   B) 18   C) 8   D) 16   E) 36

37. The number of *scores* involved in the raw data in this example must be
    A) 1   B) 24   C) 3   D) 48   E) 16

38. The total degrees of freedom for Table 3 is
    A) 12   B) 7   C) 16   D) 15   E) 1

39. The number of *row* degrees of freedom is
    A) 12   B) 11   C) 16   D) 3   E) 1

40. The number of degrees of freedom for *interaction* is
    A) 12   B) 11   C) 16   D) 15   E) 1

41. The number of degrees of freedom for *within* cell variation (or "error") is
    A) 12   B) 11   C) 4   D) 15   E) 1

42. The "mean squares for rows", or MSrow is
    A) 8   B) 32   C) 16   D) 64   E) 256

43. The mean squares for interaction is
    A) 18   B) 32   C) 16   D) 64   E) 256

44. MS_{COL} is
    A) 32   B) 12   C) 16   D) 64   E) 8

45. MSwithin (or MSerror) is
    A) 3   B) 4.5   C) 16   D) 36   E) 1.5

46. The obtained F ratio for the row variable, DRUG R, is
    A) 5.33   B) 12   C) 1.78   D) 16   E) 64

47. The obtained F ratio for the effect of *interaction* is
    A) 5.33   B) 4   C) 21.33   D) 16   E) 64

48. The critical value of F appropriate for testing the above F ratios for significance is
    A) 10.56   B) 8.53   C) 8.68   D) 9.33   E) 21.20

49. Three different null hypotheses are considered in cases such as this: ROW, COLUMN, and INTERACTION null hypotheses. Which of the three hypotheses *can be rejected* based on the data above?
    A) None of the three null hypotheses may be rejected.
    B) ROW and INTERACTION only
    C) COL and INTERACTION only
    D) ROW and COL only
    E) All three null hypotheses may be rejected.

FIGURE 1

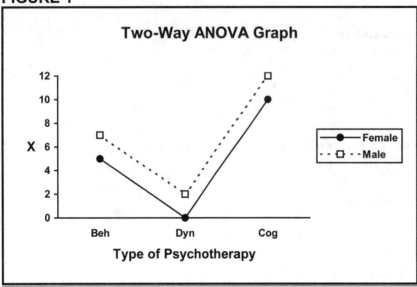

Figure 1 above is a sketch of the cell means for a two-way ANOVA.

      One independent variable is GENDER (Female or Male)

      The other independent variable is TYPE OF PSYCHOTHERAPY (Behavioral or Dynamic or Cognitive)

      The dependent variable is IMPROVEMENT after treatment.

50. In this sample, was there a *main effect* due to GENDER?
    A) Yes   B) No

51. Was there a *main effect* due to TYPE OF PSYCHOTHERAPY?
    A) Yes   B) No

52. Was there an *interaction* between GENDER and TYPE OF PSYCHOTHERAPY?
    A) Yes   B) No

----

53. In a One Way ANOVA the SS_{WITHIN} (Sum of squares *within* groups) always indicates how much variation in the sample was due to the effect of…
    A) error (*not* due to the independent variable)
    B) the independent variable
    C) error and the independent variable combined

----

54. In a two way ANOVA, suppose that…

      the grand mean is 20,   the mean of the *top row* is 15 and   the mean of the *left column* is 18

      What would you *expect* the cell mean for the *top left* cell to be, if there is *no interaction*?
      (One cell is in the top row *and* the left column. What would you expect its mean to be?)
      A) 15   B) 10   C) 12   D) 13   E) -13

Suppose that the graph below represents a different set of data that might have been obtained from the same kind of study described above. That is, The ROW variable is EXPOSURE, the COLUMN variable is TREATMENT, and the dependent variable is STRESS.

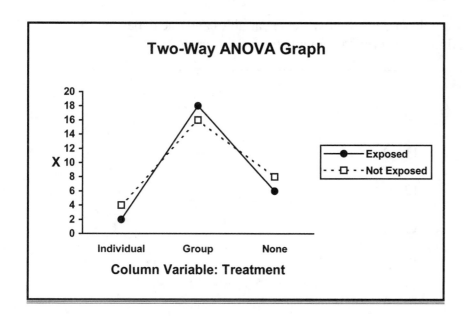

55. In this set of data, the variable TREATMENT clearly has a _____ effect than the variable EXPOSURE.

    A) weaker   B) stronger

56. In this set of data, interaction effect

    A) does not exist at all   B) exists, but it is fairly weak   C) exists and it is extremely strong

----

SCOPING OUT 2 WAY ANOVA TABLES

#1

12	16	14
0	4	2
6	10	8

#2

24	0	12
0	0	0
12	0	6

#3

6	2	4
10	6	8
8	4	6

#4

0	0	0
2	2	2
1	1	1

ABOVE ARE 4 POSSIBLE DATA SETS DESCRIBED IN TWO WAY ANOVA TABLES, SHOWING *CELL MEANS* IN THE CELLS,(NOT SCORES), *ROW MEANS* AND *COLUMN MEANS*.

57. Which table (or tables) shows some *interaction*?

    A) #1 only   B) #2 only   C) #1 and #4 only   D) #1, #2 and #3 only   E) all 4 tables

58. For which table(s) is the *row* effect stronger than the *column* effect?

    A) #1 only   B) #4 only   C) #1 and #4 only   D) #1, #2 and #4 only   E) all 4 tables

----

ANSWERS TO EXERCISES FOR CHAPTER 17

----

1. Independent variables: Blood Type, Gender

   Dependent variables: Cholesterol Level

Each two way ANOVA has two independent *nominal* scale variables and one dependent *interval* scale variable. The "*order* of finish in a sprint" is obviously *ordinal* scale.

EFFECTS OF ADS

2. D   10. C

3. C   11. B

4. A   12. C

5. B   13. D

6. C   14. B

7. B   15. A

8. E   16. E

9. E   17. B

DRUG EFFECTS: 12 PARTICIPANTS

18. E   26. A

19. B   27. B

20. A   28. E

21. B   29. B

22. D   30. A

23. C   31. D

24. B   32. C

25. D

DRUG EFFECTS: 8 PARTICIPANTS

33. A	41. C
34. A	42. A
35. A	43. A
36. B	44. A
37. B	45. B
38. B	46. C
39. E	47. B
40. E	48. E
	49. A

----
50. A) Yes

51. A) Yes

52. B) No

----
53. A) error (*not* due to the independent variable)

----
54. D) 13   The row effect is -5 and the column effect is -2. Adding these two effects to the grand mean of 20 leads us to expect a cell mean of 13.

----
55. B) stronger

56. B) exists, but it is fairly weak

----
57. B) #2 only

58. C) #1 and #4 only

COMPUTATION FOR THE PRECEDING EXERCISES

Below are all computations required for the Two Way ANOVAs in Chapter 17.

The format of the ANOVA summary table is typical of most computer programs. However, most programs *do not* show the computations. The computer program that produced the output below is available from your instructor free of charge. (It runs on any IBM compatible PC. The data must be typed in using a text editor, such as the EDIT program supplied with DOS 5.0)

Even though computer programs can make computations easier when data sets are large, it is *not* a waste of time to compute several ANOVAs "by hand" when you are *learning* to understand ANOVA techniques! Most authors and instructors agree that the intuitions that you absorb, particularly when computing the different SS values, are worth the effort required.

The notation used in these computations is simplified to allow easy printing on all printers:

Computer Printouts		Our Notation	Designates:
M	$\Rightarrow$	$\bar{X}$	The grand mean of all n cases in the sample
Mcell	$\Rightarrow$	$\bar{X}$cell	The cell mean
Mrow	$\Rightarrow$	$\bar{X}$row	The row mean
Mcol	$\Rightarrow$	$\bar{X}$col	The column mean

CH 17   EXAMPLE 1: *TESTING FOR A DRUG INTERACTION*

ROW	COL	DATA X	X-M	SSx ( )2	Mcell	SSw or SSerror X-Mcell	( )2
1	1	8.0	-2.0	4.0	9.0	-1.0	1.0
1	1	10.0	0.0	0.0	9.0	1.0	1.0
1	2	6.0	-4.0	16.0	7.0	-1.0	1.0
1	2	8.0	-2.0	4.0	7.0	1.0	1.0
2	1	4.0	-6.0	36.0	5.0	-1.0	1.0
2	1	6.0	-4.0	16.0	5.0	1.0	1.0
2	2	18.0	8.0	64.0	19.0	-1.0	1.0
2	2	20.0	10.0	100.0	19.0	1.0	1.0
		80.0	0.0	240.0	80.0	0.0	8.0

ROW	COL	DATA X	Mrow	SSrow Mrow-M	( )2	Mcol	SScol Mcol-M	( )2
1	1	8.0	8.0	-2.0	4.0	7.0	-3.0	9.0
1	1	10.0	8.0	-2.0	4.0	7.0	-3.0	9.0
1	2	6.0	8.0	-2.0	4.0	13.0	3.0	9.0
1	2	8.0	8.0	-2.0	4.0	13.0	3.0	9.0
2	1	4.0	12.0	2.0	4.0	7.0	-3.0	9.0
2	1	6.0	12.0	2.0	4.0	7.0	-3.0	9.0
2	2	18.0	12.0	2.0	4.0	13.0	3.0	9.0
2	2	20.0	12.0	2.0	4.0	13.0	3.0	9.0
		80.0	80.0	0.0	32.0	80.0	0.0	72.0

COMPUTATION

```
SSint  =     SSx   -  SSrow  -  SScol  -  SSw
       =  240.00  -  32.00  -  72.00  -  8.00
       =  128.00

df     =  n - 1 = ( 8 - 1)   =   7
dfrow  =  nrow - 1 = ( 2 - 1)   =   1
dfcol  =  ncol - 1 = ( 2 - 1)   =   1
dfint  =  (dfrow)(dfcol)  = ( 1)( 1)   =   1
dfw    =  df - dfrow - dfcol - dfint
       =  7  -  1  -  1  -  1
       =  4

MSrow  =  SSrow/dfrow  =   32.00/ 1   =  32.00
MScol  =  SScol/dfcol  =   72.00/ 1   =  72.00
MSint  =  SSint/dfint  =  128.00/ 1   = 128.00
MSw    =  SSw/dfw      =    8.00/ 4   =   2.00

Frow   =  MSrow/MSw    =   32.00/ 2.00   =  16.00
Fcol   =  MScol/MSw    =   72.00/ 2.00   =  36.00
Fint   =  MSint/MSw    =  128.00/ 2.00   =  64.00
```

ANOVA SUMMARY TABLE:

SOURCE	SS	df	MS	F	Fcrit	REJECT?
BETWEEN ROWS	32.00	1	32.00	16.00	21.20	No
BETWEEN COLS	72.00	1	72.00	36.00	21.20	Yes
INTERACTION	128.00	1	128.00	64.00	21.20	Yes
WITHIN	8.00	4	2.00			
TOTAL	240.00	7				

CH 17   EXERCISES 2 - 17   *EFFECTS OF ADS*

	DATA		SSx		SSw or SSerror		
ROW	COL	X	X-M	( )2	Mcell	X-Mcell	( )2
1	1	10.0	-1.0	1.0	13.0	-3.0	9.0
1	1	13.0	2.0	4.0	13.0	0.0	0.0
1	1	16.0	5.0	25.0	13.0	3.0	9.0
1	2	0.0	-11.0	121.0	3.0	-3.0	9.0
1	2	3.0	-8.0	64.0	3.0	0.0	0.0
1	2	6.0	-5.0	25.0	3.0	3.0	9.0
2	1	4.0	-7.0	49.0	7.0	-3.0	9.0
2	1	7.0	-4.0	16.0	7.0	0.0	0.0
2	1	10.0	-1.0	1.0	7.0	3.0	9.0
2	2	18.0	7.0	49.0	21.0	-3.0	9.0
2	2	21.0	10.0	100.0	21.0	0.0	0.0
2	2	24.0	13.0	169.0	21.0	3.0	9.0
		132.0	0.0	624.0	132.0	0.0	72.0

	DATA			SSrow			SScol		
ROW	COL	X	Mrow	Mrow-M	( )2	Mcol	Mcol-M	( )2
1	1	10.0	8.0	-3.0	9.0	10.0	-1.0	1.0
1	1	13.0	8.0	-3.0	9.0	10.0	-1.0	1.0
1	1	16.0	8.0	-3.0	9.0	10.0	-1.0	1.0
1	2	0.0	8.0	-3.0	9.0	12.0	1.0	1.0
1	2	3.0	8.0	-3.0	9.0	12.0	1.0	1.0
1	2	6.0	8.0	-3.0	9.0	12.0	1.0	1.0
2	1	4.0	14.0	3.0	9.0	10.0	-1.0	1.0
2	1	7.0	14.0	3.0	9.0	10.0	-1.0	1.0
2	1	10.0	14.0	3.0	9.0	10.0	-1.0	1.0
2	2	18.0	14.0	3.0	9.0	12.0	1.0	1.0
2	2	21.0	14.0	3.0	9.0	12.0	1.0	1.0
2	2	24.0	14.0	3.0	9.0	12.0	1.0	1.0
		132.0	132.0	0.0	108.0	132.0	0.0	12.0

COMPUTATION

$$SSint = SSx - SSrow - SScol - SSw = 624.00 - 108.00 - 12.00 - 72.00$$
$$= 432.00$$

df	=	n - 1 = (12 - 1)	=	11	
dfrow	=	nrow - 1 = (2 - 1)	=	1	
dfcol	=	ncol - 1 = (2 - 1)	=	1	
dfint	=	(dfrow)(dfcol) = (1)(1)	=	1	
dfw	=	df - dfrow - dfcol - dfint =	11 - 1 - 1 - 1 =	8	

MSrow	=	SSrow/dfrow	= 108.00/ 1	= 108.00	
MScol	=	SScol/dfcol	= 12.00/ 1	= 12.00	
MSint	=	SSint/dfint	= 432.00/ 1	= 432.00	
MSw	=	SSw/dfw	= 72.00/ 8	= 9.00	
Frow	=	MSrow/MSw	= 108.00/ 9.00	= 12.00	
Fcol	=	MScol/MSw	= 12.00/ 9.00	= 1.33	
Fint	=	MSint/MSw	= 432.00/ 9.00	= 48.00	

ANOVA SUMMARY TABLE:

SOURCE	SS	df	MS	F	Fcrit	REJECT?
BETWEEN ROWS	108.00	1	108.00	12.00*	11.26	Yes
BETWEEN COLS	12.00	1	12.00	1.33	11.26	No
INTERACTION	432.00	1	432.00	48.00*	11.26	Yes
WITHIN	72.00	8	9.00			
TOTAL	624.00	11				

```
-----------------------------------------------------------------
```

CH 17   EXERCISES 18 - 32   *DRUG EFFECTS: 12 PARTICIPANTS*

```
            DATA                    SSx              SSw or SSerror
 ROW  COL    X       X-M     ( )2      Mcell   X-Mcell    ( )2
  1    1     2.0     -6.0    36.0       5.0     -3.0      9.0
  1    1     5.0     -3.0     9.0       5.0      0.0      0.0
  1    1     8.0      0.0     0.0       5.0      3.0      9.0
  1    2     4.0     -4.0    16.0       7.0     -3.0      9.0
  1    2     7.0     -1.0     1.0       7.0      0.0      0.0
  1    2    10.0      2.0     4.0       7.0      3.0      9.0
  2    1     0.0     -8.0    64.0       3.0     -3.0      9.0
  2    1     3.0     -5.0    25.0       3.0      0.0      0.0
  2    1     6.0     -2.0     4.0       3.0      3.0      9.0
  2    2    14.0      6.0    36.0      17.0     -3.0      9.0
  2    2    17.0      9.0    81.0      17.0      0.0      0.0
  2    2    20.0     12.0   144.0      17.0      3.0      9.0
            96.0      0.0   420.0      96.0      0.0     72.0

            DATA                    SSrow                  SScol
 ROW  COL    X      Mrow    Mrow-M   ( )2     Mcol   Mcol-M   ( )2
  1    1     2.0     6.0    -2.0      4.0      4.0    -4.0    16.0
  1    1     5.0     6.0    -2.0      4.0      4.0    -4.0    16.0
  1    1     8.0     6.0    -2.0      4.0      4.0    -4.0    16.0
  1    2     4.0     6.0    -2.0      4.0     12.0     4.0    16.0
  1    2     7.0     6.0    -2.0      4.0     12.0     4.0    16.0
  1    2    10.0     6.0    -2.0      4.0     12.0     4.0    16.0
  2    1     0.0    10.0     2.0      4.0      4.0    -4.0    16.0
  2    1     3.0    10.0     2.0      4.0      4.0    -4.0    16.0
  2    1     6.0    10.0     2.0      4.0      4.0    -4.0    16.0
  2    2    14.0    10.0     2.0      4.0     12.0     4.0    16.0
  2    2    17.0    10.0     2.0      4.0     12.0     4.0    16.0
  2    2    20.0    10.0     2.0      4.0     12.0     4.0    16.0
            96.0    96.0     0.0     48.0     96.0     0.0   192.0
```

COMPUTATION

$$SSint = SSx - SSrow - SScol - SSw = 420.00 - 48.00 - 192.00 - 72.00$$
$$= 108.00$$

```
    df     =  n - 1  =  (12 -  1)   =  11
    dfrow  =  nrow - 1  = ( 2 - 1)    =   1
    dfcol  =  ncol - 1  = ( 2 - 1)    =   1
    dfint  =  (dfrow)(dfcol)  = ( 1)( 1)    =   1
    dfw    =  df - dfrow - dfcol - dfint  =  11  -  1  -  1  -  1  =   8

    MSrow  =  SSrow/dfrow   =   48.00/ 1    =   48.00
    MScol  =  SScol/dfcol   =  192.00/ 1    =  192.00
    MSint  =  SSint/dfint   =  108.00/ 1    =  108.00
    MSW    =  SSW/dfw       =   72.00/ 8    =    9.00
    Frow   =  MSrow/MSw     =   48.00/ 9.00 =    5.33
    Fcol   =  MScol/MSw     =  192.00/ 9.00 =   21.33
    Fint   =  MSint/MSw     =  108.00/ 9.00 =   12.00
```

ANOVA SUMMARY TABLE:

SOURCE	SS	df	MS	F	Fcrit	REJECT?
BETWEEN ROWS	48.00	1	48.00	5.33	11.26	No
BETWEEN COLS	192.00	1	192.00	21.33*	11.26	Yes
INTERACTION	108.00	1	108.00	12.00*	11.26	Yes
WITHIN	72.00	8	9.00			
TOTAL	420.00	11				

CH 17   EXERCISES 33 - 49   *DRUG EFFECTS: 8 PARTICIPANTS*

ROW	COL	DATA X	SSx X-M	( )2	Mcell	SSw or SSerror X-Mcell	( )2
1	2	0.0	-4.0	16.0	1.5	-1.5	2.3
1	2	3.0	-1.0	1.0	1.5	1.5	2.3
1	1	7.0	3.0	9.0	8.5	-1.5	2.3
1	1	10.0	6.0	36.0	8.5	1.5	2.3
2	2	1.0	-3.0	9.0	2.5	-1.5	2.3
2	2	4.0	0.0	0.0	2.5	1.5	2.3
2	1	2.0	-2.0	4.0	3.5	-1.5	2.3
2	1	5.0	1.0	1.0	3.5	1.5	2.3
		32.0	0.0	76.0	32.0	0.0	18.0

ROW	COL	DATA X	Mrow	SSrow Mrow-M	( )2	Mcol	SScol Mcol-M	( )2
1	2	0.0	5.0	1.0	1.0	2.0	-2.0	4.0
1	2	3.0	5.0	1.0	1.0	2.0	-2.0	4.0
1	1	7.0	5.0	1.0	1.0	6.0	2.0	4.0
1	1	10.0	5.0	1.0	1.0	6.0	2.0	4.0
2	2	1.0	3.0	-1.0	1.0	2.0	-2.0	4.0
2	2	4.0	3.0	-1.0	1.0	2.0	-2.0	4.0
2	1	2.0	3.0	-1.0	1.0	6.0	2.0	4.0
2	1	5.0	3.0	-1.0	1.0	6.0	2.0	4.0
		32.0	32.0	0.0	8.0	32.0	0.0	32.0

```
COMPUTATION
    SSint  =    SSx  -  SSrow -  SScol -   SSw
           =   76.00 -  8.00 -  32.00 -  18.00
           =   18.00

    df     =  n - 1 = ( 8 -  1)   =    7
    dfrow  =  nrow - 1 = ( 2 - 1)   =    1
    dfcol  =  ncol - 1 = ( 2 - 1)   =    1
    dfint  =  (dfrow)(dfcol)  = ( 1)( 1)   =    1
    dfw    =  df - dfrow - dfcol - dfint
           =   7 -  1 -   1 -   1
           =    4

    MSrow  =  SSrow/dfrow  =    8.00/ 1   =    8.00
    MScol  =  SScol/dfcol  =   32.00/ 1   =   32.00
    MSint  =  SSint/dfint  =   18.00/ 1   =   18.00
    MSw    =  SSw/dfw      =   18.00/ 4   =    4.50

    Frow   =  MSrow/MSw    =    8.00/ 4.50  =    1.78
    Fcol   =  MScol/MSw    =   32.00/ 4.50  =    7.11
    Fint   =  MSint/MSw    =   18.00/ 4.50  =    4.00
```

ANOVA SUMMARY TABLE:

SOURCE	SS	df	MS	F	Fcrit	REJECT?
BETWEEN ROWS	8.00	1	8.00	1.78	21.20	No
BETWEEN COLS	32.00	1	32.00	7.11	21.20	No
INTERACTION	18.00	1	18.00	4.00	21.20	No
WITHIN	18.00	4	4.50			
TOTAL	76.00	7				

17.6* ADDITIONAL TOPICS IN ANOVA

PLANNED AND POST-HOC COMPARISONS IN ANOVA

PLANNED COMPARISONS

Sometimes when conducting an ANOVA involving several groups, we know in advance that we will be particularly interested in a specific comparison between means. E.g. if the independent variable is TREATMENT, and we are comparing several types of experimental treatments in addition to two prominent ones (perhaps PROZAC vs. COGNITIVE THERAPY for obsessive compulsive disorder) we can set up a separate hypothesis test in advance to compare means for these two specific treatments.

POST-HOC COMPARISONS

On the other hand, sometimes an intriguing difference between means among the groups is only noticed *after* the data have been obtained and we can raise the question, *after the fact*, "Is this difference *significant?*"

Scheffé's Test is the most commonly used post hoc comparison. It can be used to test any hypothesis about *pairs* or *groups* of means. For example, "Is the average of the two medication treatments significantly higher than the average for the three types of psychotherapy?"

Tukey's Test is used to test *pairs* of means only. E.g. "Does the PROZAC group do significantly better than the COGNITIVE THERAPY group?"

If you see either of these used in the discussion of some experimental results, you can infer that the researchers were surprised by an apparently significant, unsuspected pattern of differences between group means.

WHY *PLANNED* COMPARISONS ARE PREFERRED

If there is an interesting difference between means, you're much more likely to be able to prove it using *planned* comparisons. That is, the *power* of planned comparisons is always higher. If there are 4 treatment groups there are more than ten different possible comparisons that might be made! Post-hoc comparisons take this into account, and require a *very strong*, convincing difference to be considered significant.

ANCOVA: ANALYSIS OF COVARIANCE

CONTROLLING FOR AN INTERVAL SCALE COVARIATE

Sometimes the interval scale dependent variable in an ANOVA is known (or suspected) to be *confounded* with another *interval* scale variable referred to as a ***covariate***. A procedure for controlling for the effect of the covariate while performing the ANOVA has been developed. As you might guess, it is very similar to

1. Removing the effect of the covariate by performing a simple *regression* (covered in Chapters 18) and computing a *residual* (Chapters 18, 20)

2. Then conducting the ANOVA using the dependent variable with the 'effect of the covariate removed'

Several covariates may be controlled for simultaneously (using multiple regression, covered in Chapter 20)

MANOVA: MULTIPLE ANALYSIS OF VARIANCE

SEVERAL INTERVAL SCALE DEPENDENT VARIABLES

Suppose people are categorized using one or more nominal scale (independent) variables, then measured on several interval scale variables (E.g., several different measures of anxiety and depression). You can analyze all these data *at once* using MANOVA. (Like conducting one ANOVA for each dependent variable.)

MANCOVA: MULTIPLE ANALYSIS OF COVARIANCE

Yes, this is an ANOVA which involves *several* interval scale *dependent* variables, with each of them having the effect of a covariate removed!

CHAPTER 18
CORRELATION and REGRESSION

18.1 CORRELATION COEFFICIENTS

CORRELATION

Recall the definition of a *relationship* between any two variables:

"A relationship exists between the variables X and Y if knowing a case's score on X, (the independent variable) will allow you to better predict the case's score on Y, (the dependent variable)."

A relationship that exists between two *numerical* variables (interval or ordinal scale) is referred to as a **correlation**.

A **correlation coefficient** is a statistic which measures the strength of a relationship between two variables. Given a set of data consisting of 10 cases' scores on the variables X and Y, a correlation coefficient computed from the data would tell you if any relationship existed between X and Y, how strong that relationship was, and possibly also, whether the relationship was positive or negative. Note that scores on *both* variables are required to compute a correlation coefficient. Statistics such as correlation coefficients, which are only meaningful when applied to *two* variables are called **bivariate statistics**.

A **positive relationship** between the numerical variables X and Y is one in which high scores on X are associated with high scores on Y, and low scores on X are aSSEciated with low scores on Y. If there's a positive relationship between X and Y, and you know Joe scored above the mean on X, you'd expect Joe to have also scored above the mean on Y. An intuitive notion of a positive relationship is that in such relationships the variables tend to *agree* about the cases. That is, X and Y tend to both rate a case high or both rate the case low. If there's a strong positive relationship between X and Y, it is *unlikely* (but possible) that one variable will rate the case high and the other will rate the same case low.

A **negative relationship** between X and Y is one in which cases that score high on X tend to score low on Y, and vice versa. Negative relationships are characterized as ones in which the variables *disagree* about the cases.

Pearson's r , or simply "r", or "the product-moment correlation coefficient" is the correlation coefficient commonly used when both variables are *interval scale* variables. It measures how much of a *linear*, or "straight-line" relationship there is between the two variables. Pearson's r tells you how well you could predict a case's score on the variable Y if you knew two things:

> 1) the case's score on the variable X, and

> 2) the equation of one line that describes the *linear* relationship between X and Y. This line is called the **regression line**.

The values of r range from -1, which indicates a perfect *negative* relationship, to +1, which indicates a perfect *positive* relationship. An r of 0 indicates that there is no linear relationship between X and Y. The interpretation of r values other than -1, 0, and +1 is tricky; examples will provide some intuitions. As usual, even if you find a strong relationship in some data using Pearson's r, you *cannot* conclude that there is a *causal* relationship between X and Y.

Pearson's r is used so often that the terms "correlation" and "correlation coefficient" are assumed to refer to Pearson's r unless the use of some other measure of correlation is specifically mentioned.

r^2, also called the **coefficient of determination**, is much easier to interpret than Pearson's r. This statistic, which is computed simply by squaring r, always indicates the *proportion* of variation in Y that could have been predicted using X. It is just like eta-squared in ANOVA.

18.2 PICTURING LINEAR RELATIONSHIPS

As usual, we'll begin by showing how to estimate the statistic using sketches and intuition. Formulas for computing the statistic precisely will follow in the next section.

SCATTERGRAMS

A **scattergram** is a pictorial representation of the relationship between the independent variable X, and the dependent variable Y. A scattergram allows you to quickly visualize and assess the relationship between X and Y. Figure 18.2.1 shows six sets of bivariate raw data, along with a scattergram for each set of data. Each case's scores on *two* variables, X and Y, are portrayed by *one* point, indicated by a bold dot, on the scattergram. All of the information in the raw data is conveyed by the scattergram, so that you could recreate the raw data from the scattergram. (Of course, if two cases got identical scores on both variables, some way of indicating that one point represented both cases would be needed.)

The **regression line,** $\hat{Y}$ = a + bX, is the line which **best** characterizes the *linear* relationship between X and Y. This line is the best fitting line in the sense that it comes as close as possible to the points that represent the cases' actual scores on X and Y. It *minimizes* r.m.s. error (and *squared* error). After viewing a number of examples, you'll be able to guess the best fitting line fairly accurately in most cases.

FIGURE 18.2.1
EXAMPLES OF SCATTERGRAMS

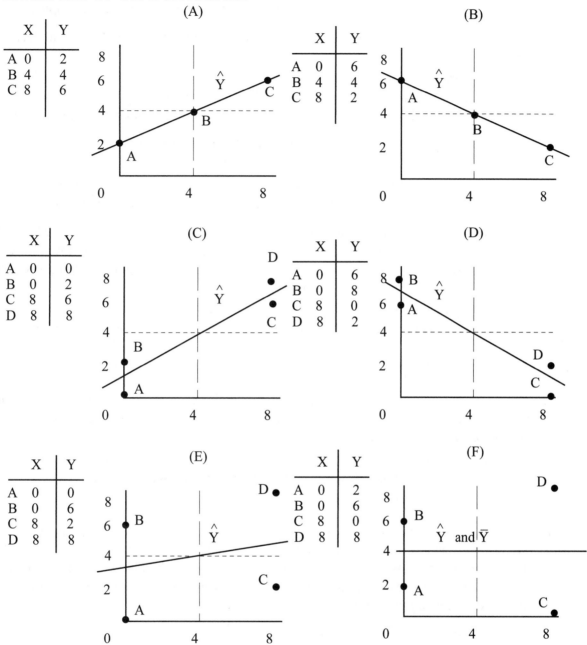

Note that three optional lines are included in each scattergram:

-- a vertical dashed line indicates $\overline{X}$, which is 4 in each case.

-- a horizontal dashed line indicates $\overline{Y}$, which is also 4 in each case.

-- a solid line, labeled $\hat{Y}$, indicates the regression line.

SUMMARY OF EXAMPLES IN FIGURE 18.2.1

Here are the exact values of r, r^2, and the regression line equations for the examples above.

(A) In this case, it is possible to draw a straight line through all data points, and it has a positive slope.

> The regression line equation is $\hat{Y} = 2 + .5X$
> $r = 1.0$, because there is a *perfect* positive linear relationship between X and Y.
> $r^2 = 1.0$, which indicates that 100% of the variation in Y can be explained by X.

(B) Here, a straight line fits through all the points, but it has a negative slope.

> The regression line equation is $\hat{Y} = 6 - .5X$
> $r = -1.0$, indicating that there is a *perfect* negative linear relationship between X and Y.
> $r^2 = 1.0$, indicating that 100% of the variation in Y can be explained by X.

(C) No straight line can fit all 4 points perfectly. A positive trend is clear, and the best fitting line, which goes through the middle of each pair of points, comes fairly close to the points. Note that cases C and D, who got high scores on X also got the high scores on Y. The variables X and Y 'agree" about all 4 cases.

> The regression line equation is $\hat{Y} = 1 + .75X$
> $r = .949$, which indicates a strong, but not perfect, positive relationship between X and Y.
> $r^2 = .90$, indicating that 90% of the variation in Y is related to X.

(D) Similar to (C), except that there is a negative trend, i.e. cases like C and D which score above the mean on X, score below the mean on Y. The variables X and Y consistently "disagree" about all 4 cases.

> The regression line equation is $\hat{Y} = 7 - .75X$
> $r = -.949$, indicating a strong negative relationship between X and Y.
> $r^2 = .90$, so 90% of the variation in Y can be attributed to X.

(E) Here a weak positive trend can be seen. The regression line misses the points by quite a lot. Predictions made using the regression line would not be very accurate.
Two cases, C and D scored above the mean on X. C scored 2 below the mean on Y, and D scored 4 above the mean on Y, so we don't see a strong, consistent pattern of agreement between the variables X and Y.

> The regression line equation is $\hat{Y} = 3 + .25X$
> $r = .316$, indicating a weak positive relationship between X and Y.
> $r^2 = .10$, indicating that only 10% of the variation in Y can be attributed to X.

(F) There is *no* line which fits the points closely, and there is no obvious positive or negative trend. X and Y seem to be unrelated.

> The regression line equation is just $\hat{Y} = 4$, i.e. $\hat{Y}$ equals $\bar{Y}$, the mean of Y.
> This can also be expressed $\hat{Y} = 4 + 0X$, which indicates that X is *useless* in predicting Y.
> $r = 0$, indicating that there is *no* linear relationship between X and Y.
> $r^2 = 0$, indicating that *none* of the variation in Y can be explained by X.

18.3 COMPUTING PEARSON'S *r*

A COMPUTATIONAL EXAMPLE

TABLE 18.3   Here's the computation of Pearson's r for example (E) above:

	DATA: X	Y	SSx $(X-\bar{X})$	$(X-\bar{X})^2$	SSy $(Y-\bar{Y})$	$(Y-\bar{Y})^2$	COVARIATION $(X-\bar{X})(Y-\bar{Y})$
A	0	0	-4	16	-4	16	+16
B	0	6	-4	16	+2	4	-8
C	8	2	+4	16	-2	4	-8
D	8	8	+4	16	+4	16	+16
			0 √	64	0 √	40	+16

The sum of squared deviations are first computed for each of the variables X and Y separately.

THE COVARIATION BETWEEN X AND Y

The new term in TABLE 18.3 is the **covariation**, the sum of the products of each case's deviation on X multiplied by its deviation on Y. The covariation term for one case is also referred to as the **cross-product** in some texts.

$$(18.3.1) \qquad \textbf{COVARIATION} = \sum (X - \bar{X})(Y - \bar{Y})$$

The covariation term for a particular case is positive whenever both variables *agree* about the case. For example, case A is *below* the mean on X and *below* the mean on Y. X and Y *agree* that case A is low, so A's covariation is *plus* 16.

Case B is *below* the mean on X but *above* the mean on Y. The variables *disagree* about B, and B's covariation is *negative* 8. Overall, the positive covariation terms outweigh the negative terms, resulting in a total covariation of plus 16.

COVARIATION will be abbreviated COV at times to improve readability.

A similar term is covariance, the "amount of covariation per case". We won't need to use this in computations below, but it is defined here because it occurs in the literature:

$$(18.3.2) \quad \textbf{COVARIANCE} = \frac{\textbf{COV}}{\textbf{N}} = \frac{\Sigma(X - \overline{X})(Y - \overline{Y})}{\textbf{N}}$$

COMPUTING PEARSON'S r

Pearson's r can be computed in several ways. We will first employ the 'product-moment' or 'mean deviation' method using the covariation:

$$(18.3.3)$$
$$\textbf{Pearson's r} = \frac{\textbf{COVARIATION}}{\sqrt{(\textbf{SSx})(\textbf{SSy})}} = \frac{\Sigma(X - \overline{X})(Y - \overline{Y})}{\sqrt{\left(\Sigma(X - \overline{X})^2\right)\left(\Sigma(Y - \overline{Y})^2\right)}}$$

In our example based on TABLE 18.3:

$$r = \frac{\text{COVARIATION}}{\sqrt{(SS_X)(SS_Y)}} = \frac{16}{\sqrt{(64)(40)}} = .316$$

The coefficient of determination, r^2, is of course computed by squaring r:

$$r^2 = (.316)^2 = .10$$

18.4 THE REGRESSION LINE EQUATION

COMPUTATION OF a AND b (Intercept and Slope)

The regression line equation, $\hat{Y} = a + bX$, is easily computed using the formulas in (18.4.1) below. These computations guarantee that the resulting line will be the optimal one, in the sense of minimizing errors.

(18.4.1) In the regression line, $\hat{Y} = a + bX$,

The slope, $\quad b = \dfrac{\text{COVARIATION}}{\text{SS}_x}$

The intercept, $\quad a = \bar{Y} - b\bar{X}$

EXAMPLE

Continuing with the computations based on (E) above, to find the regression line equation we use (18.4.1):

The slope, b, is $\quad \dfrac{\text{COVARIATION}}{\text{SS}_x} \quad = \quad \dfrac{16}{64} \quad = \quad .25$

The intercept, a, is $\quad \bar{Y} - b\bar{X} \quad = \quad 4 - (.25)4 \quad = \quad 4 - 1 \quad = \quad 3$

So the regression line equation for (E) is $\quad \hat{Y} = 3 + .25X$

Note that b, the slope of the regression line, will always have the same sign as r, the correlation coefficient. Both are computed by dividing the covariation by a positive number, and both indicate whether the relationship between X and Y is positive or negative.

PRACTICE: Verify the computation of the regression line equations for Examples (A) through (D) and (F) in Figure 18.2.1 above.

18.5 PARTITIONING THE VARIATION: REGRESSION vs RESIDUAL ERROR

THE VARIATION THAT IS "TO BE EXPLAINED" : SSy

A relationship exists between X and Y if knowing a case's score on X allows us to *better* estimate the case's score on Y.

In the case of a *linear* relationship described by a regression line, we can get more specific; we can compute precisely *how much better* estimates are when the estimates are made using the regression line. To compare one set of estimates with another it is necessary to focus on *error*. Good estimates make errors as small as possible; poor estimates make larger errors in general.

TABLE 18.5.1

DATA			(A) SSy COMPUTATION			(B) SSE COMPUTATION		
				DEVIATION			RESIDUAL ERROR	
Case	X	Y	$\bar{Y}$	$(Y-\bar{Y})$	$(Y-\bar{Y})^2$	$\hat{Y}$	$(Y-\hat{Y})$	$(Y-\hat{Y})^2$
Art	0	0	6	-6	36	2	-2	4
Bart	0	4	6	-2	4	2	+2	4
Clint	4	8	6	+2	4	10	-2	4
Dee	4	12	6	+6	36	10	+2	4
				0 √	SSY=80		0 √	SSE=16

Imagine that you had access only to the four cases' scores on Y in Table 18.5.1 above. Suppose someone picks a case at random, and you must estimate the case's score on Y. The optimal strategy is to guess the mean of Y, $\bar{Y}$. (There is a hypothetical aspect in this procedure that takes some getting used to, but this "guessing" idea does lead to all the correct intuitions regarding relationships between variables.) $\bar{Y}$ is the best guess, because you don't know the case's name, or the case's score on X, and using $\bar{Y}$ will at least minimize the typical squared error.

Suppose the case picked had been Art. We would have *guessed* the mean, which in this case is 6. Art's *actual* score on Y is 0. Here, our estimate is 6, but the true value is 0. The error in this case has a special designation: $Y - \bar{Y}$, which is -6, is called "Art's *deviation* from the mean of Y". (This is always referred to as a "deviation" not as a "residual error", to avoid confusion with the residual error described in the next section)

In general, the deviation for a case, $Y - \bar{Y}$ measures "how much error we'd make if we had estimated the case's score on Y using $\bar{Y}$ as our estimate." If we square each deviation and add we obtain the familiar SSY.

SSY (also termed "SSTOTAL") is the measure of how much total (squared) error would be made if scores on Y were estimated using $\bar{Y}$ as an estimate. It indicates **how much variation in Y there is *to be explained*.**

The term "explained" is used synonymously with "predicted" in discussions of estimation techniques in statistics. In the current example, TABLE 18.5.1 (A) shows that there are 80 units of variation in Y "to be explained". You might imagine all the unanswered questions related to differences between scores on Y, such as "Why did Dee beat Clint by 4?", "Why did Art score 6 below the mean?", etc. The SS$_Y$ of 80 is a numerical summary of the total amount of "mystery" or "randomness" or "unpredictability" in all the cases' scores on Y. If X *can* be used to predict Y better, we say that "X explains some of the variation in scores on Y" or that "X reduces the unexplained variation in Y".

THE UNEXPLAINED VARIATION: SS$_{ERROR}$ (SSE)

$\hat{Y} = a + bX$, the regression line equation, is a rule for coming up with estimates of cases' scores on the variable Y. If r is not equal to 0, then the estimates we get using this equation should be *better*, and using the $\hat{Y}$ estimates should *reduce* error.

The regression line equation for the data in Table 18.5.1 is $\hat{Y} = 2 + 2X$. We'll now look at estimates that are made using scores on X and the regression line equation. These estimates are referred to as "regression line estimates" or simply as $\hat{Y}$.

Suppose someone picks one of the four cases above, and tells you the case scored 0 on X, and you know the regression line equation. Your best guess of the case's score on Y will be $\hat{Y} = 2 + 2(0)$ = 2. That is, you just plug the case's score on X into the regression line equation to generate $\hat{Y}$ for that case. All cases that get the same score on X will of course get the same $\hat{Y}$ estimate. Suppose again that Art was the case picked. Art's actual score on Y is 0, but our $\hat{Y}$ estimate was 2. The *residual error* for Art is Y - $\hat{Y}$ or -2. If we square *all* such errors for all cases and add we get SSE, the 'sum of squared residuals'.

SSE, or **SS$_{ERROR}$** ("SS$_{RESIDUAL}$" in some texts) is the sum of squared residual errors, i.e., the sum of squared differences between actual scores on Y and $\hat{Y}$ estimates of the scores. It measures the **variation in Y that is *unexplained* by X**.

Comparing Art's deviation of -6 with his residual error of -2, we see that, for Art anyway, the residual error is smaller, i.e., we make *less* error using the $\hat{Y}$ estimate (based on X) than just guessing the mean of Y. This is the most common situation, though there may be exceptions. However we *can* always guarantee that no other line produces less total squared error than the line $\hat{Y}$:

The regression line, $\hat{Y} = a + bX$, computed as described above in Section 18.4, minimizes **SSE**. That is, no other straight line "fits" the points better, and no other line produces better estimates of scores on Y.

SSE for the data above is 16, so we'd say that "16 units of variation in Y cannot be *explained* by X", or "16 units of variation in Y could not have been *predicted* by X."

THE EXPLAINED VARIATION: SSREGRESSION (SSR)

COMPUTING SSR BY SUBTRACTION

There were 80 units of variation in Y "to be explained." 16 of those units of variation could not be explained by X, and we describe them as "residual" or "error," or "left over". The difference, 80 - 16 = 64 units of variation are termed *"explained by X"* or *"predicted by X"*.

This is true in general. The procedures above will always divide, or *partition,* the variation in Y into two parts: the part that *can* be explained by X, and the part that *cannot* be explained by X.

(18.5.1) PARTITIONING THE VARIATION IN Y

The variation in Y can always be separated into two parts, SSREGRESSION and SSERROR such that

$$SS_Y = SS_{REGRESSION} + SS_{ERROR} \text{ or}$$

$$SS_Y = SS_R + SS_E$$

This leads to a straightforward formula for computing the explained variation:

(18.5.2) COMPUTING SSREGRESSION

$$SS_{REGRESSION} = SS_Y - SS_{ERROR}$$

Equation (18.5.1) describes the **partitioning of the variation** in Y into two parts: the part that can be explained by X , and the residual error variation, which cannot be explained by X.

COMPUTING SSR DIRECTLY FROM DATA

There's another way to compute the explained variation. Recall that Art's *deviation*, the error we made estimating Art's score using $\bar{Y}$ was $\hat{Y} - \bar{Y}$, or -6. The *residual* error using $\hat{Y}$ to estimate his score was $Y - \hat{Y}$ or -2. The *change* in error when we use $\hat{Y}$ is the difference between those estimates:

$$
\begin{aligned}
\text{change in error} &= \text{deviation} - \text{residual error} \\
&= (Y - \bar{Y}) - (Y - \hat{Y}) \\
&= (0 - 6) - (0 - 2) \\
&= (-6) - (-2) \\
&= -4
\end{aligned}
$$

The residual error is 4 units smaller than the deviation, indicating that the error *decreases* 4 when the $\hat{Y}$ estimate is used. This can also be computed just by subtracting $\bar{Y}$ from $\hat{Y}$.

$$
\begin{aligned}
\text{change in error} \quad &= \quad \hat{Y} - \bar{Y} \\
&= \quad 2 - 6 \\
&= \quad -4
\end{aligned}
$$

In Table 18.5.2 the change in error, $\hat{Y} - \bar{Y}$, is computed for all cases. When these terms are squared and added the result is the SSREGRESSION or SSR.

TABLE 18.5.2 COMPUTING SSR DIRECTLY FROM DATA

DATA			SSR COMPUTATION		
Case	X	Y	$\hat{Y}$	$(\hat{Y} - \bar{Y})$	$(\hat{Y} - \bar{Y})^2$
Art	0	0	2	-4	16
Bart	0	4	2	-4	16
Clint	4	8	10	+4	16
Dee	4	12	10	+4	16
				$0\sqrt{}$	SSR=64

SUMMARY OF PARTITIONING

SSE or SSERROR measures the **variation in Y that *cannot* be explained or predicted by X**.

SSR, or SSREGRESSION measures the **variation in Y that *can* be explained or predicted by X**. It may be computed by subtracting the SSE from SSY, or by computing $\Sigma(\hat{Y} - \bar{Y})^2$.

1) Each case's *deviation from the mean* can be viewed as divided or *partitioned* into two parts:

FOR *ONE* CASE:

DEVIATION FROM MEAN = PART EXPLAINED BY X + RESIDUAL ERROR

$(Y - \bar{Y})$ = $(\hat{Y} - \bar{Y})$ + $(Y - \hat{Y})$

2) The *total variation* in Y can also be *partitioned* into two parts:

FOR *ALL* CASES COMBINED:

VARIATION IN Y   =   PART EXPLAINED BY X   +   RESIDUAL ERROR

$\Sigma(Y - \bar{Y})^2$ = $\Sigma(\hat{Y} - \bar{Y})^2$ + $\Sigma(Y - \hat{Y})^2$

PICTURING THE PARTITIONING

FIGURE 18.5.1

(A) Art's deviation from the mean, Y-Y̅

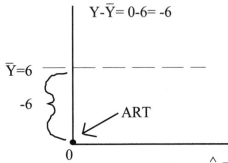

(B) Art's residual, Y-Y'

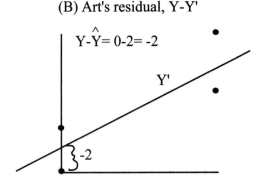

(C) The change in error for Art, Ŷ-Y̅

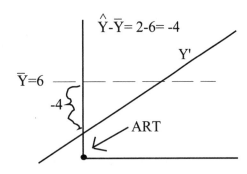

(A) Art's score on Y is 6 below the mean. If you had used Y̅ as an estimate of Art's score on Y, you would have been off by -6.

(B) Art's score on Y is only 2 below $\hat{Y}$. $\hat{Y}$ provides a better estimate of Art's score, and the error in this case is only -2.

(C) The difference between the errors in (A) and (B) is -4. This is illustrated in the figure (C). The difference between Y̅ and the line $\hat{Y}$ is -4

WHY THE REGRESSION LINE IS THE BEST LINE

The regression line has two qualities that are analogous to desirable properties of the mean. It "runs through the middle of all the points" and it "minimizes error" More precisely:

(18.5.3) The regression line $\hat{Y} = a + bX$ is an **unbiased** estimator of the cases' scores on Y. The sum of all residual errors will always be 0, i.e. $\Sigma(Y-\hat{Y}) = 0$.

(18.5.4) The regression line $\hat{Y} = a + bX$ is a *'least squares'* estimator.
No other straight line will have a *lower* sum of all squared residual errors.
$\Sigma(Y-\hat{Y})^2$, the squared error for the regression line $\hat{Y}$, is *lower than* the squared error for any other straight line.

18.6 *PROPORTIONAL REDUCTION IN ERROR*

It was mentioned above that r^2 is a more intuitive measure of the strength of a relationship than r, because r^2, called the **coefficient of determination** tells us what *proportion* of the variation in Y can be explained by X.

Statistics which indicate what *proportion* of the variation in a dependent variable can be explained by some independent variable are said to indicate **proportional reduction in error, or PRE**. r^2 is our first example of a PRE statistic.

SSE, the *sum of squares regression*, is the measure of *reduction in error* in regression examples; it measures how much the (squared) error *decreases* when you use $\hat{Y}$ instead of $\overline{Y}$ to estimate scores on Y.

(18.6.1) The *general* formula for PRE is

$$\text{Proportional reduction in error} = \frac{\text{Reduction in Error}}{\text{Total Error}}$$

In the regression case described above the proportional reduction in error can be computed several ways:

(18.6.2) Coefficient of Determination

If estimates are made using linear regression,

$$PRE = r^2 = \frac{SS_R}{SS_Y} = \frac{SS_Y - SS_E}{SS_Y}$$

So, if you have computed r, you can quickly compute the PRE by *squaring r*.

If you have *any two* of: SS_Y, SS_R, SS_E you can compute PRE by dividing, using (18.6.2) above.

If you have computed r and SS_Y and SS_R, you can *check* your computation of r, using (18.6.2)

18.7 THE STANDARD ERROR OF THE ESTIMATE (or "S.E.E")

THE IMPORTANT NOTIONS OF ERROR AND ACCURACY

You have, of course, been estimating scores, making predictions and perceiving relationships between variables all of your life, and so have all the people around you. If you tried to write a precise summary of the knowledge referred to as "common sense", or "street smarts", or "good business sense", you'd describe many situations in which information was obtained and used to make *predictions* and guide decisions.

Smart handicappers know the scores of the horses on many relevant variables, and can *predict* well the time it will take each horse to finish the race, and the ordinal position of the horse at the finish line. The smartest stockbrokers *predict* well which stocks will go up (or down) in value. Smart TV executives can *predict* the future earnings that will result from hiring David Letterman accurately, and bid for his services according to these estimates. Three friends waiting for Slow Joe, who always runs late, can each *predict* how late Joe will be today, and perhaps place bets accordingly. Studies show that children even after a little exposure to music, can *predict* quite well which notes will come next, in tunes they have never heard before.

Any time a prediction is made about a score on an interval scale variable, and we later find out the actual score, we can compute an obvious, intuitive, measure of error discussed previously: the difference between the actual score and the score that was predicted. *Accuracy* and *error* measure the same thing, though numerical measures of accuracy are less common and less intuitive. If Smith told us a month ago that IBM would close at 81 and Jones told us that IBM would close at 101, and IBM actually closed at 100, Jones' prediction shows *less* error, so of course it is *more* accurate. Jones would get even more credit if he had made this prediction in 1968, because we don't expect a high correlation between stock predictions made 25 years ago and current stock prices!

Suppose many predictions have been made for many scores, and each prediction is in error by a certain amount. As usual in statistics, we want to come up with *one* number that will characterize the *entire set* of errors, and we'd like a meaningful number that can be used to communicate "how accurate the estimates were, typically", or "how *far off* a typical estimate was".

SSE, the "error sum of squares" measures the *total* squared error, but it doesn't indicate the size of a *typical* error. For example, suppose someone told you "Jones must have inside information. He predicted the prices of some stocks a year in advance, and when we looked at the actual prices a year later, the *SSE* was only 246."   You can't really tell if 246 is good or bad. If one of the stocks was called Syntronics, you can't even guess how far off Jones' estimate of Syntronics' price was.

In a regression analysis, the partitioning of SSY into SSR (the part that *can* be explained by X) and *SSE* (the variation in Y that *can't* be explained by X) is the best way to describe the overall or *total* amount of explanation of Y that is possible using X. But to describe how accurate a *typical* estimate for one single case is, we use another statistic called the *standard error of estimate* or S.E.E. This is also referred to in some texts as the *standard error of* $\hat{Y}$, or *r.m.s. error*)

The computation of the S.E.E. is analogous to the computation of the standard deviation:

$$(18.7.1) \quad \text{S.E.E.} = s_{Y \cdot X} = \sqrt{\frac{SS_E}{n}} = \sqrt{\frac{\sum (Y - \hat{Y})^2}{n}} = SD_Y \sqrt{1 - r^2}$$

The S.E.E. is the r.m.s. (or "root-mean-square", covered in Chapter 4) of the "residual error variable", $Y - \hat{Y}$. (The residual error variable will be denoted "Y.X" below)

The S.E.E. is also the standard deviation *of the residual error variable*, $Y - \hat{Y}$.

The S.E.E. is the *typical size* of the error you make if you use $\hat{Y}$ to estimate Y.

When r is 1.0 or -1.0, the S.E.E. is 0. When r is 0, the S.E.E. is the same as the SD.

NOTE: Unfortunately, notation for the standard error of estimate is not consistent in the literature! We'll generally use S.E.E, which is also used by SPSS (Statistical Package for the Social Sciences). When it is helpful to indicate the specific independent and dependent variables used in the estimate, $s_{Y \cdot X}$ is a nice designation.

Other common designations are: $\quad S_{est\,X} \qquad S_{est} \qquad S_{Y.X}$

EXAMPLE #1

Table 18.7.1:

X	Y
0	0
0	4
3	6
3	10

$\hat{Y} = 2 + 2X$

$SS_Y = 52 \quad SS_E = 16 \quad SS_R = 36$

$r^2 = SS_R/SS_Y = 36/52 = .692 \qquad r = +\sqrt{r^2} = \sqrt{.692} = .832$

$\text{S.E.E.} = \sqrt{SS_E/n} = \sqrt{16/4} = 2$

To estimate the *population* S.E.E. from *sample data*, we need to use $\hat{\sigma}_{Y.X}$.

$$(18.7.2) \quad \hat{\sigma}_{Y.X} \text{ is the best estimate of } \sigma_{Y.X}, \text{ the population standard error of estimate, or S.E.E.}$$

$$\hat{\sigma}_{Y.X} = \sqrt{\frac{SS_E}{n-2}} = \sqrt{\frac{\sum (Y - \hat{Y})^2}{n-2}}$$

For our data, $\quad \hat{\sigma}_{Y.X} = \sqrt{SS_E/(n-2)} = \sqrt{16/2} = 2.828$

EXAMPLE #2

Table 18.7.2

X	Y
0	0
0	4
1	2
1	6
2	4
2	8
3	6
3	10

$\hat{Y} = 2 + 2X$

$SS_Y = 72 \quad SS_E = 32 \quad SS_R = 40$

$r^2 = SS_R/SS_Y = 40/72 = .555 \quad r = +\sqrt{r^2} = \sqrt{.555} = .745$

$S.E.E. = \sqrt{SS_E/n} = \sqrt{32/8} = 2$

Comparing Examples #1 and #2, we see that both cases, the distance from $\hat{Y}$ to Y is always 2. Intuitively, the S.E.E, which represents the "typical error", should be 2 in both cases, and the computation does turn out to produce a value of 2.

The SS_E, which is 16 in #1 and 32 in #2, is affected by n, the number of cases (twice as many in #2), so it *cannot* describe *one* 'typical' case's error.

Comparing the two examples also shows that the S.E.E. *cannot* be predicted from Pearson's r alone, since the S.E.E. is the *same* in both cases, but the value of r is *different*.

18.8 INFERENCE ABOUT CORRELATION

SAMPLE r and POPULATION ρ

Recall that Pearson's r is the measure of the relationship between two interval scale (continuous) variables. When r is 0, there is *no* relationship between X and Y. When r is 1.0, there is a *perfect positive* linear relationship between X and Y, and if r is -1.0, there is a *perfect negative* relationship between X and Y.

We have covered hypothesis tests for means, percents, differences between means and percents, and relationships between *nominal* scale variables. The same basic techniques can be used for testing hypotheses about the relationship between two *interval* scale variables-- only a few new computations are required to rescale r and make it have a t-shaped sampling distribution.

As usual, the important question to deal with is: If a sample seems to indicate that there is a relationship between X and Y, can we *infer* that this relationship exists in the whole population?

Also as usual, it's helpful to be able to distinguish the *sample* correlation coefficient, *r*, from the *population* correlation coefficient, which will be designated "rho", (ρ). So, ρ is just the value of Pearson's r you'd get if you computed it for *all* cases in a population-- it's computed using the same formula as for r.

SOME SAMPLES CAN BE MISLEADING

When we do inferential statistics, we always *sample* from a population, compute a *statistic* from that sample, and try to make the right inferences about a population *parameter* based on the information from the sample. When we're dealing with inferences about correlation, we sample from a population, compute Pearson's r for the sample, and then try to make the right inference about ρ (The population correlation coefficient).

It's good to keep in mind the fact there exist some samples which are misleading with regard to rho-- that is, *some* sample values of r are very far from ρ. Luckily, in practice we can usually use sample sizes large enough to make it very unlikely that the sample r will be misleading.

EXAMPLE 1

Suppose that the *whole population* consists of these 5 cases:

	X	Y
Al	0	4
Bo	0	0
Cab	2	2
Dan	4	4
Edge	4	0

FIGURE 1: SCATTERGRAM FOR THE POPULATION IN EXAMPLE 1

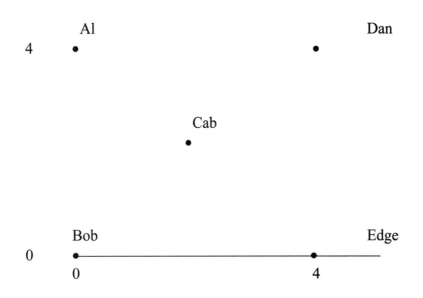

ρ for this population is *0*. There's *no* relationship between X and Y in this population.

Let's consider samples of size 3 from this population. We'll designate the cases in a sample by the first initials of the sample's three cases--e.g. "BCD" designates the sample consisting of Bo, Cab and Dan.

Check that these 4 samples are "*representative*", because for each, r is 0, the same as ρ:

ABC, BCE, CDE, ACD

But the following samples are "*misleading*" about rho:

BCD , ACE, ABD, ADE, BDE

If any of these samples were picked, we'd be *far off* if we tried to estimate rho (the *population* correlation), using r (the *sample* correlation).

THE SAMPLING DISTRIBUTIONS OF r AND "RESCALED r"

The sampling distribution of r is asymmetrical and does not correspond in shape to familiar distributions. Luckily, a rescaling formula has been devised which *rescales* r so that the *rescaled r* values have an approximately t-shaped distribution.

A simpler rescaling formula can be used when n is 30 or more, in which case the *rescaled r* values have an approximately z-shaped sampling distribution.

(18.8.1) FORMULA FOR RESCALING r

(Small samples, n less than 30)

$$t = r\sqrt{\frac{n-2}{(1-r^2)}}$$

degrees of freedom, df = n - 2

(18.8.2) FORMULA FOR RESCALING r

(Large samples, n of 30 or more)

$$z = r\sqrt{n-1}$$

TESTING HYPOTHESES ABOUT ρ

The typical null hypothesis about ρ states that it is equal to 0. The investigator usually suspects that there *is* a positive (or negative) relationship between X and Y. The skeptical position is "there's *no* relationship between X and Y in the population, so ρ is 0". Expressing these in briefer notation:

Null Hypothesis, H_0 $\rho = 0$

Alternate Hypothesis, H_1 $\rho > 0$ (or, $\rho < 0$)

EXAMPLE 1 (SMALL SAMPLE)

The yield in bushels of corn per plot was measured on 15 plots that had been fertilized with various amounts of a new fertilizer. The inventor of the new fertilizer wants to establish that there is a significant positive relationship between the amount of fertilizer and the yield. In the sample, r was .87.

NULL HYPOTHESIS: $\rho = 0$

ALTERNATE HYPOTHESIS: $\rho > 0$

RESCALED r: *t = 6.40*

$$t = r\sqrt{\frac{n-2}{(1-r^2)}} = .87\sqrt{\frac{15-2}{(1-.87^2)}} = 6.40$$

DEGREES OF FREEDOM (df): *13*
   $n - 2 = 15 - 2 = 13$

CRITICAL VALUE FOR t: *2.65*
   Because there are 13 degrees of freedom, and we assume the significance level is .01 for this one-tailed test.

CAN WE REJECT THE NULL HYPOTHESIS? *Yes,*
   Because the t value obtained from our sample (6.40) is greater than the t critical value (2.65). Therefore, *p* must be less than .01.

EXAMPLE 2   (LARGE SAMPLE)

Suppose you are trying to prove that ρ is less than 0, and you find a Pearson's r value of -.56 in a random sample of size 37. Can you reject H_0?

The data support the alternate hypothesis. We're trying to prove the correlation in the population is less than 0 and we have a sample correlation less than 0.

Rescaled r $= z = r\sqrt{n-1} = -.56\sqrt{37-1} = -3.36$

   $P(r < -.56) = P(z < -3.36) = .0004$

We can reject H_0, because $p < .01$

EXERCISES FOR CHAPTER 18.8

PRACTICE WORD PROBLEMS

In a random sample of 12 students the correlation (Pearson's r) between "hours of training" and "performance on the final exam" was .5.

Test the hypothesis that there is a positive relationship between hours of training and performance on the exam.

1. What is the null hypothesis?

    There is no relationship between hours of training and performance in the population. (or, informally "it doesn't matter how many hours of training a student receives.")

2. Can you reject the null hypothesis? Why?

    No. Rescaled r =1.83, and rescaled r has a t shaped distribution, with n-2 degrees of freedom. The critical value of t, with 10 d.f. is 2.764, so we can't reject the null hypothesis.

3. If the null hypothesis were true, would the sampling distribution of the statistic Pearson's r in this case be t shaped, or z shaped?

    No, it would have a distribution which is neither t nor z shaped.

4. Why could we use the t-table to test significance above?

    Because we rescaled r using the formula, and rescaled r is guaranteed to have a t-shaped sampling distribution.

5. Redo the above test, assuming that there were **52** students in the sample, instead of *12*.

    Either z or t can be used.

    t = 4.08, with 50 d.f., which is significant, since the t critical value is about 2.423.

    z = 3.57, so p must be less than .0003, and we can reject the null hypothesis.

6. Which has more power to reject the null hypothesis, the example with 52 students or the example with 12 students?

    The example with 52 students. All other things being equal, the larger the sample size, the higher the power.

PRACTICE RESCALING PEARSON'S r : COMPUTATIONAL EXAMPLES

For each question assume that H_1 is $\rho > 0$, and that your sample r and n are as specified.
Compute t and df (in all cases), and z (where appropriate, when n is large).
Estimate p (Based on z, or t) and state whether you can reject H_0.
For example the first question would read "Assuming that you got a Pearson's r value of .10 in a sample
of size 12, what would the value of 'obtained t' be? How many degrees of freedom are appropriate?
Would you reject the null hypothesis?

You can check your answers against those below.

Question	r	n	t	df	z	P	Reject?
7.	.10	12	0.32	10		> .01	No
8.	.10	52	0.71	50	0.71	= .2389	No
9.	.10	92	0.95	90	0.95	= .1711	No
10.	.50	12	1.83	10		> .01	No
11.	.50	52	4.08	50	3.57	< .0002	Yes
12.	.50	92	5.48	90	4.77	< .0002	Yes
13.	.90	12	6.53	10		< .01	Yes
14.	.90	52	14.60	50	6.43	< .0002	Yes
15A.	.90	92	19.59	90	8.59	< .0002	Yes
15B.	-.90	92					No!

MULTIPLE CHOICE QUESTIONS

CREATIVITY vs CONFORMITY

(Based on an actual study) A researcher named Barron in 1965 reported the results of a study designed to
investigate possible correlates of creativity.   Each of 44 women mathematicians were rated on their
creativity prior to being invited to a three day program. They were rated on "conformity" later by staff
members who did not know their rated creativity. Assume that both ratings were on interval scale
variables.

Assume that the researcher wished to prove that there is a *negative* relationship between conformity and
creativity.

The sample correlation coefficient, r was -.51, with a sample size of 44.

16. The appropriate null hypothesis in this case states that the Pearson correlation coefficient for the
          A) sample is less than 0.
          B) population is less than 0.
          C) population is greater than 0.
          D) population is equal to zero.
          E) sample is equal to zero.

17. The alternate hypothesis states that the Pearson correlation coefficient for the...
    (Use the same answer choices as in the previous question)

18. The z value which results if you rescale the sample r is
       A) -.51   B) -1.9   C) 3.34   D) -3.34   E) 1.9

19. Based on the z value in question 18, $p = ?$
       A) .0287   B) -.0004   C) .0004   D) .0005   E) -.0005

20. Based on the above data, you _____ reject the null hypothesis, because _____.
       A) can, p is less than 0.
       B) can, p is less than .01
       C) cannot, p is greater than .01
       D) can, p is greater than 0.
       E) can, p is greater than .01

NOTE: FOR THE FOLLOWING THREE QUESTIONS, ASSUME ALL OF THE ABOVE
    INFORMATION IS CORRECT, EXCEPT THAT THE SAMPLE SIZE IS 18 instead of 44.
    (Sample r = -.51)

21. Assume that the sample r was -.51, but the sample size was *18*. What value of the t statistic do
    you obtain when you rescale r in this case?
       A) 4.31   B) -4.31   C) 2.199   D) -2.199   E) -2.37

22. How many degrees of freedom (d.f.) are appropriate for the correct sampling distribution in this
    case?
       A) 18   B) 34   C) 16   D) 17   E) 49

23. Can you reject the null hypothesis based on the t value and d.f. in the two previous questions?
       A) Yes, because p is greater than .01
       B) No, because p is greater than .01
       C) Yes, because p is less than .01
       D) No, because p is less than .01
       E) No, because the data do not support the alternate hypothesis.

STUDYING WORKS!

An instructor suspects that hours of study is related to final exam score among her students. She selects a random sample of students, measures each student on both variables.

Assume that the instructor wishes to prove that there is a *positive* relationship between hours of study and exam score.

Suppose the sample correlation coefficient, r was .3, with a sample size of 82.

24. The appropriate *alternate* hypothesis in this case states that the Pearson correlation coefficient for the

      A) population is greater than 0.
      B) population is equal to zero.
      C) sample is equal to zero.
      D) sample is less than zero.
      E) population is less than 0.

25. The *null* hypothesis states that the Pearson correlation coefficient for the...
    (Use the same answer choices as in the previous question)

26. The z value which results if you rescale the sample r is
    A) .82 B) -1.8 C) -2.7 D) 2.7 E) 1.8

27. Based on the z value in question 26, $p = ?$
    A) .0359 B) .9965 C) .0035 D) .9641 E) .01

28. Based on the above data, you _____ reject the null hypothesis, because _____.
    A) can, p is less than .01
    B) cannot, p is greater than .01
    C) can, p is greater than 0.
    D) can, p is greater than .01

Suppose you were trying to show that the population Pearson's r value was greater than zero, and you obtained a Pearson's r of .8 in a sample of size 11.

29. What value of the t statistic do you obtain when you rescale r in this case?
    A) 4 B) 3 C) -4   D) -3 E) -.8

30. How many degrees of freedom (d.f.) are appropriate for the correct sampling distribution in this case?
    A) 11 B) 10 C) 9 D) 2 E) 18

31. Can you reject the null hypothesis based on the t value and d.f. in the two previous questions?
    A) Yes, because p is greater than .01
    B) No, because p is greater than .01
    C) Yes, because p is less than .01
    D) No, because p is less than .01
    E) No, because the data do not support the alternate hypothesis.

In a sample of size 27 the Pearson's r value is .6.

32. When you rescale Pearson's r to produce a value of t for this sample, what t value do you obtain?
        A) 3.75   B) 2.89   C) 2.12   D) 6.25   E) 1.61

33. What is the critical value of t appropriate in this case?
        A) 2.479   B) 2.485   C) 2.896   D) 2.821   E) 2.787

34. How many *scores* are included in the list of raw data in this case?
        A) 16   B) 20   C) 2   D) 54   E) 27

35. How many variables are involved in this study?
        A) 1   B) 2   C) 27   D) 4

36. Can you reject the null hypothesis if the alternate hypothesis is "$\rho < 0$"?
        A) No   B) Yes

37. Can you reject the null hypothesis if the alternate hypothesis is "$\rho > 0$"?
        A) No   B) Yes

DOES LITHIUM IN THE WATER SUPPLY PREVENT CRIME? (Based on an actual study!)

Lithium salts are used to treat manic-depression (bipolar disorder) and some other emotional disorders. Various trace amounts of Lithium salts occur naturally in towns and cities in the USA in Texas and Georgia. The "baths" in Lithia Springs, Georgia which are high in Lithium, have been believed since the 1800's to have curative powers. Pellegrino and Lithia Springs mineral waters have a relatively high natural Lithium Content. Several studies have been done to assess whether the amount of Lithium in the water supply (X) is *negatively* related to the crime rate (Y). Assume that 10 cities are picked at random and measured on the two variables X and Y, and the correlation coefficient in the sample is -.6. Test the appropriate hypothesis.

38. What value of the t statistic do you obtain when you rescale r in this case?
        A) -2.12   B) 3.77   C) 2.12   D) -3.77   E) -.8

39. How many degrees of freedom (d.f.) are appropriate for the correct sampling distribution?
        A) 11   B) 10   C) 9   D) 8   E) 18

40. Can you reject the null hypothesis based on the t value and d.f. in the two previous questions?
        A) Yes, because *p* is greater than .01
        B) No, because *p* is greater than .01
        C) Yes, because *p* is less than .01
        D) No, because *p* is less than .01
        E) No, because the data do not support the alternate hypothesis.

ARE "SOCIOPATHIC" TENDENCIES RELATED TO BLOOD CHEMISTRY?

(Based on an actual study)   A psychologist thinks that there is a positive relationship between a type of blood platelet reaction (BPR) and sociopathy (a tendency toward behavior that violates the rights of others) as measured by an MMPI scale. She selects a random sample of student volunteers and measures each student on both variables.

Suppose the sample correlation coefficient, r was .4, and the sample size was 50.

41. The appropriate *alternate* hypothesis in this case states that the Pearson correlation coefficient for the
> A) population is greater than 0.
> B) population is equal to zero.
> C) sample is equal to zero.
> D) sample is less than zero.
> E) population is less than 0.

42. The *null* hypothesis states that the Pearson correlation coefficient for the...
> (Use the same answer choices as in the previous question)

43. The z value which results if you rescale the sample r is
> A) .80   B) 1.60   C) 2.80   D) 2.82   E) 1.8

44. Based on the z value in the previous question, $p =$
> A) .0026   B) .9974   C) .0548   D) .9452   E) .01

45. Based on the above data, you _____ reject the null hypothesis, because .
> A) can, p is less than .01
> B) cannot, p is greater than .01
> C) can, p is greater than 0.
> D) can, p is greater than .01

ANSWERS TO EXERCISES FOR CHAPTER 18.8

MULTIPLE CHOICE QUESTIONS

(Answers for questions 1-15 are included with the questions.)

CREATIVITY vs CONFORMITY

16. D

17. B

18. D

19. C

20. B

21. E

22. C

23. B   The t critical value is -2.584. -2.37 is not as extreme
(i.e. not as far from 0) so you can't reject.

STUDYING WORKS!

24. A

25. B

26. D

27. C

28. A

----

29. A   30. C

31. C   The critical value for t is 2.821. 4 is more extreme, so you can reject.

----

32. A

33. B

34. D

35. B

36. A

37. B

DOES LITHIUM PREVENT CRIME?

38. A

39. D

40. B   The critical value for t is -2.896. -2.12 is not as extreme, so you can't reject.

----

41. A

42. B

43. C

44. A

45. A

EXERCISES FOR CHAPTER 18

---

1. 64% of the variation in Y can be explained by X.   b = -.1. What is r ?

---

2. r = -.8. What percent of the variation in Y can be explained by X ?

$$SSY = 200, \quad SSE = 72, \quad b = .3$$

3. SSR = ?

4. r^2 = ?

5. r = ?

	X	Y
A	0	0
B	10	30
C	30	10
D	40	40

6. SSX = ?

7. SSY = ?

8. In the equation $\hat{Y} = a + bX$, b = ?

9. a = ?

10. For case A, $\hat{Y}$ = ?

11. The deviation from the mean on Y for A is

12. What part of that deviation can be explained by X, i.e. what is ($\hat{Y} - \bar{Y}$) for A?

13. What part of A's deviation cannot be explained by X, i.e., what is the residual error for A?

14. The covariation value *for case A* is

15. The *total* covariation for all 4 cases is

16. SSE =

17. SSR =

18. $r^2 =$

19. SSR/SSY =

20. What percent of the variation in Y can be explained by X ?

----

21. Check the computations of the regression lines and all statistics for Example #1 in section 18.7.

22. Check the computations of the regression lines and all statistics for Example #2 in section 18.7

TABLE 1:

X	Y
0	4
0	6
1	3
2	0
2	2

23. r = ?

24. What percent of the variation in Y can be explained by X ?

25. What is the regression line equation?

26. SSY =

27. SDY =

28. SSE =

29. SSR =

30. S.E.E, or the standard error of the estimate, or the r.m.s. error of $\hat{Y}$ =

31. If you used the mean of Y to estimate cases' scores on Y, how far off would your typical estimate be?

32. If you used the regression line equation estimates, $\hat{Y}$, to estimate scores on Y, how far off would you typically be?

TABLE 2

X	Y
0	2
0	6
1	3
2	4
2	0

33. r = ?

34. What percent of the variation in Y can be explained by X?

35. What is the regression line equation?

36. SS_Y =

37. SD_Y =

38. SS_E =

39. SS_R =

40. S.E.E, or the r.m.s. error of $\hat{Y}$ =

41. If you used the mean of Y to estimate cases' scores on Y, how far off would your typical estimate be?

42. If you used the regression line equation estimates, $\hat{Y}$, to estimate scores on Y, how far off would you typically be?

Suppose we are considering only one fixed set of cases' scores on Y.

The following series of questions shows that the *closer* Pearson's r is to *1* (or *-1*) the *greater* the accuracy in predicting scores on Y.

GIVEN: $SD_Y = 10$

43. If you don't know the regression equation or the cases' scores on X, and you just use the mean of Y as an estimate of scores on Y, what will be the size of the typical error you'll make?

    The following questions all assume that you know the regression line equation, and each case's score on X, and that you use the regression line estimates, $\hat{Y}$, to estimate scores on Y.

44. If $r = 0$, the typical size of the error of your estimate will be ...

45. If $r = .5$ or $-.5$, the typical size of the error of your estimate will be ...

46. If $r = .6$ or $-.6$, the typical size of the error of your estimate will be ...

47. If $r = .7$ or $-.7$, the typical size of the error of your estimate will be ...

48. If $r = .8$ or $-.8$, the typical size of the error of your estimate will be ...

49. If $r = .9$ or $-.9$, the typical size of the error of your estimate will be ...

50. If $r = .99$ or $-.99$, the typical size of the error of your estimate will be ...

51. If $r = .999$ or $-.999$, the typical size of the error of your estimate will be ...

52. If $r = 1.0$ or -1.0, the typical size of the error of your estimate will be ...

---

53. What does SS_Y measure ?

54. What does SS_E measure ?

55. When does $SS_E = 0$?

56. When does $SS_E = SS_Y$?

57. For case A, what does $Y - \bar{Y}$ measure? What is it called ?

58. For case A, what does $Y - \hat{Y}$ measure? What is it called ?

59. For case A, what does $\hat{Y} - \bar{Y}$ measure? What is it called ?

---

60. If you standardize Bill's score on X you get -2. $Y = -3 + 5X$
    What will you get if you standardize Bill's score on Y ?

ANSWERS TO EXERCISES FOR CHAPTER 18

---

1. -.8 r^2 must be .64, so r must be -.8 or +.8. The sign of r is always the same as the sign of the slope, b. In this case, since b is *negative* r must be -.8.

---

2. 64%   The PRE is r^2 , or $(-.8)^2 = .64$.

---

3. 128   SSR = SSY - SSE = 200 - 72

4. .64 r^2, the coefficient of determination, also is equal to SSR/SSY.
SSR/SSY = 128/200 = .64

5. +.8   See #1 above

---

6. 1000

7. 1000

8. .6 $b = COV/SS_x = 600/1000 = .6$

9. 8 $a = \bar{Y} - b\bar{X} = 20 - .6(20)$

10. 8 $\hat{Y} = 8 + .6X = 8 + .6(0) = 8$

11. -20 $Y - \bar{Y} = 0 - 20 = -20$

12. -12 $\hat{Y} - \bar{Y} = 8 - 20 = -12$

13. -8 $Y - \hat{Y} = 0 - 8 = -8$

14. +400 $(X - \bar{X})(Y - \bar{Y}) = (-20)(-20)$

15. +600

16. 640

17. 360

18. .36 $r = 600/1000 = .6$, so $r^2 = .36$

19. .36   360/1000 = .36 Note that this equals r^2, which is what we'd *expect* based on the definitions of r^2, SSR and SSY. r^2, the coefficient of determination, is supposed to *equal* the proportion of variation in Y that can be explained by X, and SSR/SSY *is* the proportion of variation in Y that can be explained by X.

20. 36%

---

21. EXAMPLE #1: $\hat{Y} = 2 + 2X$, SSY, SSE, etc. are provided below Table 18.7.1.

22. EXAMPLE #2: $\hat{Y} = 2 + 2X$, SSY, SSE, etc. are provided below Table 18.7.2

---

23. -.8944 OR -.89

24. 80%

25. $\hat{Y} = 5 - 2X$

26. 20

27. 2

28. 4

29. 16

30. .8944 $\text{S.E.E.} = \sqrt{\text{SSE}/n} = \sqrt{4/5} = .8944$ or,

                    $\text{S.E.E.} = \text{SD}_Y\sqrt{1 - r^2} = 2\sqrt{1 - (-.8944)^2} = .8944$

31. 2   The SD of Y

32. .8944   The S.E.E. of $\hat{Y}$

---

33. -.447

34. 20%

35. $\hat{Y} = 4 - 1X$ or $\hat{Y} = 4 - X$

36. 20

37. 2

38. 16

39. 4

40. 1.79

41. 2

42. 1.79

---

43. 10   This is SD$_Y$, which was given as 10.

44. 10   If r is 0, knowing X doesn't help, and you'll still typically be off by one SD of Y.

45. 8.66   S.E.E. $= SD_Y\sqrt{1-r^2} = (10)\sqrt{1-(.5)^2} = 8.66$

46. 8.00   See previous answer-- the same formula is used.

47. 7.14

48. 6.00

49. 4.36

50. 1.41

51. 0.45

52. 0

----

53. The total (squared) error you'd make if you tried to estimate all cases' scores on Y, and you used the mean of Y as your estimate for all cases.

54. The total (squared) error you'd make if you estimated all cases' scores on Y, using $\hat{Y}$ as your estimate of Y. In this case you assume you know the case's score on X and the regression line equation.

55. When Pearson's r is -1.0 or 1.0.

   When there's a perfect linear relationship between X and Y.

   When SSR = SSY, because *all* the variation in Y can be explained by X.

56. When Pearson's r is 0, and there is no relationship between X and Y.

   When SSR = 0, because no variation in Y can be explained by X.

57. How much you'd be "off by" if you estimated A's score on Y using the mean of Y.

   The deviation of A's score from the mean.

58. How much you'd be "off by" if you estimated A's score using $\hat{Y}$.

   The residual error for A.

59. How much of A's deviation on Y was 'explained' by X.

The 'regression" term for A, or A's "reduction in error".

60. -2

This takes some thinking! If Bill is 2 standard deviations below the mean on X, he'll still be two standard deviations below the mean on Y, so his standard score on Y will also be -2. E.g., suppose the mean of X is 100, SDx is 10, and Bill scored 80. His standard score on X is:

$$(80 - 100)/10 = -2$$

Y will have a mean of 497 and a SD of 50. Bill will score 5(80)-3 = 397 on Y. Bill's 397 on Y will still correspond to a standard score on Y of -2:

$$(397 - 497)/50 = -2$$

CHAPTER 19

REGRESSION and PREDICTION

19.1 THE CONCEPT OF REGRESSION TOWARD THE MEAN

HOW CASES' SCORES "REGRESS" TOWARD THE MEAN

Chapter 18 showed how to compute the coefficients a and b of the regression line equation, $\hat{Y} = a + bX$. If you know this equation and a case's score on X you can *estimate* the case's score on Y by computing $\hat{Y}$ for that specific case. $\hat{Y}$ is the *best linear estimate* of Y based on X, because it minimizes error.

In this chapter we'll see how $\hat{Y}$ also *optimally* balances the two kinds of effects:
- the effect of the independent variable X, and
- the effect of "error" or "chance" or unexplained random factors.

If scores on Y are *not* related to X at all, r will be 0, and the best estimate of an case's score on Y will just be $\bar{Y}$. The regression line equation will be $\hat{Y} = \bar{Y} + 0X$, or $\hat{Y} = \bar{Y}$. In this case, it appears that scores on Y are affected *entirely* by "chance". So, when r is 0, $\hat{Y}$ is $\bar{Y}$, "the mean".

On the other hand, when r is -1 or +1, $\hat{Y}$ is typically *far from* $\bar{Y}$. In this case, scores on Y are determined *entirely* by X, with *no* chance error involved.

EXAMPLE

Considering a specific example may make these points clearer. Suppose the means of X and Y are *both* 100 and the standard deviations are *both* equal to 20. Also, suppose Aimee scored 140 on X.

If r = 0, we'd estimate that Aimee scored 100 on Y. This estimate is affected *entirely* by $\bar{Y}$ and *not at all* by X. This estimate won't be perfect, but the mean of Y is the best guess we can make.

If r = 1.0, we'd estimate Aimee's score on Y to be 140, the same as her score on X. In a sense, this estimate is based *entirely* on X. She'll score *exactly* 2 standard deviations above the mean on Y, just as she did on X. The prediction will be *perfect*, with *no* residual error due to chance.

If r is *between* 0 and 1.0 (but not equal to 0 or 1.0) $\hat{Y}$ will be somewhere *between* 100 and 140. Aimee's score in this case is affected both by X (which tends to make her score 140) and by *chance* (which would tend to make her score about 100). The closer r is to *1.0*, the closer the $\hat{Y}$ estimate will be to 140. The closer r is to *0*, the closer the estimate will be to 100, the mean of Y.

The estimated scores will always be *closer to the mean* of Y when r is *weaker*. This is called **regression toward the mean** of the dependent variable.

The regression line is guaranteed to produce $\hat{Y}$ estimates that have just the right amount of regression toward the mean. Examples below will demonstrate how b, the regression line *slope*, is related to Pearson's r in a way that makes the $\hat{Y}$ estimates "regress" *correctly* toward the mean.

THE REGRESSION FALLACY

Suppose r is .2. We'd conclude that there is a positive, but weak, relationship between X (a math achievement test) and Y (a music achievement test), and that only .04 of the variation in Y is related to X. Assume that the variables X and Y both have means of 100 and SD's of 10, and suppose that Joe scored 120 on X. His standard score on X is +2, i.e. he's "2 standard deviations above the mean"on X. What should he expect to get on *Y*, based on all this information?

As explained above, *regression toward the mean* implies that he shouldn't expect to get as high as 120 on Y, because Y is only *slightly* affected by X. On the other hand, he can expect to score *above* the mean on Y, because he scored *above* the mean on X, and X and Y are *positively* correlated. If he scored 118 on Y and concluded "I expected to get 120 based on my Math test score, I must not have tried as hard on the music test" he would be subject to the *regression fallacy.*

The *regression fallacy* occurs when someone misinterprets (or does not expect) regression toward the mean, and erroneously concludes that one specific *cause* is responsible when a score on the dependent variable Y is closer to the mean than expected.

ESTIMATING THE AMOUNT OF REGRESSION TOWARD THE MEAN

19.1.1 ESTIMATING STD Y
The best *estimate* of STD Y, a case's *standard score* on Y, is *r times* the case's standard score on X.
$$\text{(Estimated STD Y)} = r(\text{STD X})$$
$$\text{STD } \hat{Y} = r(\text{STD X})$$

EXAMPLE

Aimee's score on X is 140. The means of X and Y are both 100 and the SD's are both 20.
r = .4
   a) What can you conclude about Aimee's score on STD Y?
   b) What can you conclude about Aimee's score on Y?

ANS: a) We can estimate that Aimee's standard score on Y would be approximately .8.
     Her standard score on X is +2, so

ESTIMATED STD Y =

STD $\hat{Y}$ = r (STD X)

= (.4)(2)

= .8

b) By "unstandardizing" her score on Y, we can *estimate* her score on Y to be 116:

ESTIMATED SCORE ON Y = $\bar{Y}$ + (*ESTIMATED* STD Y)(SD$_Y$)

= 100 + (.8)(20)

= 116

REMEMBER: COMPUTATIONS BASED ON *ESTIMATES* ALWAYS PRODUCE *ESTIMATES*!

19.2 RESCALING AND REGRESSION

PEARSON'S *r* IS UNAFFECTED BY POSITIVE LINEAR TRANSFORMATIONS!

EXAMPLE 19.2.1
SDY = 2   SDX = 4

EXAMPLE 19.2.2
SDY = 4   SDX = 2

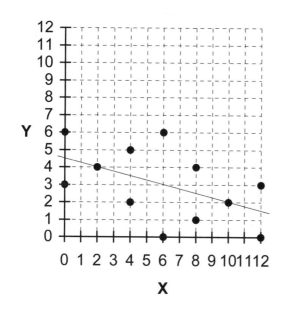

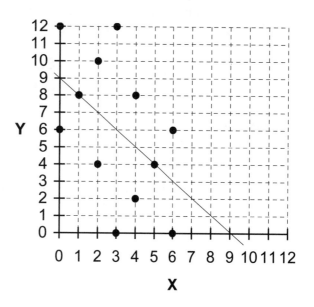

$\hat{Y}$ = 4.5 - .25X

$\hat{Y}$ = 9 - 1.0X

r = -.5

r = -.5

Check this new equation:

Check this equation:

$$b = r\frac{SD_Y}{SD_X} = (-.5)\frac{2}{4} = -.25 \ \sqrt{}$$

$$b = r\frac{SD_Y}{SD_X} = (-.5)\frac{4}{2} = -1.0 \ \sqrt{}$$

Compare the figures for EXAMPLE 19.2.1 and EXAMPLE 19.2.2 above. EXAMPLE 19.2.2 was created from EXAMPLE 19.2.1 by rescaling X and Y. Each score on X was *divided* by 2, and each score on Y was *multiplied* by 2. (Note that this does have an effect on the standard deviations: SDx *decreases* from 4 to 2 and SDY *increases* from 2 to 4.)

The examples above illustrate two general rules:

(19.2.1)   Positive linear transformations of the variables X and Y do not affect Pearson's r.

(19.2.2)   The SD formula for the regression line slope, b

The slope, b, can be computed from r, SDY and SDx :

$$b = r\,\frac{SD_Y}{SD_X}$$

Below the figures, we check that formula (19.2.2) could have been used to compute b in these cases. That is, in these examples, we get the same answer computing b whether we use the short formula COV/SSx, or this new "SD formula for b". This is true in general, there are two ways to compute b:

$$b = \frac{COV}{SS_X} = r\,\frac{SD_Y}{SD_X}$$

EXAMPLE

Suppose Pearson's r = -.4, SDY = 10 and SDx = 2. What is the slope of the regression line?

$$b = r\frac{SD_Y}{SD_X} = -.4\,\frac{10}{2} = -2.0$$

19.3 STANDARDIZATION, CORRELATION AND REGRESSION

The effects of standardizing X and Y

EXAMPLE 19.3.1
STD Y vs STD X

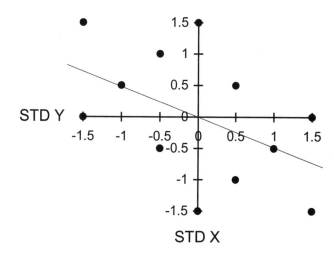

STD X

Regression line equation for predicting STD Y using STD X:

Estimate of (STD Y) = 0 + -.5(STD X)

r = -.5

As usual, we can verify:

$$b = r \frac{SD_Y}{SD_X} = (-.5)\frac{1}{1} = -.5 = \text{Pearson's r !}$$

EXAMPLE 19.3.1 above shows what happens to r, b and a when we standardize *either* EXAMPLE 19.2.1 *or* EXAMPLE 19.2.2:

r remains unchanged. It is still -.5

b, the slope of the regression line, becomes *equal to* Pearson's r

a, the intercept is (The mean of STD Y) - b(The mean of STD X) = 0 - b(0) = 0

The SD formula for b shows that any time $SD_X = SD_Y$, b will equal r.

In particular, if X and Y are standard variables (both with means of 0 and SD = 1), then b will equal r and a must equal 0.

(19.3.1) EFFECTS OF STANDARDIZATION

If Std. X and Std. Y are both *standard* variables, and we compute
the regression equation relating Std. X and Std. Y,

the regression line slope, b, will equal r,
the intercept a, will be 0, so
the regression line equation will be   Std. $\hat{Y}$ = r(Std. X)

$$\text{Pearson's } r = \frac{\sum(\text{Std. X})(\text{Std. Y})}{n}$$

We don't need to standardize the whole distribution of scores, we can just standardize one case's
score on X and estimate that case's standard score on Y by multiplying by r:

19.4 SUMMARY and EXAMPLES

SUMMARY OF FREQUENTLY USED EQUATIONS

Real-world problems (and word problems on exams) often combine concepts from *regression,
standardization,* and/or *standard normal estimation.* Students with extensive recent experience
with algebra and word problems may only need to skim the following examples. Some formulas
covered above are restated here for easier reference.

A few equations are used repeatedly. Recall that in the regression line equation:

(19.4.1) $\hat{Y}$ = a + bX

$\hat{Y}$ is the best estimate of Y based on X, *b* is the slope, and a is the intercept, i.e., *a* is the estimate
of Y when X = 0.

(19.4.2) $b = \dfrac{\text{Change in } \hat{Y}}{\text{Change in X}}$

This equation just describes the usual interpretation of the slope of a line: The regression line
slope b indicates how much of a change in $\hat{Y}$ corresponds to a given change in X.

(19.4.3) $b = r\,\dfrac{SD_Y}{SD_X}$

This equation gives an alternate method of computing the regression line slope, when you know r
and the standard deviations of both X and Y.

Since $\hat{Y}$ represents an "estimate of Y," these equations follow from (19.4.2):

(19.4.4)   **(Estimated *change* in Y) = b (*Change* in X)**

(19.4.5)   **(Estimated *change* in X) = (*Change* in Y)/b**

In using these equations, you typically know the values on the right hand side of the equation, and your task is to come up with the estimate described on the left hand side.

(19.4.6)   **(Estimated *standard score* on Y) = r (*Standard score* on X)**

(19.4.7)   **(Estimated *standard score* on X) = r (*Standard score* on Y)**

These handy equations can be derived from (19.4.4)-(19.4.5) and the definition of a standard score.

The following examples may be used for practice. See if you can obtain the answers, referring to the equations on the previous page if necessary.

COMPUTING b

EXAMPLE 19.4.1

Joe beat Karen by 4 on the independent variable X. Dr. Smith estimated, using a regression line, that Karen would beat Joe by 12 on Y. What was b, the slope of the regression line?

To relate a statement like "Joe beat Karen by 4" to the slope of a line it's helpful to think of the statement as describing a *change* of +4.

Consider the "change" from Karen to Joe. On X, it's +4; but on $\hat{Y}$, it must be -12. (Since Karen beat Joe on $\hat{Y}$, when you go from Karen to Joe you are decreasing.)

Using (19.4.2),   b = (Change in $\hat{Y}$)/(Change in X) = -12/4 = -3   ANS: -3

EXAMPLE 19.4.2

Given: r = -.5   SDy = 100   SDx = 10.   What is b?

Using (19.4.3), b = r (SDy)/SDx = (-.5)(100)/10 = -5   ANS: -5

ESTIMATING A CHANGE IN Y (OR A DIFFERENCE IN Y)

EXAMPLE 19.4.3

Suppose that after many experiments, the engineers at Dodge are convinced that the slope of the regression line equation relating engine horsepower (HP) to the 0-60 mph elapsed time (ET) for their new model car, the Viper, is -.005. That is, the equation is

$$ET' = a + -.005(HP), \quad \text{for some intercept } a$$

With a 360 hp engine the elapsed time is 5.2 seconds.
A) What change in elapsed time would you expect if the HP is increased to 420?
B) Would you expect the car to go 0-60 mph in less than 5 seconds with 420 HP?

The independent variable is HP and the dependent variable is ET. HP gets increased from 360 to 420, a change of +60. Using (19.4.4), with HP for X and ET for Y,

(Estimated change in ET) = b (Change in HP) = (-.005) (+60) = -.3

A) We expect the ET to *decrease* by .3 seconds.
B) Yes. Since the old ET was 5.2 seconds, we expect the new ET to be 5.2 -.3 = 4.9 seconds.

EXAMPLE 19.4.4

The instructor has said that the slope of the regression line relating the independent variable Hours of Diligently Solving Practice Questions (H) to the dependent variable Final Exam Score (F) is 12. How much of an increase in her Final Exam Score should Sheila expect if she decides to Diligently Practice for an additional 4 hours?

Using (19.4.4) with F for Y and H for X:

(Estimated Change in F) = b (Change in H)
                         = 12 (+4) = 48

So she can expect an improvement of 48 points on the final exam.

EXAMPLE 19.4.5

(See previous question for definitions of the variables H and F.)
Elle studies 4 hours more than Al. If the slope of the regression line relating H to F is 12, as in the previous question, how would you expect Elle and Al's Final Exam Scores to compare?

You'd expect Elle to beat Al by 48 points. The computation is identical to that in the previous example. The *difference* between Elle and Al must be interpreted as the "change" referred to in the formula.

ESTIMATING A CHANGE IN X (OR A DIFFERENCE IN X)

EXAMPLE 19.4.6

(See Example 19.4.3 for information and definitions)
The Dodge engineers expect Viper buyers to be in a big hurry! Estimate how much you'd need to increase the Viper's horsepower by to allow it to go 0 to 60 mph in 4 seconds flat. (That's faster than a Porsche Turbo Carerra!)

When the HP is 360, the ET is 5.2. We want the dependent variable ET to go down to 4.0, i.e., to decrease by 1.2. We want to know what change in the independent variable HP can be expected to produce a change of -1.2 in the dependent variable.
With ET for Y and HP for X in (19.4.5):

$$
\begin{aligned}
(\text{Estimated Change in HP}) &= (\text{Change in ET})/b \\
&= (-1.2)/(-.005) \\
&= +240
\end{aligned}
$$

So, we'd estimate that 240 additional horsepower would be required, for a total of 600 hp.

ESTIMATING A STANDARD SCORE ON Y

EXAMPLE 19.4.7

Joe scored 4 standard deviations above the mean on X. The correlation between X and Y is -.25. Estimate Joe's standard score on Y.

Joe's standard score on X is +4. Using (19.4.6),

$$
\begin{aligned}
(\text{Estimated standard score on Y}) &= r\ (\text{Standard score on X}) \\
&= (-.25)(+4) \\
&= -1
\end{aligned}
$$

We estimate Joe's standard score on Y to be -1, i.e., we estimate that Joe will score 1 SD *below* the mean on Y.

ESTIMATING A PERCENTILE RANK ON Y

EXAMPLE 19.4.8   [GIVEN A STANDARD SCORE ON X]

*Joe's standard score on X was -1.5.   r is -.3. Estimate Joe's percentile rank on Y.
Y is known to be approximately normal, but X is not!*

First we must carefully determine whether a meaningful estimate is *possible*.
Recall the following rule:

(19.4.8) RULE FOR STANDARD NORMAL APPROXIMATIONS

**If the Standard Normal Table is used to *estimate* a percentile rank or a
percentile for some real world variable, X, then the variable X *must* have a
distribution that is *approximately normal* in shape (approximately
symmetrical and bell shaped)**

**If X *does not* have an approximately normal shape, then estimates
of percentiles or percentile ranks for X will be inaccurate and misleading.**

We estimate Joe's standard score on Y using (19.4.6). Note that X is not required to be
approximately normal to use equation (19.4.6):

$$\text{(Estimated standard score on Y)} = r\,(\text{Standard score on X})$$
$$= (\,-.3\,)\,(\,-1.5\,)$$
$$= +.45$$

Joe's standard score on Y is estimated to be +.45, and since Y has a distribution which is
approximately normal, we can look up +.45 as a z score, and estimate his percentile rank on Y to
be 67.36 %.

EXAMPLE 19.4.9 [GIVEN A PERCENTILE RANK ON X]

Ed' s percentile rank on X is 97%. The correlation between X and Y is +.1.
  A) Estimate Ed's percentile rank on Y.
    Assume both X and Y are known to be approximately normal.
  B) Explain why Ed's predicted percentile rank on Y is lower than on X.

1) We estimate Ed's standard score on X to be 1.89, by finding the 97th percentile in the standard normal distribution. (This is legitimate because X is approximately normal.)

2) We estimate Ed's standard score on Y, using (19.4.6):
   (Estimated standard score on Y) = r (Standard score on X)
$$= (.1) (1.89)$$
$$= .189$$

3) We estimate Ed's percentile rank on Y, by looking up the percentile rank of .189 in the z table. This is OK because Y is known to be approximately normal in shape.

   A) The answer is 57.53 % (Using a z score of .19 in our z table.)

   B) Ed's score on Y should exhibit *regression toward the mean.*
      Clearly, factors other than X must be affecting scores on Y. Otherwise r would be higher than .1! We can't expect Ed to score higher than average on the other factors. So Ed's score on Y should be affected *slightly* by his (known) high performance on X, and *greatly* by his (unknown) possibly mediocre performance on other unknown variables affecting Y. The effect of his *unknown* performance on the *unknown* variables is expected to drag him *down* toward the mean on Y.

EXERCISES FOR CHAPTER 19

----

1. Regression toward the mean occurs
   A) whenever r is not 1.0 or -1.0
   B) only when r is very high
   C) only when X and Y are both normal

Linda's percentile rank on X is 3%. The correlation between X and Y is -.5.
Assume that X is known to be approximately normal.

2. Linda's standard score on X
   A) can be *estimated* to be *approximately* -1.88
   B) *is* -1.88
   C) can be *estimated* to be *approximately* 1.88
   D) *is* 1.88
   E) cannot be estimated or computed

3. Linda's standard score on Y
   A) can be *estimated* to be *approximately* -.94
   B) *is* -.94
   C) can be *estimated* to be *approximately* .94
   D) *is* .94
   E) cannot be estimated or computed

4. *Based on the information given above*, Linda's percentile rank on Y
   A) can be *estimated* to be *approximately* 17.36%
   B) *is* 17.36%
   C) can be *estimated* to be *approximately* 82.64%
   D) *is* 82.64%
   E) cannot be estimated or computed

5. In addition to the information above, *assume Y is also known to be approximately normal.*
   Linda's percentile rank on Y
   A) can be *estimated* to be *approximately* 17.36%
   B) *is* 17.36%
   C) can be *estimated* to be *approximately* 82.64%
   D) *is* 82.64%
   E) cannot be estimated or computed

6. Linda's predicted percentile rank on Y is closer to 50% than her percentile rank on X because
   A) the mean of Y is less than the mean of X
   B) Y is negatively skewed
   C) of regression toward the mean, i.e., the effect of unknown variables other than X.

Suppose a study is done of a large set of retail stores, and it is found that the correlation between the 'amount spent on Sunday newspaper advertising' (AD) and the 'gross sales the following week' (GROSS) is .5. That is, Pearson's r, computed for the independent variable AD and the dependent variable GROSS, is .5.

Assume that both AD and GROSS have distributions which are approximately normal in shape.

Suppose that Mr. Jones' Acme Market spent $100 on advertising last week, and that placed his store in the bottom 5% of all stores on the variable AD.

That is, Acme Market's percentile rank on AD was 5%.

7. Acme Market's *standard score* on the variable AD
    A) is definitely 1.64
    B) can be estimated to be approximately -1.28
    C) is definitely -1.64
    D) can be estimated to be approximately -1.64
    E) can neither be computed nor estimated

8. Acme Market's *standard score* on the variable GROSS
    A) is definitely -.64
    B) can be estimated to be approximately -.64
    C) is definitely -.82
    D) can be estimated to be approximately -.82
    E) cannot be estimated or computed.

9. Acme Market's *percentile rank* on the variable GROSS
    A) cannot be estimated or computed
    B) is approximately 20.61%
    C) is exactly 26.11%
    D) is approximately 26.11%
    E) is exactly 20.61%

----

10. Al beat 97% of all people on the variable X. The correlation of X with Y is moderately negative. Al's percentile rank on Y...
    A) Could be estimated if we knew r. It'll be between 3% and 50%
    B) Could be estimated if we knew r. It'll be between 50% and 97%
    C) Will be 97%
    D) Will be 3%
    E) Could not be estimated without additional information, even if we knew r.

----

11. Al beat 97% of all people on the variable X. The correlation of X with Y is moderately negative. X and Y are both approximately normal. Al's percentile rank on Y...
    A) Could be estimated if we knew r. It'll be between 3% and 50%
    B) Could be estimated if we knew r. It'll be between 50% and 97%
    C) Will be 97%
    D) Will be 3%
    E) Could not be estimated without additional information, even if we knew r.

SOME EXAMPLES BASED ON THE FILM INDUSTRY

The next six questions refer to this kind of situation:

> Suppose a number of films are being rated on a scale from 0 to 100 by a test audience in a "preview house" in Hollywood. We'll call a film's average rating it's score on the variable RATING.
>
> The goal is to estimate, before a film is released, the film's future 'gross', how much money the film will make in wide release. The preview RATING is the independent variable used to estimate the money the film will 'take in at the box office', which we'll call GROSS. Actual film grosses are published on Tuesdays in the LA times.
>
> Being able to accurately estimate how much a film will gross is helpful in the film business, because that knowledge can affect decisions about which films to release widely, how many copies (or 'prints') of the film will be needed, which films will need a lot of advertising, etc. Sometimes a decision is made to not even bother releasing a film to theatres, and to "banish" it instead directly to video stores or Cable stations! This embarrasses the actors, the director and others who worked to make the film.
>
> Assume that all film grosses are measured in millions of dollars.

----

12. Suppose the new 'Heaven's Great!' scored 10 with the preview audience, and that the regression line equation relating RATING to GROSS is $\hat{Y} = 2 + .6X$. The film company, MGM, wants to release the film only if it can be expected to make more than 9 million dollars. (Which is not much these days! 'Home Alone' made about 250 million dollars.)
    Should 'Heaven's Great!' be released?

----

13. Suppose the new film 'Snow Man' scores in the 10th percentile on the variable RATING. The producers want to release it only if it would *not* be expected to gross below the bottom 15% of all films released. Suppose the correlation between RATING and GROSS is .7, and suppose the producer were to ask you to use statistical techniques to estimate the film's percentile rank on GROSS and decide if it should be released.
    You, as an upstanding former student in this class, would reply... (Really consider, what would be the correct reply, and why?)

14. Suppose the producer responds... "*Why not? Can't you use statistics to get an estimate here? What am I paying you for? Get me some results or I'll see that you never do statistics in this town again!*", you'd patiently respond by explaining, ".....

15. Suppose that after 'Snow Man' is released, the boss of the advertising agency that handled the publicity for the film states:

> "We *saved* that film from totally bombing! The previews rated it in the bottom 10%, but after *our* ad campaign, it beat out 16% of the other films in gross box office. Our ads helped it do more than 150% better than expected."

Is there any evidence that the ad campaign was what caused the film to gross above the 10th percentile? HINT: What would you have expected the percentile rank of the film's gross to be, assuming both variables are approximately normal?

16. What is the ad boss' kind of (erroneous) reasoning called?

_____

17. Suppose a new film "9 ½ seconds", starring Mickey Rourke and Brooke Shields, is about to be released. Two versions of the film are previewed at Preview House in Hollywood.were previewed. The 3-D version rated 15 points higher on the variable RATING. If $r = .8$, the SD of RATING is 5, and the SD of GROSS is 10, how much more money would you expect the 3-D version to make? If it costs 5 million dollars more to release the 3-D version, does it look as is that 5 million should be spent on the film?

(*These* data and films are *hypothetical* of course! However, Mickey and Brooke *were* originally slated to appear in the real film "Wild Orchid" together, which would have been one of those very *un*predictable, *low* probability events!)

Here are 3 scores on the variable X:

	X	$\hat{Y}$
Amy	0	?
Bob	3	?
Cat	5	?

Suppose a regression equation, $\hat{Y} = a + bX$ had been computed, and that by using the equation, you would have *estimated* that:

> Amy's score on Y is 8 (I.e., $\hat{Y}$ for Amy is 8)
> Bob beat Cat on Y by 6 (I.e. $\hat{Y}$ for Bob is 6 greater than for Cat)

18. In the regression line equation, $\hat{Y} = a + bX$, *a* tells you

    A) the intercept, the value of X when $\hat{Y} = 0$.
    B) the intercept, the value of $\hat{Y}$ when X = 0.
    C) the slope, the (Change in X)/(Change in $\hat{Y}$)
    D) the slope, the (Change in $\hat{Y}$)/(Change in X)

19. What must the value of *a* be in this case ?

    A) -3   B) 3   C) 6   D) 8   E) 0

20. In the regression line equation, $\hat{Y} = a + bX$, b tells you

      A) the intercept, the value of X whan $\hat{Y} = 0$.

      B) the intercept, the value of $\hat{Y}$ when $X = 0$.

      C) the slope, the (Change in X)/(Change in $\hat{Y}$)

      D) the slope, the (Change in $\hat{Y}$)/(Change in X)

21. What must the value of *b* be in this case?

      A) -3   B) 3   C) 6   D) 8   E) 0

----

22. Given: $r = -.8$ $SD_Y = 10$ $SD_X = 50$. What is b, the slope of the regression line?

      A) -.16   B) -4   C) 4   D) .2   E) 5

----

23. Moe scored 1.5 standard deviations below the mean on X. The correlation between X and Y is -.50. Moe's standard score on Y...

    A) can be *estimated* to be *approximately* .75

    B) *is* .75

    C) can be *estimated* to be *approximately* -.75

    D) *is* -.75

    E) cannot be estimated or computed

----

24. Flo scored .75 standard deviations below the mean on X. The correlation between X and Y is 1.0. Flo's standard score on Y...

    A) can be *estimated* to be *approximately* .75

    B) *is* .75

    C) can be *estimated* to be *approximately* -.75

    D) *is* -.75

    E) cannot be estimated or computed

Zoe scored 112 on X.

$\bar{X}$ is 100 and SDx is 20. $\bar{Y}$ is 400 and SDy is 50

r is -.8.

X *is* known to be approximately normal, but Y is *not*!

25. Zoe's *standard score* on X

      A) can be *estimated* to be *approximately* .6

      B) *is* .6

      C) can be *estimated* to be *approximately* -.6

      D) *is* -.6

      E) cannot be estimated or computed

26. Zoe's *percentile rank* on X
    A) can be *estimated* to be *approximately* 27.43%
    B) *is* 27.43%
    C) can be *estimated* to be *approximately* 72.57%
    D) *is* 72.57%
    E) cannot be estimated or computed

27. Zoe's *standard score* on Y
    A) can be *estimated* to be *approximately* .-.48
    B) *is* -.48
    C) can be *estimated* to be *approximately* .48
    D) *is* +.48
    E) cannot be estimated or computed

28. Zoe's *score* on Y
    A) can be *estimated* to be *approximately* 376
    B) *is* 376
    C) can be *estimated* to be *approximately* 324
    D) *is* 324
    E) cannot be estimated or computed

29. Zoe's *percentile rank* on Y
    A) can be *estimated* to be *approximately* 68.44%
    B) *is* 68.44%
    C) can be *estimated* to be *approximately* 31.56%
    D) *is* 32.56%
    E) cannot be estimated or computed

Suppose that after many studies the Surgeon General estimates that, for men 40 years old, the slope of the regression line equation relating the independent variable Cigarettes Smoked Per Day (CIG) to the dependent variable Life Expectancy (LE) in years is -.5. I.e.,

$$\text{Estimate of LE} = a -.5(\text{CIG}), \quad \text{for some intercept } a$$

(In reality an equation like this would only be applicable to all men who smoked a limited number of cigarettes per day-- perhaps some number between 0 and 50)

30. What change in Life Expectancy would result if a 40 year old man *decreased* the number of cigarettes smoked per day from 40 to 20?
    A) an increase of *exactly* 10 years-- he'd live exactly 10 years longer.
    B) an increase of about 10 years (estimated)
    C) a decrase of *exactly* 10 years-- he'd live exactly 10 years longer.
    D) an decrease of about 10 years (estimated)
    E) cannot be computed or estimated

Suppose a typical 40 year old man who *does not smoke at all* has a life expectancy of 32 years.

31. In that case, the regression line equation must be Estimate of LE = ?
     A) 16 - .5(CIG)
     B) 32 - .5(CIG)
     C) cannot be computed

32. If Smoky Joe is 40 and smokes 40 cigarettes a day, how many more years can he expect to live?
     A) 72   B) 12   C) 52   D) cannot be estimated

33. To expect to live to the (estimated) age of 62, Smoky Joe would have to *decrease* his cigarette consumption by _____ cigarettes per day.
     A) 10   B) 40   C) 30   D) 20   E) cannot be estimated

ANSWERS TO EXERCISES FOR CHAPTER 19

----

1. A

----

2. A

3. C

4. E

5. C

6. C

----

7. D

8. D

9. B

----

10. E

11. A

FILM RATINGS

12. No! You'd expect it to make "only" 8 million dollars, because 2 + .6(10) = 8.

13. "I don't know!. (That is, you'd reply "any estimate might be misleading."
    Estimation can't be done without more information!)

14. "I'd need to assume that *both* RATING and GROSS are *approximately normal* distributions to estimate a percentile rank for GROSS form a percentile rank on PRE. *If* the distributions are approximately normal, then we'd expect 'Snow Man' to earn a GROSS at or above approximately 18% of all films. Since you *wouldn't* expect it to gross below 15% of all films, it *should* be released.

    Of course the 18% is an *estimate*, not an exact figure. Any time you use the standard normal table in a computation related to *real-world data* that was actually collected, the results are *estimates* or *approximations*.

    The estimation is done as follows: We use the percentile rank of 10% on RATING, and the z table to estimate that Snow Man's standard score on RATING is -1.28. The standard score on GROSS is then estimated to be r(std. score on RATING), or .7(-1.28) = -.896. Looking up the z score of -.89, we obtain an estimated percentile rank on GROSS of 18.67%.

15. No. Just by chance, because of regression toward the mean, we'd expect the film to beat or tie about 18.41% of other films. That's *without* any ad campaign, so the film actually did slightly worse than would have been predicted, not better!

16. The regression fallacy.

17. You'd expect the 3-D version to make 24 million dollars more, and it would seem that it's worth it to spend the 5 million.

    $$b = r(SD_Y/SD_X) = .8(10/5) = 1.6$$

    $$\text{Estimated Change in GROSS} = b(\text{Change in RATING})$$
    $$= 1.6(+15)$$
    $$= +24$$

---

18. B

19. D   Amy got 0 on X and $\hat{Y}$ for Amy was 8. So we know that when $X = 0$, $\hat{Y} = 8$

    When $X = 0$, the value of $\hat{Y}$ *is* the intercept, a. So a must be 8

    The regression line must be $8 + bX$, because when $X = 0$, $\hat{Y} = 8$

20. D

21. A   Cat beat Bobby 2 on X (Bob's 5 vs. Cat's 3). So if we "change" from Cat
             to Bob on X we go *up* by 2.

             Bob beat Cat by 6 on $\hat{Y}$, so if we go from Cat to Bob on the regression line, we go
             down by 6

             The slope is b $= \dfrac{\text{Change in } \hat{Y}}{\text{Change in X}} = \dfrac{-6}{2} = -3$

----

22. A

$$b = r\frac{SD_Y}{SD_X} = (-.8)\frac{10}{50} = -.16$$

----

23. A
             (19.4.6)   (Estimated *standard score* on Y) = r (*Standard score* on X)
                                                              = (-.5)(-1.5)
                                                              = .75

----

24. D   (19.4.6)   (Estimated *standard score* on Y) = r (*Standard score* on X)
                                                              = (1.0)(-.75)
                                                              = -.75
                             In this case, because r = 1.0, we know the 'estimate' is exactly correct

----

25. B   STD X $= \dfrac{X - \overline{X}}{SD} = \dfrac{112 - 100}{20} = .6$

             This is a calculation, no estimation is involved.

26. C   We know that X is approximately normal.

27. A   (19.4.6)   (Estimated *standard score* on Y) = r (*Standard score* on X)
                                                              = (-.8)(.6)
                                                              = -.48

28. A   We can 'unstandardize' the standard score on Y:

             Score on Y $= \overline{Y} +$ (STD Y)(SD$_Y$)
                         = 400 + (-.48)(50)
                         = 376
             376 is only an *estimate*, because it was computed using -.48 which was an
             estimate.

29. E   Y is not approximately normal! To estimate a percentile rank, the variable involved must
             be known to be approximately normal.

----

30. B

31. B

32. B $32 - .5(40) = 32 - 20 = 12$

33. D   He'd live to *52* smoking 40 a day (See previous question)
             Living to *62* would be an increase of 10 on the dependent variable.
                    (Change in X) = (Change in Y)/(b)
                                  = (+10)/(-.5)
                                  = -20

CHAPTER 20

MULTIPLE REGRESSION and PARTIAL CORRELATION

20.1 MULTIPLE REGRESSION

USING MORE THAN ONE INDEPENDENT VARIABLE

The linear regression techniques presented in the last chapter showed you how to come up with a regression equation for estimating a case's score on Y (the dependent variable) based on the case's score on X (the independent variable).

Multiple regression is a very useful extension of those regression techniques. The new thing about multiple regression is that *more than one* independent variable may be used to try to predict Y. This can make the predictions much better! In many real world cases we know that there are actually several different variables that might influence or affect the dependent variable. The area of statistics that handles cases like this, with *more than one independent variable* is called **multivariate statistics**.

Often the independent variables are informally called *factors*, in statements such as

1) "Success on exams is due to several *factors*: ability, motivation, and practice."

> Independent Variables: ability
> motivation
> practice
> Dependent Variable: success on exams

2) "The severity of a psychotic episode is related to several *factors*: the number of previous episodes, the patient's age, recent abuse of stimulant or psychedelic drugs."

> Independent variables: number of previous episodes
> patient's age
> recent abuse of stimulant drugs
> recent abuse of psychedelic drugs
> Dependent Variable: severity of a psychotic episode

Using statistical terminology, we'd say "Statements 1 and 2 are each stating that there's a relationship between *several* independent variables (the 'factors') and one *single* dependent variable of interest."

You have so much real-world experience at making predictions based on several independent variables that you probably don't notice you are doing it! One aspect of your practical intelligence surely is knowing which are the relevant factors necessary to predict scores on variables that are important in your life. This ability enables you to make smart *decisions*, based on good predictions.

On the other hand, you can easily spot *bad* decisions. For example, suppose Moe said to you,

> "I think I'll take the job in DC. I *predict* it'll be a good job overall, 'cause the *employee benefits* are good, although the *boss* is an inconsiderate tyrant, and the *pay* is low, and the plant *smells* like those chemicals they mix, which they are pretty sure are not related to those *tumors* the employees were getting, like the guy I'd be replacing..."

You could respond to Moe in a number of different ways, depending on your patience, your relationship with Moe, Moe's psychiatric history, etc. But if you tried to *reason* with Moe (e.g. by arguing that his prediction is inaccurate!), or if you tried to understand *his reasoning*, (he must place a tremendous weight on *employee benefits*!) what you'd be doing would be analogous to multiple regression: You'd be trying to analyze a *prediction* based on *several* relevant factors.

We all know Moe's reasoning seems strange because we all have similar world knowledge about how to combine a job's 'scores' on variables like 'benefits', 'the boss', 'pay' and 'environment' to come up with a *prediction* of 'how good' the job will be.

Multiple regression is just a systematic and accurate way to combine information about several factors (independent variables) to make the best possible predictions. In those situations where multiple regression is appropriate to use, it can be shown mathematically that, under the appropriate assumptions, **no other technique produces more accurate estimates in general**.

THE MULTIPLE REGRESSION EQUATION

(20.1.1) Multiple regression equation

$$\hat{Y} = a + b_1X_1 + b_2X_2 + b_3X_3 + ...$$

This general form of a multiple regression equation indicates that Y will be predicted by combining information about several independent variables (X_1, X_2, etc.). The " + ... " term in the equation indicates that any number of additional X's may appear. The different independent variables are referred to as "the X_i". Each of the independent variables X_i in a multiple regression is handled just like the single independent variable X is in a simple linear regression; that is, each X_i is multiplied by a number called a 'slope'. The slope for X_1 is designated b_1, the slope for X_2 is designated b_2, etc. And just as in simple linear regression, there is one intercept designated a.

20.2 MULTIPLE REGRESSION ANALYSIS COMPUTATIONS

EXAMPLE 20.2.1: PREDICTING EXAM SCORES *VERY WELL*

TABLE 20.2.1 STUDENT DATA

	X_1: Ability	X_2: Motivation	X_3: Practice	Y: Test Score
Al	0	0	2	0
Ben	0	2	0	4
Carol	2	0	0	2
Dan	2	2	2	18

Suppose the data above were obtained when four students were measured on the independent variable*s ability*, *motivation* and *practice*, and the dependent variable *test score*.

In a typical real situation requiring multiple regression techniques you'll have data available such as that in Table 20.2.1 above. That is, you'll have scores on *more than one* interval scale independent variable and *one* interval scale dependent variable.

You'd then simply type the data into a computer and run one of the well known statistical programs (E.g., SPSS, BMD, SYSTAT or STATA) to produce the following regression equation for the data in TABLE 1:

(20.2.1) $\hat{Y}$ = -6 + 4X_1 + 5X_2 + 3X_3

When you performed linear regression analyses with *one* independent variable (Chapter 9), *you* computed the regression coefficients *a* and *b*.

In the multiple regression case, *you* won't need to compute regression coefficients. In this class they'll be provided (except on one homework assignment, in which you are asked to *guess* them!). If you need to compute them later you'll use a computer. So Equation (20.2.1), with the slopes +4, +5, and +3, and the intercept, -6, would be given to you. (**Bold** numbers will be used in this chapter to designate values that would usually be provided for you.)

However, once you are given the multiple regression equation, you should be able to use it, along with the data, to compute all of the following statistics, in much the same way you did in Chapter 18 where you used only one independent variable.

REVIEW OF NOTATION

$\hat{Y}$ The regression equation estimate. In the multiple regression example above, this represents the best estimate of an case's score on Y, based on information about *all three* independent variables X_1 (Ability), X_2 (Motivation), and X_3 (Practice)

$SS_Y = \Sigma(Y - \bar{Y})^2$ The sum of squared deviations from the mean for the dependent variable
(The *total variation* we'll try to explain using the independent variables)

$SS_E = \Sigma(Y - \hat{Y})^2$ The *residual* variation which *cannot* be explained by the independent variable (or *variables*)

$SS_R = SS_Y - SS_E$ The variation in Y that *can* be explained by the independent variables.

$R^2 = SS_R/SS_Y$ The *multiple* coefficient of determination

$R = +\sqrt{R^2}$ The *multiple* correlation coefficient

SEE   The standard error of the estimate $= \sqrt{SS_E/n} = SD_Y\sqrt{1-R^2}$

EXAMPLES OF COMPUTATION

The computations below demonstrate the use of the above formulas to obtain all required statistics for the multiple regression analysis:

MULTIPLE REGRESSION ANALYSIS:

GIVEN: The multiple regression equation (This *always* will be provided)

$$\hat{Y} = 4X_1 + 5X_2 + 3X_3 - 6$$

RESIDUAL COMPUTATION (Based on STUDENT DATA in TABLE 20.2.1)

	X_1	X_2	X_3	Y	$\hat{Y}$	$Y-\hat{Y}$	$(Y-\hat{Y})^2$
Al	0	0	2	0	0	0	0
Ben	0	2	0	4	4	0	0
Carol	2	0	0	2	2	0	0
Dan	2	2	2	18	18	0	0

$$SSE = 0$$

Note that the $\hat{Y}$ values are obtained by plugging the cases' scores on *all 3* independent variables into the regression equation.

For example, for Dan,

$$\hat{Y} = 4X_1 + 5X_2 + 3X_3 - 6$$
$$= 4(2) + 5(2) + 3(2) - 6$$
$$= 18$$

OTHER MULTIPLE REGRESSION COMPUTATIONS:

$SS_Y = 200$ and $SS_E = 0$, so $SS_R = SS_Y - SS_E = 200 - 0 = 200$

$$SEE = \sqrt{SS_R / n} = \sqrt{0/4} = 0$$

$R^2 = SS_R/SS_Y = 200/200 = 1.0$ $\qquad R = + \sqrt{R^2} = 1.0$

OPTIONAL "STEPWISE" VERSION OF EXAMPLE 1

The following table summarizes an (optional) four step process, comparing four different ways of predicting Y. As discussed in class, this type of summary clearly shows the *increasing accuracy* of the estimates as you go from *no* independent variables (Row 1), to *one* independent variable (Row 2), to *two* independent variables (Row 3) to *three* independent variables (Row 4).

Note that as you go down the Total Error column, the error *decreases* from 200 to 0, and similarly the Typical Error decreases from 7.07 to 0.

Row 4 represents an ideal case, the full multiple regression described above, in which 100% of the variation in Y gets explained by the three independent variables.

PRACTICE: You should be able to compute all numbers in this summary except the bold numbers (which are the multiple regression coefficients)

'STEPWISE' MULTIPLE REGRESSION (STUDENT DATA from TABLE 20.2.1)

Estimate of Y	Total squared error	Typical Error	Proportion Explained	Correlation
1) $\bar{Y}$	$SS_Y = 200$	SD $= 7.07$		
2) $\hat{Y} = \mathbf{2} + \mathbf{4}X_1$	$SS_E = 136$	$SEE = 5.83$	$r^2 = .32$	$r = .57$
3) $\hat{Y} = \mathbf{-3} + \mathbf{4}X_1 + \mathbf{5}X_2$	$SS_E = 36$	$SEE = 3.00$	$R^2 = .82$	$R = .91$
4) $\hat{Y} = \mathbf{-6} + \mathbf{4}X_1 + \mathbf{5}X_2 + \mathbf{3}X_3$	$SS_E = 0$	$SEE = 0$	$R^2 = 1.0$	$R = 1.0$

20.3 BETA WEIGHTS: STANDARDIZED REGRESSION COEFFICIENTS

EXAMPLE 20.3.1: COMPARING THE *STRENGTH* OF PREDICTORS

TABLE 20.3.1 STUDENT DATA

	X_1: Ability	X_2: Motivation	X_3: Practice	Y: Test Score
Al	0	4	0	2
Ben	0	0	8	6
Carol	2	0	0	0
Dan	2	4	8	12
Ed	0	4	0	2
Fred	0	0	8	6
Glee	2	0	0	0
Hal	2	4	8	12

REGRESSION COEFFICIENTS ARE <u>NOT</u> COMPARABLE

Suppose the data above were obtained when *eight* students were measured on the independent variables *ability*, *motivation* and *practice*, and the dependent variable *test score*.

Here's the correct regression equation for predicting Y from X_1, X_2 and X_3

$$\hat{Y} = \text{-2} + 1X_1 + 1X_2 + 1X_3$$

People often ask, "Can you look at the regression coefficients and get an idea how *important* each independent variable is in predicting Y?"

For example, the regression coefficients are all *equal* here. b_1, b_2 and b_3 all equal +1. To estimate Joe's score on Y, you'd start with -2, then you'd add *1* times Joe's score on X_1 and *1* times his score on X_2 and *1* times his score on X_3. Does this mean that each of the independent variables contributes *equally* to the prediction of Y? *No!*

Regression coefficients are *not* comparable to each other *unless* all of the independent variables have the same standard deviation. In this example, the standard deviation of X_3 is *twice as large* as that of X_2, and the standard deviation of X_2 is *twice as large* as that of X_1. When you add 1 times X_3 to your estimate, you're adding much more variation compared to adding 1 times X_2, so X_3 is contributing much more to your estimate.

STANDARDIZED REGRESSION COEFFICIENTS (BETA WEIGHTS) *ARE* COMPARABLE

Suppose you standardized each of the variables above, before conducting the multiple regression. This would guarantee that all variables had the same standard deviation, 1, and that the intercept in the regression equation would be zero.

Here's the regression equation which results when each of the previous variables is standardized before computing the regression coefficients.

$$\text{Estimate of STD Y} = \mathbf{0} + \mathbf{.218}\,(\text{STD } X_1) + \mathbf{.436}\,(\text{STD } X_2) + \mathbf{.873}\,(\text{STD } X_3)$$

These coefficients are called **beta weights**, and are denoted β_1, β_2, β_3, etc., to distinguish them from the original (unstandardized) coefficients). The general form of the standardized regression equation is then:

$$\text{Estimate of STD Y} = \beta_1\,(\text{STD } X_1) + \beta_2\,(\text{STD } X_2) + \beta_3\,(\text{STD } X_3)\ldots$$

NOTE: Some older texts just denote beta weights with upper case "B's".

Beta weights *can* be compared to find out the relative strength of the different independent variables.

To estimate Joe's standard score on Y, you'd add *.218* times Joe's standard score on X_1 and *.436* times his standard score on X_2 and *.873* times his standard score on X_3.

In this example we *can* compare the .436 beta coefficient for X_2 with the .218 beta coefficient for X_1 and conclude that "in the multiple regression using X_1, X_2 and X_3 to predict Y, the contribution of the variable X_2 is *twice* that of the variable X_1."

Beta weights are routinely included in the output of statistical software programs such as SPSS.

20.4 INFERENCE ABOUT MULTIPLE CORRELATION

THE BEST POINT ESTIMATE OF POPULATION R^2 : 'ADJUSTED R^2 '

EXAMPLE 1

In the example above based on Table 20.2.1, if we had used only the first two independent variables, X1 (Ability) and X2 (Motivation) to predict Y (Test Score), we would have succeeded in explaining .82 of the variation in Y. I.e., for *this set* of data, R^2 = .82, and R = .91. If we assume that the data were obtained from a random sample, what can we conclude about the *population* in question? We'll show how to estimate the *population* R^2, and then show how to perform a hypothesis test on R^2.

The *sample* squared multiple correlation coefficient, R^2 , is *not* the best estimate of the squared multiple correlation in the *population* the sample was drawn from.

'R^2_*', often referred to as *adjusted R^2* , denotes the best estimate of population R^2 based on sample data.

**20.4.1   The best estimate of ρ^2 (Population R^2)
          based on sample data is *adjusted R^2* ,or**

$$R^2_* \ = \ 1-(1-R^2)\left(\frac{n-1}{n-k-1}\right)$$

Where
**R^2 is the sample squared multiple correlation
coefficient**
n is the sample size
k is the number of independent variables

The multiple regression technique is a powerful way of predicting scores on a dependent variable. In a small sample, using several independent variables, you'll automatically obtain a *high* multiple correlation in the *sample*, even if there's *no* relationship in the *population*.

R^2_* adjusts for this "ad hoc" aspect of multiple correlation, reducing the estimate, which makes it more conservative and more realistic.

*There is no generally accepted designation for the *population* R^2 ! *Consistency* would dictate
    that it should be called "P^2". "P" is the upper case version of ρ, the Greek letter rho, but the
    use of that notation is rare. We'll use ρ^2 or "population R^2 " and "sample R^2 ".

In our example,

$$R^2* = 1 - (1 - R^2)\left(\frac{n-1}{n-k-1}\right)$$

$$= 1 - (1 - .82)\left(\frac{4-1}{4-2-1}\right)$$

$$= 1 - (.18)\left(\frac{3}{1}\right)$$

$$= 1 - (.54) = .46$$

The best estimate of the ρ^2 or population R^2 is only *.46*, and the best estimate of R is the square root of .46, which is only *.6782!* This is understandable in this simple case. We were estimating Y scores for *only 4* cases, using our choice of any *3* different values to use in our regression equation (a, b1, and b2). You can guarantee that your *sample* R^2 fairly close to R^2* if you follow this common rule of thumb: Have *at least 10* cases in your sample for each independent variable. I.e., if you make n equal to at least 10 times k, the sample R^2 will almost never be unrealistically high.

EXAMPLE 2

Suppose we had ten times as many cases in our sample, compared to EXAMPLE 1 above. That is, suppose sample R^2 is .82, but there are n = *40* cases in the sample, not *4*. Assume that we use k = 2 independent variables.

What will R^2* , our best estimate of the population R^2 , be?

$$R^2* = 1 - (1 - R^2)\left(\frac{n-1}{n-k-1}\right)$$

$$= 1 - (1 - .82)\left(\frac{40-1}{40-2-1}\right)$$

$$= 1 - (.18)\left(\frac{39}{37}\right)$$

$$= 1 - (.18)(1.054) = .8103$$

In this case, adjusted R^2 , the best estimate of the *population* R^2 is *.8103*, close to the *sample* R^2 value of .82.

USING ANOVA TO TEST HYPOTHESES ABOUT R

After computing a *sample* R , it's natural to ask, "Is this convincing evidence that the *population* R is greater than zero?" or "Is this convincing evidence that in the population, X_1 and X_2 are related to Y?". ANOVA techniques may be used to test the null hypothesis that "Population R $= 0$" against the alternate hypothesis that "Population R $\neq 0$". The F Ratio corresponds in this case to $MS_{REGRESSION}/MS_{RERROR}$. Here's an outline of the computations in the ANOVA summary table:

COMPUTATIONAL FORMAT: ANOVA SIGNIFICANCE TEST FOR R^2

Source	SS	df	MS	F
Multiple Regression (Explained)	SS_R	k	SS_R/k	$\dfrac{SS_R/k}{SS_E/(n-k-1)}$
Residual (Error)	SS_E	n-k-1	$SS_E/(n-k-1)$	
Total	SS_Y	n-1		

The SS due to the effect of the independent variables is 'SS_R' in this case. The error SS is SS_E. The numerator df is k and the denominator df is n-k-1.

DATA REQUIREMENTS
These requirements must be satisfied in order to perform a hypothesis test on a multiple correlation coefficient.

1. Independence of scores.

Each case's score on a variable is not affected by any other case's score.

2. Normality

For each possible *combination* of specific scores on the independent variables, X_1, X_2, etc, there's a group of all cases in the population that got that particular set of scores on the independent variables. Each of these groups must have an approximately normal distribution on Y, the dependent variable.

3. Homoscedasticity (Homogeneity of Variance)

For each possible *combination* of specific scores on the independent variables, X1, X2, etc, there's a group of all cases in the population that got that particular set of scores on the independent variables. Each of these groups must have the same variance.

EXAMPLE

As in EXAMPLE 2 above, suppose that the sample R^2 is .82, and there are n = 40 cases in the sample. Assume that k = 2 independent variables were used.
Assume that SSY, the total sum of squares for Y, is 2000, and that SSR is 1640.
Is this convincing evidence that there is a relationship in the population?

H_0 : Population R^2 = 0

H_1 : Population $R^2 \neq 0$

COMPUTATION:

Source	SS	df	MS	F	P
Multiple Regression (Explained)	1640	2	820	84.28	<.01
Residual (Error)	360	37	9.73		
Total	2000	39			

The critical value of F at the .01 level of significance is $F_{2,37}$ = 5.39. We *can* conclude that P<.01 in this case and reject H_0, because the *obtained* value of F is greater than the *critical value* for F. (We use $F_{2,30}$ as an approximation to $F_{2,37}$. Here is the general rule when you need to approximate: You never assume you have *more* degrees of freedom than you actually have.)

20.5 PICTURING and INTERPRETING RESIDUALS

Table 20.5.1 shows hypothetical (but not unrealistic) data for four automobiles. There are *two* independent variables, HP, or engine horsepower, (labeled X_1) and WEIGHT (labeled X_2). There is one dependent variable, ET, the 'elapsed time' or time it takes the automobile to accelerate to a speed of 60 mph, (Labeled Y).

TABLE 20.5.1 AUTOMOBILE DATA

	X_1 : HP	X_2: WEIGHT*	Y: ET (seconds)
BMW	200	33	7
FORD	200	37	11
CORVETTE	280	38	4
LINCOLN	280	40	6

* Weight is in *hundreds* of pounds

You probably have acquired some intuitions about automotive physics-- increasing a car's *power* generally makes it *quicker*; and increasing a car's *weight* generally makes it *slower*. Cars with higher horsepower would be expected to have *lower* ET's, and cars that weigh more would be expected to have *higher* ET's. These intuitions are correct! Below, they will help you to see how tricky it can be to interpret multivariate data.

THE RESIDUAL VARIABLE

Suppose you perform a simple linear regression analysis on the Automobile Data above, using only the single independent variable HP (X_1) . The regression equation will be:

$$\hat{Y} = 19 - .05X_1$$

	X_1 : HP	Y: ET	$\hat{Y}$	**Y-$\hat{Y}$**	$(Y-\hat{Y})^2$
BMW	200	7	9	**-2**	4
FORD	200	11	9	**+2**	4
CORVETTE	280	4	5	**-1**	1
LINCOLN	280	6	5	**+1**	<u>1</u>

SSE = 10

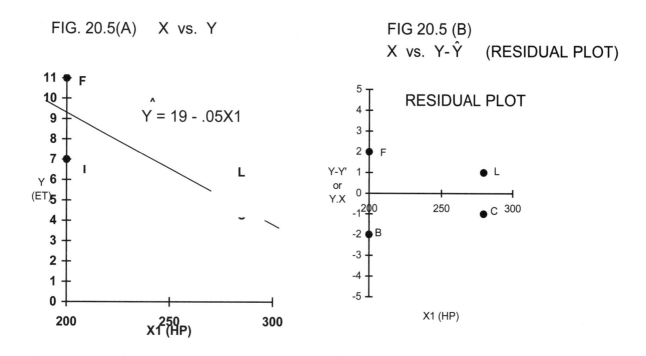

FIG. 20.5(A)   X vs. Y

FIG 20.5 (B)
X vs. Y-$\hat{Y}$ (RESIDUAL PLOT)

$\hat{Y} = 19 - .05X1$

Figure 20.5A is the usual scattergram showing the relationship between X1 (HP) and Y (ET). We see a clear negative relationship between HP and ET, as expected.

Figure 20.5B shows the corresponding **residual plot.** The horizontal axis is the same as in the scattergram, but the vertical axis is Y-$\hat{Y}$, (or Y.X), the *residual*. That is, the residual plot shows, for each case, the case's score on Y *with* $\hat{Y}$ *subtracted.* Recall that $\hat{Y}$ represents the best estimate of Y based on the effect of the independent variable X. So the residual, Y-$\hat{Y}$, represents Y, *with the effect of X removed.* It is also referred to as *Y, after X has been controlled for,* or *Y with X* **partialled out.**

Here's yet another intuitive way to think of Y-$\hat{Y}$. The scattergram on the left above shows cars' ET's when the cars have been affected by engines of different horsepower. Of course, the cars with higher horsepower have lower ET's. We might ask how the cars' ET's might compare if they all had *identical* engines, so we could see how the other differences among the cars affected their ET's. (The cars have different weights, tires, air drag coefficients, transmissions, etc.) If we *remove* the effect of the different engine HP, the differences due to these *other* factors will be more obvious. Computing Y-$\hat{Y}$ shows us what the ET's would look like if the cars all had equal engines installed. The only differences between the cars' ET's in the variable Y-$\hat{Y}$ are due to the *other* factors.

Note how the diagonal trend shown by the regression line in the scattergram, is *not* present in the residual plot (because this trend represents the effect of X, which has been *removed*).

Inspection of the residual plot makes it clear that the correlation of X with Y-$\hat{Y}$ is 0. This is just what you'd expect, since Y-$\hat{Y}$ *is not* supposed to be influenced by X *at all!*

EXERCISES   CHAPTER 20.1 - 20.5

MULTIPLE REGRESSION

TABLE EX 20.1

	X_1	X_2	Y
Arnie	-1	+1	0
Barnie	+1	-1	4
Carnie	+1	+1	12
Darnie	-1	-1	0

TABLE EX 20.1 above shows scores for four cases that were measured on the two independent variables X_1 and X_2, and the dependent variable Y.

1. How much variation is there in Y to be explained? What is SSy?

2. If you picked one of the four cases, and estimated that case's score using $\bar{Y}$, how far off would you typically be? What is SDy?

PART 1 : SIMPLE REGRESSION OF Y WITH X_1 *ONLY*

Questions 3 - 9 refer to Table EX 20.1 and the following (review) task only:
   Do a simple linear regression using only X_1 as the independent variable and Y as the dependent variable.

3. What is the regression line equation?

4. How much variation in Y cannot be explained by X_1 ? I.e., what is SSE ?

5. How much variation in Y can be explained by X_1 ? I.e., SSR = ?

6. r^2 = ?

7. r, the simple linear correlation of X_1 with Y is ?

8. What percentage of the variation in Y can be explained *by X_1 alone*?

9. If you estimated scores on Y using $\hat{Y}$ predictions *based on X_1 alone*, how far off would your estimates typically be?   That is, what is the S.E.E. ?

PART 2 : SIMPLE REGRESSION OF Y WITH X₂ *ONLY*

These questions refer to Table EX 20.1 and the following (review) task only:

Do a simple linear regression using *only* X_2 as the independent variable and Y as the dependent variable. That is, for Part 2, (Questions 10-16) just ignore X_1 and act as if X_2 were the only independent variable.

10.. What is the regression line equation?

11. How much variation in Y cannot be explained by X_2. ? I.e., what is SSE ?

12. How much variation in Y can be explained by X_2 ? I.e., SSR = ?

13. r^2 = ?

14. r, the linear correlation of X_2 with Y is ?

15. What percentage of the variation in Y can be explained *by X₂ alone*?

16. If you estimated scores on Y using $\hat{Y}$ predictions *based on X₂ alone*, how far off would your estimates typically be ? I.e., what is the SEE ?

PART 3 : MULTIPLE REGRESSION OF Y WITH X₁ AND X₂ COMBINED

These questions continue to refer to Table EX 20.1.

Using this *multiple* regression equation,

$$\hat{Y} = 4 + 4X_1 + 2X_2$$

Answer the following questions below.

That is, Part 3 is about the *multiple* regression in which *both* X_1 and X_2 are used to predict Y.

17. How much variation in Y cannot be explained using X_1 and X_2 together? I.e., what is SSE ?

18. How much variation in Y can be explained by X_1 and X_2 together? I.e., SSR = ?

19. R^2 , the *multiple* coefficient of determination, is ?

20. R, the *multiple* correlation coefficient = ?

21. What percentage of the variation in Y can be explained *by X₁ and X₂ combined*?

22. If you estimated scores on Y using $\hat{Y}$ predictions *based on X₁ and X₂ combined* , how far off would your estimates typically be? I.e., what is the SEE ?

RESIDUALS

If all the scores on the variable $Y - \hat{Y}$ are zero you can conclude that...

23. (In a multiple regression), R =

24. (In a simple regression), r =

25. SSE =

26. SSR/SSY =

----

27. Suppose $Y - \hat{Y}$ for Sue is +5, and $Y - \hat{Y}$ for Al is -2. We'd say that 'Sue scored 5 more than expected' and 'Al scored 2 less than expected'. What is the difference between these two residuals due to?

ANSWERS TO EXERCISES   *CHAPTER 20.1 - 20.5*

----

1. 96

2. 4.9

   PART 1

3. $\hat{Y} = 4 + 4X_1$

4. SSE = 32

5. SSR = 96 - 32 = 64

6. .6666   SSR/SSY = 64/96 = .6666

7. +.82

8. 66.67 %

9. 2.82 $\sqrt{SSE/n} = \sqrt{32/4} = \sqrt{8} = 2.82$

   PART 2

10. $Y - \hat{Y} = 4 + 2X_2$

11. SSE = 80

12. SSR = 16

13. .1666

14. +.41

15. 16.67 %

16. 4.47 $\sqrt{SSR/n} = \sqrt{80/4} = \sqrt{20} = 4.47$

PART 3

17. SSE = 16

18. SSR = 80

19. .8333

20. .91 $+ \sqrt{.8333}$

21. 83.33 %

22. 2.0 $\sqrt{SSR/n} = \sqrt{16/4} = \sqrt{4} = 2$

RESIDUALS

----

23. R = 1.0

24. r = -1.0 or +1.0

25. SSE = 0

26. SSR/SS_Y = 1.0   (SSR must equal SS_Y, because SSR = SS_Y + SSE, and SSE is 0)

----

27. The effects of variables *other than* the independent variable(s). This is referred to as 'chance error'.

20.6 PARTIAL CORRELATION

DEFINITION
So far we have covered two kinds of correlation coefficients for interval scale variables:

- Pearson's *r*, (simple linear correlation), which indicates the strength and direction of a linear relationship between *one* independent variable (usually designated X) and *one* dependent variable (usually designated Y). When it is necessary to specify which two variables are being correlated we list the variables after the *r*, as in "r_{XY}".

- *R*, the *multiple* correlation coefficient, which indicates the strength (but not the direction) of a relationship between *two or more* independent variables and *one* dependent variable.

The last important correlation coefficient is the *partial* correlation coefficient:

(20.6.1) The Partial Correlation Coefficient, $r_{XY.Z}$ indicates the strength and direction of the relationship between the variables X and Y, *after* the effect of the variable Z is first *removed* from both X and Y.

> **X is the independent variable.**
> **Y is the dependent variable.**
> **Z is the *control* variable, an additional independent variable.**

COMPUTATION
  A) *DIRECT*, BASED ON THE DEFINITION:

$$r_{XY.Z} = \text{the correlation of X.Z with Y.Z}$$

Steps in computation
  1) **Compute X.Z, the *residual* in the regression with Z as independent variable and X as dependent variable.**
  2) **Compute Y.Z, the *residual* in the regression with Z as independent variable and Y as dependent variable.**
  3) **Compute Pearson's r using X.Z as the independent variable and Y.Z as the dependent variable. That is, compute the correlation between the residual from Step 1 with the residual from Step 2.**

B) *SHORTCUT* FORMULA USING CORRELATION COEFFICIENTS

$$r_{XY.Z} = \frac{r_{XY} - r_{XZ}\, r_{YZ}}{\sqrt{(1 - r^2_{XZ})(1 - r^2_{YZ})}}$$

NOTATION:

- X.Z will be used to designate the *residual variable* which results when the *dependent* variable X is estimated using the *independent* variable Z. (This kind of notation is necessary whenever the independent and dependent variables are not the usual X and Y respectively).

  Similarly, Y.Z is used to designate the *residual variable* which results when the *dependent* variable Y is estimated using the *independent* variable Z.

- r^2_{XY} designates $(r_{XY})^2$ This common notation is unambiguous, and it saves space and parentheses.

Here's a description of the value of partial correlation from a widely used book, *SPSS: Statistical Package for the Social Sciences* (Nie, Norman H., *et al*, 2nd Ed., 1975):

> Partial correlation can be used in a wide variety of ways to aid the researcher in understanding and clarifying relationships between three or more variables. When properly employed, partial correlation becomes an excellent technique for uncovering spurious relationships, locating intervening variables, and can even be used to help the researcher make certain types of causal inferences.

USE OF THE PARTIAL CORRELATION COEFFICIENT

The *partial* correlation provides a clear and precise answer to a question that comes up often: "What would the relationship between X and Y look like *if we control for the effect of Z?*"

Z is typically a variable that we suspect is *confounded with* the independent variable X. We want to see if a relationship between X and Y might really be *spurious*, and is really due to the effect of Z on both of the variables X and Y.

(20.6.2) SPURIOUS RELATIONSHIPS

A) In general:

A *spurious* relationship is said to exist between an independent variable X and a dependent variable Y if the relationship disappears, becomes weaker, or reverses when we control for some third variable, Z.

B) For *linear* relationships between *interval scale* variables:

If $r_{XY.Z}$ (the partial correlation controlling for Z) is much *closer to 0* than r_{XY}, or *different in sign*, then the relationship between X and Y is called *spurious*.

EXAMPLE 20.6.1   SHOWING THAT WEIGHT DOESN'T *CAUSE* QUICKNESS!

The goals of this example are to show

- how a real, possibly *causal* relationship between X and Y can be *obscured* (or *masked*, or *hidden*) by the effects of a third, *confounding* variable, Z

- how to use $r_{XY.Z}$ to *test for* a spurious relationship between X and Y

- how to interpret a correlation matrix and inspect it for possible confounded variables

Suppose Mario inspects the automobile data in Table 20.5.1 and finds a surprising, unintuitive *negative* relationship between WEIGHT and ET among the cars tested. It is generally believed that adding weight to a car will cause it to take longer to accelerate from zero to sixty miles per hour, so Mario would have expected to find a *positive* relationship between WEIGHT and ET. Mario remembers how to *compute* Pearson's r, but not how to *interpret* it correctly. He computes Pearson's r, finds it to be -.23, and concludes (incorrectly) that, at least for these cars, increasing weight *causes* the cars to be 'quicker'.

Mario describes his data and conclusions to his colleague Manuel, who paid more attention when he took statistics. Manuel says, "You're *right* that there is a negative relationship between WEIGHT and ET, but you're *wrong* to conclude that it's a causal relationship. I think we can analyze the data and *prove* that the relationship is *not* causal, by controlling for the cars' horsepower (HP). If the relationship is causal it will remain the same when we control for HP. If it disappears or reverses when we control for HP, then we'll know it's *spurious*. If it's spurious, it can't be causal."

Manuel reorders and renames variables from Table 20.6.1 into this more convenient form:

TABLE 20.6.1   AUTOMOBILE DATA
(Set up to compute partial correlation, $r_{XY.Z}$)

	X: WEIGHT	Z: HP	Y: ET (seconds)
BMW	33	200	7
FORD	37	200	11
CORVETTE	38	280	4
LINCOLN	40	280	6

We'll designate the control variable Z throughout, for easy identification. This is the variable suspected of being confounded with X and Y.

A) COMPUTATION OF $r_{XY.Z}$ USING THE 'DIRECT' METHOD

STEP 1) Compute X.Z , the *residual* in the regression with Z as *independent* variable and X as *dependent* variable.

	Z HP	X WEIGHT	X-$\hat{X}$	X.Z RESIDUAL
BMW	200	33	35	-2
FORD	200	37	35	+2
CORVETTE	280	38	39	-1
LINCOLN	280	40	39	+1

We need to remove the effect of the control variable Z from the variable X. The computations are the same as the usual simple regression computations, *except* that the independent variable is Z (instead of the usual independent variable X) and the *dependent* variable is X (Which is usually the **in**dependent variable!) The goal is just to find the four values of the residual, X-$\hat{X}$, for use in Step 3 below. We denote this residual X.Z to make it clear that is the effect of the variable Z which has been removed from X.

$\hat{X}$ in the table above represents "the best estimates of WEIGHT based on HP". The values were computed using the simple regression equation

$$\hat{X} = 25 + .05Z$$

This regression equation was obtained from the data above. Here are the relevant scattergram and residual plot:

FIGURES FOR STEP 1 : FINDING X.Z

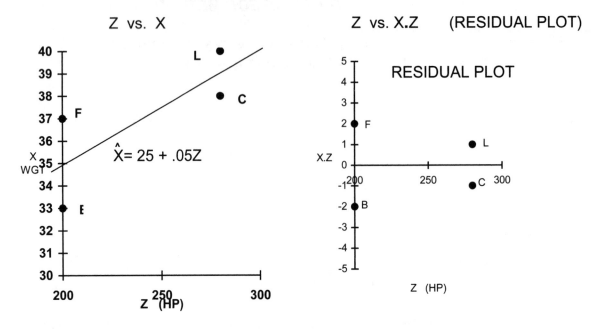

Note that the vertical and horizontal axes do not cross at the usual (0,0) point. The intercept in the regression line equation, 25, is correct. It is the value of $\hat{X}$ when Z, the independent variable equals 0. We have just *not shown* that part of the scattergram, so that the data points would be more visible.

PRACTICE: Check the computation of the regression line equation $\hat{X}$ = 25 + .05Z
        Hint: Use Formula 18.4.1 in Section 18.4 (But you must designate Z as the
                independent variable, and X as the *dependent* variable.)

**STEP 2) Compute Y.Z , the *residual* in the regression with Z as
         independent variable and Y as *dependent* variable.**

	Z HP	Y ET	$\hat{Y}$	Y.Z RESIDUAL
BMW	200	7	9	-2
FORD	200	11	9	+2
CORVETTE	280	4	5	-1
LINCOLN	280	6	5	+1

We need to remove the effect of the control variable Z from the variable Y. The computations are the same as the usual simple regression computations, *except* that the independent variable is called Z (instead of the usual independent variable X). The goal here is just to find the four values of the residual, $Y-\hat{Y}$, for use in Step 3 below. We denote this residual $(Y-\hat{Y})_z$ to make it clear that is the effect of the variable Z which has been removed from Y.

$\hat{Y}$ in the table above represents "the best estimate of ET based on HP". The values were computed using the simple regression equation

$$\hat{Y} = 19 - .05Z$$

This regression equation was obtained from the data above. Here are the relevant scattergram and residual plot:

FIGURES FOR STEP 2 : FINDING Y.Z

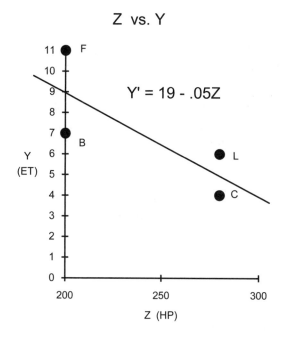

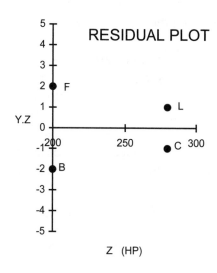

STEP 3) Compute Pearson's r using X.Z as the *independent* variable and Y.Z as the *dependent* variable. That is, compute the correlation between the residual from Step 1 with the residual from Step 2.

	X.Z X RESIDUAL (From Step 1)	Y.Z Y RESIDUAL (From Step 2)
BMW	-2	-2
FORD	+2	+2
CORVETTE	-1	-1
LINCOLN	+1	+1

$$r_{XY.Z} = +1.0$$

Step 3 just requires that we take the residual variable computed in Step 1 as the independent variable, and the residual from Step 2 as the dependent variable, and compute Pearson's r.

This makes sense, because $r_{XY.Z}$ is supposed to be "the correlation between X and Y, if the effect of Z is removed from X and Y." Step 1 removes the effect of Z from X. Step 2 removes the effect of Z from Y. Step 3 then computes the partial correlation using the residual variables computed in Steps 1 and 2.

In this case the residual variables are clearly perfectly related, since they are identical. In most cases it would be necessary to do the calculations described in Chapter 18 to obtain Pearson's r.

INTERPRETING $r_{XY.Z}$

Comparing the two correlation coefficients,

r_{XY} = -.23   The correlation between WEIGHT and ET

$r_{XY.Z}$ = +1.0   The correlation between WEIGHT and ET, *controlling for HP*

Manuel has proved that the relationship between WEIGHT and ET is *spurious* (and therefore not causal). The relationship *reverses* when HP is controlled for.

$r_{XY.Z}$ might also be described in this case as "the correlation that would exist between WEIGHT and ET *if* all cars had the *same* HP."

In this particular example, Manuel could also claim, "The effect of HP was *masking* the strong positive relationship between WEIGHT and ET." This is because the strong ***positive*** relationship, **+1.0**, only appears *after* we control for HP.

INTERPRETING A CORRELATION MATRIX

TABLE 20.6.2 CORRELATION MATRIX FOR AUTOMOBILE DATA

	X WEIGHT	Z HP	Y ET
X WEIGHT	1.0		
Z HP	+.784	1.0	
Y ET	-.231	-.784	1.0

A *correlation matrix* for a set of variables shows the correlation of each of the variables with every other variable. The column and row headings each list the entire set of variables. The value in a cell of the table is the correlation of the column variable with the row variable. E.g., the correlation of X (first column) and Z (second row) is +.784. Each value in a correlation matrix must be computed in the usual way. (Described in Chapter 18)

Since the statistic Pearson's r is *symmetrical*, $r_{XY} = r_{YX}$ for any two variables X and Y. I.e., if you switch the independent and dependent variables, you'll get the same value of r. So it is only necessary to show values below the diagonal in the table. All values on the diagonal are 1.0, since the correlation of any variable with itself is 1.0.

Inspecting a correlation matrix such as this can quickly show whether confounding might be occurring. If Z is a variable that is correlated with both X and Y then it is possible that controlling for Z will show that the relationship between X and Y is spurious. In Table 20.6.2, we see that Z and X are correlated +.784 and the correlation between Z and Y is -.784, so it is not surprising that the relationship between X and Y turns out to be spurious.

B) SHORTCUT COMPUTATION OF $r_{XY.Z}$ USING CORRELATIONS

There's probably no way to really understand the partial correlation coefficient completely without following the three steps of computation above at least once. There is, however, a less obvious, but quicker shortcut procedure to compute $r_{XY.Z}$ using three correlation coefficients:

$$r_{XY.Z} = \frac{r_{XY} - r_{XZ}\, r_{YZ}}{\sqrt{(1 - r^2_{XZ})(1 - r^2_{YZ})}} = \frac{-.231 - (.784)(-.784)}{\sqrt{(1-(.784)^2)(1-(-.784)^2)}} = +1.0$$

The three correlation coefficients needed may be obtained from a correlation matrix (Table 20.6.2 in this case), or they may be computed directly from the data if necessary.

EXERCISES   CHAPTER 20.6

OLDER PEOPLE PARTICIPATE TOO!

	X AGE	Z EDUCATION	Y CIVIC PARTICIPATION
X AGE	1.0		
Z EDUCATION	-.55	1.0	
Y CIVIC PARTICIPATION	-.30	.49	1.0

Suppose a set of people is surveyed, and each person's AGE, years of EDUCATION, and "level of CIVIC PARTICIPATION" is measured. The correlation matrix for these variables is computed and is displayed above. (From *Fundamentals of Social Statistics*, 2nd ed., Kirk Elifson, *et al*, 1990)

1. Is there a negative relationship between AGE and CIVIC PARTICIPATION?

2. What percent of the variation in CIVIC PARTICIPATION is due to AGE?

3. A possible problem with the survey was that the people available might not be representative-- in particular it is suspected that it accidentally contained too many poorly educated older people and/or too many highly educated younger people. Does it seem that this might have happened? (I.e., is age negatively correlated with education?)

4. $r_{XY.Z} = $? I.e., what is the correlation between AGE and CIVIC PARTICIPATION if you *control for* EDUCATION?

5. Does the relationship between AGE and CIVIC PARTICIPATION seem to be *spurious*?

6. If you *control for* EDUCATION, then what proportion of the variation in CIVIC PARTICIPATION is due to AGE? (Square $r_{XY.Z}$)

STAY IN SCHOOL!

	X PARENTAL $	Z OFFSPRING'S EDUCATION	Y OFFSPRING $
X PARENTAL $	1.0		
Z OFFSPRING'S EDUCATION	.53	1.0	
Y OFFSPRING $	.45	.69	1.0

Suppose a set of *pairs* of people is surveyed, each pair consisting of a parent and an adult daughter or son, and for each pair the parent's wealth, the daughter or son's years in school completed, and the daughter or son's wealth are measured. The correlation matrix for these variables is computed and is displayed above.

7. Is there a positive relationship between parent's wealth and offspring's wealth?

8. What percent of the variation in offspring's wealth seems to be related to parent's wealth?

9. Suppose the researcher believes that offspring's wealth derives almost entirely from a combination of two factors
        A) transfer of wealth from parents to children, and
        B) wealth accumulated by offspring from their own income, which should be related to their educational level.

    Do the data above indicate that offspring's educational level is related to offspring's wealth?

10. $r_{XY.Z}$ = ? That is, what is the correlation between parent's wealth and offspring's wealth, if you *control for* the offspring's educational level?

11. If you *control for* the offspring's educational level, then what proportion of the variation in the offspring's wealth is due to the parent's wealth (Square $r_{XY.Z}$, then convert to a percent)

12. Does most of the variation in offspring's wealth seem to be due to education, or to direct transfers of wealth from their parents?

CHECKING THE *VALIDITY* OF A PERSONALITY TEST

A test is called **valid** if it correctly measures what it was designed to measure. A way of *checking* the validity of a personality test is to compare test *scores* with some *criterion measure* of the trait that the test is supposed to measure. The objective measure is called a criterion. So, if test scores correlate highly with the criterion then the test is called valid.

Suppose a generally accepted criterion measure of resistance to authority in an adolescent mental hospital ward is the number of POINTS LOST due to violation of ward rules. Suppose two personality test scores are available for each adolescent, in addition to the POINTS LOST during the last month: a PSYCHOPATHY scale score, which is supposed to measure resistance to authority (along with other traits) and a LIE scale score, which is supposed to measure a tendency of the person being tested to "fake good" and deny any problems.

TABLE EX 20.6.1 PERSONALITY TEST DATA

(Not their real) NAMES	X PSYCHOPATHY	Z LIE SCALE	Y POINTS LOST
Angry Al	3	5	20
Bad Ben	7	5	40
Cranky Carol	7	10	5
Devious Dan	13	10	35
Edgy Ed	14	15	5
"Friendly" Frank	16	15	15

13. What is the correlation between PSYCHOPATHY and POINTS LOST?

14. Does it seem that the PSYCHOPATHY scale is valid ?

15. The LIE scale may be confounded with the PSYCHOPATHY scale -- patients who are *high* in PSYCHOPATHY may also tend to "*fake good*." Do the data indicate that this happened?

Compute $r_{XY.Z}$ using the DIRECT computation:

STEP 1) Compute X.Z, the *residual* in the regression with Z as independent variable
         and X as dependent variable.

> 16. What is the regression equation, $\hat{X}$ = a + bZ ?

> 17. What is the residual variable X.Z ?

STEP 2) Compute Y.Z , the *residual* in the regression with Z as independent variable
         and **Y** as dependent variable.

> 18. What is the regression equation, $\hat{Y}$ = a + bZ ?

> 19. What is the residual variable Y.Z ?

STEP 3) Compute Pearson's r using X.Z as the independent variable and Y.Z as the
         dependent variable. That is, compute the correlation between the residual from
         Step 1 with the residual from Step 2.

> 20. What is $r_{XY.Z}$?

> 21. What kind of relationship does this reveal between PSYCHOPATHY and POINTS LOST?

> 22. Create the correlation matrix for X, Y and Z.

> 23. Check your computation of $r_{XY.Z}$ using the shortcut formula.

CREATING A NEW, IMPROVED, VALID SCALE (USING MULTIPLE REGRESSION)

The multiple regression equation that best predicts Y (POINTS LOST) based on *both*
X (PSYCHOPATHY) *and* Z (LIE SCALE) is

$$\hat{Y} = 40 + 5X - 7Z$$

> 24. What is R, the multiple correlation ?

> 25. What percentage of the variation in POINTS LOST can be explained by the *two* scales
>   PSYCHOPATHY and LIE SCALE *combined*?

> 26. Suppose you create a new scale called "TRUE PSYCHOPATHY" by combining the
>   questions from the PSYCHOPATHY and LIE scales. You find a patient's score on this
>   new scale by taking the PSYCHOPATHY scale score and multiplying by 5, then subtracting
>   7 times the LIE SCALE score, then adding 40. Would this new scale be *valid* (using
>   POINTS LOST as the criterion variable, for the patients in this group? Why or why not?

REVIEW QUESTIONS

MULTIPLE REGRESSION

TABLE 1

X_1	X_2	Y
0	2	12
0	0	6
2	2	2
2	0	0

The following questions refer to the multiple regression in which X_1 and X_2 are the two independent variables, and Y is the dependent variable.

THE MULTIPLE REGRESSION EQUATION IS $\hat{Y} = -4X_1 + 2X_2 + 7$

27. $SSE =$ A) 16   B) 80   C) 52   D) 4   E) 1

28. $SSR =$ A) 4   B) 52   C) 80   D) 56   E) 16

29. What proportion of the variation in Y can be explained by X_1 and X_2 combined ?
    That is, what is R^2?
               A) .928   B) 1.0   C) .952   D) .007   E) -.928

30. R, the multiple correlation coefficient, is
               A) 1.00   B) 0   C) -1.0   D) .98   E) .96

31. S.E.E., the standard error of $\hat{Y}$, is
               A) 4   B) .25   C) 2.24   D) 1   E) -1

RESIDUAL VARIABLE

32. Suppose you do a regression with one independent variable X and a dependent variable Y.
    You then compute the residual variable $Y-\hat{Y}$.
    There will be _____ relationship between X and the residual variable $Y-\hat{Y}$, because $Y-\hat{Y}$ _____.
       A) a negative ... is negatively related to X.
       B) a positive ... is positively related to X.
       C) a weak ... is less variable than Y.
       D) no ... has had the effect of X removed from it.
       E) a strong ... represents the very essence of X-ness.

ANSWERS TO EXERCISES   CHAPTER 20.6

OLDER PEOPLE PARTICIPATE TOO!

1. Yes

2. 9%

3. Yes, the correlation between AGE and EDUCATION was -.55.

4. $r_{XY.Z} = \dfrac{r_{XY} - r_{XZ} r_{YZ}}{\sqrt{(1 - r^2_{XZ})(1 - r^2_{YZ})}} = \dfrac{-.30 - (-.55)(.49)}{\sqrt{(1 - (-.55)^2)(1 - (.49)^2)}} = \dfrac{-.03}{\sqrt{.53}} = -.04$

5. Yes, it becomes much *weaker* (closer to 0) when we control for EDUCATION.

6. 0.16% $(-.04)^2 (100\%) = (.0016)(100\%)$

STAY IN SCHOOL!

7. Yes

8. 20.25% $(.45)^2(100\%)$

9. Yes, the correlation between these variables is +.69.

10. $r_{XY.Z} = \dfrac{r_{XY} - r_{XZ} r_{YZ}}{\sqrt{(1 - r^2_{XZ})(1 - r^2_{YZ})}} = \dfrac{.45 - (.53)(.69)}{\sqrt{(1 - (-.53)^2)(1 - (.69)^2)}} = .14$

11. 1.96% $(.14)^2(100\%)$

12. Most of the variation in offspring's wealth seem to be due to OFFSPRING'S EDUCATION , because when we control for OFFSPRING'S EDUCATION, then OFFSPRING'S WEALTH no longer has much relationship to PARENTS' WEALTH.

CHECKING THE *VALIDITY* OF A PERSONALITY TEST

13. $r = -.160$

14. No, to be valid it would have to correlate highly with POINTS LOST, the criterion variable.

15. Yes. The correlation between LIE SCALE and PSYCHOPATHY is $+.884$.

16. $\hat{X} = Z$ That is, $\hat{X} = 0 + 1.0(Z)$

STEP 1) Compute X.Z, the *residual* in the regression with Z as
         independent variable and X as dependent variable.

17.

	Z LIE SCALE	X PSYCHOPATHY	$\hat{X}$	X.Z RESIDUAL
A	5	3	5	-2
B	5	7	5	+2
C	10	7	10	-3
D	10	13	10	+3
E	15	14	15	-1
F	15	16	15	+1

18. $\hat{Y} = 40 - 2Z$

   STEP 2) Compute $(Y - \hat{Y})_Z$, the *residual* in the regression with Z as
   independent variable and Y as dependent variable.

19.

	Z LIE SCALE	Y POINTS LOST	$\hat{Y}$	Y.Z RESIDUAL
A	5	20	30	-10
B	5	40	30	+10
C	10	5	20	-15
D	10	35	20	+15
E	15	5	10	-5
F	15	15	10	+5

   STEP 3) Compute Pearson's r using $(X - \hat{X})_Z$ as the independent variable and
   $(Y - \hat{Y})_Z$ as the dependent variable. That is, compute the correlation
   between the residual from Step 1 with the residual from Step 2.

	X.Z X RESIDUAL (From Step 1)	Y.Z Y RESIDUAL (From Step 2)
A	-2	-10
B	+2	+10
C	-3	-15
D	+3	+15
E	-1	-5
F	+1	+5

20. $r_{XY.Z} = +1.0$

21. A perfect positive linear relationship.

22.

	X PSYCHOPATHY	Z LIE SCALE	Y POINTS LOST
X PSYCHOPATHY	1.0		
Z LIE SCALE	.884	1.0	
Y POINTS LOST	-.160	-.603	1.0

23. $r_{XY.Z} = \dfrac{r_{XY} - r_{XZ}\, r_{YZ}}{\sqrt{(1 - r^2_{XZ})(1 - r^2_{YZ})}} = \dfrac{-.160 - (.884)(-.603)}{\sqrt{(1 - (.884)^2)(1 - (.603)^2)}} = +1.0$

24. R = +1.0

25. 100%

26. Yes, it would correlate 1.0 with POINTS LOST. (Actually, it would be *equal to* POINTS LOST!)

     This is actually how some personality test scales on the most widely used personality test (MMPI) were constructed-- with a correction to compensate for "faking," based on multiple regression.

REVIEW QUESTIONS

----

27. D

28. C

29. C $\dfrac{SS_Y - SS_E}{SS_Y} = \dfrac{84 - 4}{84} = .952$

30. D

31. D

RESIDUAL VARIABLE

32. D   The residual variable *never* has any correlation with the independent variable.

CHAPTER 21

USING CORRELATION AND REGRESSION WISELY

21.1 CORRECT USES OF CORRELATION AND REGRESSION

The correlation and regression techniques covered in the previous chapters are valuable in two ways:

1) They are extremely *general*, that is, they can really be applied to very many real world situations; and

2) Learning about correlation and regression helps you understand the ideas of *relationship*, *prediction* and *explanation* in a clear, precise, objective way.

When you first learn about these techniques it is easy to forget some of the main goals as you learn the details involved in the computation of SS_E, SS_R, SEE, etc.

A review of some of the main concepts and their correct application follows in this section.

In the next section, some frequent errors in using correlation and regression techniques will be presented, with appropriate warnings and advice.

MEASURING A RELATIONSHIP BETWEEN TWO VARIABLES

Two variables are related if information about a typical case's score on one variable enables you to better predict the case's score on the other variable. You could imagine that two people, looking at the same set of scores on X and Y, might still disagree about the existence of, or the strength of, a relationship between the two variables.

Pearson's r eliminates the possibility of such debate by providing one precise, objective measure of the strength and direction of a *linear* relationship between two *interval scale* variables, for a given set of cases that have been measured on each variable. (R does the same thing for *any number* of independent variables and one dependent variable).

Pearson's r and R are *objective*, because any two people doing the computations correctly will come up with the same value. These values are not matters of opinion or viewpoint. Once you learn to compute r, your values will agree with those computed by any expert throughout the world. Pearson's r, computed just as you have learned to compute it, appears in articles and books in all published languages.

Also, because of the mathematical properties of r, no one is likely to suggest that some other statistic should have been used instead of r, to assess the strength of a linear relationship.

QUALITIES OF r, r², R, and R²

There's another quality r has which makes it more generally useful and easier to interpret:

Pearson's r measures the degree of relationship between two variables without being influenced by the measurement scale used:

> **(21.1.1) If either variable X or Y, or both, is rescaled using a positive linear transformation, r will remain the same.**
>
> **The same applies to r², R and R² . *None* of these statistics depends on the choice of a particular scale of measurement.**

EXAMPLE

Suppose the correlation between the weight of a car and its speed after accelerating for 10 seconds is found to be -.432 by an engineer in the US who has measured weight in pounds and speed in miles per hour. Can you say what Pearson's r will be if a British engineer measures the same set of cars (assume that they are equally heavy and equally fast) using kilograms to measure weight and kilometers per hour? How about if the weight were measured in ounces and the speed in meters per second?

ANSWER

The correlation will be -.432 in all cases.

Our intuition leads us to expect a causal relationship here. The speed measured should be influenced by the weight of the cars, by a certain amount, and *that relationship's* is what r should measure. r really does get at whether these cases are related on the variables. r is *not* influenced by arbitrarily chosen units of measurement.

PEARSON'S r IS SYMMETRICAL

For any two variables X and Y: $r_{XY} = r_{YX}$. You'll always obtain the same value of r if you reverse the independent and dependent variables.

PROPORTIONAL REDUCTION IN ERROR (PRE)

The notion of a reduction in error is fundamental to understanding relationships between variables. Information about scores on X must help us estimate scores on Y with more accuracy (and less error) if X is related to Y. Using X should produce a *reduction* in error.

r and R do not have any obvious interpretation in terms of reduction in error. But r² and R² do! Recall the important definition of PRE in general:

> **(21.1.2) Proportional Reduction in Error (PRE) =**
>
> $$\frac{\text{Reduction in error made when X is used}}{\text{Error made in predicting Y without using X}}$$

The PRE is an intuitive measure of the strength of relationship between any two variables, of any scale types. It's a ratio that compares the error made in predicting Y, with and without information about X. (Assuming as usual that Y is the dependent variable we are trying to predict.) In the case of *interval* scale variables, the PRE is easily computed.

> **(21.1.3)** r^2 = **SSE/SSY is the PRE statistic when both X and Y are interval scale variables.**
>
> R^2 **is the PRE statistic when there are *several* independent interval scale variables and one interval scale dependent variable.**

COMPUTING THE REGRESSION LINE

Seeing the regression line helps you visualize the relationship between two variables. You can use it to make predictions of scores on Y based on scores on X.

As with r, you could imagine two people seeing the same bivariate data, each person with a different guess about 'the' best fitting line. The computational techniques presented in Chapter 18 for computing a and b, the intercept and slope of the line $\hat{Y}$, *guarantee* that the equation you come up with, $\hat{Y} = a + bX$, will be *best*.

The computer programs for obtaining the multiple regression coefficients can make the same guarantee.

QUALITIES OF THE REGRESSION LINE

These qualities of the regression line indicate why we can claim it is "*best*" :

> **(21.1.4) The sum of residuals, $\Sigma(Y - \hat{Y})$ is always 0.**

This indicates that the $\hat{Y}$ values lie in the 'middle' of the Y values, since the positive errors exactly cancel the negative errors. This fact can be used to check computations: The sum of the $Y - \hat{Y}$ column should always be 0.

> **(21.1.5) The sum of squared residuals, $\Sigma(Y - \hat{Y})^2$ is minimal.**

This indicates that if you compute a and b as specified in Chapter 8, the total squared error is as *small as possible* when you use $\hat{Y}$ as an estimate of Y. (This applies only to *linear* estimates; there's no better-fitting *straight line*). The same applies to estimates obtained from multiple regression equations. Because of this property, estimates made using regression techniques are called *least-squares* estimates.

INTERPOLATION AND EXTRAPOLATION

Suppose that you find the regression line for the data sketched below to be $\hat{Y} = 4 + .5X$, based on the six cases A - F.

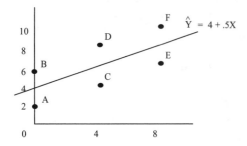

You can use the regression line to make estimates for *new* cases, that were *not* in the original data set, based on their scores on X. (However, so far no claims can be made about the *accuracy* of these estimates, which will be discussed later)

EXAMPLE 1

Based on the data illustrated above what would be your best estimate of the score on Y of a new case G, whose score on X was 6.

ANSWER

7,   because $4 + .5(6) = 7$

EXAMPLE 2

Suppose some new case, G, scored 100 on X. Estimate G's score on Y.

ANSWER

54, because $4 + .5(100)$ is 54

The first example, representing *interpolation*, seems reasonable, if G was chosen from the same population of individuals that A - F were.

The second example, representing *extrapolation* (far beyond the original range of data!) should raise concerns about accuracy-- it is the best *estimate* we can make based on these data, but we wouldn't claim that it is accurate to within the SEE (which is 2 in this case). The SEE of course, only refers to the typical accuracy of estimates for the *original* 6 data points.

CONTROLLING FOR X BY COMPUTING THE RESIDUAL

Computing the residual variable $Y - \hat{Y}$ and graphing it in a residual plot shows us:

- The variation in Y that cannot be explained by X.
- What scores on Y would have looked like if they had not been affected by X.
  (This is particularly helpful when we believe X has a causal relationship with Y.)
- Y, controlled for X.
- The variation in Y that may be explainable by *other* independent variables,
  but not by X.

Examples in which residuals are computed and graphed provide the best intuitions about the *control* of variables. There's no clearer, more elegant way to see what it means to "*control* for the effect of the variable X" than to *remove* the effect of the variable X using regression methods, and see what remains.

EXAMPLE

Suppose Nicolette runs a race at a high altitude in 307 seconds. Her rival Kira runs the same distance at a much lower altitude in 304 seconds, and calls Nicolette and suggests that she find another hobby. Nicolette predicts that in an upcoming meet, when they compete at the same altitude, Nicolette will beat Kira by 2 seconds, because when you *control for the effect of altitude*, Nicolette's time is really 2 seconds *faster* than Kira's. Nicolette FAXes the following figures to back up her claim.

Figure 1 shows the results of numerous races run at different altitudes, including Nicolette and Kira's last races. Figure 2 shows (roughly) what the residuals would look like.

If $Y - \hat{Y}$ for Kira is +1 and $Y - \hat{Y}$ for Nicolette is -1, our best estimate would be that at *equal* altitude Nicolette would be 2 seconds *quicker*.

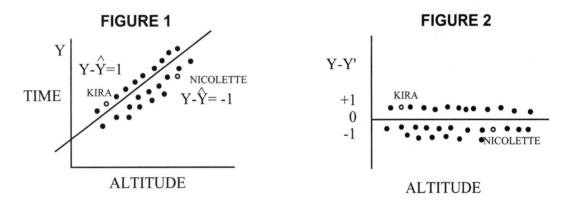

21.2 AVOIDING SOME COMMON PITFALLS

DON'T INFER CAUSALITY!

Correlation and regression techniques received a 'bad name' for many years because of articles in which authors found variables to be correlated, and then erroneously concluded that the independent variable must be having a *causal* effect on the dependent variable. For a while journals would routinely turn down any article which involved computation of correlations, particularly if the studies were observational.

Pearson's r and other measures of correlation are meaningful and useful! But an r of 1.0 or -1.0 does ***not*** imply that the relationship measured was causal, even in part.

The stringent requirements to assess causality will be discussed later, meanwhile, when in *doubt, don't*! (Conclude causality.)

NOTE THE EFFECT OF OUTLIERS

Outliers have a strong effect on interval scale statistics such as the mean, the standard deviation, as well as Pearson's r and regression coefficients. You should always look at the scattergram and visually check for unusual atypical scores which may represent errors in data entry or failures in measurement apparatus. Only a few erroneous data points can cause significant *underestimation* or *overestimation* of r.

FIGURE 21.2.1

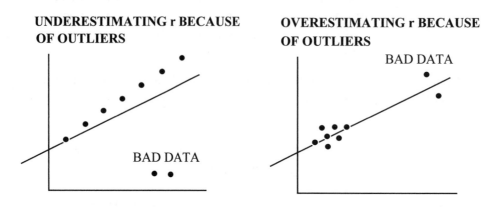

UNDERESTIMATING r BECAUSE OF OUTLIERS

OVERESTIMATING r BECAUSE OF OUTLIERS

FACE THE CHALLENGE OF NONLINEAR RELATIONSHIPS

Regression techniques we have used guarantee the best *straight line* fit to the data. If a scattergram reveals an obvious curved trend, more advanced techniques which use more complicated equations than $\hat{Y} = a + bX$, should be investigated. They will result in a better understanding of the relationship between the variables, lower residual error, and better prediction of Y based on X.

To fit *curved* trends in data neatly may require using equations with logarithmic functions, or higher powers of X such as X^2 or X^3 instead of just X. This will require going beyond the level of an introductory course, but such techniques are explained pretty clearly in the books that come with computer programs such as the SPSS, SYSTAT and BMD packages.

FIGURE 21.2.2

EXAMPLES OF DATA SHOWING CURVED TRENDS

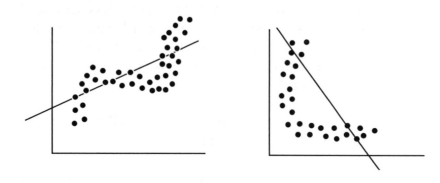

USE ECOLOGICAL CORRELATIONS CORRECTLY

Ecological correlation are correlations in which the *scores* are themselves statistics computed for groups of individuals and the *groups* are the cases under consideration. There is nothing wrong or inherently misleading about ecological correlations, as long as conclusions are only drawn about the actual cases involved. However, erroneous conclusions are often based on ecological correlations, and these cases always involve computing r for one set of cases and then applying it to a different set of cases.

FIGURE 21.2.3

CORRELATIONS AMONG GROUPS OF INDIVIDUALS

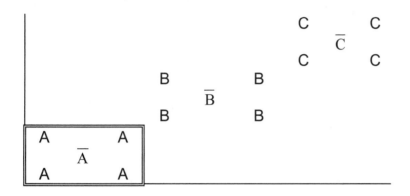

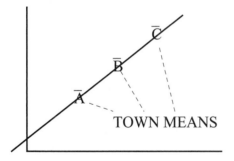

TOWN MEANS

Suppose first that the 12 points sketched on the left represent people from three towns, A, B, C, which together comprise an entire county. The points A, B, C represent the *town means* on X and Y, for each of the 3 towns. Suppose the horizontal axis represents educational level and the vertical axis represents income.

Consider just the four points representing people in Town A. Among those four people there's no correlation between X and Y. That is, r = 0 in Town A.

Similarly, in Town B, r = 0; and in Town C, r = 0.

Now look at all twelve points, representing all twelve residents of the County. In the entire County, there's a positive, but not perfect relationship. Suppose r in the entire County is .7.

Compare those results with this *ecological* correlation. Consider a different correlation in which there are only three cases, the three towns, and each towns score on X is the town mean of its four residents on X, and similarly for Y. This is sketched on the right. r = 1.0 for the ecological correlation between the three towns.

Now we have correlations of 0 (among individuals within each town), .7 (among individuals within the entire county), and 1.0 (ecological correlation between towns within the county). Yet no errors have been made; this does represent a situation that could conceivably occur.

Here's the common mistake that is often made. A consumer of statistics, being told that the *ecological* correlation, say between education and income, is 1.0, concludes that *a person* from town A whose education is above average probably has an above average income, compared to the other people *within* that town. This is an error-- the correlation in Town A is 0! The mistake occurs because a correlation based on one set of cases (towns) is applied to a different set of cases (people in Town A).

RESTRICTED VARIABLES CAN BE MISLEADING

See Figure 21.2.3 above. Suppose you are trying to compute the correlation for the whole County, but you only have access to individuals whose educational level is in the *top third* (i.e., in this case the four residents of Town C) You'd compute r to be 0, and the regression line to be a horizontal line through the average Y score for Town C.

In general, *restricting the range* of scores on X in this way will *usually* (but not always!) lead to *underestimating* r and *underestimating* the steepness of the regression line, as it does in this case. (In less typical cases restricting the range *could* also lead to *over*estimation.)

INFERENCES ABOUT SUBGROUPS ARE SUSPECT

Refer to Figure 21.2.3 again. Suppose someone knew the correlation for the whole county was .7, and based on that concluded "someone in Town A whose educational level is above the mean for Town A probably has an income level higher than Town A's average." The conclusion is erroneous-- there's no correlation in Town A. The mistake here is to assume that a correlation which exists within a large group holds for small subgroups.

This error was also illustrated in Homework 8, an assignment involving employment testing.

INFERENCES ABOUT POPULATIONS REQUIRE RANDOM SAMPLES!

But the techniques for drawing conclusions about population correlations based on correlations found in random samples were covered in previous chapters. The necessity of choosing random samples cannot be overemphasized. Subgroups which are not *random* samples from the *entire* population can't tell you anything about the entire population.

EXERCISES   CHAPTER 21

Suppose a study is done of a large set of retail stores. In each store the average (or mean) salary and the average (or mean) level of employee job satisfaction is computed.

Then a correlation is computed using the stores as cases, the mean salary for each store as the independent variable and the average employee job satisfaction as the dependent variable. The correlation is .8.

1. The type of correlation is referred to as
    A) canonical
    B) discriminatory
    C) teleological
    D) logical
    E) ecological

2. Suppose Joe's salary is higher than the average employee's salary at the store at which Joe works. *Based on the data described above*, we could conclude that Joe's job satisfaction is
    A) definitely higher than the average employee at his store
    B) probably higher than the average employee at his store
    C) definitely higher than the average of employees at all stores.
    D) probably higher than the average of employees at all stores.
    E) none of the above.

3. Suppose Ken's store had a mean salary well above the typical store's. We can conclude based on the data above that the mean employee job satisfaction at Ken's store, compared to the other stores studied, is...
    A) probably higher than the average store's
    B) definitely higher than the average store's
    C) none of the above

ANSWERS TO EXERCISES, CHAPTER 21

----

1. E   It's a correlation among a group of *statistics*, with each statistic summarizing a number of employees.

2. E   You can't conclude anything about what relationships are like among employees *within one* of the stores. We've only been given information about a relationship *between* a bunch of stores, not about individual employees in a specific store.

3. A

           This statement relates to the information given. We know that there's a positive correlation between stores average salary and average employee satisfaction. So we can conclude that if this store's average salary is relatively high (compared to other stores) we can expect its average employee satisfaction to be relatively high also.

INDEX

TABLE A1

STANDARD NORMAL DISTRIBUTION (z)
CUMULATIVE PROPORTIONS

z scores are in the margins.
Table entries indicate the <u>cumulative</u> <u>proportion</u> for each z score.

z	.00	.01	.02	.03	.04	.05	.06	.07	.08	.09
-3.4	.0003	.0003	.0003	.0003	.0003	.0003	.0003	.0003	.0003	.0002
-3.3	.0005	.0005	.0004	.0004	.0004	.0004	.0004	.0004	.0004	.0003
-3.2	.0007	.0007	.0006	.0006	.0006	.0006	.0006	.0005	.0005	.0005
-3.1	.0010	.0009	.0009	.0009	.0008	.0008	.0008	.0008	.0007	.0007
-3.0	.0013	.0013	.0013	.0012	.0012	.0011	.0011	.0011	.0010	.0010
-2.9	.0019	.0018	.0018	.0017	.0016	.0016	.0015	.0015	.0014	.0014
-2.8	.0026	.0025	.0024	.0023	.0023	.0022	.0021	.0021	.0020	.0019
-2.7	.0035	.0034	.0033	.0032	.0031	.0030	.0029	.0028	.0027	.0026
-2.6	.0047	.0045	.0044	.0043	.0041	.0040	.0039	.0038	.0037	.0036
-2.5	.0062	.0060	.0059	.0057	.0055	.0054	.0052	.0051	.0049	.0048
-2.4	.0082	.0080	.0078	.0075	.0073	.0071	.0069	.0068	.0066	.0064
-2.3	.0107	.0104	.0102	.0099	.0096	.0094	.0091	.0089	.0087	.0084
-2.2	.0139	.0136	.0132	.0129	.0125	.0122	.0119	.0116	.0113	.0110
-2.1	.0179	.0174	.0170	.0166	.0162	.0158	.0154	.0150	.0146	.0143
-2.0	.0228	.0222	.0217	.0212	.0207	.0202	.0197	.0192	.0188	.0183
-1.9	.0287	.0281	.0274	.0268	.0262	.0256	.0250	.0244	.0239	.0233
-1.8	.0359	.0351	.0344	.0336	.0329	.0322	.0314	.0307	.0301	.0294
-1.7	.0446	.0436	.0427	.0418	.0409	.0401	.0392	.0384	.0375	.0367
-1.6	.0548	.0537	.0526	.0516	.0505	.0495	.0485	.0475	.0465	.0455
-1.5	.0668	.0655	.0643	.0630	.0618	.0606	.0594	.0582	.0571	.0559
-1.4	.0808	.0793	.0778	.0764	.0749	.0735	.0721	.0708	.0694	.0681
-1.3	.0968	.0951	.0934	.0918	.0901	.0885	.0869	.0853	.0838	.0823
-1.2	.1151	.1131	.1112	.1093	.1075	.1056	.1038	.1020	.1003	.0985
-1.1	.1357	.1335	.1314	.1292	.1271	.1251	.1230	.1210	.1190	.1170
-1.0	.1587	.1562	.1539	.1515	.1492	.1469	.1446	.1423	.1401	.1379
-0.9	.1841	.1814	.1788	.1762	.1736	.1711	.1685	.1660	.1635	.1611
-0.8	.2119	.2090	.2061	.2033	.2005	.1977	.1949	.1922	.1894	.1867
-0.7	.2420	.2389	.2358	.2327	.2297	.2266	.2236	.2206	.2177	.2148
-0.6	.2743	.2709	.2676	.2643	.2611	.2578	.2546	.2514	.2483	.2451
-0.5	.3085	.3050	.3015	.2981	.2946	.2912	.2877	.2843	.2810	.2776
-0.4	.3446	.3409	.3372	.3336	.3300	.3264	.3228	.3192	.3156	.3121
-0.3	.3821	.3783	.3745	.3707	.3669	.3632	.3594	.3557	.3520	.3483
-0.2	.4207	.4168	.4129	.4090	.4052	.4013	.3974	.3936	.3897	.3859
-0.1	.4602	.4562	.4522	.4483	.4443	.4404	.4364	.4325	.4286	.4247
-0.0	.5000	.4960	.4920	.4880	.4840	.4801	.4761	.4721	.4681	.4641

STANDARD NORMAL DISTRIBUTION (z)

z	.00	.01	.02	.03	.04	.05	.06	.07	.08	.09
0.0	.5000	.5040	.5080	.5120	.5160	.5199	.5239	.5279	.5319	.5359
0.1	.5398	.5438	.5478	.5517	.5557	.5596	.5636	.5675	.5714	.5753
0.2	.5793	.5832	.5871	.5910	.5948	.5987	.6026	.6064	.6103	.6141
0.3	.6179	.6217	.6255	.6293	.6331	.6368	.6406	.6443	.6480	.6517
0.4	.6554	.6591	.6628	.6664	.6700	.6736	.6772	.6808	.6844	.6879
0.5	.6915	.6950	.6985	.7019	.7054	.7088	.7123	.7157	.7190	.7224
0.6	.7257	.7291	.7324	.7357	.7389	.7422	.7454	.7486	.7517	.7549
0.7	.7580	.7611	.7642	.7673	.7703	.7734	.7764	.7794	.7823	.7852
0.8	.7881	.7910	.7939	.7967	.7995	.8023	.8051	.8078	.8106	.8133
0.9	.8159	.8186	.8212	.8238	.8264	.8289	.8315	.8340	.8365	.8389
1.0	.8413	.8438	.8461	.8485	.8508	.8531	.8554	.8577	.8599	.8621
1.1	.8643	.8665	.8686	.8708	.8729	.8749	.8770	.8790	.8810	.8830
1.2	.8849	.8869	.8888	.8907	.8925	.8944	.8962	.8980	.8997	.9015
1.3	.9032	.9049	.9066	.9082	.9099	.9115	.9131	.9147	.9162	.9177
1.4	.9192	.9207	.9222	.9236	.9251	.9265	.9279	.9292	.9306	.9319
1.5	.9332	.9345	.9357	.9370	.9382	.9394	.9406	.9418	.9429	.9441
1.6	.9452	.9463	.9474	.9484	.9495	.9505	.9515	.9525	.9535	.9545
1.7	.9554	.9564	.9573	.9582	.9591	.9599	.9608	.9616	.9625	.9633
1.8	.9641	.9649	.9656	.9664	.9671	.9678	.9686	.9693	.9699	.9706
1.9	.9713	.9719	.9726	.9732	.9738	.9744	.9750	.9756	.9761	.9767
2.0	.9772	.9778	.9783	.9788	.9793	.9798	.9803	.9808	.9812	.9817
2.1	.9821	.9826	.9830	.9834	.9838	.9842	.9846	.9850	.9854	.9857
2.2	.9861	.9864	.9868	.9871	.9875	.9878	.9881	.9884	.9887	.9890
2.3	.9893	.9896	.9898	.9901	.9904	.9906	.9909	.9911	.9913	.9916
2.4	.9918	.9920	.9922	.9925	.9927	.9929	.9931	.9932	.9934	.9936
2.5	.9938	.9940	.9941	.9943	.9945	.9946	.9948	.9949	.9951	.9952
2.6	.9953	.9955	.9956	.9957	.9959	.9960	.9961	.9962	.9963	.9964
2.7	.9965	.9966	.9967	.9968	.9969	.9970	.9971	.9972	.9973	.9974
2.8	.9974	.9975	.9976	.9977	.9977	.9978	.9979	.9979	.9980	.9981
2.9	.9981	.9982	.9982	.9983	.9984	.9984	.9985	.9985	.9986	.9986
3.0	.9987	.9987	.9987	.9988	.9988	.9989	.9989	.9989	.9990	.9990
3.1	.9990	.9991	.9991	.9991	.9992	.9992	.9992	.9992	.9993	.9993
3.2	.9993	.9993	.9994	.9994	.9994	.9994	.9994	.9995	.9995	.9995
3.3	.9995	.9995	.9996	.9996	.9996	.9996	.9996	.9996	.9996	.9997
3.4	.9997	.9997	.9997	.9997	.9997	.9997	.9997	.9997	.9997	.9998

COMMONLY USED z-TABLE VALUES

CONFIDENCE	Confidence Level	90%	95%	99%	99.9%
INTERVALS	z-values	1.65	1.96	2.58	3.29
HYPOTHESIS	Type I Error Risk α	.10	.05	**.01**	.001
TESTS	Two-tailed Test z =	1.65	1.96	2.58	3.29
	One-Tailed Test z =	1.28	1.65	**2.33**	3.09

TABLE A2: Binomial Table

BINOMIAL COEFFICIENTS

n	\multicolumn{11}{c}{k (Number of successes in n trials)}										

n	0	1	2	3	4	5	6	7	8	9	10
0	1										
1	1	1									
2	1	2	1								
3	1	3	3	1							
4	1	4	6	4	1						
5	1	5	10	10	5	1					
6	1	6	15	20	15	6	1				
7	1	7	21	35	35	21	7	1			
8	1	8	28	56	70	56	28	8	1		
9	1	9	36	84	126	126	84	36	9	1	
10	1	10	45	120	210	252	210	120	45	10	1
11	1	11	55	165	330	462	462	330	165	55	11
12	1	12	66	220	495	792	924	792	495	220	66
13	1	13	78	286	715	1267	1716	1716	1287	715	286
14	1	14	91	364	1001	2002	3003	3432	3003	2002	1001
15	1	15	105	455	1365	3003	4005	6435	6435	5005	3003
16	1	16	120	560	1820	4368	8008	11440	12870	11440	8008
17	1	17	138	680	2380	6188	12376	19448	24310	24310	19448
18	1	18	153	816	3060	8568	18564	31824	43758	48620	43758
19	1	19	171	969	3876	11628	27132	50386	75582	92378	92378
20	1	20	190	1140	4845	15504	38760	77520	125970	167960	184756

TABLE A3

STUDENT'S *t* DISTRIBUTIONS

		Level of Significance			
		Probability in tail(s)			
Confidence		90%	95%	98%	99%
Two-tailed →		.10	.05	.02	.01
One-tailed →		.05	.025	.01	.005
	df				
	1	6.314	12.706	31.821	63.657
	2	2.920	4.303	6.695	9.925
	3	2.353	3.182	4.541	5.841
	4	2.132	2.776	3.747	4.604
	5	2.015	2.571	3.365	4.032
	6	1.943	2.447	3.143	3.707
	7	1.895	2.365	2.998	3.500
	8	1.860	2.306	2.896	3.355
	9	1.833	2.262	2.821	3.250
	10	1.812	2.228	2.764	3.169
	11	1.796	2.201	2.718	3.106
	12	1.782	2.179	2.681	3.055
	13	1.771	2.160	2.650	3.012
	14	1.761	2.145	2.625	2.977
	15	1.753	2.131	2.602	2.947
	16	1.746	2.120	2.584	2.921
	17	1.740	2.110	2.567	2.898
	18	1.734	2.101	2.552	2.878
	19	1.729	2.093	2.540	2.861
	20	1.725	2.086	2.528	2.845
	21	1.721	2.080	2.518	2.831
	22	1.717	2.074	2.508	2.819
	23	1.714	2.069	2.500	2.807
	24	1.711	2.064	2.492	2.797
	25	1.708	2.060	2.485	2.787
	26	1.706	2.056	2.479	2.779
	27	1.703	2.052	2.473	2.771
	28	1.701	2.048	2.467	2.763
	29	1.699	2.045	2.462	2.756
	30	1.697	2.042	2.457	2.750
	40	1.684	2.021	2.423	2.704
	60	1.671	2.000	2.390	2.660
	120	1.658	1.980	2.358	2.617
z Distribution:	∞	**1.65**	**1.96**	**2.33**	**2.58**

TABLE A4: Chi Square Table

.01 Critical Values for Chi Square Distributions

df	Significance Level (α)	
	.05	.01
1	3.841	6.635
2	5.991	9.210
3	7.815	11.345
4	9.488	13.277
5	11.070	15.086
6	12.592	16.812
7	14.067	18.475
8	15.507	20.090
9	16.919	21.666
10	18.307	23.209
11	19.675	24.725
12	21.026	26.217
13	22.362	27.688
14	23.645	29.141
15	24.996	30.578
16	26.296	32.000
17	27.587	33.409
18	28.896	34.806
19	30.145	36.191
20	31.404	37.568
21	32.671	38.932
22	33.924	40.289
23	35.173	41.638
24	36.415	42.980
25	37.625	44.314
26	38.885	45.642
27	40.113	46.968
28	41.337	48.278
29	42.557	49.588
30	43.773	50.892
40	55.759	63.691
50	67.505	76.154
60	79.082	88.379
70	90.531	100.425
80	101.879	112.329
90	113.145	124.116
100	124.342	135.807

TABLE A5: F Table
.01 Critical Values for F Distributions

df Error	df Due to Independent Variable(s)										
	1	**2**	**3**	**4**	**5**	**6**	**7**	**8**	**9**	**10**	**11**
1	4052	4999	5403	5625	5764	5859	5928	5981	6022	6056	6082
2	98.49	99.01	99.17	99.25	99.30	99.33	99.34	99.36	99.38	99.40	99.41
3	34.12	30.81	29.46	28.71	28.24	27.91	27.67	27.49	27.34	27.23	27.13
4	21.20	18.00	16.69	15.98	15.52	15.21	14.98	14.80	14.66	14.54	14.45
5	16.26	13.27	12.06	11.39	10.97	10.67	10.45	10.27	10.15	10.05	9.96
6	13.74	10.92	9.78	9.15	8.75	8.47	8.26	8.10	7.98	7.87	7.79
7	12.25	9.55	8.45	7.85	7.46	7.19	7.00	6.84	6.71	6.62	6.54
8	11.26	8.65	7.59	7.01	6.63	6.37	6.19	6.03	5.91	5.82	5.74
9	10.56	8.02	6.99	6.42	6.06	5.80	5.62	5.47	5.35	5.26	5.18
10	10.04	7.56	6.55	5.99	5.64	5.39	5.21	5.06	4.95	4.85	4.78
11	9.65	7.20	6.22	5.67	5.32	5.07	4.88	4.74	4.63	4.54	4.46
12	9.33	6.93	5.95	5.41	5.06	4.82	4.65	4.50	4.39	4.30	4.22
14	8.86	6.51	5.56	5.03	4.69	4.46	4.28	4.14	4.03	3.94	3.86
16	8.53	6.23	5.29	4.77	4.44	4.20	4.03	3.89	3.78	3.69	3.61
20	8.10	5.85	4.94	4.43	4.10	3.87	3.71	3.56	3.45	3.37	3.30
24	7.82	5.61	4.72	4.22	3.90	3.67	3.50	3.36	3.25	3.17	3.09
30	7.56	5.39	4.51	4.02	3.70	3.47	3.30	3.17	3.06	2.98	2.90
40	7.31	5.18	4.31	3.83	3.51	3.29	3.12	2.99	2.88	2.80	2.73
50	7.17	5.06	4.20	3.72	3.41	3.18	3.02	2.88	2.78	2.70	2.62
100	6.90	4.82	3.98	3.51	3.20	2.99	2.82	2.69	2.59	2.51	2.43
200	6.76	4.71	3.38	3.41	3.11	2.90	2.73	2.60	2.50	2.41	2.34
∞	6.64	4.60	3.78	3.32	3.02	2.80	2.64	2.51	2.41	2.32	2.24

df Error	df Due to Independent Variable(s)										
	12	**14**	**16**	**20**	**24**	**30**	**40**	**50**	**100**	**200**	**∞**
1	6106	6142	6169	6208	6234	6258	6286	6302	6334	6352	6366
2	99.42	99.43	99.44	99.45	99.46	99.47	99.48	99.48	99.49	99.49	99.50
3	27.05	26.92	26.83	26.69	26.60	26.50	26.41	26.30	26.23	26.18	26.12
4	14.37	14.24	14.15	14.02	13.93	13.83	13.74	13.69	13.57	13.52	13.44
5	9.89	9.77	9.68	9.55	9.47	9.38	9.29	9.24	9.13	9.07	9.02
6	7.72	7.60	7.52	7.39	7.31	7.23	7.14	7.09	6.99	6.94	6.88
7	6.47	6.35	6.27	6.15.	6.07	5.98	5.90	5.85	5.75	5.70	5.65
8	5.67	5.56	5.48	5.36	5.28	5.20	5.11	5.06	4.96	4.91	4.86
9	5.11	5.00	4.92	4.80	4.73	4.64	4.56	4.51	4.41	4.36	4.31
10	4.71	4.60	4.52	4.41	4.33	4.25	4.17	4.12	4.01	3.96	3.91
11	4.40	4.29	4.21	4.10	4.02	3.94	3.86	3.80	3.70	3.66	3.60
12	4.16	4.05	3.98	3.86	3.78	3.70	3.61	3.56	3.46	3.41	3.36
14	3.80	3.70	3.62	3.51	3.43	3.34	3.26	3.21	3.11	3.06	3.00
16	3.55	3.45	3.37	3.25	3.18	3.10	3.01	2.96	2.86	2.80	2.75
20	3.23	3.13	3.05	2.94	2.86	2.77	2.69	2.63	2.53	2.47	2.42
24	3.03	2.93	2.85	2.74	2.66	2.58	2.49	2.44	2.33	2.27	2.21
30	2.84	2.74	2.66	2.55	2.47	2.38	2.29	2.24	2.13	2.07	2.01
40	2.66	2.56	2.49	2.37	2.29	2.20	2.11	2.05	1.94	1.88	1.81
50	2.56	2.46	2.39	2.26	2.18	2.10	2.00	1.94	1.82	1.76	1.68
100	2.36	2.26	2.19	2.06	1.98	1.89	1.79	1.73	1.59	1.51	1.43
200	2.28	2.17	2.09	1.97	1.88	1.79	1.69	1.62	1.48	1.39	1.28
∞	2.18	2.07	1.99	1.87	1.79	1.69	1.59	1.51	1.36	1.25	1.00

\multicolumn{4}{c}{**SUMMARY OF ONE-VARIABLE HYPOTHESIS TESTS** (ALSO CALLED 'ONE POPULATION', 'ONE SAMPLE', 'CASE I')}

HYPOTHESIS TEST	VARIABLE TYPE	STATISTIC	NULL HYPOTHESIS
HT for mean of one population (t-test, one population)	INTERVAL	MEAN	$H_0: \mu = \mu_0$
HT for proportion of one population	NOMINAL (2 CATEGORIES)	PROPORTION	$H_0: p = p_0$
One Variable χ^2	NOMINAL (2 OR MORE CATEGORIES)	χ^2	$H_0: p_A = p_{A0}$, $p_B = p_{B0}$, etc.

APPENDIX B2

SUMMARY OF HYPOTHESIS TESTS FOR *RELATIONSHIPS* BETWEEN VARIABLES (ALSO CALLED 'TWO GROUP', 'TWO SAMPLE', 'CASE II')				
NAME OF TEST	**INDEPENDENT VARIABLE**	**DEPENDENT VARIABLE**	**STATISTIC**	**NULL HYPOTHESIS**
Pearson's r	INTERVAL: X	INTERVAL: Y	Pearson's r	H_0: $\rho = 0$
Multiple R	SEVERAL INTERVAL: X_1, X_2, X_3, etc.	INTERVAL: Y	Multiple R	H_0: $\rho = 0$ (or, $\beta_1 = 0$ $\beta_2 = 0$, etc.
Two variable χ^2	NOMINAL: ROW	NOMINAL: COL	χ^2	H_0: $\chi^2 = 0$
t-test, two groups t-test for difference between means	DICHOTOMOUS NOMINAL (Often: Treatment vs. Control group	INTERVAL: X	$\bar{X}_A - \bar{X}_B$ sample difference	H_0: $\mu_A - \mu_B = 0$
ONE WAY ANOVA	NOMINAL: i	INTERVAL: X	F ratio	H_0: $\mu_A = \mu_B = \mu_C$, etc.
TWO WAY ANOVA	TWO NOMINAL: ROW, COL	INTERVAL: X	Three F ratios	H_0: No row effect H_0: No col. effect H_0: No interaction